RELIGION AND
PRACTICAL REASON

330

SUNY Series, Toward a Comparative Philosophy of Religions
Frank E. Reynolds and David Tracy, editors

RELIGION AND PRACTICAL REASON

*New Essays in the Comparative
Philosophy of Religions*

edited by

Frank E. Reynolds

and

David Tracy

WITHDRAWN

UTSA Libraries

State University of New York Press

Published by
State University of New York Press, Albany

For information, address State University of New York Press,
State University Plaza, Albany, N.Y. 12246

Production by Marilyn P. Semerad
Marketing by Fran Keneston

Library of Congress Cataloging-in-Publication Data

Religion and practical reason: new essays in the comparative philosophy of
    religions /   edited by Frank E. Reynolds and David Tracy.
        p.   cm. — (SUNY series, toward a comparative philosophy of
    religions)
    Includes bibliographical references and index.
    ISBN 0-7914-2217-8 (alk. paper). — ISBN 0-7914-2218-6 (pbk.   :
alk. paper)
    1. Religion—Philosophy—Comparative studies. 2. Philosophy,
Comparative. 3. Reason. I. Reynolds, Frank, 1930–   . II. Tracy,
David. III. Title: Practical reason. IV. Series.
BL51.R3475   1994   94-7298
210—dc20   CIP
                            10 9 8 7 6 5 4 3 2 1

For Arthur W. H. Adkins,
a pioneer who has helped us find our way

Contents

PART IV
Practical Reason and the Negotiation of Difference

Concluding Reflections

A Note on Transliterations of Foreign Words

Although the editors have striven for uniformity in the English spellings of foreign words and the use of diacritical marks, they have given the authors final authority in the matter. As a result of this deference to the authors' individual preferences, there are some inconsistencies between articles (particularly those dealing with Arabic sources) in the transliteration of some words.

Introduction

Frank E. Reynolds

Religion and Practical Reason: New Essays in the Comparative Philosophy of Religions is the third and culminating collection of essays generated by a series of nine international conferences on the comparative philosophy of religions. Held from 1986 to 1992, these conferences were sponsored by the Institute for the Advanced Study of Religion at the Divinity School of the University of Chicago and were largely funded by a grant from the Booth-Ferris Foundation. When it became clear that a ninth conference was needed, supplementary support was made available by the Divinity School.

Like this third volume of collected essays, the first two were both edited by David Tracy and myself and were published in the SUNY *Toward a Comparative Philosophy of Religions Series.* Like the first two collections, this one contains both programmatic essays that focus on broad ranging proposals for re-envisioning a discipline of comparative philosophy of religions and a number of case studies that focus on the interpretation of particular religio-historical data from comparatively oriented philosophical perspectives.[1]

Since the nine conferences were attended by a relatively stable group of thirty scholars (approximately half from the University of Chicago, and half from other universities in the United

1

States, Canada, and Europe), a certain trajectory of development can be traced. Discussions at the earliest conferences generated a set of essays on the topic of *Myth and Philosophy*
(SUNY Press, 1990) that accomplished at least two purposes.
These essays demonstrated the value of rethinking positions
that presume or seek to defend any kind of simplistic or overly
hierarchical dichotomy between myth and philosophy, both in
the academy and in the religio-philosophical traditions being
studied. These same essays also pointed to the need to focus
much more specific attention on the ways in which both myth
and philosophy are related to practice.

In the middle phase of the project, the group moved on to
a set of discussions that produced a second volume of essays
entitled *Discourse and Practice* (SUNY Press, 1992). Here, once
again, two closely related results were achieved. The collection
served to demonstrate the interpretive power of approaches
which examine the philosophical discourse of the academy and
the philosophical discourse of religious traditions as different
but related modes of practice. In addition, the collection provided a background against which the group was able to identify "practical reason" as a term that could provide a creative
locus around which the study of such practice-oriented approaches to the comparative philosophy of religions could be
further pursued and enriched.

As Sally Gressens suggests in her summary report of the
discussions that occurred during the last of the nine conferences:

> "practical reason" is not a certain "something"—not, say,
> Aristotelian practical versus theoretical reason—which has
> attracted our attention. Rather, "practical reason" (or "prac-
> tical theory") is a motto of sorts. It signals our interest in a
> realm where those details of contingent human life that we
> include in "practice" actually *meet* the sorts of disciplined
> thinking we mean by "theory," where excellence in one is
> linked to excellence in, or an understanding of, the other.[2]

Among the chapters in the present volume (all of which
are revised versions of papers presented at one of the final conferences), the two that I have included in Part 1, "Self-Under-

standing and Issues of Practice" are, at first glance, a very un-
likely pair. However, I have chosen to place Franklin Gamwell's
"A Foreword to Comparative Philosophy of Religion" and Steven
Collins' "What Are Buddhists *Doing* When They Deny the Self?"
together at the beginning of the collection for two different but
complimentary reasons. The first is that each represents one of
two major poles of interest that have structured the *Toward a
Comparative Philosophy of Religions* project since its inception—
namely, a more formalist and normatively oriented pole on the
one hand, and a more historically and descriptively oriented
pole on the other. The second reason is that, despite this very
basic tension between the two chapters, they share a number of
common themes.

Gamwell's chapter is a bold attempt—by the person who
originally suggested and secured funding for the Chicago
project—to lay out a philosophically sophisticated "general understanding" of the kind of activities in which those involved in
comparative philosophy of religion should be engaged. In order
to achieve this purpose he sets forth a set of closely interlocking
definitions of religion, of philosophy, and of comparative philosophy of religion.

For Gamwell, religion is a form of culture that structures a
specific kind of primary human activity; philosophy is a human
intellectual activity that is characterized by critical reflection;
and comparative philosophy of religion is a form of interreligious dialogue that has become critical reflection. In his discussion Gamwell defends the claim that there is a single *comprehensive* question with which all of them deal. This question
goes as follows: "What is the valid comprehensive self-understanding, or what is human authenticity as such?"

Though Gamwell does not use the term *practical reason,*
he makes it clear that from his perspective the central tasks of
religion, philosophy, and comparative philosophy of religion
are all essentially practical or pragmatic. According to his argument, the answer to the "comprehensive question" (the way in
which human purposes and authenticity are understood) functions, in each philosophical or religious instance, as the norm in

terms of which all forms of religious and moral practice are valorized or condemned.

Collins' chapter, in contrast to Gamwell's, is a study of a particular religious tradition (Theravāda Buddhism). And Collins, in his discussion, differentiates much more sharply than Gamwell between the philosophically informed but essentially historical and interpretive task of the academic investigator and the essentially philosophical, religious, and moral concerns of the tradition being studied. But despite these differences, Collins focuses his attention on themes that directly parallel the themes that Gamwell has identified as basic for comparative philosophy of religion. These include: (1) claims for universality, (2) understandings of selfhood, and (3) the relationship between notions of selfhood and modes of religious and ethical practice.

Although Collins is concerned to highlight the fact that the Buddhists' claims for the universality of their message—concerning what Gamwell would call "the valid comprehensive self-understanding"—are historically located and culturally conditioned, he respects these claims and discusses them with great sophistication. He directs his primary attention to a particular Buddhist discourse about selfhood (which, in the final analysis, denies the self as any kind of substantive or permanent entity) which the Theravādins claim has universal validity despite the fact that they recognize certain contexts in which its employment is inappropriate. His contention is that this no-self notion of selfhood is the key element in the kind of "secondary theory" that Theravādins identify with the ultimate level of truth.

In the final section of his chapter Collins argues that, for Theravādins, the recognition of this notion of the universal validity of the no-self notion of selfhood provides the definitive norm for the kind of behavior that both leads to and manifests the ultimate goal of enlightenment. According to Collins, this religio-moral process is a mode of self-cultivation "that might be summarized as a certain kind of textual meditative introspection, occurring within a specific, 'performed' social and behavioral environment."

Part 2 of this volume, entitled "Types of Reasoning and Issues of Practice," contains essays by Paul Walker and Charles Hallisey that explore the philosophical and religious significance of the distinction between two modes of reasoning and truth in the thought of two philosophers, one a Muslim who lived in the tenth century C.E., and one a Theravāda Buddhist who lived in the twelfth century C.E. Although the distinctions that are made in the two instances are by no means identical, the two modes of reason that are discussed by Walker in "Al-Farabi on Religion and Practical Reason" and the two modes that are discussed by Hallisey in his "In Defense of Rather Fragile and Local Achievement: Reflections on the Work of Gurulugomi" have a great deal in common.

Walker highlights the tension in al-Farabi's philosophy between philosophy as represented primarily by Aristotle and religion as represented primarily by Islam. Walker shows how al-Farabi both expressed and mediated this tension through a fundamental distinction and correlation between what he called "theoretical reason" and what he called "practical reason." For al-Farabi philosophy is a "science of certainty" that works with an essentially metalinguistic and metacultural type of theoretical reason that seeks, through logically structured demonstrations, to gain knowledge of realities that are unchanging. Religions, on the other hand, are brought into being through the actions of founders and lawgivers. According to al-Farabi these founders and lawgivers are masters of practical reason who use the power of imagery, poetry, and persuasive rhetoric to embed the eternal and universal truths concerning reality in the thought and life of a particular historical community. What is perhaps most fascinating about Walker's essay is his account of the ways in which al-Farabi affirms the necessity of nurturing both philosophy (with its characteristic use of theoretical reason) and religion (with its characteristic use of practical reason), and, further, the ways in which al-Farabi portrays the interactions between them.

Charles Hallisey's chapter "In Defence of Rather Fragile and Local Achievement: Reflections on the Work of Gurulugomi" is one of the richest and most complex in the entire collection. In the course of this fascinating chapter Hallisey presents important Buddhist philosophical material from a source that has previously been ignored, even by Buddhologists. At the same time, in the process of introducing and exploring the Gurulugomi material he brings to the foreground three general issues that are of central importance for comparative philosophers of religions.

The first of these issues concerns the coexistence and interrelationships of dual or multiple types of rationality. Hallisey suggests that it is important, but not sufficient, to recognize the existence and the character of the dual or multiple modes of rationality that are operative within a particular culture or a particular philosophical perspective. He contends that it is crucial to move on to explore the multiple ways in which, within the culture or philosophical perspective in question, particular types of reasoning and associated notions of truth are correlated and contrasted.

With this approach in mind, he turns his attention to the Theravāda tradition in general and to the work of Gurulugomi in particular. He takes note of the existence of a clear distinction between an "ultimate truth" associated with an analytic type of reasoning and a "conventional truth" associated with more emotive and mundane uses of language and argument. But he then proceeds to spell out a variety of ways, some of them quite surprising for those who have a stereotyped view of Theravāda "orthodoxy," in which the two types of reasoning and truth were, in fact, correlated and contrasted.

The second general issue that Hallisey raises is more directly focused on the relationship between theory and practice. Here he draws a distinction between two very different "models" that can be used to illumine this relationship: "One treats theory outside of practice as an action guide, while the other includes theory within practice as a constitutive part of a process of character-formation and moral education." Hallisey demonstrates that Gurulugomi portrays and uses both conventional theory *and* ultimate, Abhidhammic theory in ways that are congruent with the second model rather than the first. What is more, he argues that Gurulugomi's way of valuing and utilizing both types of truth and associated modes of reasoning in accord with their distinctive pedagogical efficacy is one from which modern virtue theorists could learn a great deal.

The third general issue that Hallisey raises is perhaps the most important, since it concerns not just an element *within* the comparative philosophy of religions, but the basic character of the enterprise itself. At the outset of this portion of his essay, Hallisey highlights what he takes to be the two most prominent options that have been proposed by contemporary scholars for characterizing the activity that should constitute the discipline. The first (as explicitly exemplified in Gamwell's chapter discussed above) identifies the primary activity as "critical reflection on the claims made by or about religions." The second (as explicitly exemplified in Bantly's chapter discussed below) identifies the primary activity as one that "uses the resources of a religious tradition that is not the author's 'own' to address issues of his or her own milieu."

Drawing on insights from Gurulugomi and from Buddhaghosa—a famous Theravāda predecessor of Gurulugomi who characterized one important mode of philosophy as "study as of a treasurer"—Hallisey proposes the element of "preservation" as an aspect which constitutes an indispensable component in any comparative philosophical activity that in our present situation can be justified, either intellectually or morally. More specifically, he turns to an approach set forth by several contemporary philosophers— including Heidegger, Wittgenstein, and Rorty—in which philosophy is conceptualized and justified as a continuation of inherited conversations rather than as a guest for objective truth. But Hallisey suggests that we must take a further step, that we must think in terms of a past that is much more inclusive and much more expansive than the purely western past that previous proponents of this viewpoint have had in mind. As he puts it,

> the most novel aspect of the collective project of any comparative philosophy, including the comparative philosophy of religions, will be to create contexts in which we can learn how to "continue conversations" that are not "our own" (or

at least not yet our own) in the light of the invented traditions within which we habitually do philosophy today.

Part 3, "Practical Reason and the Flow of Time," which is by far the longest section in the collection, contains three chapters: one by a philosopher who is an intellectual historian (Aziz Al-Azmeh), one by a historian of religions (Laurie Patton), and one by an anthropologist (Fitz John Porter Poole). Yet all three chapters focus on an issue that is central to a comparative philosophy of religions that takes empirical studies of religious traditions seriously into account. This issue is the character of the strategies of practical reasoning used by the adherents of various religious traditions (or particular strands of those traditions) to confront the reality of temporality and historicity. It is an issue that involves the mechanisms that are used to assure continuity, and, in some cases, those that are employed to achieve the creative management of change.

Aziz Al-Azmeh, in the intriguing title that he has chosen for his chapter ("Chronophagous Discourse: A Study of Clerico-Legal Appropriation of the World in an Islamic Tradition"), signals the basic thesis that he sets forth and defends. According to Al-Azmeh, the tradition of legal discourse that emerged in Islam in the tenth century C.E. and culminated in the fourteenth-century C.E. writings of Shāṭibī is a "chronophagous discourse"— that is, a discourse in and through which temporality and all of the everyday activities (both devotional and secular) that are embedded within it are "eaten" or "consumed."

Al-Azmeh begins his chapter with a discussion of the notion of salvation history that developed in the great monotheistic traditions that originated in the Middle East and indicates that his discussion of legal theory is designed to highlight a particular consequence generated by the monotheistic universalism espoused there. In addition, he highlights the fact that his study of the anatomy of traditionalist argumentation, taken in conjunction with accompanying comparisons with scholasticism, is intended to provide elements of a general theory of dogmatic discourse.

In the main body of his chapter, Al-Azmeh brilliantly demonstrates how—in the particular tradition on which he has chosen to focus—the broad range of temporally contingent, everyday activities is robbed of its reality through clerically administered modes of genealogically structured practical reasoning. More specifically, he shows how in this system the clerico-legal elite is able to use various modes of intricate hermeneutical reasoning to "subsume" or "consume" these temporally contingent, everyday activities and occurrences into a set of supposedly eternal archetypes embedded in the canon. According to Al-Azmeh's interpretation of Shāṭibī, these supposedly eternal archetypes are promulgated in a Koranicly legitimated myth of origins that is—or at least is intended to be—absolutely totalizing in its scope.

Laurie Patton, in the chapter that follows ("Dis-solving a Debate: Toward a Practical Theory of Myth, with a Case Study in Vedic Mythology"), pursues an important issue that Al-Azmeh's discussion brings vividly to the fore.[3] Is it necessary, she asks, to identify myth as an exclusively universalizing, totalizing phenomena as some recent theorists of myth seem—at least to their more historicizing opponents—to suggest? Or is it possible to develop a theory of myth which takes this universalizing, totalizing tendency into account but recognizes that myth can draw upon the realities of material experience in such a way that it challenges the drive to hegemony and domination?

In order to "dis-solve" the debate between the philosophers, who tend to theorize about the universalizing aspects of myth, and the historians, who tend to reduce myth to the dimensions of difference and materiality, Patton proposes a "practical theory of myth based upon a practice of reading." Using distinctions developed by Lee Yearley in *Mencius and Aquinas* (SUNY Press, 1990), she identifies practical theory as a mode of evaluative and regulatory theory that is situated between the kind of secondary theory that tends toward totalizing explanations and the kind of primary theory that is correlated with matters that are directly related to the material exigencies of everyday life. She then turns to a critical examination of the work of Walter Benjamin as a resource that enables her to specify more clearly how it is that myth is able to function at this practical level *both* as a totalizing instrument of repression *and* as a liberating illumination of the significance of the particular and the profane. She concludes her study with an incisive "reading" of several successive stages of the Vedic and later Hindu myth of the drought. In this "reading" she focuses her attention on specific points in the process of retelling where elements of repression can be discerned and on other specific points in the process where elements of liberation are brought to the fore.

The third chapter in this section is Fitz John Porter Poole's "The Reason of Myth and the Rationality of History: The Logic of the Mythic in Bimin-Kuskusmin 'Modes of Thought.' "[4] Poole explores how the leading elders (and particularly one pre-eminent elder named Trumeng) in a nonliterate tribe in the mountains of Papua New Guinea utilized creative processes of practical reason to maintain cultural meaning and balance in the midst of unprecedented historical events and rapid social change.

Poole reports that according to some native informants there was a time before "the great destruction" (a reference to a series of disastrous historical events that occurred in the 1940s) when a relatively coherent complex of mythic narratives provided an established secondary theory that enabled the tribal elders to subsume or to render meaningless contingent historical events and to maintain traditional patterns of ritual and social practice. Beginning with "the great destruction," the elders found that the secondary theory constituted by the traditional mythology was no longer adequate and that changes in secondary theory and in the traditional modes of practical reasoning were needed in order to maintain both a genuine continuity with past traditions and a meaningful engagement with changing historical conditions. In his narrative, Poole provides an extremely rich and compelling account of the process through which Trumeng and his colleagues incorporated elements of skepticism and a "logos" orientation at the level of secondary theory. In so doing Poole highlights the ways in which, through the creative use of practical reason, they were able to provide meaningful interpretations of unprecedented historical events and to initiate and legitimate significant changes in basic patterns of ritual and social practice.

Part 4, "Practical Reason and the Negotiation of Difference," pairs two essays that focus on the problems and possibilities involved in negotiating conflicts or gaps in understanding between groups who hold world views that are often presumed to be "incommensurable." Although the conflicts or gaps considered in the two essays by Jeffrey Stout and Francisca Cho Bantly are quite different in kind, the arguments that are made by each author identify creative possibilities for practical wisdom (Stout's term) and practical reason (Bantly's term) in situations which, in the view of some, have been or can be resolved only through an exercise of raw power or intellectual imperialism.

Stout, in his chapter "The Rhetoric of Revolution," begins his discussion with a careful review of Thomas Kuhn's *The Structure of Scientific Revolutions* and Jon P. Gunnemann's *The Moral Meaning of Revolution.* In his review, Stout focuses attention on the notion (suggested by some of Kuhn's statements in regard to science, and explicitly affirmed by Gunnemann in the political sphere) that revolutionaries and their opponents are operating out of frameworks of principle and value so radically incommensurable that there are no agreed upon rules of discourse and that, as a result, rational communication and persuasion are impossible. But Stout is not satisfied with this kind of conclusion and suggests that a more accurate and satisfying position can be forged by picking up and greatly extending those of Kuhn's comments which point toward a broader view of rationality. He argues in favor of moving much further in the direction of an Aristotelian notion that "practical wisdom has the capacity to make reasonable choices in matters that cannot be determined simply by consulting agreed upon rules." This, he contends, lays a basis for the view that rhetoric and persuasion can, in fact, play a creative role in the resolution of revolutionary conflict.

With this position established, Stout goes on to develop his notion of practical wisdom as a virtue (*phronesis* or *prudentia*) and to indicate how, like other virtues, it must be cultivated as a skill. He spells out ways in which the efficacious application of practical reason involves the employment of a very wide range of rhetorical techniques that deserve to be carefully studied and evaluated by ethicists and historians of ethics. He concludes that the proper cultivation and use of these rhetorical techniques offers a viable hope for meaningful communication between revolutionaries and their opponents. It does this by providing a creative alternative to the kind of devastatingly divisive and destructive "Manichean rhetorical cycle" that intense revolutionary conflicts tend to generate and perpetuate.

Francisca Cho Bantly, in her chapter entitled "The Fear of *Qing:* Confucian and Buddhist Discourses on Desire," is concerned with very similar issues of commensurability and communication across the gap between different frameworks of principle, conception, and value.[5] But here the issues arise in the context of the recent western academic concern with "the Other" or "Otherness," and with the problems and possibilities of understanding, interpreting, and engaging in conversation with the representatives of cultures (either past or present) that are not our own. From Bantly's perspective the extended soul-searching in the academy over issues of Otherness has "tended to vitiate rather than charter the praxis of comparative scholars." Her paper is an effort to move beyond the obstacles that this soul-searching has generated by proposing an appropriately self-reflexive approach to comparative studies.

Bantly's basic thesis is that comparative study can itself "formulate action guides for modern scholars and even illuminate something of the process through which action guides are derived." She begins her defense of this thesis with a study of the Buddhist and Confucian discourse on *qing* (desire) which demonstrates how, in sixteenth-century China, the long-standing indigenous notion concerning the incommensurability of Confucian and Buddhist philosophy was overcome through the exercise, by certain literati, of practical reason (which she identifies as an intellectual skill or virtue that operates within the enlarged context of what Lee Yearley has called practical theories and pragmatic purposes). She then draws an analogy between the intellectual practices of the sixteenth-century Chinese literati and the intellectual practices of the modern academy; using this analogy, she argues that modern scholars can best break through the supposed incommensurability between their own perspectives and those of the traditions they study through the development of a comparative studies approach that gives a central position to the use of practical reason. Her contention is that comparative philosophers of religions both can and should use practical reason as a means of giving legitimation and direction to their enterprise, as a mechanism for the generation of more specific action guides, and as a basic strategy in the actual process of interpretation.

Bantly concludes her study with a future-oriented summarizing comment with which, I believe, Jeffrey Stout would (despite some minor terminological reservations) wholeheartedly agree:

> The virtue of practical reasoning as a model of cultural encounter is that it nuances the power issue into pragmatically mediated instances of contingency and creativity. I hope future applications of practical reason to contexts in which ideological systems clash will reveal that the process of understanding is not wrought by zero-sum strategies of intellectual warfare. Rather, understanding is gained through the creation of options whose best recommendation is a rationale for action.

The concluding chapter in the collection is a reflective overview by Richard Parmentier entitled "Comparison, Pragmatics, and Interpretation in the Comparative Philosophy of Religions." In the retrospective section that constitutes the main body of the chapter, Parmentier begins by setting the *Toward a Comparative Philosophy of Religions* endeavor in the context of more general comparative studies. He then identifies three different strands that can be discerned in the perspectives that have been set forth by the various participants in the project—one that emphasizes a comparatively oriented *philosophy* of religions, a second that emphasizes the *comparative* study of philosophies of religion broadly conceived, and a third that emphasizes a kind of comparative study that is specifically focused on the comparative philosophies that have been generated (either explicitly or implicitly) by religions themselves. He summarizes this segment of his discussion with the observation that:

> The rich cross-disciplinary fertilization that is revealed in the final papers results from a tacit agreement that these three perspectives should be held in "essential tension," a collective decision that allows for a "preventive pluralistic methodology" in which historians, philosophers, ethnographers and theologians are all welcome.

Parmentier continues his retrospective discussion in a section that he entitles "Comparison and Interpretation as Practical Reason." Under this rubric he provides a fascinating and constructively critical survey of the way in which various contributors have formulated their understanding of the role of practical reason, both in the traditions they have studied and in their own enterprises of interpretation and comparison.

In the final, prospectively oriented pages of his chapter Parmentier highlights the need for the participants in the emerging discipline of the comparative philosophy of religions to give priority to two quite specific issues. The first is a crucially important substantive issue that has thus far received little explicit attention. In his phrasing this issue is "the bi-causal relationship between philosophical discourse and the cultural traditions in which that discourse emerges." The second is a methodological issue or set of issues that requires ongoing attention and clarification. According to Parmentier, priority must be given to further and more sophisticated reflection concerning the kinds of traditions that can fruitfully be compared (and on the justifications and motivations that are involved in each case), on the scope of the units of comparison that can appropriately be employed, and on the "grounds" or "criteria" on which appropriate comparative strategies can be based.

There are many other substantive and methodological issues that must receive serious and sustained attention. These include issues that are raised but not resolved within particular essays in the present volume. They include issues that are made evident by the differences (even conflicts) between the approaches and/or conclusions that are propounded by the various authors. They include still other issues that have emerged in the context of oral discussions but have not yet been seriously addressed in any of the written materials that the project has produced. In addition, there are certainly a host of other issues that have not yet been fully perceived and formulated, issues that will come to the fore more clearly and urgently as the development of the discipline proceeds.

Much progress has been made in the three volumes of collected essays that have appeared in the *Toward a Comparative Philosophy of Religions Series* (*Myth and Philosophy* published in 1990 as Volume 1, *Discourse and Practice* published in 1992 as Volume 3, and the present collection on *Religion and Practical Reason* designated as Volume 7). Much additional progress has been made in and through the three single-author books that have been published in the series during the same time period (Lee Yearley's *Mencius and Aquinas* published as Volume 2 in 1990, Francis X. Clooney's *Theology after Vedanta* published as Volume 4 in 1993, and Ben-Ami Scharfstein's *Ineffability* published as Volume 5 in 1993). And still more progress will be evident in the two additional volumes in the series that are presently in press (José Cabezón's *Buddhism and Language,* Volume 6, which will be available late in 1994, and Paul Griffiths' *On Being Buddha: The Classical Doctrine of Buddhahood,* Volume 8, which will be available sometime in late 1994 or early 1995).

The set of nine international conferences that launched the *Toward a Comparative Philosophy of Religions Series* has now come to a conclusion, and the last of the papers presented at these conferences has now appeared in print. But the project itself will continue in the ongoing work of the participants, in the new Philosophy of Religions area of study that has recently been established at the University of Chicago Divinity School, and, we are hopeful, in the work of many new colleagues from other institutions as well.

Notes

1. David Tracy and I would like to thank four persons who have provided invaluable administrative assistance in the process through which this volume has been conceived and produced. Francisca Cho Bantly, then a student in the History of Religions program at the University of Chicago, was the project assistant who helped to organize and host the conferences at which most of the essays in the collection were presented and discussed. Paul Powers, a younger student in the History of Religions, took over the duties of project assistant when Ms. Bantly moved on to become assistant professor in the Department of Theology at Georgetown University. Mr. Powers has effectively carried out the very demanding responsibilities of editing many of the articles, of preparing the index, and of shepherding the volume through the various stages of the publication process. Kathryn Kueny and Jacob Kinnard, both doctoral candidates in the History of Religions, also provided crucial assistance at various points.

2. "Conference Summary" printed July 1, 1992. This summary was distributed to all conference participants and played a significant role in guiding the final revisions of the papers that appear in this volume. The editors are extremely grateful for the contribution that Ms. Gressens has made to the intellectual quality and coherence of the collection as it has finally developed.

3. During the time Laurie Patton was a student in the History of Religions program at the University of Chicago (and also since she has assumed her present position as assistant professor in the Department of Religion at Bard College) she has made a major and continuing contribution to the Chicago project and to the *Toward a Comparative Philosophy of Religions Series*. She assisted in organizing and hosting several of the project conferences; she wrote the summary reports on conferences four through six (see Francisca Cho Bantly, *Deconstructing/Reconstructing the Philosophy of Religions* published by the Divinity School of the University of Chicago in 1989); and she published an excellent essay, "Hymn to Vāc: Myth or Philosophy?" in *Myth and Philosophy*.

4. Readers should be aware that Poole has also contributed an essay to *Discourse and Practice* entitled "Wisdom and Practice: The Mythic Making of

Sacred History among the Bimin-Kuskusmin of Papua New Guinea." Although this essay provides material directly relevant to the discussion in "The Reason of Myth and the Rationality of History," this second essay is fully independent and can be read without reference to the earlier text.

5. In addition to Francisca Cho Bantly's role in organizing and hosting the final conferences in the Chicago series (see n. 1), she has also made many other contributions to the *Toward a Comparative Philosophy of Religions* project. While Ms. Bantly was a student in the History of Religions program at Chicago, she served for more than four years as the project assistant; she co-authored an essay article about the project entitled "Hedgehogs and Foxes: Rethinking the Philosophy and History of Religions" (*Criterion* 27, no. 2 [Spring 1988]); she wrote a superb summary report on the third conference; she edited a volume containing the summary reports on the first six conferences (the *Deconstructing/Reconstructing the Philosophy of Religions* volume mentioned in n. 3 above); and she published an impressive article on "Buddhist Philosophy in the Art of Fiction" in *Discourse and Practice*. It is clear that she deserves much of the credit for any success that the Chicago project and the *Toward a Comparative Philosophy of Religions Series* may have achieved.

Part I

Self-Understanding and Issues of Practice

Chapter 1

A Foreword to Comparative Philosophy of Religion

Franklin I. Gamwell

The present volume of essays and the series to which it belongs seek to contribute to a "comparative philosophy of religions." This common purpose includes not only contributions that exemplify such philosophy but also, in part through those exemplifications, an attempt to understand generally the practice or activity so named. The present essay pursues directly that general understanding. My particular purpose is to help clarify the task of comparative philosophy of religion, and I will seek to do so by defending the following thesis: Comparative philosophy of religion may be identified as interreligious dialogue that has become critical reflection. In saying this, I mean that comparative philosophy of religion and interreligious dialogue are distinguished from other forms of human activity by the same question, and the two differ solely in the fact that the first is and the second is not critical reflection.

At the outset, I will identify the inclusive philosophical task simply as critical reflection on the most general understandings of human activity. On the assumption that forms of reflection may be identified in terms of the questions they address, we may also say that philosophy critically asks and answers the question: What most general understandings of human activity are valid? It should be noted that "most general understandings of human activity" is ambiguous, because it may itself be understood as either an objective genitive or subjective genitive phrase. As the former, the phrase intends understandings of which human activity is the object and, as the latter, human activity's understandings. I will assume that the character of human activity generally is the object of philosophical inquiry. Given that humans live with understanding, however, to comprehend the most general character of their activity is to comprehend the most general understandings of which it is the subject. Hence, I mean to include both senses of the phrase "most general understandings of human activity" in the question by which philosophy is identified.

This formulation, I judge, is explicitly neutral to most contemporary disagreements, at least in Western thought, regarding the task of philosophy. If some say, with Karl-Otto Apel, that philosophy pursues "fundamental grounding,"[1] and others say, with Richard Rorty, that philosophy is at best "muddling through on a large scale,"[2] this disagreement may be represented as a difference between claims about the most general understandings of human activity, in both senses of the phrase. Again, the claim that philosophy's proper object is in some sense language may be reformulated as the claim that the most general character of human activity and, therefore, its most general understandings are themselves properly understood in or through an understanding of language and its use.

Assuming that there is something properly called "philosophy of religion," then, this specific form of philosophy may be initially defined as critical reflection that addresses the question: What most general understandings of religious activities are valid? *Comparative* philosophy of religion, in turn, may be initially defined as critical reflection that asks: What most general understandings of the similarities and differences among religious activities are valid? This last question may be reformulated, somewhat more economically: What are the most general similarities and differences among religions? It is apparent that a clarification of the task so identified requires a philosophical definition of religion. It is worth noting, then, that the attempt to define religion philosophically asks about a most general similarity among all religions. Assuming that there is something properly called "comparative philosophy of religion," in other words, the attempt critically to clarify its task is itself a part of that very task.

But the assumption that there is something properly called "comparative philosophy of religion" is widely suspect. Many scholars in religious studies find that the phenomena properly or plausibly called "religious" are so varied and complex as to preclude the possibility of any general definition. As a consequence, these scholars choose to study one or some but not all instances of such phenomena and insist that any explicit or implicit definition of religion will be selective, so that it can be justified only with respect to some particular purpose in religious studies. This conclusion is also implied in the claim that "religion" is a "family-resemblance concept" in the sense that each of its referents "is similar in important respects to some others in the family, though not in all respects to any or in any respect to all."[3] Since phenomena, not all of which are similar in at least one respect, do not exemplify a single definition, one or another definition of religion will be justified only with respect to some particular purpose in religious studies. Even if one allows that religion can be generally defined, moreover, one might hold that its definition is not among or implied by the most general understandings of human activity that are valid and, therefore, does not permit comparative philosophy of religion.

Still, the conclusion that religion cannot be philosophically defined is itself a philosophical claim. To say that an understanding of religious activity is not included in or implied by the most general understandings of human activity that are valid is itself to assert a most general understanding of human activity, so that this is a claim subject to philosophical assessment. Nor is the result of this assessment dictated by the fact, if it is a fact, that the term "religion" is commonly used in reference to phenomena so varied that all are in no respect similar to each other. For critical reflection on the most general understandings of human activity is not bound simply to report the common use of terms but, rather, is required to assess whether the common use should, in the interests of philosophical understanding, be reformed.

Of course, it might be asked how or in relation to what philosophy might assess the claim that religion cannot be philosophically defined. The answer can only be that this claim is assessed in relation to a philosophical definition of human activity, because philosophy is critical reflection on the most general understandings of human activity. I will assume as noncontroversial that "religious activity," however varied its applications, is not another term for human activity in general or as such, so that applications of this term may be distinguished from instances of political or scientific or other specific human activities or aspects thereof. The question to be pursued, then, is whether a general definition of human activity includes or implies certain distinctions among its specific forms or aspects, that is, whether human activity as such is self-differentiating, and, if so, whether one of its forms or aspects can be defended as an appropriate referent of "religious."

This approach requires that one first develop a general understanding of human activity, and that is the course I will attempt to follow. In the first section of this chapter, I will seek to clarify and defend an understanding of human activity as such, at least in the measure and manner that our present purpose requires. In the second section, I will argue that human activity so understood is self-differentiating, in the sense that it implies certain specific forms or aspects, and that one such differentiation is properly called "religious." In the final section, then, I will pursue the implications of this definition of religious activity for an understanding of comparative philosophy of religion.[4]

1. Human Activity

It is widely agreed that human existence is distinguished by self-reflection or self-understanding. Humans, as has often been said, not only *are* but also *understand that they are.* Of course, human beings or human individuals are not always aware of themselves. We sleep and can become unconscious in a manner that excludes all understanding. More precisely, then, a human individual may be distinguished as one that has the capacity for self-understanding. At those times when individuals are aware of themselves, they are, we may say, in their distinctively human state. I will define human activity to mean this distinctively human state, that is, human activity is activity constituted by a self-understanding. A human individual, then, is a series or succession of activities, all of which exemplify the identity of that individual and at least some of which are distinctively human.[5]

Because a human activity understands itself, it also understands at least some other reality, at least in some measure. This is because understanding necessarily distinguishes; to understand anything at all is to distinguish what is understood from other things that it is not, so that the other things are also understood. In one sense, then, it makes no difference whether we say that human activity is constituted by a self-understanding or simply constituted by understanding—since to understand others as others is to distinguish them from the self and, thereby, to understand the self. In terms of *what* is understood, however, self-understanding is the inclusive term, because the self includes its relations to others, at least insofar as the others are understood. In other words, the self that understands is constituted by relations to others or is internally related to at least some others in some measure, whereas the others that are understood are not necessarily constituted by relations to the self.

Moreover, a self-understanding also includes an understanding, at least in some measure, of some larger reality of which the self and others are parts, because it is only with respect to this larger reality that understanding distinguishes between self and others. To distinguish is to identify not only difference but also similarity; complete or absolute difference is not a definite difference at all and, therefore, not an understanding of different things.[6] But to understand the similarity of self and others is, in one respect, to identify some larger reality in which both are somehow included. In order to avoid misunderstanding, I should perhaps underscore that I mean by "a larger reality" nothing other than whatever is implied by that fact of similarity between things that are understood. Thus, for instance, one might hold that the similarity implies nothing more than a mere collection of self and others. It remains, in that event, that this collection is the larger reality with respect to which one understands its members. Summarily, then, human activity is constituted by an understanding of itself and, therefore, of the larger reality of which it is a part.

Granting that understanding of self, others, and some larger reality occurs, some may still contest the claim that this understanding *constitutes* such activity. Some modes of thought attempt to treat understanding as an "epiphenomenon," such that no mention of or reference to it is required in order to identify any given activity, and human science may proceed "objectively" or in a manner that seeks causal relationships similar to those pursued by the sciences of nonhuman existence. But to treat self-understanding as an epiphenomenon is in truth to deny that it occurs, because an activity that understands itself must in some measure thereby determine itself. Whatever effects other things may have on the activity, others cannot effect an understanding of their effects. Self-understanding, in other words, necessarily transcends other-determination, and, therefore, an activity in which self-understanding occurs is in some measure a product of self-determination or is constituted by that understanding. This is not to deny that a human activity, because it includes an understanding of other things, is internally related to and, therefore, determined in some measure by them. However extensive that other-determination, it remains that the completion of a human activity waits on how it chooses to understand itself.[7]

One might ask how an activity's self-understanding differs from its understanding of other things. When one understands oneself, *what* is it that one understands in addition to the others to which one is internally related? The answer, I judge, can only be one's purpose. If to understand others is to understand those by which one is determined, then to understand oneself is to understand that by which others will be determined. The choice of a self-understanding can only be the choice with understanding of a particular purpose. To complete the self is to determine the effects one pursues, and our distinctive activity, we may say with Alfred North Whitehead, "arises as an effect facing its past and ends as a cause facing its future."[8] Alternatively stated, an activity unifies its relations to others in a particular purpose, so that it *is* its purpose. On this account, then, all understanding is pragmatic, that is, understanding is always a part of some chosen purpose.[9] The choice of a self-understanding is the way in which a human activity chooses to add itself or make a difference to the larger reality of which it is a part.

So to define distinctively human activity, however, is not to say that its understanding is in all respects *explicit.* I mean by "explicit understanding" one's conscious thoughts. It is, I assume, undeniable that the conscious thought constituting any given human activity is partial or fragmentary, that is, no human activity explicitly understands all things completely. As a consequence, every human activity also includes or is constituted by understandings that are only implicit, that is, those excluded from conscious thought and without which conscious thought could not be what it is. One's explicit understanding may attend, for instance, to certain aspects of the nonhuman world or to the activities of certain other humans, so that one's understanding of self remains implicit. Alternatively, one's conscious thought may attend to one's purpose, so that some of one's understandings of other things remain implicit.

In part, the understandings implicit in a particular activity were explicit in some previous activity or activities of the individual in question. As I have suggested, we may understand an individual as a series or succession of activities, each of which includes or inherits from its predecessors the identifying character of that individual. With respect to any given conscious moment, then, we may distinguish between understandings explicit in the activity of the moment and understandings that were previously explicit in the individual's existence and are nonconsciously remembered in the present. If, for instance,

Abraham Lincoln's activity in signing the Emancipation Proclamation was explicitly constituted by whatever conscious
thoughts he had at the time, this activity was also constituted
by an extensive complex of implicit interpretations of the Union,
its order and disorder, that had been conscious thoughts at one
time or another in Lincoln's previous activity. In general, we
may say that the measure and respects in which explicit understanding is possible for a given activity depend on the measure
and respects in which prior learning is implicitly understood.

Some may claim, further, that the implicit understandings
of any given activity are exhausted by the individual's prior
learning, that is, new understandings must be explicit before
they can subsequently be implicit in an individual's activity.
But this claim entails that self-understanding could never be
implicit, because a self-understanding is always a new understanding. Since a human activity is self-determined, every human activity is something new, so that a self-understanding is a
new understanding. Were implicit understandings exhausted
by prior learning, moreover, there could never be new explicit
self-understandings either, because new thoughts have new implications. Lincoln, for instance, could not have conceived of his
signing the Emancipation Proclamation, because, in doing so,
he implicitly conceived of a certain future for the United States,
namely, one in which all future events would be conditioned by
the event of the Proclamation, and that implicit understanding
of the Union's future was not a possible understanding prior to
his conception of the event.

This is not to deny that the possibility of Lincoln's new
thought and its new implications depended on his prior learning. The point is that the understanding constituting a given
activity, explicit or implicit, depends also on the self-understanding, explicit or implicit, the activity chooses, for instance, what
Lincoln chose to do with his prior learning. Thus, if implicit
understandings are those excluded from conscious thought and
without which conscious thought could not be what it is, they
are those so excluded without which the self-understanding
could not be what it is—and these include the logical implica-

tions of its choice, whether or not they were previously learned by the individual in question.[10]

Still, an activity's implicit understanding, like its conscious thought, is always fragmentary. Since implicit understandings are those excluded from conscious thought and without which self-understanding could not be what it is, these implicit understandings could be complete rather than fragmentary only if the self to be understood were constituted by complete relations to all things. I will assume as noncontroversial that the activities of human individuals are always fragmentary, that is, never related to all things completely. Indeed, if there are activities completely related to all things, then they are, it seems proper to say, divine rather than human. Accordingly, the understandings implicit in any human activity are also partial. We might formulate this point by saying that explicit understanding represents a fragment of an activity's fragmentary understanding. To be sure, this formulation says that what is understood explicitly is also understood implicitly, but, given the dictum that any proposition implies itself, that consequence need not be troubling.

It is because all understanding is fragmentary, moreover, that both explicit and implicit understandings are fallible. If we understood all things completely, then it would not be possible to misunderstand anything. Since our understandings are partial, we may attribute to some things features that in truth belong or could belong to others. In other words, we misrepresent things by confusing their characteristics. For instance, one misunderstands Abraham Lincoln if one believes that he defended slavery in the Lincoln-Douglas debates. One correctly understands that a defense of slavery is a characterization that does or could belong to some human activities, but, failing to understand all things completely, one attributes this characterization to the relevant activities of Lincoln.

Fallibility with respect to self-understanding merits special attention. Given that a human activity chooses its particular purpose with understanding, one can never be simply ignorant of that purpose; since to understand oneself is to understand one's purpose, we can never be simply ignorant of ourselves. To be sure, our conscious or explicit self-understandings may be incorrect, in the sense that one may understand one's particular purpose to be other than it is. If this occurs, however, one's conscious thought can only be a misrepresentation of the implicit self-understanding by which one's activity is constituted. Given that distinctively human purposes are chosen, the falsity of one's explicit self-understanding implies the choice of another understanding of oneself.

Accordingly, the fallibility of explicit self-understanding includes the possibility of self-deception. Having learned the possibility of exploiting other individuals for her or his own maximal advantage, for instance, an individual presently attempts to do so and believes explicitly that she or he pursues what is best for the other individuals. The individual's activity explicitly deceives itself or conceals from its explicit attention the implicit self-understanding by which it is constituted. Moreover, self-deception means that one's implicit self-understanding is self-convicting or duplicitous; that is, one chooses a purpose of which one also disapproves or that one proscribes. Seeking to exploit other individuals, for instance, one may also implicitly believe that one ought not to do so, and it is by virtue of this implicit duplicity that one explicitly conceals one's true purpose. In order to be what it is, the conscious understanding that is false excludes the following implicit self-understanding: to exploit others notwithstanding that I ought not to do so and, therefore, to deceive myself implicitly.[11]

If the fallibility of explicit self-understanding means that one's implicit self-understanding may be explicitly misrepresented, then it may seem to follow that one's implicit self-understanding must be infallible. But I have also said that all human understanding is fallible, and the sense in which this is the case with implicit self-understanding must be explained. It is certainly true that one's implicit self-understanding is correct, in the sense that one understands the purpose by which one is constituted, because this purpose is chosen, at least implicitly, with understanding. Still, we may say that this self-understanding is fallible precisely because, as we have just seen, it may be duplicitous. One may choose an understanding of oneself that one also understands to be invalid; one may choose a purpose that one understands to be morally wrong. To be sure, duplicity is a possibility for all human activities only if human activity as such is bound by a norm that our self-understandings might contradict. But we are now in a position to see that our choices are always moral choices because every particular self-understanding includes, at least implicitly, a comprehensive self-understanding.

Because every human activity chooses its particular self-understanding, it also chooses, at least implicitly, an understanding of human activity in general. This is simply an application of the logical dictum that the particular implies the general. To understand that something is a plant or an animal is to understand that it is an example of things that are alive. Similarly, the particular self-understanding by which a given activity is distinguished implies an answer to the general question: What are the characteristics common to the diverse, particular self-understandings of all human activities, actual and possible? In other words, each activity understands itself, at least implicitly, to exemplify the character that all other human activities, each in its own way, also exemplify. We might express this point by saying that every human activity is constituted, at least implicitly, by a general hermeneutical understanding, that is, an understanding of self-understanding as such. To be sure, one may ask whether there are or, if there are, whether it is possible to identify characteristics common to all particular self-understandings. But this question answers itself, since self-understanding and, therefore, understanding in some measure of others and some larger reality are precisely such characteristics.

To choose a particular self-understanding is, I have said, to choose with understanding a particular purpose; to understand oneself is to choose with understanding how one will make a difference to the larger reality of which self and others are parts. Given that every particular self-understanding implies an understanding of human activity in general, we may also say that every human activity chooses, at least implicitly, an understanding of human purpose as such, the common character or characteristics of all particular purposes. In other words, every human activity is constituted, at least implicitly, by an understanding of the purpose by which the human adventure is identified, and I will call this understanding an activity's "comprehensive self-understanding." We may also make this point by saying that every activity chooses an understanding of the *material* character of human activity as such, in distinction from its *formal* character, which I have defined as the choice with understanding of some or other particular purpose.

Since the material character of human activity as such is implied by any given activity, the valid comprehensive self-understanding is understood implicitly by all human activity. Still, any given human activity may so choose its particular purpose that it is also constituted, at least implicitly, by an invalid comprehensive self-understanding. If, for instance, the purpose of the human adventure is, with John Dewey, the pursuit of the democratic ideal,[12] an individual's activity might so understand itself as to pursue the wealth or pleasure of that individual at the expense of democratic association, so that the activity's implied comprehensive self-understanding includes not only the valid but also an invalid understanding of human purpose as such. In other words, one's comprehensive self-understanding may be duplicitous, so that one's activity is pragmatically self-contradictory.[13]

It now follows that the valid comprehensive self-understanding is the comprehensive moral norm. Every human activity ought to be constituted without duplicity by this self-understanding, or, again, the particular purpose by which any given activity is identified ought to exemplify without duplicity the comprehensive purpose. The valid comprehensive self-understanding is a norm precisely because it is valid; that is, the choice of an understanding is rationally bound by the norm of validity. This same self-understanding is a practical norm because it is a norm for human purpose; and it is a moral norm because it is categorical, that is, its prescription cannot be defeated by any choice that a human might make.[14] In order to express the moral character of the valid comprehensive self-understanding, I will say that it identifies human authenticity as such.

But if every human activity is constituted by an understanding of human authenticity as such, this includes an understanding of reality as such. I previously argued that any self-understanding is also an understanding at least in some measure of some larger reality in which self and others are distinguished or of which self and others are parts. It then follows that an understanding of self-understanding as such is an understanding of the larger reality in which self and all *conceivable* others, all others that might be understood, are distinguished, and this is an understanding of reality as such. In other words, the valid comprehensive self-understanding includes a valid metaphysical understanding. The character of human authenticity as such is a relation of human activity to reality as such.[15]

We may now reformulate the task of philosophy. As critical reflection on the most general understandings of human activity, philosophy is a form of critical reflection identified by the question: What is the valid comprehensive self-understanding, or what is human authenticity as such? I will call this the comprehensive question. Answers to it constitute the most general understandings of human activity, in the sense that human activity is the object of understanding. Just because human activity as such asks and answers the question, at least implicitly, answers to the question include the most general understandings of human activity, in the sense that human activity is the subject of understanding. So identified, then, philosophy includes both a hermeneutical, or moral, and a metaphysical aspect, where the former asks about the characteristics of self-understanding as such, and the latter asks about the characteristics of reality as such—and, because self-understanding is inclusive, the hermeneutical or moral question is the inclusive philosophical question. In sum, critical reflection on the material character of human activity as such is the inclusive philosophical task. Accordingly, philosophy, inclusively understood, may be called pragmatic; that is, its task is critically to understand the comprehensive purpose.

2. Religion

In order to achieve a philosophical definition of religion and, subsequently, to clarify the task of comparative philosophy of religion, I have sought, first, to develop an understanding of human activity as such. This course has been taken because religious activity will be philosophically defined if we show that human activity as such is self-differentiating, in the sense that it implies certain forms or aspects of itself, and that one such differentiation is properly called "religious." Still, it may be doubted whether a definition of religious activity is the same as a definition of religion. In the first instance, at least, "religion" generally refers to a specific form of culture rather than to a specific form of activity. Before asking about specific forms of human activity, then, we require some attention to the relation between activity and culture.

Considerable discussion in more recent philosophy has focused on the relation between understanding and language. If distinctively human activity is constituted by understanding, many have argued, then activity cannot be human without participation in language, because understanding cannot be or become explicit without being linguistically mediated. Even without seeking precision regarding this claim, we have good reason to affirm one of the principal conclusions to which, for many, it leads: Because language is always a particular cultural creation, human activity is mediated in part by a particular culture.

I take this conclusion to be convincing, because it follows from the fact that human understanding is fragmentary. Given this fact, as we have seen, the measure and respects in which explicit understanding is possible for a given activity depend on the measure and respects in which the individual's prior learning is nonconsciously remembered or implicitly understood. Learning, we may now add, depends on relation to other human individuals, and, therefore, the possibilities for explicit understanding in any given activity depend on the individual's participation in human association. Understanding is always intersubjective, dependent on communication. But, now, communication between or among human individuals is also fragmentary, and, for this reason, occurs in terms of the particular concepts and symbols with which individuals express themselves to others. Thus, we may say that conscious thought depends on an individual's participation in a particular cultural lifeworld, including especially its language.

As I have already mentioned, explicit understanding also depends on the choice of a self-understanding and, therefore, may be or include a new understanding. Insofar as explicit understanding is new, however, it is culturally creative, that is, new as an addition or possible addition to the cultural lifeworld in which it participates. New conscious thoughts occur in terms of new concepts and symbols that allow those understandings to be communicated to others who also participate in that particular culture. In other words, explicit understandings generally are not only created by but also creative of a particular culture. Thus, it remains that explicit understandings and, insofar, human activity are mediated by a particular culture, and we may identify the relation between human activity and culture in the following general way: Culture consists in the concepts and symbols in terms of which human activities explicitly understand themselves and other things and the larger reality of which both are parts.

On the assumption that "religion" generally refers to a specific form of culture, then, activity is specifically religious when it understands explicitly in terms of the concepts and symbols of a particular religion. But if this brief discussion identifies for present purposes the relation between activity and culture, it leaves the question of whether religious activity and, therefore, religion can be philosophically defined. Accordingly, we must now proceed in asking whether human activity as such is self-differentiating and, if so, whether one of its specific forms or aspects can be defended as an appropriate identification of activity that understands itself in the terms of some or other religion.

That the philosophical definition of human activity is self-differentiating has, in fact, already been confirmed by the preceding discussion. Because the understanding constituting any given activity is fragmentary, it implies the distinction between explicit and implicit understandings. Still, this distinction is analytic, in the sense that there is no human activity that does not include both. In other words, this distinction refers to aspects of any human activity and never to a difference between some human activities and others. In contrast, religious activity seems to be a kind of activity in the sense that some human activities may be religious and some may not. I will reserve the term *specific form of human activity* to mean a kind of activity in this sense; that is, the distinction between one specific form and any other is nonanalytic. The question remains, then, whether the philosophical definition of human activity implies any distinctions among its specific forms.

But, now, it is the analytic distinction between explicit and implicit understandings that may be used to explain how specific forms of human activity might be differentiated. Because explicit understanding is always fragmentary, such forms may be distinguished in terms of the differences between their explicit understandings. On the assumption that understandings may be represented as the answers to questions, different forms of human activity may be distinguished in terms of the questions that they explicitly ask and answer or address. Thus, for instance, one might distinguish political activity from all other forms of activity in terms of the question of the state, so that politics asks and answers explicitly the question of what the state should do.[16] Similarly, then, other specific forms of human activity may be distinguished in terms of the questions that are explicitly addressed.

Still, this possibility does not yet confirm that any such forms of activity are implied by the general definition of human activity, that is, does not show that self-understanding as such is self-differentiating in the sense pertinent to a philosophical definition of religion. It may be objected, for instance, that the identification of political activity I have suggested is not implied by human activity as such, because the kind of association to which we refer with the term *state* is not universal to human existence but is, rather, historically emergent and, therefore, specific to certain historical conditions. More generally, the objection is that any and all questions with which specific forms of human activity are distinguished will include concepts and symbols, the referents of which are historically specific, so that activity in which those questions are explicitly asked and answered is not implied by human activity as such.

But this objection, I judge, cannot be sustained even with respect to political activity. If the term *state* is historically specific, we may substitute for it the general term *governing association,* that is, an association whose distinctive purpose is to order or unify all associations and activities of a particular group of individuals. Although I will not pursue the matter here, I believe that all of the central concepts defining a governing association (namely, 'association,' 'particular group of individuals,' and 'purposeful ordering of associations and activities') are implied in the concept of human activity as the choice with understanding of a purpose. If so, then activity in which a particular group of individuals explicitly decides on an answer to the question of its own governing association may be considered a self-differentiation of human activity as such.

Whatever merit the objection does or does not have with respect to political activity, however, the previous discussion has identified at least one specific form of human activity that is implied by human activity as such, namely, the activity of philosophy. The general definition of human activity as the choice of a particular self-understanding and, thereby, a comprehensive self-understanding implies the question: What is the valid comprehensive self-understanding? Accordingly, the specific form of activity that occurs insofar as this question is explicitly asked and answered in a critical manner is implied by the general definition of human activity, and the distinction between philosophy and all other activities is a self-differentiation of that general definition.

One might doubt this conclusion on the ground that *critical* reflection is not a kind of activity implied by human activity as such. But this doubt can be removed through the recognition that every choice of a self-understanding claims to be valid and, therefore, implies an assessment in relation to a norm of validity. When this assessment is explicit, the reflection is critical. In other words, I understand critical reflection to be a secondary form of human activity in the sense that it seeks explicitly to

assess or validate understandings or claims and, therefore, presupposes a primary form of activity in which understandings
are asserted or claims are made, explicitly or implicitly. A specific form of activity, then, may be identified not only in terms
of the distinguishing question that is explicitly addressed but
also in terms of the manner in which this is done. The general
distinction in manner important to the present discussion is between critical and precritical or, as I will also say, decisive reflection. Decisive reflection is, then, the primary form of human
activity. This is simply to repeat that all understanding is pragmatic. A self-understanding is the choice with understanding of
some purpose, so that human activity is constituted inclusively
by claims that it makes, explicitly or implicitly. In the nature of
the case, all implicit understanding is precritical or decisive and,
therefore, all critical reflection is explicit. But this leaves the
possibility that human activity may explicitly ask and answer
questions in a decisive manner.[17]

Because the activity of philosophy is *critical* reflection that
addresses the comprehensive question, the distinction between
critical and decisive reflection implies another self-differentiation of human activity as such that addresses that same question. I now wish to suggest that this latter form of activity is
appropriately called "religious." On this account, activity is religious insofar as it asks and answers explicitly and *decisively* the
question of human authenticity as such. If we assume that the
term *religion* refers to a form of culture rather than a form of
activity, then we may now define religion as the primary form
of culture in terms of which the comprehensive question is explicitly asked and answered.[18]

If religious activity addresses explicitly and decisively the
same question that philosophy addresses critically, then it may
seem that philosophy as such is philosophy of religion, that is,
critical reflection on the understandings or claims that identify
religious activity. But this conclusion ignores the fact that *every*
human activity makes a claim, at least implicitly, in answer to
the comprehensive question; human activity as such is constituted by a comprehensive self-understanding. In contrast, religious activity is a specific form of activity in which this question

is addressed *explicitly*. Thus, the activities on which philosophy as such critically reflects are not simply those that are religious but, rather, all human activity.

Just because all human activities are not religious, the claim that religion may be philosophically defined does not imply that all human individuals or all societies are religious—however pervasive religion may be in human history. If a specific form of activity is philosophically defined, in other words, then the *possibility* of this kind of activity is implied by the character of human activity as such; this possibility can be identified without reference to any specific historical conditions or circumstances. Still, the recognition that every human activity is implicitly constituted by asking and answering the comprehensive question allows one to clarify the specific function of religion as a form of culture. Since one's implicit self-understanding may be duplicitous, the specific function of religion is so to represent in concepts and symbols the valid comprehensive self-understanding that religious adherents choose it in all of their activities, that is, choose particular purposes without duplicity. In other words, religious activity addresses the comprehensive question explicitly and decisively in order to cultivate in the lives of religious adherents authentic self-understanding as such.

As does philosophy, then, religion includes both hermeneutical, or moral, and metaphysical aspects, and the hermeneutical, or moral, aspect is inclusive. Hence, the religious question may also be called the most general moral question.[19] In order to emphasize that it includes the question of reality as such, however, the comprehensive question may also be formulated: What makes human activity as such authentic? On the one hand, the character of reality as such makes human activity as such authentic, at least in the sense that the larger reality permits human authenticity. On the other hand, human activity makes itself authentic, because self-understandings are chosen.

Granting that the form of culture that I have called "religion" is a form the differentiation of which is philosophical or is implied by human activity as such, one must still give some reason why this is appropriately understood as the referent of "religion." I take the most apparent reason to be that each of the so-called axial or post-axial religions more or less obviously illustrates the definition. I have in mind especially Buddhism, Christianity, Confucianism, Hinduism, Islam, and Judaism. To be sure, each of these traditions is internally complex, so that, in each case, it is an open question whether we should speak of one religion or more than one that claim the same name. If the latter, however, I expect that the inner complexity of any such tradition results in two or more traditions or cultural systems, each of which consists in concepts and symbols in terms of which the comprehensive question is explicitly and decisively asked and answered.

Moreover, I judge that the comprehensive question allows one to distinguish the specifically religious character of these traditions or cultural systems from others generally considered nonreligious, for instance, political cultures. This is not to deny that one or more of the traditions in question may include terms in which questions other than the comprehensive one are explicitly asked and answered. On my account, as I have mentioned, a distinction between specific forms of human activity is nonanalytic in the sense that it *may* distinguish between particular human activities. Hence, religions and the activities and associations distinguished thereby may in a given society be more or less culturally and socially differentiated. As a matter of fact, religions are rather highly differentiated in most modern societies and have been more or less diffuse in some premodern situations. In the latter, then, cultural formations and activities properly called "religious" are also properly called, say, "political"—although they are religious and political in differing aspects.

The appeal to so-called axial or post-axial religions as apparent illustrations may elicit the objection that the definition I have offered excludes so-called pre-axial or archaic religions. I am not competent to discuss this objection in an informed way, but I suspect that it is not finally as telling as it may initially seem to be. If the point is that a pre-axial religion is particularistic in the sense that its understanding of human authenticity is limited to a particular collectivity, then it might be argued that such particularism includes a belief about other collectivities— either that authenticity is not possible in other collectivities or that authenticity in other collectivities is of an entirely different order. Beliefs such as these are, perhaps, among those that adherents of axial religions are especially concerned to reject, and this suggests that pre-axial religions in their own way ask and answer the comprehensive question. Be that as it may, however, a philosophically differentiated form of culture that the axial religions more or less obviously exemplify and that allows one to identify the specifically religious character of these traditions commends itself as an appropriate definition in terms of which to clarify the comparative philosophy of religion.

It is important to note that this understanding of religion, whether or not it seems in some sense exclusive, is more inclusive than use of the term sometimes intends. Thus, for instance, at least some forms of nationalism or humanism might be understood as cultural systems in terms of which the question of human authenticity is explicitly and decisively addressed. In contrast, "religion" is often reserved, both in academic discussion and in that of the wider public, to mean traditions or cultural systems from which such nationalism and humanism are thought to be distinguished as examples of secularism. On this usage, in other words, religion is defined in terms not only of the comprehensive question but also of a certain kind of answer to that question, such that secularistic answers are another kind. Alternatively stated, my account may be called a "functional definition"; that is, religion is identified as a philosophically differentiated function of cultures. In contrast, common usage implies a substantive definition; that is, religion is identified as a specific kind of performance of the function in question.[20]

Generally speaking, I judge, those who attempt to distinguish religion from secularism intend a definition of the former something like the following: Religion is the form of culture in terms of which the comprehensive question is explicitly and decisively asked and answered and in which human authenticity is derived from the relation to reality as such. Whether reality as such is understood as Yahweh, Allah, "emptiness," or in some other way, its character grounds the distinction between human authenticity and inauthenticity and, in that sense, authorizes authentic human activity. In contrast, then, secularism is the form of culture in terms of which the comprehensive question is explicitly and decisively asked and answered and in which the distinction between authentic and inauthentic human activity is not authorized by reality as such, so that reality as such is understood to be indifferent or hostile to, even if it also permits, human authenticity.

So far as I can see, the putative distinction between religion and secularism as substantively different kinds or classes of answers to the comprehensive question, each with more than one member, is not a coherent distinction. Because the valid answer to this question is implied by any self-understanding at all, invalid answers are always self-contradictory. In other words, every invalid claim of the form "the authentic character of human activity as such is X" is self-refuting because human activity as such implies the valid comprehensive self-understanding. But there can be no coherent distinction in terms of content among incoherent claims, and, therefore, invalid answers to the comprehensive question cannot be coherently distinguished into classes. This is not to say that the question of whether reality as such does or does not authorize human authenticity cannot be coherently answered. On the contrary, human authenticity either is or is not authorized by reality as such, and the valid answer to the comprehensive question asserts, without contradiction, the alternative that is valid. But all other answers are self-contradictory, and, therefore, assert both alternatives, at least implicitly. The same must be the case with any other characteristic, the affirmation or denial of which is said to distinguish religion and secularism in the sense here in question.

Hence, the only pertinent distinction among different answers to the comprehensive question is between the valid answer and all others. In other words, the putative distinction between religion and secularism has no significance for human activity. What matters is the distinction between human authenticity and inauthenticity as such. For this reason, the philosophical definition of religion must resist any more narrow understanding and identify religion in terms of the comprehensive question itself.

3. Comparative Philosophy of Religion

We are now in a position to pursue directly an understanding of comparative philosophy of religion, which, as I stipulated at the outset, is identified by the question: What are the most general similarities and differences among religions? In order to clarify more fully the task that is thereby distinguished, it will be useful to make explicit the sense in which the philosophical enterprise as such is necessarily comparative of human activities. Because its inclusive task is critical reflection on the comprehensive character of human activity, philosophy seeks critically to understand the most general similarities and differences of all human activities. Alternatively stated, philosophy seeks critically to understand the character of authentic self-understanding as such, and, since every human activity is a particular exemplification of just that self-understanding, the object of philosophy's inquiry must be a variable in terms of which all human activities may be compared. It might be asked how the variable of human authenticity as such can compare all human activities, since the self-understandings by which activities are constituted may be inauthentic. But this question has already been addressed, because I have argued that an inauthentic self-understanding is duplicitous. It implies the understanding of human authenticity as such that it also denies. Accordingly, the authentic self-understanding as such is a moral ideal and compares all self-understandings, not only authentic but also inauthentic ones, in the manner that a moral ideal compares better and worse.

In the respects that human activity as such implies specific forms of activity, philosophy also is self-differentiating. On the assumption that political activity may be philosophically defined, for instance, one may speak of political philosophy. Since philosophy as such is comparative, the same is the case with such self-differentiations. Political philosophy, for instance, critically asks and answers the question: What are the most general similarities and differences among activities insofar as they are political? It now follows that philosophy of religion is also necessarily comparative; its distinguishing question may be formulated: What are the most general similarities and differences among religions? In this sense, at least, "comparative philosophy of religion" is redundant.

But if all forms of philosophy are comparative in the sense that has been explained, there is also a distinctive sense in which philosophy of religion compares religions. We may approach a clarification of this claim by underscoring that philosophy compares activities because it assesses them. Since critical reflection is a secondary form of activity that seeks to validate claims that are made, any form of philosophy is concerned to assess understandings constitutive of human activities. To say this is simply to repeat that the question philosophy as such critically asks and answers is the comprehensive question of human authenticity as such. But philosophy of religion is the one form of philosophy that *fully* assesses the explicit understandings identifying its subject activities. The explicit understandings by virtue of which human activities are political at least includes understandings of some more or less particular aspects of human or nonhuman reality, and the same is true of the subject activities of any specific form of philosophy other than philosophy of religion. In other words, these activities explicitly ask and answer questions about empirical conditions or characteristics in distinction from the character of human activity or reality as such.

Political philosophy, for instance, seeks critically to understand the most general ideal in terms of which all activities may be compared insofar as they are political and, in that respect, assesses political activities. But this is not a full assessment of the explicit understandings of any political activity. Since those understandings attend to some particular governing association, a full assessment of them requires a specification of the ideal to the empirical conditions or characteristics in question, and this specification is not a philosophical task. Political philosophy, then, seeks to assess its subject activities only insofar as they include an understanding of the most general political ideal, and this understanding may be only implicit in any given political activity.

In contrast, human activity is specifically religious precisely insofar as it explicitly and decisively asks and answers the question of human authenticity as such. This means that philosophical reflection on religion is reflection on explicit answers to the very question that distinguishes philosophy itself. Religions are themselves explicit claims about the terms in which all religions should be compared and assessed. Hence, the comparison that identifies philosophy of religion can only be a full assessment of the explicit understandings identifying its subject activities. In other words, the question What are the *most general* similarities and differences among religions? is equivalent to the question What are *the* similarities and differences among religions? Because the similarities and differences among religions are similarities and differences with respect to the most general terms for comparing and assessing religions, philosophy of religion is the one specific form of philosophy in which an answer to its identifying question is a full comparison of the understandings identifying its subject activities.

We might also formulate this point by saying that philosophy of religion requires philosophical theology. With the latter term, I mean nothing other than the attempt to reflect on all human activity and culture so as critically to ask and answer the comprehensive question. Of course, to define "philosophical theology" in this way is simply to make it another name for the inclusive philosophical task; philosophy itself *is* philosophical theology. Since every self-differentiation of philosophy (for instance, political philosophy) requires philosophy itself, we may also say that any specific form of philosophy requires philosophical theology. Still, there may be a rhetorical reason to emphasize this point with respect to philosophy of religion. Given that philosophical theology is generally understood to include a critical assessment of religious claims, to say that philosophy of religion requires philosophical theology expresses the distinctive character of the former, namely, its full assessment and, therefore, full comparison of the understandings identifying its subject activities.

Again, we may say that philosophy of religion is the one form of philosophy identified by explicit discussion with the activities on which it reflects. Other specific forms of philosophy may be only implicit discussions with their respective subject activities, because those forms seek to assess general similarities and differences that may be only implicit in the understandings of those activities. But religious understandings are candidate answers to the philosophical theological question, so that philosophy of religion is an explicit discussion with its subject activities. In the case of "comparative philosophy of religion," one might say, the redundancy is a useful one because it emphasizes the full comparison and assessment that identifies this form of philosophy.[21]

But if comparative philosophy of religion is the one form of philosophy identified by explicit discussion with its subject activities, then it may also be defined as a discussion among religious activities that has become critical reflection. A discussion among religious activities may be called "interreligious dialogue," and I understand this to be an activity in which adherents of two or more religions each seek to understand the other or others in the terms of her or his own religion. Precisely because religious activity asks and answers the comprehensive question not only explicitly but also decisively, each of the participants in an interreligious dialogue seeks so to understand the terms in which others ask and answer that question that the similarities and differences are understood and, therefore, assessed in her or his own religious terms. As a form of human activity, in other words, interreligious dialogue is also identified by the question: What are the similarities and differences among religions? Accordingly, this form of activity is distinguished from comparative philosophy of religion solely in the fact that the former asks and answers the question precritically.[22]

What this understanding denies, then, is the claim sometimes advanced that philosophy of religion is reflection of a different order than the reflection identifying religious activity. Of course, I have already said that the two are indeed different in the sense that philosophy is a secondary or critical form of activity. But the claim I mean to deny is that the two differ because religious activities explicitly ask and answer a different question than does philosophy. On this account, for instance,

religious understandings are said to be culturally and historically specific or, alternatively, subrational or transrational convictions in some sense that does not permit of philosophical
validation. Accordingly, religions are not candidate answers to
the philosophical question, and comparative philosophy of religion at best reports general similarities and differences in a manner that is not an assessment of religious claims. To the contrary, I conclude that comparative philosophy of religion may
be identified as interreligious dialogue that has become critical
reflection.

So to define comparative philosophy of religion suggests
that it is not the only form of critical reflection on religion. One
may also distinguish a form of reflection identified by asking
critically about the validity of a particular religion, and this form
is generally called "theology" or, at least an aspect of theology.[23]
In distinction from comparative philosophy of religion, then, theology is necessarily qualified by the name of some or other particular religion, for instance, Christian theology or Islamic theology. But just because it is critical reflection on the claims of a
particular religion, theology is similar to comparative philosophy
of religion in that both require philosophical theology.

We might say that theology is identified by explicit discussion with the activities identified in terms of a particular religion, and this discussion is important to the religious activities
in question precisely because they claim to represent the valid
answer to the comprehensive question. In other words, religious adherents have reason to seek the validation of their understandings, and, accordingly, the results of theological reflection sometimes assume a religious character, that is, become a
part of the cultural system in terms of which religious adherents decisively ask and answer the comprehensive question. Since
comparative philosophy of religion is also a validation of the
understandings identifying its subject activities, it follows that
this critical activity is also important to the adherents of the
religions that it compares. Given this importance, there is all the
more reason to say that comparative philosophy of religion may
be identified as interreligious dialogue that has become critical
reflection.

On the assumption that we have properly identified the task of comparative philosophy of religion, we may also clarify the relation between this task and historical or empirical study of religion. Given that religions are cultural systems, the concepts and symbols in terms of which the comprehensive question is religiously asked and answered are always some or other historically specific creation. Moreover, the identifying function of religious activity is to cultivate authentic understandings of the comprehensive purpose. Given this function, it is characteristic of religions that the terms they provide assume different rhetorical forms than do the terms proper to philosophical reflection. Religions at least frequently include highly symbolic forms of expression in distinction from the literal terms without which philosophy cannot critically reflect on the comprehensive question.

For both of these reasons, then, comparative philosophy of religion is dependent on the results of historical study of religion. Essential to the critical task of comparing and thereby assessing religious understandings is the task of understanding what these understandings are, that is, understanding the meaning of the claims represented in diverse religions. Given that religions are particular cultural creations and, moreover, that their rhetorical form is at least often highly symbolic, comparative philosophy of religion is dependent on answers to particular hermeneutical questions that only critical historical reflection on religions can provide.

But if comparative philosophy of religion is dependent on historical study of religion, it also follows that the latter is dependent on philosophical theology. Because all human understanding implies some answer to the comprehensive question, this is also the case with particular hermeneutical inquiries; every such inquiry is informed by some or other understanding of human activity or self-understanding as such. When the understandings that historical study seeks to understand are themselves attentive to empirical matters (for instance, in political history), it is not necessarily the case that hermeneutics must explicitly attend to its own understanding of human activity as such. In the case of the historical study of religion, however, the understandings that one seeks to understand are themselves answers to the comprehensive question. Accordingly, the terms in which historical study of religion seeks to make explicit the meaning of religious understandings are themselves the terms of some or other answer to the comprehensive question. When the subject activities are religious, then, the validity of particular hermeneutical inquiries depends on a valid understanding of human authenticity as such that is explicit, and, in that sense, the historical study of religion is also dependent on philosophical theology. Since comparative philosophy of religion requires philosophical theology, historians and philosophers who study religion have good reason to seek each other's company. Moreover, since comparative philosophy of religion may be identified as interreligious dialogue that has become critical reflection, both historians and philosophers of religion have good reason to keep company with theologians.

Notes

1. Karl-Otto Apel, "The Problem of Philosophical Fundamental-Grounding in Light of a Transcendental Pragmatic of Language," *Man and World* 8 (1975):239–75.

2. Richard Rorty, *Consequences of Pragmatism* (Minneapolis: University of Minnesota Press, 1992), 168.

3. John Hick, *An Interpretation of Religion: Human Responses to the Transcendent* (New Haven: Yale University Press, 1989), 3–4.

4. In the discussion that follows, I am immensely indebted to the work of Schubert M. Ogden. Above all, the definition of religion for which I will argue is his definition, with only a verbal change. But this means that the understanding of human activity that I attempt to develop, including especially the distinctions between explicit and implicit understandings and between religion and critical reflection upon it, is simply an attempt to appropriate his formulations and arguments within the context of the present purpose. See Schubert M. Ogden, *The Point of Christology* (San Francisco: Harper & Row,

1982), especially chap. 2; *On Theology* (San Francisco: Harper & Row, 1986), chaps. 1, 4, 6; *Is There Only One True Religion or Are There Many?* (Dallas: Southern Methodist University Press, 1992), especially chap. 1.

5. I recognize that the terms *human activity* and *self-understanding* may be used such that one has broader application than the other. Some might insist, for instance, that human activity but not self-understanding occurs when a human individual is asleep or unconscious. Others may attribute self-understanding to the activity of creatures or existents that we do not call human, for instance, certain nonhuman animals. My stipulation identifies the occurrence of self-understanding with human activity in order to simplify the presentation of the present argument. I judge that no substantial conclusions would be altered by stipulating any other plausible extensions for the two terms.

I also recognize that some formulations of theism assert that the divine reality is constituted by a self-understanding. My identification of self-understanding with human activity is meant neither to deny theism nor to call God human. Neither is intended, because I am convinced by the argument of Schubert M. Ogden that psychic terms, including the term *self-understanding*, properly apply to God, if God is, only as symbols and, therefore, not literally. See Schubert M. Ogden, "The Experience of God: Critical Reflections on Hartshorne's Theory of Analogy," in *Existence and Actuality: Conversations with Charles Hartshorne*, ed. John B. Cobb, Jr., and Franklin I. Gamwell (Chicago: University of Chicago Press, 1984), 16–37.

6. To understand something positive about X (for instance, that X is human) and to say that Y is absolutely different is to identify Y as merely not-X (for instance, not human). But not-X is insofar solely negative, that is, not the identification of another thing.

7. It is sometimes argued that the notion of self-determination is paradoxical or self-contradictory, because the self that determines must be different than the self that is determined, and yet the two must be one. But the apparent paradox disappears, I believe, if one understands the self that is determined as an activity that might have been (in the sense of real, not merely logical, possibility) different than it is. When Robert Frost, facing two roads that diverged, chose the one less traveled by, he did not simply walk down the less traveled road; on the contrary, his activity was walking down the less traveled road when it might have been walking down the well-worn path. The inclusion of the rejected alternative as something that was rejected is what made the activity the distinct thing that it was, as Frost's poem clearly expresses, and this inclusion of the alternative or alternatives that are not chosen makes the self that is determined and the self that determines the same self.

It is also sometimes argued that the notion of self-understanding or self-reflection is paradoxical or self-contradictory, because the self that reflects must be different than the self on which it reflects, and yet the two must be one. But the same notion of something related to itself is, I believe, involved in the concept of determination by others. If X is determined by others, then X is internally related to them; and if X is internally related to others, then X is both its *relations* to others and a *term* constituted by those relations. One might speak of X in the latter sense as a relation to its relations. More precisely, perhaps, X as the term constituted is the manner in which X is related to others. Hence, we may say that understanding is the distinctively human manner of being internally related to others. But then understanding one's own relations to others becomes self-understanding in that the manner of relating to others is self-determined. Understanding is a relation of X to its relations to others because it is also a choice to be X rather than X' or X", all of which are consistent with being internally related to the others in question. To choose what one is or becomes with understanding is self-understanding.

8. Alfred North Whitehead, *Adventures of Ideas* (New York: The Free Press, 1961), 194.

9. If this is so, then one might formulate the so-called pragmatic theory of meaning in something like the following manner: If a putative understanding cannot sensibly be a part of one's choice of purpose—that is, if one cannot sensibly say how this understanding constitutes one's choice—then it is not a sensible understanding at all. For instance, the claim that all things are completely determined by things other than themselves cannot sensibly be a part of one's choice of purpose and, therefore, is not a sensible understanding. I also believe, to illustrate the point again, that "nothing exists" is not a sensible understanding, because one cannot sensibly say how this understanding constitutes one's choice.

10. Indeed, if all implicit understandings were previously learned, then *that* claim would be implied by all explicit understandings, and each of us would have to learn the truth of that claim before we could have any conscious thoughts at all.

11. To say that an explicit misunderstanding of oneself *may be* is not to say that it always or in all respects *is* self-deception. One's implicit self-understanding may not express duplicity or, as I will also say, may be authentic, and its explicit misrepresentation may be the result of ignorance or mistake. Consciously, one simply formulates incorrectly what one implicitly knows about oneself. For instance, one may implicitly believe that one ought so to act as to pursue in some specified way the well-being of others and may in fact so act. But one may also explicitly misrepresent this as simply what one wants to

do or enjoys doing rather than what one ought to do—because, say, one has learned to associate morality with some rigid or oppressive moralism that one rightly rejects. Thus, one's implicit purpose is more fully characterized as follows: to pursue in the specified way the well-being of others and to formulate this purpose explicitly as best one can. This is not to deny the importance of an explicit mistake in self-understanding, since one may subsequently believe it implicitly, such that implicit self-understanding becomes an expression of duplicity. For instance, one may subsequently choose not to pursue the well-being of others because, in some situation, one does not enjoy it.

12. See John Dewey, *Reconstruction in Philosophy* (Boston: Beacon Press, 1957), 186.

13. I understand a pragmatic self-contradiction to be an understanding or claim that denies what is implied in every act of making the claim, that is, the valid comprehensive self-understanding. If, as the text will argue in a moment, philosophy is the critical attempt to make explicit the valid comprehensive self-understanding, a claim is shown to be a valid philosophical claim by showing that its denial is pragmatically self-contradictory.

A valid philosophical claim may be stated as a hermeneutical claim, a claim of the form "self-understanding is X," or as an existential claim, a claim of the form "something that is X exists." If a valid philosophical claim is stated as a hermeneutical claim, then its denial is not only pragmatically but also logically self-contradictory, that is, the propositional content of the denial implies what it denies. This follows because the comprehensive character of self-understanding is denied. One might object that "self-understanding exists" is pragmatically self-contradictory but not logically self-contradictory. But this claim is not of the form "self-understanding is X," which may be reformulated "if it exists, self-understanding is X." In other words, "self-understanding exists" is an existential claim that, if stated hermeneutically, is expressed "if it exists, self-understanding exists"—and, in this formulation, its denial, "if it exists, self-understanding does not exist," is logically self-contradictory. It now follows that every valid philosophical claim may be stated as an existential claim, a claim of the form "something that is X exists," and, given this form, its denial is pragmatically but not necessarily logically self-contradictory. Hence, philosophy is, in the broad sense, metaphysics.

In the sense that the denial of a valid philosophical claim is pragmatically self-contradictory, I hold that the philosophical task is transcendental. In saying this, I have been educated by and agree with Karl-Otto Apel (see Apel, "Philosophical Fundamental-Grounding"). In distinction from Apel, however, I also hold that one must distinguish within the class of valid transcendental claims those that are valid metaphysical claims in the strict sense, that is, valid claims about reality or existence as such. These are hermeneutical claims that, when stated as existential claims, cannot be denied without logical self-contradiction. In other words, a claim of the form "something that is X exists" is a valid metaphysical claim in the strict sense if its denial is not only pragmatically but also logically self-contradictory. I have attempted a more extended clarification in *The Divine Good: Modern Moral Theory and the Necessity of God* (San Francisco: HarperCollins, 1990), chaps. 4, 6. Although, as I have noted, one may use the term "metaphysical" in both a broad and a strict sense, my use of it in the text will be limited to the strict sense.

14. On my reading, the insight that self-understanding as such is categorically prescriptive for human activity is Kant's abiding contribution to moral thought, so that the imperative "act only on that maxim whereby thou canst at the same time will that it should become a universal law" (Immanuel Kant, *Fundamental Principles of the Metaphysic of Morals* [Indianapolis: Bobbs-Merrill, 1949], 38) means "act only on that understanding of yourself that is a consistent exemplification of self-understanding as such."

15. In saying that the valid comprehensive self-understanding includes a valid metaphysical understanding, I depart from Kant. But this departure was implied in the claim that one's choice of a self-understanding is nothing other than the choice of one's purpose. On my reading, it was precisely because Kant denied metaphysical knowledge (in the strict sense of "metaphysics"; see n. 13) that he insisted on a purely formal moral law, that is, a categorical imperative that is independent of any purpose. For Kant, in other words, the "end in itself" (ibid., 45) can be "conceived only negatively, as that which we must never act against" (ibid., 54), namely, the rational freedom of every person. To the best of my reasoning, however, this putative independence from any purpose or any material character means that human authenticity as such "can be conceived only negatively," and what can be conceived only negatively is nothing. I have discussed this point more extensively in *The Divine Good,* especially chap. 2.

The same point is at issue if one says that the valid comprehensive self-understanding is an understanding of reality only *insofar as it can be understood.* For those who add it, this qualification is important because they seek to distinguish, as Kant did, between reality as understandable or conceivable and reality as it is. It is precisely this distinction that expresses Kant's denial of metaphysical knowledge and, therefore, his affirmation of a purely formal law. But I hold, with Whitehead and against Kant, that "the unknowable is unknown" (Alfred North Whitehead, *Process and Reality,* corrected edition, ed. David Ray Griffin and Donald Sherburne [New York: The Free Press, 1978], 4). To claim that something inconceivable is possible is to claim that one can conceive of the inconceivable. I have discussed this point in *The Divine Good,* chap. 4.

16. I recognize that this may be considered a narrow definition of *political,* since the term is often defined in terms of the larger cultural and social struc-

ture. But this distinction between narrow and broad meanings of *political* is not germane to the present discussion.

17. To be sure, the distinction between critical and decisive reflection is a relative one, because an activity seeking to validate claims that are made or implied in other activities may itself involve other claims that are simply asserted. For instance, given human activities may be constituted by understandings about empirical regularities in the nonhuman world. If the critical reflection on such claims is called "natural science," this activity may itself include explicit or implicit claims about reality as such that are not themselves the object of critical reflection and would become so only in the activity of philosophy. Moreover, any critical activity itself implies the claim that this critical activity is important or worthwhile. But the relative character of a distinction does not gainsay that distinction, as the example just given also illustrates, because it serves to distinguish between scientific and nonscientific understandings of empirical regularities, as well as between science and philosophy.

It is worth noting that there is one question on which human activity cannot reflect critically without at the same time reflecting decisively—namely, the comprehensive question. Since every human activity asks and answers this question decisively, philosophical activities cannot avoid doing so. This is, I judge, at least one way to understand the claim that philosophical activity is "self-referential" (see, for instance, Apel, "Fundamental Grounding"). It does not follow, however, that philosophy is always "ideological" or "rationalizing" in a sense that prevents it from being critical. For the activity of thinking philosophically may be, at least so far as the character of the thinking is concerned, authentic.

18. Cf. Ogden: " 'Religion' . . . [is] the primary form of culture in terms of which we human beings explicitly ask and answer the existential question of the meaning of being for us" (Ogden, *Is There Only One True Religion?*, 5). Ogden means by "the existential question" what I mean by "the comprehensive question."

19. Although this formulation is logically proper, one might recommend against it if certain rhetorical considerations assume prominence. One might hold that explicitly moral claims are expressed in a different "voice" or have a different "illocutionary load" than is the case with explicitly existential claims, notwithstanding that a given moral claim and a given existential claim are, all implications taken into account, identical in propositional content. For instance, one might hold that "human activity as such ought fully to pursue the divine telos" and "human activity as such is the object of God's redemption,"

even if the two imply each other, differ in illocutionary load. Since the former prescribes and the latter describes, one might argue, the religious affections that each seeks to evoke are in the first instance different—loyalty or commitment in the one case, trust or gratitude in the other. I will not attempt to pursue this matter here, since my principal intent is to clarify the logic of the comparative philosophy of religion.

In calling the question that religious activity explicitly asks and answers the most general moral question, I should underscore that this is the question of human authenticity as such and, therefore, a transcendental question. On another use of the term, *moral* is limited to questions about more or less particular purposes or actions in which one's understanding of human authenticity as such is expressed. I do not deny but, rather, insist that every human activity asks and answers not only the most general moral question but also another moral question to which the more limited use of the term *moral* refers.

20. Cf. Peter Berger, *The Sacred Canopy: Elements of a Sociological Theory of Religion* (Garden City, N.Y.: Doubleday and Company, 1967), 175–77.

21. It should be noted that comparison in philosophy of religion includes an assessment of religions with respect to the function of religion. Given that religious activities ask and answer the comprehensive question explicitly and *decisively,* the function of religion is to cultivate in the lives of religious adherents authentic understandings of human activity as such. One might say that religious representations claim to be not only adequate to the content of authentic human activity as such but also religiously fitting. That a religion is fitting is, one should note, in some respects a matter particular to historical time and place. One might hold, for instance, that both Buddhism and Judaism represent the valid answer to the comprehensive question, each in its own set of concepts and symbols, and also properly conclude that one or the other is not fitting in some specified historical circumstances. Because it makes reference to specific historical circumstances, this conclusion cannot be validated by philosophy alone. But the function of religion generally is implied by the character of human activity as such, and, therefore, there must be general characteristics of a fitting religion. Since any religion claims to exemplify these general characteristics, philosophy of religion includes critical reflection on these claims and, insofar, on such matters as sacred texts, myth, ritual, and religious associational patterns. Here, too, philosophy of religion is distinguished from other forms of philosophy by explicit discussion with its subject activities, precisely because a religion includes the claim that its answer to the comprehensive question is fitting to the function of religion.

In addition to whatever other inadequacies it includes, the present essay suffers from the fact that it is not an explicit discussion with any religion. Since I have said that a clarification of philosophy of religion is itself a task within philosophy of religion, the claim that this form of philosophy is comparative in the special sense that I have identified implies that the conclusions of this essay are properly subject to explicit discussion with the material claims of diverse religions. The absence of this discussion is one reason why I have titled this essay "A Foreword to Comparative Philosophy of Religion."

22. I do not mean to say that either interreligious dialogue or comparative philosophy of religion occurs only when individuals are actually having a discussion with each other. I speak of "discussion" or "dialogue" in a general sense, so that they mean any attempt explicitly to understand the understandings of other individuals, even if those other individuals are not currently present. Actual discussion or dialogue is, we may say, the mutual public expression of the dialogue that each individual may pursue privately. Interreligious dialogue, then, means any attempt by a religious adherent explicitly to understand the similarities and differences between or among religions in her or his own religious terms. Accordingly, I do not mean to confine either interreligious dialogue or comparative philosophy of religion to religions that currently have adherents.

23. This last qualifying phrase intends to acknowledge that *theology* is often used to mean not only reflection that seeks to validate the answer identifying a particular religion. On this broader meaning, theology as a form of critical reflection also includes the relevant hermeneutical question—What is the answer identifying a particular religion?—and, perhaps, relevant practical questions—How should this answer be expressed in particular purposes?

References

Apel, Karl-Otto. 1975. "The Problem of Philosophical Fundamental-Grounding in Light of a Transcendental Pragmatic of Language." *Man and World* 8:239–75.

———. 1979. "Types of Rationality Today." In *Rationality Today,* edited by Theodore Gereats, 307–40. Ottawa: University Press.

Berger, Peter. 1967. *The Sacred Canopy: Elements of a Sociological Theory of Religion.* Garden City, New York: Doubleday and Company.

Dewey, John. 1934. *A Common Faith.* New Haven: Yale University Press.

———. 1948. *Reconstruction in Philosophy.* Boston: Beacon Press.

Gamwell, Franklin I. 1990. *The Divine Good.* San Francisco: HarperCollins.

Hartshorne, Charles. 1970. *Creative Synthesis and Philosophic Method.* LaSalle, Ill.: Open Court.

Hick, John. 1989. *An Interpretation of Religion: Human Responses to the Transcendent.* New Haven: Yale University Press.

Kant, Immanuel. 1949. *Fundamental Principles of the Metaphysic of Morals.* Indianapolis: Bobbs-Merrill.

———. 1960. *Religion within the Limits of Reason Alone.* New York: Harper & Brothers.

Rorty, Richard. 1979. "Transcendental Arguments, Self-Reference, and Pragmatism." In *Transcendental Arguments and Science,* edited by Peter Bieri, Rolf Horstman, and Lorenz Kreuger, 77–103. Dortrecht, Holland: D. Reidel.

———. 1982. *Consequences of Pragmatism.* Minneapolis: University of Minnesota Press.

Ogden, Schubert M. 1982. *The Point of Christology.* San Francisco: Harper & Row.

———. 1984. "The Experience of God: Critical Reflections on Hartshorne's Theory of Analogy." In *Existence and Actuality: Conversations with Charles Hartshorne,* edited by John B. Cobb, Jr., and Franklin I. Gamwell, 16–37. Chicago: University of Chicago Press.

———. 1986. *On Theology.* San Francisco: Harper & Row.

———. 1992. *Is There Only One True Religion or Are There Many?* Dallas: Southern Methodist University Press.

Whitehead, Alfred North. 1961. *Adventures of Ideas.* New York: The Free Press.

———. 1974. *Religion in the Making.* New York: Meridian.

Chapter 2

What Are Buddhists *Doing* When They Deny the Self?

Steven Collins

In this chapter the word *Buddhism* refers to the Theravāda tradition(s) of South and Southeast Asia, in what I call its traditional period.[1] The argument draws on historical and textual data and also on modern ethnographic reports. This is not unproblematic methodologically, I realize, but I think it is defensible: given the comparative intentions of the volumes published in this series, and the fact that most readers are not specialist Buddhologists, it is not inappropriate to write from a general and in some ways simplified—but not, I hope, misleading—perspective. The chapter has three parts: Buddhist Universalism, the Discourse of Not-self, and the Practice of Not-self.

Buddhist Universalism

One obvious characteristic of what are often called "world religions" or "great traditions" is universalism: they offer visions of the world which claim to be true universally and aims to be achieved which are available universally. In Buddhism it is said that the fundamental nature of things as depicted in its teaching exists always and everywhere, whether or not there is a Buddha at any given time and place to teach it (S II 25, A I 286). But while some of the characteristics of life, such as impermanence and suffering, are readily known to all, the truth of not-self must be discovered and made known by a Buddha (Vbh-a 49–50). One can therefore delineate a specific attitude to history and religious authority: unlike what became the dominant tradition of Vedic Hinduism, on the one hand, which holds the Vedas to be ahistorical and without any author (either human or divine),[2] Buddhism locates its "revelation" in the experiences and statements of a historical human. On the other hand, unlike Christianity and Islam, the historicity of a unique founding figure is not intrinsic to the salvific message: all Buddhas are, in this sense, the same and interchangeable, in that they rediscover the same Truth.[3] Accordingly, while there is in Buddhism, unlike Hinduism, an extensive tradition of historiography, its historical consciousness—while undeniable—is of a different kind from that of Christianity and Islam.

I should like to look a little more closely at some differences in the other aspect of universalism just mentioned, that of universal availability. One might be tempted to say that the aims offered by such religions are meant for anyone and everyone; however, Buddhist soteriology, while immediately applicable to and relevant for anyone, is not for everyone: that is, not everyone all at once. There are, one might say, two kinds of universalism, which claim either

(1) everyone can and should do X; or

(2) everyone is permitted to do X (if individually capable), but no one is required to do X.

The first has tended to be more characteristic of Christianity and Islam, the second of Buddhism. As claims to universal truth, all three systems have conflicted with other competing views; thus Buddhism has had terms and concepts which parallel the categories of "heathen," "pagan," and "infidel."[4] But the monotheist exclusivism[5] of Christianity and Islam has led them to compete with, and for the most part proscribe, not only the beliefs and practices of alternative soteriologies, but also—in theory if not always in practice—any interaction with other religious or supernatural resources. Their message is both available to and exclusively mandatory for all individuals, in any society or culture.

In the Buddhist case, allegiance to Buddhism as an ultimate, soteriological system has not excluded participation in other forms of religion (by which I mean interaction with supernatural beings, mediated by non-Buddhist religious specialists); moreover, it is simply not feasible for everyone to attempt to achieve the goals of Buddhist soteriology. Salvation *(nirvāṇa)* requires a celibate, monastic life (since it involves the eradication of desire, seen as impossible to those sexually active), which obviously can have little future as a blueprint for human society. Moreover, Buddhist monastic law forbids monks (and nuns, when they existed) to acquire and cook their own food or to handle money. They are thus dependent on the existence of a lay society which can produce the surplus food and wealth needed to sustain monasticism and reproduce the next generation of members of the monastic Order.[6] Historically, probably only a small minority of monks and nuns has in fact aimed directly at *nirvāṇa,* and in the broader range of goals envisaged by Buddhist practice both laity and monks share many activities and concerns. But it remains true that the monastic life has been seen as a necessary condition for final salvation.

I shall return later to what one might call this restricted universalism in Buddhism; for the moment I want to describe two contexts in which the universal truth of Buddhism has replaced or complemented more particularistic ideas. In the volume of summary reports of the earlier conferences in this series, I am recorded (accurately) as having said that an essential function of the idea of a universal religious truth is to be a weapon in a particular arsenal, in a historically specific situation of dispute.[7] As it stands, this was perhaps an extreme way to express the point; on the same occasion Stephen Toulmin made the more elegant suggestion that "claims to universality themselves have to be contextualised, seen as rhetorical claims within a rhetorical context."[8] I will discuss two such contexts here: first, ancient

India at the time of the Buddha, where Buddhist universal ethics countered the relativist particularism of Brahmanical society and religion; and second, the ongoing sociocultural position of Buddhism in South and Southeast Asia, where it has provided teachings, symbols, and institutions of translocal value.[9]

At the time of the Buddha, Brahmanical religion was successfully disseminating over the north of India its social ideology of separate classes or estates: *brahmin* priests, *kṣatriya* warriors, *vaiśya* farmers, and *śūdra* servants.[10] (It is noteworthy that the scheme did not at first contain merchants; it was formulated originally for a nomadic pastoralist and then rural agricultural society, and it had difficulty accommodating the rise of urban trading and political centers. Merchants were eventually classed in the *vaiśya* group.) The overriding concept of morality or religious duty *(dharma)* was particularized into different individual duties (*svadharma,* also translatable as "essential nature"): it was as much the nature and duty of a *brahmin* to perform ritual, or a *vaiśya* to farm, as it was for fish to swim, cows to give milk, the sun to shine, and so on. There was no universal notion of human nature shared by the different groups or species (this being one meaning of the word *jāti,* also translatable as "caste"). Access to religious truths and Brahmanical sacrificial rituals was regulated by a hierarchical set of entitlements *(adhikāra)* distributed across this social spectrum. The Buddha seems to have spent much time in cities and with merchants and to have rejected Brahmanical ideology and social practices in two ways. First, although he did not set out to change caste society, caste background was irrelevant both to entry into the monastic order and to the universal ethical rules which applied to all, regardless of social position.[11] "Do not ask about caste," runs a famous verse, "ask about behaviour" (Sn 462). Second, his soteriological scheme was centered around the concept of *dukkha* (Sanskrit *duḥkha*), usually translated "suffering" but better "unsatisfactoriness," both the truth and the transcendence of which were to be found in the human body and mind, in experience shared or shareable by all individuals. "In this fathom-long carcase with its perceptions and ideas," the

Buddha is alleged to have said, "there is the world, the arising and the cessation of the world, and the way leading to the cessation of the world" (S I 62). Thus the Buddha's teaching that there was a universal humanity and a universal method for attaining salvation, available to any individual, arose not as a context-free intellectual option but as a specific maneuver in an arena of contestation and competition.

As Buddhism spread over the whole of South and Southeast Asia, its universalism came to have other dimensions. As mentioned earlier, what we might call Buddhism, what the tradition calls the *sāsana*—that is, both Buddhist teaching and the historical institutions which transmit its timeless truth—has always coexisted in lived practice with other forms of religion, which I prefer to call localized supernaturalism; that is to say, interaction with supernatural beings whose sphere of activity is always, to a greater or lesser degree, concentrated on a particular geographical area. The aims of such interaction tend to be immediate and practical: health, agricultural success, etc. The aims of Buddhist soteriology, on the other hand but complementarily, are displaced from the present: better rebirth or the final understanding and transcendence of suffering and death. (These two types, localized supernaturalism and Buddhist soteriology, are abstractions from a behavioral field, better seen not as separate systems but as two ends of a spectrum.) In this context, the perspective and goals of Buddhism—offering an overall, context-free vision of life, death, and ultimate happiness—sit on top, as it were, of the immediate problems and localized solutions offered by interaction with supernatural beings. Buddhist universal truth exists as the most over-arching, least localized level within a field of religious concerns and solutions. To speak of a soteriology, a "system of salvation," is to emphasize two points: it is not only a system of *salvation,* offering final solutions to ultimate problems; it is also a *system* of salvation, in the sense that it provides the possibility of organizing the universe conceptually and of seeing the manifold polytheism of everyday life[12] in the perspective of a single, hierarchically ordered world view.

Although the dynamics of Buddhist history and culture
are for some purposes best understood in relation to its settled
position in the agricultural societies of South and Southeast
Asia,[13] it has also been associated, in its beginnings and throughout history, with urban centers of trade and political authority
and has often been adopted as an ideology by kings in the
process of establishing or consolidating their kingdoms (kingdoms of course always in conflict and in danger of
disestablishment). There is a connection, I think, between the
role of Buddhism as a soteriology in the sense just outlined and
its political significance. Kingship provided in politics the symbols and institutions of translocal power and authority which
Buddhist teaching provided on the religious level; one might
say, borrowing Max Weber's famous term, that there has been
in Buddhist cultures an elective affinity between the possibility
of conceiving the universe and its inhabitants in terms of a single,
overall religious ideology and the idea that political organization could and should be large-scale, ordered, and focused ultimately on one person or lineage. In inscriptions and texts kings
were rhetorically associated both with the lineage of the Buddha and with that of the great Indian emperor Aśoka, while the
legitimacy of their power was expressed, *inter alia,* in the possession of Buddha relics and Buddha images. The universality
of Buddhist truth and the expansive aspirations of Buddhist
polities have co-existed in one and the same practical and rhetorical context.

The Discourse of Not-self

Central to Buddhist soteriology is the doctrine of not-self (Pali
anattā, Sanskrit *anātman;* the opposed doctrine of *ātman* was
central to Brahmanical thought). Put very briefly, this is the
doctrine that human beings have no soul, no self, no unchanging essence.[14] What appear to be stable and unitary persons are
in fact collections of impersonal and impermanent events, arising and disappearing in a beginningless process of conditioning, a process which includes both physical causation and the

spiritual causation of *karma,* action and its results. Connectedness across a series of lives occurs through the continuity of consciousness, seen as a constantly changing series of momentary events, in which both memory and temporary coherence of personality can be found, but no enduring self. It has often been remarked that this doctrine (aside from the belief in rebirth) bears some resemblance to the thought of David Hume; recently Derek Parfit, a philosopher in the same tradition, has claimed in his book *Reasons and Persons* that his reductionist view of personal identity agrees with that of the Buddha. I mention these alleged similarities in order to introduce a specific point.

In Hume's work, there are two quite different ways in which he speaks of self and person. In the first book of his *Treatise of Human Nature,* "Of the Understanding," he arrives at sceptical conclusions about the nature of personal identity, claiming that human beings are "nothing but a bundle or collection of different perceptions." In books Two and Three, on the other hand, "Of the Passions" and "Of Morality," his psychological and ethical reflections are carried on in terms of a unitary "self, or individual person, of whose actions and sentiments each of us is intimately conscious."[15] Social relations and sentiments are described in terms of a straightforward distinction between self and other. He seems to lack either a way of connecting the two kinds of discussion of self in a single discourse or a theory which can account for the co-existence of separate discourses of the self.[16] Derek Parfit is explicitly concerned to connect his view of personal identity with his discussion of moral problems, but as Steven Lukes points out in a review of the book, Parfit's " 'persons,' linking 'experiences' and acting on 'reasons,' are curiously disconnected from any recognisable social context: their *social* identity—how they are seen by and how they relate to others—does not enter into his 'reductionist' view" (italics in original). Parfit's arguments proceed, *inter alia,* through various thought experiments, more or less science fictional, in which, for example, brain bisection and transplantation make it theoretically possible that one self should be divisible into a number of descendant selves. Peter Strawson, in another review, also notes that Parfit pays "relatively little attention to [a] person's place in society or his relation to others"; and he remarks:

> If I am the same person as X, then all X's rights and duties and other social relations are mine: his property is mine, his wife and children, his office, his status and his friends. But what if I am divided up [as Parfit suggests is possible]? No doubt an equitable arrangement could be arrived at in some cases. Property can be divided. Families present more difficulty. And which of my two "psychological inheritors," if either, will command my regiment? Or present himself, with a reasonable hope of welcome, at the door of my lover, if I have one? Perhaps the two should fight a duel about it.[17]

Buddhism cannot countenance, because of the strictly individual nature of karmic causality, the possibility of selves separating; the Buddhist view is, in fact, much less drastically reductionist than Parfit's.[18] But there is an analogous problem. In what ways can Buddhism's selfless persons interact? What is the relation between the Buddhist denial of self and the ongoing fact of Buddhist monks—those who attempt to realize the truth of not-self—existing as social agents, related both to other monks and to lay society?

Within Buddhist thought, there is an apparently simple answer to the problem. Two levels or kinds of language and truth are distinguished: the conventional and the ultimate. It is true "ultimately" that there is no self, but "conventionally" it is possible to designate the temporary psycho-physical configurations of impersonal events we think of as persons by proper names, pronouns (including "I"), definite descriptions, and other means of reference. Buddhism thus has what Hume lacked: an explicit meta-theory which can account, in its own terms, for the co-existence of separate discourses of the self. In a characteristically Indian solution to a dilemma, two apparently incompatible alternatives are both kept but ordered into a hierarchy. For my purposes the distinction between these two kinds of discourse, when seen without its hierarchical ordering, can point us to the fact that the denial of self is meant to describe directly only certain kinds of experience and agency. I want to ask: Which discourses within Buddhism are intended to describe which kinds of agency? What can we learn about the discourse of not-self by a study of its social location?

Let me start by citing an article by Michael Carrithers. Commenting on a lecture by Marcel Mauss, entitled "A Category of the Human Mind: The Notion of Person [personne]; The Notion of Self [moi]," Carrithers distinguishes between what he calls personne-theories, conceptual construals of the person, and moi-theories, conceptual construals of the self. (This use of the words is meant purely as a heuristic device, not as a commentary on the actual use of the terms in ordinary language.) A personne-theory, he says, is

> a conception of the individual human being as a member of a (1) significant and (2) ordered collectivity. [Such a collectivity] has a specific form which bears a clear relationship to the conception of the personne which goes with it. ... [A moi-theory is] a conception of (1) the physical and mental individuality of human beings within (2) a natural or spiritual cosmos, and (3) interacting with each other as moral agents.[19]

One might say that human beings are articulated conceptually as agents, by themselves and in relation to each other, in different ways, in different discourses. Carrithers suggests, and I agree, that the Buddhist doctrine of not-self is a moi-theory, not a personne-theory: "The Buddhist analysis of the moi is one which is profoundly moral and social, but the society it envisages is that of all living beings interacting face to face."[20] That is to say, although there are extensive, indeed intrinsic moral dimensions of the teaching, this morality is not one whose application is restricted to agency within a specific social system, actual or ideal. It applies to any individual interacting with any other(s) anywhere, not only to an agent in the particular circumstances of, and with the particular relations determined by, for instance, the Indian caste system, a given kinship formation or patron-client matrix, citizenship in a modern bureaucratic nation-state, or any other such situation in which the agents are defined in terms of their position within an ordered collectivity, with the rights and duties (which may or may not be encoded legally) afforded by that position. Buddhist soteriology has existed in a variety of different forms of society throughout Asia. Just as the "ultimate" solutions of Buddhist soteriology have co-existed with localized religious solutions to immediate problems, so too the universal truth of not-self applies to all individuals regardless of any other kinds of agency enabled and constrained by the various social arrangements of their different collectivities.

Before modern times, it had never been supposed that lay-persons should apply the doctrine of not-self directly to them-selves.[21] In traditional Buddhist societies, to be ordained as a monk is, on the formal level at least, to change one's social identity from that enabled and constrained by one's place in a specific kinship group, patron-client matrix, or other local rela-tionships, to that afforded by the translocal, universal monastic role. Of course in practice things are more complex, and many qualifications have to be made to this statement. For example, continuing relations and obligations between a monk and his parents have always been accepted. In mainland Southeast Asia it is customary for young boys and men to enter the monkhood temporarily; they obviously remain, in the longer term, clearly within their previous kinship group. In Sri Lanka, a village mon-astery is frequently inhabited by only one monk, along with his sister's son as pupil and successor.[22] But from the analytical perspective I am adopting here, I think it is reasonable to ignore such facts and to accept the formal, institutional change of iden-tity, as it is represented in the Buddhist language which de-scribes the situation. The change of social role from layman to monk is not in itself, of course, a change in ontological status.[23] The ordination ceremony provides someone with a new name and a new position in civil law—and in contemporary societies with a new identity card. Not only are monks subject to the civil law of their societies, but they take on the new rights and duties afforded by the monastic rule, the *Vinaya*. In both kinds of legal code the facts of responsibility, contractual relations, and so on, apply to named and enduring individuals; in monastic law, the only provision for impaired identity is the lack of responsibility ascribed to those who have committed infractions while *acittaka,* literally "mindless" or "unconscious," but perhaps better here "not in their right minds," or "without *mens rea.*" The etiquette vocabularies of Buddhist societies prescribe that special forms of language (honorific verbs, pronouns, and so on) be used in relation to monks; it is interesting, for example, that modern "nuns" in Burma—women who deserve that designation in many ways in practice, but not in either Buddhist or civil law—seem to be described and addressed sometimes in the style appropriate to monastics, and sometimes in that appropriate to laity, which reflects precisely their ambiguous social status.[24]

Buddhist monks as social agents, therefore, are unitary and enduring persons. It is not simply a convenient (or "conventional") fiction to use ordinary language to refer to such persons. There is, *in principle,* an analysis of such agency which can dispense with reference to persons, but such a reductionist discourse cannot serve the social, legal, or behavioral purposes of the nonreductionist discourse which it can, *in principle,* replace. There are, likewise, many kinds of Buddhist literature in which the identity and agency of monks are depicted as being those of recognizable, named individuals; this literature simply could not exist as reductionist discourse. In the historical chronicles, for example, individual monks are often portrayed as major characters, sometimes simply mentioned as names in monastic lineages—those lineages through which the chronicles seek to demonstrate that one monastic group is the authentic heir of the Buddha's teaching and authority. The same thing is true of two genres of literature extremely widespread in Buddhist culture: narrative texts and collections of ethical and practical maxims. In narratives, whether canonical or commentarial stories, *Jātaka*-s or *Apadāna*-s (stories of the past lives of the Buddha and of famous monks and nuns), or other texts, it is obviously a constitutive necessity that characters appear and act as persons, albeit persons whose karmic identity can be carried across different lifetimes. The genre of ethical and practical maxims contains sentiments which are pan-Indian rather than specifically Buddhist, and texts of this kind are usually called *nīti,* "good policy," or *subhāṣita,* "elegant sayings"; they seem to have formed a major part of traditional monastic education. Their proverbs and advice—roughly, the Sanskrit and Pali equivalents of "a friend in need is a friend indeed," "one good turn deserves another," and the like—presuppose enduring agents, notably in the quasi-contractual notions of friendship which are so frequent in them.

There is one kind of Buddhist canonical literature which deals directly not with conventional but with ultimate truth. The first two of the three divisions of the canon, the monastic disciplinary rules and the Buddha's sermons, as narrative texts are mostly worded in terms of persons and their agency; but the third, the *Abhidhamma,* contains for the most part elaborations of the ubiquitous lists in Buddhist teaching which are held to describe, reductively and exhaustively, the ultimate truth of the impersonal events which make up the things and persons of everyday life. But it also contains, as an apparent anomaly, a work called *Puggala-paññatti* ("Designations of Persons," or "Character Types") in which various moral and practical predicates are ascribed to different kinds of person (this kind of character depiction is common in many other texts also). This text is indeed anomalous on the level of classification; but its content can be seen to correspond to many important and familiar practical issues in the life of the monkhood: for example, the spiritual status of different individuals, which kinds of pupil fit which kinds of teacher, and, perhaps most important, which meditation subject is to be chosen for which kind of person. This last issue is elaborated in other texts in terms of the differing temperaments (or "behaviors," *cariya*) of different persons (e.g., Vism 97–115).

There are, then, a number of texts and contexts in which the discourse of not-self is inapplicable, both for specifically Buddhist purposes and for the purposes of social description in different collectivities. It is noteworthy that there is no Buddhist *personne*-theory in Carrithers' sense. Buddhist texts are quite happy to make use of local categories of description in their accounts of what it is to be a member of a "significant and ordered collectivity" (most notably those of caste in India and Sri Lanka). It might well be argued that the monastic Order itself is the Buddhist *personne*-theory. It is certainly a significant and ordered collectivity, with clearly defined roles and statuses: elder, novice, preceptor-teacher, pupil, etc. But although the Order is the necessary venue for the individual realization of not-self (as I shall discuss later), agency within it is determined not by the metaphysical and psychological theory of not-self, but by the monastic Code and is attributed to the persons who are defined by the Code. One example of this distinction: for monks, sexual thoughts in dreams and nocturnal emissions, being as far as ordinary agency is concerned unintentional, do not breach monastic law (Vin III 39, 112, 116); but on the metaphysical-psychological level, they are counted as facts of residual desire, and so as actions *(karma)*, which necessarily produce a karmic result (Sp 521, Mp III 3178, Vbh-a 408). Moreover, the monastic Order is, in sociological terminology, a formal organisation; that is, it is not a naturally evolving human community but a particular association "established for the explicit purpose of achieving certain [specific] goals."[25] As such a formal organization, it can exist alongside of, or more accurately within, any kind of natural society. One might say that there is in this sense—and despite what I called earlier the elective affinity between Buddhist soteriology and kingship—no such thing as a *Buddhist* social *theory;* that is, there is no account of an ideal, self-reproducing human community whose members are defined in terms of, and in which social agency is deduced from, Buddhist first principles. Despite this lack of a *theory* of social persons in Buddhism, there are, as I have said, many Buddhist discourses in which persons do and must appear. But what, then, are the texts and contexts in which not-self, Buddhism's *moi*-theory, *is* immediately applicable?

Before answering this question empirically, let me make use of another distinction made by an anthropologist, Robin Horton. In a much-discussed paper called "African Traditional Thought and Western Science," originally published in 1967, he contrasted in both contexts "two distinct yet intimately complementary levels of thought and discourse." Originally, these were called the "commonsense" or "everyday" level and the "theoretical," but in later writing he has accepted many of the criticisms made of this formulation and replaced it with a distinction between "primary" and "secondary theory."[26] Some of the main differences between them are as follows:

1. "Primary theory really does not differ very much from community to community or from culture to culture," whereas "there are startling differences" between different cultures' secondary theories.

2. Primary theory "gives the world a foreground filled with middle-sized (say between a hundred times as large and a hundred times as small as human beings) enduring, solid objects. These objects are interrelated, indeed interdefined, in terms of a 'push-pull' conception of causality, in which spatial and temporal contiguity are seen as crucial to the transmission of change."

3. Primary theory "makes two major distinctions amongst its objects: first, that between human beings and other objects; and second, among human beings, that between self and others," whereas secondary theory may not make these distinctions.

4. "Whilst the entities and processes of primary theory are thought of as directly 'given' to the human observer, those of secondary theory are thought of as somehow 'hidden.' "

5. Finally, secondary theory attempts to "transcend the limited causal vision of primary theory," by postulating "a 'hidden' or 'underlying' realm of entities and processes of which the events of everyday experience, as described in primary-theory terms, are seen as manifestations."

While anthropologists and others may no doubt want to criticize or to extend Horton's formulations,[27] for my present purposes his distinction can help us get a better grip on the social location of the Buddhist doctrine of not-self. There is a tolerably clear correspondence between the conventional and ultimate truths of Buddhism and Horton's primary and secondary theory. Not-self is a secondary theory. In Buddhism human beings are "directly given" as embodied persons and social agents, both monastic and lay; the ultimate truth of the changing, transmigrating flux of consciousness and karmic causality is hidden, and must be discovered through meditation. Like other forms of secondary theory, such as African spiritualistic or modern scientific discourses, it is largely the preserve of trained specialists, in whose activities and articulations direct knowledge (and, where contextually appropriate, verification) of it are actualized. Just as everyone in a spiritualistic world "knows" of the spirits and their effects, and everyone in a scientific world "knows" of the processes of physics, chemistry, and biology, so everyone in the Buddhist world "knows" of the truth of not-self. But these secondary explanatory theories exist alongside the discourse of primary theory, rather than replacing it, for the majority of people all of the time, and for everyone most of the time. The occasions when secondary theory actually replaces primary theory are necessarily those of specialized practices conducted by trained experts: exorcisms and spirit lore, laboratories and academic publications, and in the Buddhist case the monastic practices of meditation and scholarly textual activity.

The Practice of Not-self

In considering the practice of not-self in general, it would be necessary to discuss the whole of Buddhist ethics; as Carrithers stressed in making the distinction between *moi-* and *personne-* theories, there are extensive moral dimensions and implications of not-self. But my concern here is more limited: in accordance with the previous discussions in the seminars which have produced the *Toward a Comparative Philosophy of Religions Series,* I want to consider how the philosophy of not-self is itself directly a form of practice. As a form of scholarly textual activity, of course, not-self is part of the ideology of Buddhism, preserved and transmitted in the texts of the *Abhidhamma,* and in commentarial and other exegetical works. It would be interesting to explore the transmission of Buddhist learned culture as a system of education, along the lines of the intriguing account of educational practice in the Chinese neo-Confucian tradition given by Judith Berling. But my concern here will instead be with the virtuoso religious life of asceticism and meditation as a form of practice in which not-self is intended to be directly realized and embodied in experience and action.

As I have said, in traditional Buddhism the practice of not-self has been thought to require a celibate monastic life. This in itself is enough to call it a form of asceticism; but this term has suffered an impoverishment in modern colloquial usage, where it tends simply to mean some form of self-restraint or even self-punishment. In classical Greek, *askêsis* had the general meaning of a course of training, as practiced physically by athletes or more generally by anyone following a special mode of life leading to some chosen goal. The verb *askeô*, from which it is derived, meant primarily to work raw material, to form something artistically. It is useful, I think, to retain these wider senses of the term *asceticism* when it is applied to religious exercises. Two Indian terms which correspond well to *askêsis* in this sense are *sādhana* and, especially in the Buddhist case, *bhāvanā*, both terms which can be rendered "religious practice." *Sādhana* is from the root *sādh*, meaning to guide something straight or well, to bring it to a successful conclusion; *bhāvanā* is a causative form from *bhū*, to be, and so means the process of bringing something into being, creating. The monastic, meditational lifestyle, then, is a form of spiritual training oriented towards the realization or creation of selflessness, *nirvāṇa*. This lifestyle has both social and individual dimensions.

Buddhist practice as a whole can be subsumed in what are called the Four Foundations of Mindfulness: meditation on the body, feelings, states of mind, and "mental objects." This is a form of insight meditation *(vipassanā)*, which is held uniquely to lead to the realization of selflessness. The general point, of course, is to analyze all states of body and mind into their constituent parts, and so to realize that the psycho-physical individual is in fact a collection of impermanent processes, not an enduring self. I will concentrate here on the first of the four, meditation on the body. First I will sketch briefly the arguments of another paper[28] in which I have tried to reflect more generally on the place of the body in Theravāda Buddhist monasticism. On the one hand, in meditation, the body is mentally analyzed into its constituent parts, all of which are described as impure and repulsive, largely but not only because they are subject to decay and death. Moreover, the ascetic effort to subdue bodily desires is not merely expressed in the fact of celibacy; as mentioned earlier, all sexual thoughts, even in dreams, are for monks forms of bad *karma*. On the other hand, the monk's social behaviour and deportment, subject to extensive regulation by the monastic Rule and a matter of considerable public concern amongst the laity, require him to be clean and decorous, and to offer a "spotless performance."

Thus one may juxtapose the deconstruction and rejection of the body in meditative analysis with the construction of it in social behavior as a unified and valued public object. This strategy, this form of socioreligious theater, has a number of results. First, I suggest, the monastic rules, the meditations on the body, and the effort to eradicate all desire for material and sexual existence serve to create in the Buddhist monastic practitioner the space for an individualized, privatized, and subjectivized analysis. Insofar as salvation is conceived as a spiritual state manifested in both mind and body, the attempt wholly to inhibit all sexual drives and thoughts, and not merely to avoid overt sexual activity, necessarily induces psychic conflict, a conflict which opens up the interior terrain for which texts and doctrines provide the map. In this private zone of operations the desexualized, and thus in one sense desocialized individual can embody in imagination the immateriality posited in the doctrines of Buddhism, and in this way, as the Buddhist phrase has it, "touch the deathless with the body." Second, the social position and image of the monastic Order, both in theory and as played out in behavior and in the prescribed social interactions with laity, facilitate monks' being construed, by themselves and others, as independent, autonomous, and individual agents; the orientation towards a purely personal and immaterial goal both differentiates them from the laity, bound up in networks of material concern, and creates the actual behavioral space in which the subjectivized interiority inculcated by meditative practices can take place.

I suggested in the first part of this paper that the universalism of Buddhism was a restricted one: anyone can become a member of the monastic Order but not everyone at the same time. From the present perspective, I hope, it is clear that the practice of not-self by monks requires the active cooperation of laity in their mutually performed socioreligious theater. (I do not intend this term, by the way, to be either pejorative or reductivist.) The whole behavioral field is required to provide the individual monk with the space for subjectivized self-analysis. This self-analysis is what I am calling the practice of not-self. Earlier I cited the alleged parallels with the thought of Hume and Parfit. A common criticism made of their approach to personal identity is that they view it almost exclusively from the first-person perspective; whether or not the critical animus is justified on the conceptual level, I think that this is an accurate and significant description of Buddhist practice. Although the texts state that meditative reflection on not-self is to be done both in relation to oneself and to others (the terms are *ajjhattaṃ* and *bahiddhā,* literally "internally" and "externally"), and although the truth of not-self is of universal scope, as an experiential process it is necessarily focused on the monk's own immediate experience.

To meditate on the body, the monk is to begin by reciting the textual lists of bodily parts (there are thirty-two). This recitation is always to be done first aloud, even by those who have already learned the texts by heart; it is then to be repeated mentally, for only thus, it is said, can full understanding of the body's characteristics, its foulness and so on, be gained.[29] This is a small-scale version of a standard tripartite description of Buddhist religious training: it consists in learning *(pariyatti),* practice *(paṭipatti),* and understanding or penetration *(paṭivedha).*

Although in the history of the tradition, debates have been recorded as to the relative importance of learning or practice for the preservation of Buddhism,[30] it is clear from this example that it would be false always to oppose the oral learning and transmission of texts to meditative practice, since the former here is a condition of the latter. Such lists—more usually of psychological factors—are ubiquitous in Buddhist texts, especially in the *Abhidhamma*. This is no doubt to be explained in part by the fact that they facilitate memorization; but the practice of oral learning and recitation—the two activities can be designated by the same verb, *sajjhāyati*, since students learned by repeating aloud after a teacher—continued after the introduction of palm-leaf (and other) manuscripts. Paul Griffiths has usefully called the *Abhidhamma* "metaphysical catechesis"; the term is apposite because of the common question-and-answer format and the oral nature of those texts. We may also see an immediate meditative use of such catechetical recitation: to recite the texts, verbally and mentally, with or without a manuscript, is itself part of the meditation process. Here as so often in Buddhism (indeed in Indian religion generally), the activities designated by our verbs *reading, reciting,* and *thinking* can be very much more closely related to each other than our use of the terms suggests.[31]

The second and third Foundations of Mindfulness, the meditations on feelings and states of mind, similarly consist in the introspective classification of these events in terms of the categories of the *Abhidhamma;* all of them are to be seen as impermanent, conditioned, and therefore unsatisfactory and without enduring self. The fourth Foundation I translated above as "mental objects," which renders a complex and polyvalent term, *dhammā*. Here the term denotes both the contents or events of consciousness, good and bad, the presence of which is simply to be noted by the meditator as an impersonal fact, and also items of Buddhist doctrine, the truth of which is to be seen and known "as it really is" *(yathābhūtaṃ)*. Thus the meditator knows, for example, the Four Noble Truths: *dukkha*, suffering or unsatisfactoriness, desire as the cause of *dukkha*, the ending of desire as the ending of *dukkha* (*nirvāṇa*), and the way leading to that goal. These "mental objects" are, therefore, both elements of the normative system of Buddhism and the objects of experience in meditation;[32] from an external interpretative perspective, the meditator successfully introjects the categories of Buddhist thought and sees the world and experience of it through them; from the internal, Buddhist perspective, this is simply how one comes to know that what Buddhism teaches is true.

What kind of "knowledge" is this? On an immediate level, of course, it is the knowledge that certain propositions (such as the Four Noble Truths) are true; it is also the cognitive or (to use William James' term) noetic events in which that knowledge is instantiated. But the practice of mindfulness is supposed to be neither simply a matter of knowledge nor of knowledge-events which exist only for a certain length of time, as one might enter into a meditative trance for a specific period; rather, it is supposed to become a continuous form of awareness, present throughout any and every activity. We might, I think, profitably regard training in mindfulness as akin to learning a skill or skills, as an education in certain capabilities and dispositions.[33] It is as much a fact or process of self-cultivation as of self-knowledge. I think it is useful to consider this in relation to the familiar distinction between knowing *how* and knowing *that*, which has become customary in English-language philosophy following Gilbert Ryle. The former kind of knowledge refers not only to nonpropositional skills such as knowing how to swim or ride a bicycle; many features of this kind of knowledge are required for even the most abstract and formal cognitive operations. These skills are also forms of practice: they have to be learned through trial-and-error training, and they can be performed more or less successfully, more or less intelligently, more or less wisely. It seems to me sensible to interpret the Pali words for "knowledge"[34] as denoting various forms of knowing how, as well as the knowledge that certain propositions are true. To practice for enlightenment is to train oneself in living selflessly, without suffering; the capacity to live and act thus, and the fact of doing so, are an essential part of what it means to *know* that there is no self. To adapt R. R. Marett's well-known remark about religion, Buddhist enlightenment is not only thought out, but also danced out.

In the first section of this paper, I tried to show how and where the universal truth of Buddhist doctrine has been located in history and culture. In the second, I argued that although not-self is a universal truth, it is not a discourse which can be universally implemented: in other kinds of nonreductionist discourse monks (and *a fortiori* others) must be construed as enduring individuals, whose agency and responsibility are not directly that of the universal and impersonal law of *karma,* but rather what is enabled and constrained by the rights and duties assigned to the subjects of such discourse; in the third, I have tried to show how not-self, as a secondary theory, becomes a form of *practice* in which its truth is realized, a practice which might be summarized as a certain kind of textualized meditative introspection, occurring within a specific, performed social and behavioral environment. All of these perspectives, from the most general to the most specific, seem to me necessary to begin to answer the question, What are Buddhists *doing* when they deny the self?

Notes

1. For this periodization, which distinguishes pre-Aśokan, traditional and modern Buddhism, see S. Collins, Introduction to *Buddhist Monastic Life,* by M. Wijayaratna (Cambridge: Cambridge University Press, 1990), and "On the Very Idea of the Pali Canon," *Journal of the Pali Text Society* 15 (1990): 89–126. Abbreviations for texts are those used by the *Critical Pali Dictionary;* texts are cited from Pali Text Society editions. I am grateful to Paul Griffiths, Janet Gyatso, Charles Hallisey, and Matthew Kapstein for helpful comments on an earlier draft of this chapter.

2. See S. Pollock, "Mīmāṃsā and the Problem of History in Traditional India," *Journal of the American Oriental Society* 109 (1989): 603–10.

3. It is even said that full salvation is possible for some individuals without the teaching of a Buddha; such a person (called *pacceka-buddha*) cannot, however, proclaim the salvation thus attained.

4. Examples are: *micchādiṭṭhi* (wrong view) and *titthiya* or *titthakāra*, literally an adherent or founder of a religious sect, but used in Buddhist texts in the pejorative sense of heretic, and usually thus translated.

5. For this use of the term see B. Wilson, *Religion in Sociological Perspective* (Oxford: Oxford University Press, 1982), esp. chap. 3.

6. The order of Buddhist nuns died out in the medieval period. Here I shall either refer to "monks," meaning both monks and, when appropriate, nuns, or use a general phrase such as "the monastic Order."

7. F. Bantly, *Deconstructing/Reconstructing the Philosophy of Religions* (Chicago: The University of Chicago Divinity School, 1990), 132.

8. Ibid.

9. I take this term from D. Swearer, "Buddhism in Southeast Asia," in M. Eliade, ed., *The Encyclopedia of Religion* (New York: Macmillan, 1987).

10. For the argument of this paragraph see M. Carrithers, *The Buddha* (Oxford: Oxford University Press, 1983), 12–28, and R. F. Gombrich, *Theravāda Buddhism* (London: Routledge and Kegan Paul, 1988), 32–55.

11. For both these points, see, for example, the *Aggañña Sutta* (D, 3, 80–98), translated with annotations in S. Collins, "The Discourse on What Is Primary *(Aggañña Sutta):* An Annotated Translation," *Journal of Indian Philosophy* 21(1993): 301–93.

12. A phrase I take from the Christian philosopher S. Clark, *The Mysteries of Religion* (Oxford: Basil Blackwell, 1986).

13. See M. Carrithers, "The Modern Ascetics of Lanka and the Pattern of Change in Buddhism," *Man* 14 (1979), on what he calls "the domestication" of the monastic order, and the discussion in Strenski 1983.

14. For an extended discussion, see S. Collins, *Selfless Persons* (Cambridge: Cambridge University Press, 1982).

15. D. Hume, *A Treatise of Human Nature,* ed. Selby-Bigge (Oxford: Oxford University Press, 1888), 252, 268.

16. He does say, in book One (p. 253), that "we must distinguish betwixt personal identity, as it regards our thought or imagination, and as it regards

our passions or the concern we take in ourselves. The first is the present subject"; but he does not explain why his own philosophy is able to work with such a distinction.

17. P. Strawson, "The Parfit Connection," *The New York Review of Books,* June 14, 1984.

18. N. Tetley, "The Doctrine of Rebirth in Theravāda Buddhism" (D. Phil. thesis, University of Bristol, England), has made me see this. In a previous paper ("Buddhism in Recent British Philosophy and Theology," *Religious Studies* 21 [1985]) I had argued that the Buddhist view does resemble Parfit's. For certain purposes I still think this is true, but the similarity is limited in important ways.

19. M. Carrithers, "An Alternative Social History of the Self," in *The Category of the Person,* ed. M. Carrithers, S. Collins, and S. Lukes (Cambridge: Cambridge University Press, 1985), 235–36.

20. Ibid., 254.

21. One of the characteristics of Buddhist modernism has been the adoption of meditation practice by laity; see, for example, R. F. Gombrich, "From Monastery to Meditation Centre: Lay Meditation in Contemporary Sri Lanka," in *Buddhist Studies Ancient and Modern,* ed. P. Denwood and A. Piatigorsky (London: Curzon Press, 1983); R. F. Gombrich and G. Obeyesekere, *Buddhism Transformed* (Princeton: Princeton University Press, 1988); S. J. Tambiah, *The Buddhist Saints of the Forest and the Cult of Amulets* (Cambridge: Cambridge University Press, 1984), chap. 12.

22. For this, see R. Gothoni, *Modes of Life of Theravāda Monks* (Helsinki: Finnish Oriental Society, 1982).

23. See Collins, *Selfless Persons,* 260–61.

24. See H. Kawanami, "The Religious Standing of Burmese Buddhist Nuns," *Journal of the International Association of Buddhist Studies* 13 (1990).

25. This phrase is from Y. Ishii, *Sangha, State and Society* (Honolulu: University of Hawaii Press, 1986), 5–6, from whom I have taken this point. Ishii's discussion of the monkhood, however, is marred by his acceptance of the modern myth (invented by Sukumar Dutt) of the evolution of the order from a primitive wandering band of ascetics, living away from human society, to a 'cenobitic Sangha' involved with it (ibid.); see Collins, "Introduction."

26. R. Horton, "Tradition and Modernity Revisited," in *Rationality and Relativism*, ed. M. Hollis and S. Lukes (Oxford: Basil Blackwell, 1982), 228–30.

27. As does L. Yearley, *Mencius and Aquinas* (Albany: State University of New York Press, 1990). In the seminars which have preceded this publication, there was considerable discussion of this point, producing the title *Religion and Practical Reason*. This may be a convenient place for me to offer some remarks—written after the article—on the issue.

All such conceptual distinctions, I contend, are tools constructed for certain purposes, and the categories they produce should not then be hypostatized as describing data independent of the particular analytical question(s) which they answer. For example, the very dichotomy between practical and theoretical reason serves to distinguish between what one should do and how one should think; but as soon as one reflects that thinking is a kind of *activity* (rule-governed, historically situated, etc.), the distinction breaks down. Nonetheless, for many other purposes the dichotomy is a useful one. Horton's distinction was made for a particular purpose: to compare and contrast African traditional thought and Western science. Thus he concentrated on observable data and nonobservable descriptive and explanatory concepts. He did not address the issue of moral terminology, so whether it can be fitted into his scheme, whether it is in any sense universal, etc., is debatable. Yearley's purposes, as stated in his book, are not only descriptive and comparative, but normative: he wants to derive from his consideration of Mencius and Aquinas a usable moral vocabulary of "the virtues." (It is not clear to me whether this is for us now or all of mankind at all times.) For this reason he wants to construct a level of discourse which can refer to the universal world of primary theory but is not constrained by the incommensurable secondary theories of the two thinkers. I do not share this goal; for my analytical purpose here, the dichotomy between observable agents and nonobservable not-selves is simple and sufficient. I detect a tendency in Yearley's book, and in some of the contributions to this volume, to treat the notions of "practical theory" and "practical reason" (this is itself a confusing ambiguity) as not tied to the specific and varying purposes of analysis, but as independent and given forms of thought or behavior which are always and everywhere "out there."

28. S. Collins, "The Body in Theravāda Buddhist Monasticism," in *Religion and the Body*, ed. S. Coakley (Cambridge: Cambridge University Press, forthcoming). I use some phrases here taken directly from that paper. The points I make here have been inspired in part by M. Foucault, "The Battle for Chas-

tity," in *Western Sexuality,* ed. P. Ariès and A. Bejin (Oxford: Basil Blackwell, 1985).

29. For references and discussion of the points made in this paragraph, see S. Collins, "Notes on Some Oral Aspects of Pali Literature," *Indo-Iranian Journal* 35 (1992).

30. Mp 1:92–93; see W. Rāhula, *History of Buddhism in Ceylon* (Colombo: M. D. Gunasena, 1956), 158 ff.

31. Far from being an anomaly in the history of religions, I suspect that before the practice of silent reading, and the invention of printing, both absent from pre-modern culture in India as in Europe, this was probably the norm. William Graham, in his recent book *Beyond the Written Word* (Cambridge: Cambridge University Press, 1987) has illustrated extensively what he calls both the oral/aural aspects of religious scripture, and thereby the "sensual dimension" of religion. One might put it this way: in traditional Buddhism, texts were more often phenomena experienced through the voice and ears than through the hands and eyes, as are our books. Relevant to my point here is Louis Bouyer's argument that in early Christianity, the Greek term *mustikos,* and related words, from which we derive the concept "mysticism," were used in very close connection to reflective concentration on both scriptural and liturgical discourse. Bouyer insists, not unreasonably for a theologian, that such concentration was no mere "bookish understanding," but "a profound communion with the realities of which they speak" ("Mysticism/An Essay on the History of the Word," in *Understanding Mysticism,* ed. R. Woods [New York: Image Books], 50–51). To use a familiar Buddhist opposition, it is understanding not merely the letter *(vyañjana)* of the texts, but also their spirit or meaning *(attha).* All religious traditions tell us that at some point spiritual understanding must go beyond words, for its object is ineffable; but the words which it goes beyond are very clearly specified, usually well known, and always the place from which nondiscursive understanding begins.

32. See Collins, *Selfless Persons,* 115.

33. I owe this idea to Hal Roth (personal communication), who used it analogously when speaking of pre-Buddhist Chinese traditions (and attributed it to his teacher, A. C. Graham).

34. Examples include *aññā,* which is a technical term for enlightenment, or *paññā,* insight *(vipassanā),* "seeing things as they really are" *(yathābhūta-dassana).*

References

Bantly, Francisca, ed. 1990. *Deconstructing/Reconstructing the Philosophy of Religions.* Chicago: The University of Chicago Divinity School.

Berling, Judith. 1991. "Embodying Philosophy: Some Preliminary Reflections from a Chinese Perspective." In *Discourse and Practice (Toward a Comparative Philosophy of Religions Series* vol. 2), edited by F. Reynolds and D. Tracy. Albany: State University of New York Press.

Boyer, Louis. 1980. "Mysticism/An Essay on the History of the Word." In *Understanding Mysticism,* edited by R. Woods. New York: Image Books.

Carrithers, Michael. 1979. "The Modern Ascetics of Lanka and the Pattern of Change in Buddhism." *Man,* n.s. 14:294–310.

———. 1983. *The Buddha.* Oxford: Oxford University Press.

———. 1985. "An Alternative Social History of the Self." In *The Category of the Person,* edited by M. Carrithers, S. Collins, and S. Lukes. Cambridge: Cambridge University Press.

Clark, Stephen. 1986. *The Mysteries of Religion.* Oxford: Basil Blackwell.

Collins, Steven. 1982. *Selfless Persons.* Cambridge: Cambridge University Press.

———. 1985. "Buddhism in Recent British Philosophy and Theology." *Religious Studies* 21:475–93.

———. 1990. Introduction to M. Wijayaratna, *Buddhist Monastic Life.* Cambridge: Cambridge University Press.

———. 1990. "On the Very Idea of the Pali Canon." *Journal of the Pali Text Society* 15:89–126.

———. 1992. "Notes on Some Oral Aspects of Pali Literature." *Indo-Iranian Journal* 35:121–35.

———. 1993. "The Discourse on What Is Primary *(Aggañña Sutta):* An Annotated Translation." *Journal of Indian Philosophy* 21:301–93.

————. Forthcoming. "The Body in Theravāda Buddhist Monasticism." In *Religion and the Body,* edited by S. Coakley. Cambridge: Cambridge University Press.

Foucault, Michel. 1985. "The Battle for Chastity." In *Western Sexuality,* edited by P. Ariès and A. Bejin. Oxford: Basil Blackwell.

Gombrich, Richard F. 1983. "From Monastery to Meditation Centre: Lay Meditation in Contemporary Sri Lanka." In *Buddhist Studies Ancient and Modern,* edited by P. Denwood and A. Piatigorsky. London: Curzon Press.

————. 1988. *Theravāda Buddhism.* London: Routledge and Kegan Paul.

Gombrich, Richard F., and Gananath Obeyesekere. 1988. *Buddhism Transformed.* Princeton: Princeton University Press.

Gothoni, Réné. 1982. *Modes of Life of Theravāda Monks* (Studia Orientalia 52). Helsinki: Finnish Oriental Society.

Graham, William. 1987. *Beyond the Written Word.* Cambridge: Cambridge University Press.

Griffiths, Paul J. 1990. "Denaturalizing Discourse." In *Myth and Philosophy* (*Toward a Comparative Philosophy of Religions Series* vol. 1), edited by F. Reynolds and D. Tracy. Albany: State University of New York Press.

Horton, Robin. 1982. "Tradition and Modernity Revisited." In *Rationality and Relativism,* edited by M. Hollis and S. Lukes. Oxford: Basil Blackwell.

Hume, David. 1888. *A Treatise of Human Nature.* Edited by Selby-Bigge. Oxford: Oxford University Press.

Ishii, Yoneo. 1986. *Sangha, State and Society.* Honolulu: University of Hawaii Press.

Kawanami, Hirakawa. 1990. "The Religious Standing of Burmese Buddhist Nuns." *Journal of the International Association of Buddhist Studies* 13:17–39.

Lukes, Steven. 1984. "The Expendable I" (review of Parfit). *The Observer.* London, June 24.

Parfit, Derek. 1983. *Reasons and Persons.* Oxford: Oxford University Press.

Pollock, Sheldon. 1989. "Mīmāṃsā and the Problem of History in Traditional India." *Journal of the American Oriental Society,* 109: 603–10.

Rāhula, Walpola. 1956. *History of Buddhism in Ceylon.* Colombo: M. D. Gunasena.

Strawson, Peter F. 1984. "The Parfit Connexion" (review of Parfit). *The New York Review of Books,* June 14.

Strenski, Ivan. 1983. "On Generalized Exchange and the Domestication of the *Sangha.*" *Man,* n.s. 18:463–77.

Swearer, Donald. 1987. "Buddhism in Southeast Asia." In *The Encyclopedia of Religion,* edited by M. Eliade. New York: Macmillan.

Tambiah, Stanley J. 1984. *The Buddhist Saints of the Forest and the Cult of Amulets.* Cambridge: Cambridge University Press.

Tetley, Nigel. 1990. "The Doctrine of Rebirth in Theravāda Buddhism." D. Phil. thesis, University of Bristol, England.

Wilson, Bryan. 1982. *Religion in Sociological Perspective.* Oxford: Oxford University Press.

Yearley, Lee. 1990. *Mencius and Aquinas (Toward a Comparative Philosophy of Religions Series* vol. 3). Albany: State University of New York Press.

Part II

Types of Reasoning and Issues of Practice

Chapter 3

Al-Farabi on Religion and Practical Reason

Paul E. Walker

I. Introduction

The conflict between philosophy and religion was not readily apparent in the earliest period of Islam because philosophy was completely unknown at that time in the region of Arabia where Muhammad began his mission. It developed soon enough, however, and increased in intensity throughout the first four or five Islamic centuries as philosophy assumed an ever more prominent role in the education and intellectual makeup of Muslim scholars. The attraction of philosophy, although not everywhere felt to the same degree, produced over this period, in addition to outright hostility and rejection, a few scholars who accepted it wholly and exclusively. In one notorious case, it even caused a major thinker to deny the special importance of prophets and of revealed religion altogether.[1] To spurn prophetic religion in favor of philosophy was not merely an act of heresy but one of obstinate refusal to recognize the value of religious traditions in almost any form. Needless to say it happened rarely. On the other side of this conflict, many devout Muslims carefully segregated philosophy from religion, labeling it and the contents of treatises propounding it as "foreign" in contradistinction to the "Islamic" sciences that arose solely in the Arabo-Islamic study of Islam and its law and scripture. It was commonly taken, for example, that the non-Islamic sciences included physics, mathematics, metaphysics, and logic, all of which had appeared only when the Arabs came into contact with the Greeks and other foreigners, whereas the Islamic sciences were language and grammar and the various doctrinal and legal techniques for studying and interpreting the religious tradition. On this basis alone the two camps would have remained forever antagonistic, with no method of accommodation: revealed religion would have continued to reject and vilify philosophy and philosophy would have had little or no use for a religion based on sacred law and scripture.

Nevertheless, the importance and usefulness of philosophical modes of thought were not easily denied or suppressed, especially as the proponents of philosophy themselves gained sophistication both in their knowledge of philosophy and in their appreciation of the impossibility of ignoring the role of religion in society. But while Islamic thought slowly accepted the importation of philosophy—a sign of the broadening and maturing of an increasingly cosmopolitan culture—philosophy as it was studied in the Islamic world took a sharp, clearly discernible turn in its view of religion, particularly revealed religion, a turn that boldly sought to define and to embrace it from within the perspective of philosophy. In place of the philosopher who rejected religion, the new philosopher began to treat religion philosophically. Religion and religions thus finally entered the realm of philosophical inquiry. One result was a philosophy of religion, born on Islamic territory, that far from denigrating religion now took it as an essential facet of all human social interaction and, more to the point, of what it means to be human.

The founder of this philosophy of religion is the important tenth-century writer, Abu Nasr al-Farabi (d. 950 C.E.), whose achievement in several areas of philosophy—his appreciation of religion included—easily outstripped any before him in the Arabic world. His disciples, including Avicenna, Ibn Tufayl, Averroes, and Maimonides, saw in him a philosophical eminence they had recognized in no one since Aristotle.[2] Significantly, moreover, al-Farabi was also the first in more than a millennium to attempt the revival of political philosophy.[3] Because, in his thought, the constituent base of politics and of religion is the same, the efforts of al-Farabi to resurrect political philosophy in the Islamic milieu of his own time almost inevitably assumed the interchangeability of the two.[4] In contrast to the somewhat tepid religious problems confronting Plato, al-Farabi faced the massive cultural force that was not merely the religion brought into being by the Quran and the Arabian prophet (a cultural force which now ruled most of the known world) but that encompassed, in addition, the whole series of Semitic religions and of the prophets who had been responsible for each in turn. If al-Farabi was to engender a philosophical understanding of politics, he could not ignore the crucial role of the religious prophet and lawgiver, either for a given religion in a single period or for the flow of history across many religions.

Like many heirs to the Aristotelian tradition within philosophy, al-Farabi's understanding of the sciences—whether those acquired from the Greeks or those indigenous to the Arabs and their Muslim co-religionists—hinges on the distinction between theoretical and practical reason. In contrast to the standard Arabic division of the sciences into foreign and local, al-Farabi views them all as theoretical, practical, or both. For example, mathematics has, for him, both a theoretical component and a practical application. The domain of practical reasoning is that of action and of deliberation conducive to action. Therefore, deliberative and moral or ethical faculties are practical, and hence so too are politics and religion, insofar as they are aimed toward some goal requiring activity. Moreover, for al-Farabi there is, in addition to this notion of the practical, also a concept that arises from a further distinction between theoretical reason as a demonstrative science that yields certainty and various other "sciences" or modes of thought that produce mere opinions and beliefs. Such opinions and beliefs are, in his view, purely practical and cannot be considered as theoretical. Thus religious views about God, for example—as is the case for all other elements of religious belief—are a part of practical reason. Both the acts and the opinions engendered by religion are aspects of practical reasoning rather than theoretical reasoning *per se,* except insofar as they attempt to imitate the latter. This is a principle that al-Farabi would apply universally; each religion and each element of religion is susceptible to the same treatment. All are examples of the practical application of theoretical knowledge, and they can be compared accordingly.

The available literature about al-Farabi has grown considerably in recent years.[5] Consequently, interpretations of his ideas vary, ranging from a narrow, slavish attention to the nuances of textual discrepancies to a wider appreciation of what his contributions might suggest by implication. Such problems in reading al-Farabi are not at all new; medieval authors faced them, and their interpretations of his teachings show the same wide variations. Following the careful but restricted road is the more technically accurate, since al-Farabi is notoriously cryptic and not infrequently appears to suggest irreconcilable doctrines concerning a single problem. That approach, however, is not particularly fruitful in this context. Here, in contrast, it seems preferable to expand his ideas as far as they can reasonably be stretched without deliberately traversing the bounds he himself set. The liberties taken in what follows are based on suggestions given by al-Farabi but only developed explicitly by one or another of his medieval followers.

The materials available are, however, not systematically arranged by their author, and, in order to avoid falling into confusion and chaotic uncertainty—something al-Farabi's writings easily engender—it is essential to confine the exposition of his ideas to key questions and to develop these with a special purpose in mind. His notion of what constitutes practical and theoretical reasoning is crucial, and, fortunately, it holds a large place in his writings. A number of other issues which are less obvious need further elucidation and must be approached somewhat elliptically. But without reviewing each of those problems and the textual basis for them in various interpretations of his writings, a direct approach is, if not impossible, at least full of agonizing ambiguity. Al-Farabi simply is not yet fully or conclusively studied in modern scholarship, and many of his Arabic writings have been published for the first time only in the last three decades.[6] Therefore, to undertake a source-critical study, although admittedly needed, would lead to a mountain of evidence with few conclusions. Rather than heed the trail of al-Farabi's own words, it seems better to confront simply and directly the major themes that contribute, either explicitly or implicitly, to al-Farabi's philosophy of religion. This will allow us to extract some further conclusions about its enduring value quite apart from an importance that derives solely from its historical novelty.

The heart of the matter, although never explicitly put this way by al-Farabi, involved envisioning a hypothetical meeting of Aristotle and Muhammad as the paradigm of the meeting of philosophy and religion. His concept of founder and lawgiver, as will be seen, presupposes a personal agency: neither philosophy nor religion would exist without uniquely gifted individuals who create them. This core issue serves as a point of departure in this chapter. Following that we return (in the third and fourth sections below) to some of the questions raised in this initial confrontation by examining the implications of, first, the philosophical acceptance of practical reason and what that implies about religion viewed from the perspective of philosophy, and, second, the other side of this problem, which concerns the source and value of religious truth. For the latter investigation—on the origin, development, evaluation, and improvement of religion and religions in relation to their philosophical counterpart—al-Farabi turns to a historical solution. Thus, whereas the third section of this chapter looks at al-Farabi's *philosophy* of religion, the fourth considers what he presents as a *history* of religion. A final section steps away from the historical perspective necessitated by the close study of al-Farabi and examines what his ideas about the relationship of philosophy to religion, of theory to practice, and of reason to discourse might imply in the broader context of a comparative philosophy of religion.

II. The Meeting of Muhammad and Aristotle

When the Islamic world encountered philosophy, Muslim scholars assumed initially that it was exclusively Greek, as its Greek
name implied. Muslims in later centuries, however, could not
and did not obstruct the importation of what was for them
essentially an alien mode of thought. In contrast to nearly all of
his Muslim predecessors and contemporaries, however, al-Farabi
was concerned with the reverse perspective. He did not write as
a Muslim but as a philosopher. Nevertheless, he accepted prophecy and revelation as valid elements to be explained in reference to the establishment and propagation of religion. His purpose, therefore, was to explain the place of the prophet and
prophecy in philosophy, and secondarily, the role of philosophy in religious legislation; all this was explained from the perspective of philosophy, not of religion.

Although a confrontation between the Arab prophet and
Aristotle is only implied in al-Farabi's discussions of the supreme
philosopher-prophet, we, like his contemporaries and successors,
need to envision this possibility in order to understand the con-
text of his own abstract discussion of the principles at play. In the
Islamic world, Aristotle fairly often appeared in a similar role in
dreams. A famous example is the twelfth-century philosopher
Suhrawardi, who claims to have had an extended discussion with
Aristotle which he recorded prominently in one of his books.[7]
Aristotle was also frequently represented by proxy, as in Ibn
Tufayl's fictitious story of the autodidact, Hayy Ibn Yaqzan, who
is in part a surrogate for Aristotle in his meeting with Asal, the
ascetic follower of a prophetic religion who embodies the position of Muhammad.[8] These authors promoted this device for exactly the same effect that it may serve here. However, while al-
Farabi recognized Aristotle as the first master of philosophy, he
nowhere credited Muhammad, as opposed to other lawgiving
revelators, with unique status. That al-Farabi was Muslim, however, we do not doubt; therefore, using Muhammad as the consummate example of religious achievement is certainly appropriate. It must be taken as an assumed premise—a premise al-Farabi's
Muslim audience fully appreciated.

A more important question is whether Aristotle and Muhammad meet as equals. Aristotle is the undisputed master of philosophy and hence theoretical knowledge. Muhammad, we assume, is the supreme instance of a religious lawgiver. They are on the surface utterly dissimilar, and in order to argue that they are equals it is necessary to hold that either both are philosophers or both are religious lawgivers. Yet Aristotle is not known to have created a religion, and Muhammad never mentioned anything about philosophy. Another possibility is to accept that religion and philosophy are somehow related and that both men are masters of both subjects, even if each chose to speak exclusively about only one of them. This is al-Farabi's answer.

If the meeting were to take place, al-Farabi's understanding of theoretical reason means that Aristotle and Muhammad, insofar as either individual is capable of such thinking, share a common intellectual base that corresponds exactly or nearly so in both men. This base exists outside of all references to specific linguistic or cultural material; it is not rooted in, nor dependent on, ordinary, natural languages. It is also not temporally or geographically localized. Aside from elemental linguistic differences, the communication between Muhammad and Aristotle presents no problems. The rules by which theoretical communication takes place are logical, not grammatical.[9] These two figures share logic, which provides the basis of their mutual exchange of ideas. When Aristotle writes in Greek, however, he must descend into a mode of communication that no longer exactly corresponds to what he thinks; it is no longer exactly what he perceives theoretically. The situation for Muhammad is the same. When he uses Arabic, his utterances assume the grammatical reality of the Arabs. But if Muhammad talks to Aristotle, both men comprehend an identical thought; Muhammad's theoretical reasoning is no different from Aristotle's.

Of course, by holding that Aristotle and Muhammad think alike, al-Farabi assumes a great deal. While al-Farabi may be guilty of excessive optimism, he holds this position because of his own personal ability to comprehend completely both Aristotle and Muhammad. He reads Aristotle and understands what

Aristotle states to be theoretically true; he also fully appreciates the religion of the prophet. Moreover, al-Farabi did not arrive at this view naively. He does recognize some important limitations to his position. Although mathematics would represent an obvious area of shared thought and common theoretical understanding between the two men—as, for example, would such primary concepts as the whole is equal to the sum of its parts, or two sums each equal to a third are themselves equal—whether the axiomatic certainty in these elemental principles extends to other fields, such as ethics or metaphysics, is another matter. Al-Farabi admitted that there are limitations to theoretical reasoning and that Muhammad and Aristotle must rely to a certain extent on dialectical, rather than apodictical, methods in the communication of areas not entirely amenable to the latter. These are not truly theoretical, although they are often very close to it. The goal of each, however, is always to approximate the standard of perfect demonstration. Both thinkers fully understand where and why they must resort to the employment of dialectic as an aid to achieving eventual certainty and consensus—that is, to arrive at true theoretical knowledge. A difference automatically indicates that the two men have not reached theoretical understanding and that they must temporarily resolve the discrepancy by dialectical methods. Comparative reasoning is always dialectical, but it can lead to proper demonstration.

Naturally, when Muhammad and Aristotle exchange information at the theoretical level, very little in their discussion requires harmonization. The material of theoretical reasoning does not allow difference; it is not subject to opinion and belief. For al-Farabi the fact that the sum of the interior angles of a triangle is 180 degrees, and that this is a fact just as true for Muhammad as for Aristotle precludes rational diversity between them.

Yet, because full theoretical knowledge is available only to a trained philosopher (unless an equivalent intellectual gift was bestowed somehow with little or no training), all this implies that Muhammad was, in the estimation of al-Farabi, also a fully qualified philosopher. Although al-Farabi never said as much about Muhammad, he implied this in his claims about the law-givers who are the founders of religions. An equally interesting problem is whether he considered Aristotle to be a prophet and therefore just as able to create a religious order as was Muhammad. This problem cries out for an answer, in part, be-cause Aristotle looms so large in al-Farabi's writings. However, it is one he fails to confront directly, leaving the reader wonder-ing about the proper "religious" role of the Greek master. That one of them, in fact, did fashion a religion and the other did not does not seem to matter to al-Farabi; he appears to believe that all true philosopher-prophets possess that ability, even if noth-ing comes of it.[10]

Are we to conclude from al-Farabi's remarks about phi-losopher-prophets that all great intellectual "founders" and *imams* (intellectual leaders) share a similar philosophical sta-tus?[11] Presumably, if Muhammad and Aristotle participate in a form of reasoning that is identical, then no other great thinker is excluded from it. Al-Farabi concludes one of his discussions of the ideal philosopher-prophet by stating outright that "the idea of *Imam,* Philosopher and Legislator is a single idea,"[12] and further, "let it be clear to you that the idea of the Philosopher, Supreme Ruler, Prince, Legislator, and *Imam* is but a single idea."[13]

It was already widely assumed by Muslims that the proph-ets who predated Muhammad, such as Jesus and Moses, be-longed to the same tradition as Islam. Had they met Muhammad, neither of these religious figures would have faced any obstacle—barring minor linguistic problems—that could prohibit the com-plete exchange of knowledge with him. Muslims at times ex-tend this principle to encompass not merely all of the Semitic prophets, but others from Iran and India as well. Al-Farabi goes beyond even this. By including Aristotle (and Plato), he sub-stantially broadens what he means by a lawgiver—the person who creates the laws that form a given religion or moral re-gime. In sum, Aristotle and Muhammad represent two poles of a fairly comprehensive line from the supreme philosopher with-out a religion, at one end, to the consummate prophet without philosophy, at the other. Yet the line forms a continuum and presumably includes between its extremes all great intellectual innovators.

However, if Muhammad and Aristotle can communicate on the basis of theoretical reason—perfected, according to al-Farabi, by Aristotle—what then do they say to each other about Muhammad's religion? Can Aristotle understand and appreciate what Muhammad has created? For some Muslim authors faced with a similar quandary, the solution was to convert Aristotle. If, they argue, Aristotle had lived in the time of Islam, he would have accepted it. This is not al-Farabi's solution. Aristotle, being Greek and a member of a non-Arab, non-Islamic religious culture, would likely find no reason to reject his own tradition in favor of Islam. But what is much more important, since Aristotle has mastered theoretical reasoning, which is by its very nature metalinguistic and metacultural, he does not require the regimen of a specific religion. Thus if he speaks to Muhammad, both men see the religion of Muhammad from the perspective of theoretical, not practical, speculation. Nevertheless, Aristotle would know that Muhammad possesses a special gift in his ability to formulate the material of a particular religion. He recognizes that Muhammad's special talent lies in the practical application of reason. In this Muhammad may outclass Aristotle, who seemed to communicate almost exclusively in theoretical terms, appearing unable or perhaps unwilling to reformulate his teaching in purely practical language.

The religion of Muhammad, in contrast to the theory of Aristotle, arises in response to the cultural peculiarity of his time, tribe, and place. It must, therefore, be practical as opposed to theoretical. The role of religion is normative and explanatory; it serves to lead a given community to an ultimate happiness after which all members aspire together. Its social application does not allow it to function theoretically.

Although al-Farabi tends to confine religion within a typically Muslim notion of law, as in the Arabic term shari`a,[14] laws, in his view, exist because lawgivers created them. All religions were originally founded by a prophet-legislator who arose within a specific cultural context. (Each prophet-legislator had a mission to induce his community to apply a religion in order to obtain some portion of the anticipated ultimate happiness.) This would be true of any religion, even those outside the normal purview of the fairly cosmopolitan scholars of tenth-century Baghdad at the time of al-Farabi, a purview which already included most religions of the Near East as well as some of Asia. Regional traditions in any religion may, however, differ radically—even those within a single cultural sphere—partly in accord with local conditions, but partly because of corruption and deviation. Still, for al-Farabi, the role of a prophet-founder is the link between all these particular instances of religions and the theoretical realm that they imitate, because he is privy to both and can translate from one to the other.

Perhaps *shari`a*—as understood through the English sense of the word *law*—as the basis of religion offers too narrow an interpretation of what al-Farabi means when he speaks about the function of a lawgiver. His normal usage is *wadi` al-nawamis,* neutral language for *legislator.* In Arabic, moreover, *shari`a* is a term for the safe path to water in the desert. Far more than a formal legal code, the Islamic *shari`a* contains not only rules governing rites and rituals, but also those regulating social contracts. Religion, moreover, must provide correct images of all divine matters and thus promote valid opinions and beliefs about them. In short, it is hard to see why al-Farabi's concept of law and lawgiver should not be taken in the broadest sense, even if he is thinking only in Islamic terms, which generally he is not. He does not privilege Islam nor, taking what he says liberally, does he exclude nonrevelatory religions. The founder of any religion institutes as complete an expression of all these matters as he (or she) can, given conditions of time and place and the demands or requirements of a specific community.

Yet al-Farabi conceives religion, even though broadly encompassing a full range of spiritual and ritual elements, to be a part of practical reason. To al-Farabi the material of religion appears to include items requiring theoretical content, and that is as it should be. Religion must cover theoretical matters as well as acts and deeds of a purely individual and temporal sort. Muhammad's religion contains a complete description of the cosmos, of creation, of God, and of all divine matters. However, the method of description is itself religious, that is, practical rather than theoretical. To explain the order of the heavens, for example, Muhammad had to speak rhetorically, even poetically, so that his description would carry meaning for those who can comprehend this type of thing only by imagining a convenient or familiar similitude of the real thing. For another example, God must have a face, a back, and hands; an eternal, placeless, bodiless abstraction will serve no purpose for the ordinary believer who knows nothing of philosophy and theoretical reason.

Thus al-Farabi's approach to a general theory of religion does not begin with Muhammad or his religion, but rather with the distinction between theoretical and practical reason. Although the meeting of Muhammad and Aristotle begins to explain how religion and philosophy may be joined without conflict, it does not necessarily show how the two are connected philosophically. It is essential, therefore, to turn now to that subject and particularly to analyze what practical reason is for al-Farabi, what connects theoretical and practical discourse, and how this relationship creates religions.

III. A Philosophy of Practical Reason

According to al-Farabi a basic difference between theoretical and practical reason is that the former concerns knowledge of things or beings we cannot make or transform, whereas the latter is a source of knowledge of objects and events that owe their existence to human volition.[15] Theoretical reason investigates, for example, the principles of mathematics in the abstract without qualification; practical reason applies those rules to artificial bodies, created or manipulated by human art and will. Knowledge of what is theoretical, in this sense, might be accumulated solely from extensive experience with and interpretation of what occurs practically. Thus reasoning that is itself not rooted in the theoretical can lead to a theoretical understanding, because there is a connection between the two forms of reasoning, although it is not necessarily dependent on the temporal priority of practical experience which may, in fact, spawn erroneous conclusions.

Deliberation produces generalizations either through the ability to reason or the operation of imagination. A judgement results from the observation of a number of particulars followed by the forming or recognition of a universal. That universal, however, may be only rhetorically or poetically conceived, and thus represent merely an imagined similitude of the actual intelligible object or principle. In true theoretical reasoning, the principles of instruction and of communication are the same as the principles of being. Conversely, in other modes of thought, the principles of being are necessarily divorced from the methods or principles of instruction and of communication.

For al-Farabi, theoretical knowledge is always primary and its status does not depend on the method ordinary thinkers use to explain or to discover it. Once demonstration (the apodeictic syllogism, Arabic *burhan*)—the proper vehicle of theoretical reasoning—is understood, theoretical reason follows, and theoretical knowledge can be communicated on this basis from one individual to another, provided each has the capacity for demonstrative thinking. The practical application of theoretical knowledge or a nondemonstrative communication of it involves a secondary form of reasoning which is distinctly inferior.

A useful example helps explain what al-Farabi means. The motions of the heavens or the laws of physics do not vary according to human wishes, but the ways humans conceive of such motions or such laws do. For example, many individuals perceive the model of the heavens by imagining a practical representation of it that may only remotely correspond to the true physical reality. In this sense practical reason functions to a degree in all human endeavors and informs all social activity. Politics, religion, economics, and even many areas of the natural and physical sciences may, in fact, fall into this category. There is obviously a sense in which all languages, for example, are practical (as opposed to theoretical) vehicles for the exchange of knowledge, whether the knowledge itself is theoretical or merely a practical adaptation of it.

What al-Farabi understands as philosophy is primarily a theoretical perfection and demonstrative certainty.[16] The art and science of demonstration is, he maintains, "most emphatically prior in dignity and superior."[17] Philosophy, then, would seem to preclude practical reason. But if that were so, how can he connect it with the variable particularity of voluntary things? His understanding of philosophy as first of all a theoretical inquiry into being solely insofar as it is existent being would not necessarily produce a requirement also to investigate how, if at all, this is connected with the knowledge of practical actions. But, for him, in arriving at the philosopher's theoretical goal, one discovers that the use of theoretical knowledge and hence the theoretical virtues provides the incentive for and a means to attain an ultimate happiness.[18] Whereas knowledge of ultimate truths constitutes perfection, and the theoretical virtues consist of the sciences whose purpose is only to make beings and what they contain intelligible with certainty,[19] when one seeks such ultimate perfection and certainty, there occur two concomitant results: first, failure to attain certainty in all problems and hence confusion between the portion that is certain and the rest in which the only possibility is belief and opinion; second, the necessity (implied by perfection itself) of realization, that is, of having to bring it into being. For al-Farabi, to attain the fullest degree of perfection, one must exploit other natural beings. Thus, to achieve whatever perfection is possible for each individual, a person must associate with others. From this al-Farabi concludes, "There emerges now another science and another inquiry that investigates these intellectual principles and the acts and states of character with which one labors toward this perfection."[20] This is the philosophy or science of religion. Theoretical perfection comprises knowledge of the things by which citizens attain supreme happiness. What remains is for these things to be realized and to have actual existence while conforming to the account of them given previously in theoretical form.[21]

For al-Farabi, the methods of realization, of instruction, and of obtaining conviction, are a part of practical reason, even while they involve a "deliberative virtue"[22] that is itself susceptible to philosophical investigation. If theoretical principles are known by demonstration, he says, they are philosophy; but "if they are known by imagining them through similitudes that imitate them, and assent to what is imagined of them is caused by persuasive methods," that is religion.[23] Religion becomes, therefore, a practical imitation of philosophy.[24]

The ability to receive theoretical intelligibles either as they are or by imitating them constitutes revelation or what, according to al-Farabi, ought to be called "revelation."[25] That is all that revelation is for him; it is not a unique nor inaccessible type of epistemology. Nevertheless, it occurs solely in the uniquely endowed mind because its source is purely intellectual. Ordinary humans cannot comprehend these things as they are and therefore must merely accept an imitation of them. While these things themselves are one and immutable, the methods of imitation, each grounded in the peculiarities of a time and a place, must be many and therefore will vary for each group or nation. Thus the forms by which common people apprehend the abstract intelligibles differ for every nation, and hence this difference is a condition of religions as well.[26] Every nation and every culture will have its own religion.

But the supreme "instructor" in these practical matters is, for al-Farabi, a lawgiving philosopher-prophet, a person who possesses the ability to make particular instances of the virtues actually exist in nations and cities.[27] A more complete statement of his general theory follows in this well-known passage:

> Once the images representing the theoretical things demonstrated in the theoretical sciences are produced in the souls of the multitude and they are made to assent to their images, and once the practical things (together with the conditions of the possibility of their existence) take hold of their souls and dominate them so that they are unable to resolve to do anything else, then the theoretical and practical things are realized. Now these things are *philosophy* when they are in the soul of the legislator. They are *religion* when they are in the souls of the multitude. For when the legislator knows these things, they are evident to him by sure insight, whereas what is established in the souls of the multitude is through an image and a persuasive argument.[28]

Religion then is more than a mere imitation of philosophy; it is the perfection of a practical, deliberative virtue, requiring action. Philosophy of religion becomes a science of poetical and rhetorical method, of the power to persuade, to instill virtue, and to inculcate the means to achieve whatever portion of true happiness is possible for each citizen of every state.[29]

These and other statements indicate that the lawgiver is master of both the theoretical sciences, which are established by demonstration, and the knowledge of how the practical matters may be implemented. A lawgiver knows the particulars of how to encourage virtue and moral habits in cities and nations according to a certain order to be practiced by the whole citizenry. At the very least the true philosopher-prophet understands, on the basis of theoretical reason, what constitutes real happiness as opposed to a spurious happiness that is mistakenly thought to be real. Using that test, a lawgiver judges the actions, ways of life, and moral habits in particular instances of a particular city or nation.

Strictly from the perspective of logic, the key to al-Farabi's analysis of the function of practical reasoning is his acceptance of an expanded Aristotelian *organon* that comprises—in addition to the *Posterior Analytics* and the *Topics*—the *Rhetoric* and the *Poetics*. The superiority of demonstration remains, and thus the ancient evaluation of the ranks of the parts of logic is the same. But to this he adds not only dialectic (the *Topics*) but rhetoric and poetics as well. Without this step there might be no philosophical understanding of the latter two. Al-Farabi's viewpoint in this instance, however, regards both rhetorical and poetical discourse as possible tools of logic, which is to say that syllogistic reasoning may operate in or through them as well. Theoretical reason is philosophy, and theoretical reason depends on logic as the tool of thinking philosophically. But an extension of logic to explain rhetorical and poetical expression expands the area of philosophical discourse.[30] Of course, the syllogism in a poetic metaphor lacks a great deal as a tool of logic when judged against a true apodeitic form. Nevertheless, it constitutes a type of reasoning, or perhaps more properly a form of imagining that operates like reasoning. It mimics reason. Hence religion, which relies almost exclusively on rhetorical and poetical methods of persuasion in order to attain conviction and assent (one Arabic term for this is *tasdiq*), can be investigated philosophically.

Once the relative ranking of these lesser logical arts is properly understood, those that produce less certainty can be seen for what they are in relation to dialectic and demonstration. Nonetheless, they retain a formal function that must be known to the founder of a religion. The lawgiver's goal is to find an apt method of persuasion and through it to bring about such conviction and assent. In many instances this desired result may occur immediately and uncritically. Conviction in its simplest form is the domain of rhetoric, a realm of the sensible and particular. Assent so achieved is by its nature rhetorically based. Its techniques employ analogy and concept formation *(tasawwur).* Where such immediate assent on the basis of rhetorical communication is impossible, imagination *(takhyil)* must operate. Poetics relies on the evocation of imagination. Acceptance of imagined forms thus may replace the rhetorically induced act of assent. The poetic syllogism is an act of imagination.

In sum, al-Farabi seems to regard religion as the totality of imaginative and rhetorical devices brought by a lawgiver to promote the common quest for an ultimate good which is itself an intellectual perfection. And this, then, is the philosophical base of al-Farabi's view of religion in general. At this point his position allows no criterion for discrimination among religions except in the vague recognition that all religions ultimately depend on the same (superior) theoretical base. But the existence of that base and the recognition of it allows for comparative analysis and evaluation. A relative value must be present in the manner by which a given religion imitates philosophy. Religions differ both in the methods—the nearness or remoteness, appropriateness or inappropriateness of the images and similitudes they employ—by which they render theoretical into practical knowledge, and in the type and quality of philosophy they imitate. These are factors in how al-Farabi chooses to explain religious diversity. The relationship of a given religion to a given form of philosophy and the strength or weakness of the resulting religion are things al-Farabi interestingly presents on the grounds of a "historical" development. Therefore, al-Farabi's concept of religions also contains a historical dimension, and in order to explain this, we must next examine his discussion of the origin of religions—a subject he examines as a parallel to his own account of the history of philosophy.

IV. A History of Religion

Prophecy and ultimate happiness are comprehensive for both theoretical and practical modes of reasoning. True theoretical virtue is, in essence, simply the power to "define things and actions that direct people toward happiness."[31] This definition is valid for all humans, both those capable of philosophical thought and those who are not. Therefore, because the latter group is included, at all times a form of religion must exist, and it will necessarily imitate whatever philosophical model is then available. For al-Farabi the development of religion follows the development of philosophy.[32]

For him philosophy arose first when inquiry was limited to rhetorical methods. A key point was reached when people desired to know the causes of things. (Apparently al-Farabi did not recognize—at least not explicitly—a pre-rhetorical stage which might have been confined to poetic forms.) A further stage beyond rhetorical investigation involved the application of dialectic—a stage resulting from the constant use of rhetoric and the continuing quest for greater certainty which ultimately led to the discovery of dialectical methods. Next, following the gradual realization that dialectic is insufficient, a third stage commenced which led to the completion of philosophy by the addition of demonstration. During the third stage, demonstration continued to be mixed with dialectic, especially in political and religious affairs, although the dialectic here was almost firm enough to qualify as demonstration. Al-Farabi identifies this stage as the one which existed at the time of Plato. Finally, in

the days of Aristotle, scientific investigation completed both theoretical *and* practical philosophy. The only step remaining is the
issuing of laws *(nomoi)* that are in accord with this true philosophy. In this fourth stage, knowledge of the methods of practical
reason was so firmly grounded that laws issued thereafter would
create the ultimate, perfect religious order.[33] In the perfect religious order laws can accurately reflect both those things discovered by demonstration and practical affairs discerned through
the faculty of prudence. Al-Farabi expresses some ambiguity
about this anticipated fifth stage. Certainly, it is the best and
most desirable, although it seems to remain, for him, condi-
tional and hypothetical.

Each of these stages produced a religion that corresponds
to the kind of philosophy then available. However, only religion that is based on complete philosophy is correct. A religion
founded in accordance with a philosophy that is not yet demonstrative will, like that philosophy, contain a mixture of true and
untrue opinions and correct and incorrect beliefs. Moreover, the
use of similitudes and images for the instruction of the masses
must, in these cases, result in many examples of unperceived
corruptions. In addition there may exist a lawgiver who avoids
the most advanced philosophy of his time in favor of an older
standard; his religion will be corrupted accordingly. Thus correct religion can exist only after true philosophy, but not all
religion in a subsequent period is inevitably sound. However,
once philosophy reaches fruition, a religion can and should follow from it.[34] Whether it does or does not may be an open
question, because al-Farabi appears not to insist that it has happened or will happen.

Presumably, this "historical" pattern applies also to the religion of Muhammad. He did, after all, create his religion at a
time when Aristotle's perfection of philosophy was established
fact. Yet, in another sense, Muhammad's religion came before
philosophy in terms of the advancement of philosophical methods strictly within the cultural heritage of the Arabian tribes to
whom he preached. But the situation of Muhammad is only one
of many complex examples that seem to involve the transfer of

philosophy (or the transfer of religion) from one nation to another. In other situations, the lawgiver in question, al-Farabi
admits, may have gone abroad, learned philosophy or a foreign
religion, and then returned to institute a religion for his own
people. Such a development might occur at any stage.

But what exactly does al-Farabi imply in the case of Islam?
That is an especially awkward question which al-Farabi certainly did not answer directly. Is the actual relationship of perfect philosophy to the religion of Islam merely hypothetical,
both for us and for him? An answer may be that the meeting of
Muhammad and Aristotle did not and does not produce only
one result but rather several, each of which is equally useful.
The first realization growing from this encounter is that, although Muhammad has fashioned a religion based on true and
complete philosophy, in order to communicate with the Arab
tribes he conveyed the entirety of that philosophy in poetically
and rhetorically generated similitudes. Because the Arabs were
not prepared to accept purely theoretical concepts, Muhammad
necessarily maintained a silence concerning them. But in so doing he failed to indicate to his people that their religion was
founded on a sound philosophical base. Consequently, Muslims
came to believe that the similitudes were actually the reality
which they, in fact, only describe. Muslims concluded that the
symbols and myths of their religions are the truths in and of
themselves. Subsequently, when philosophy arrived in the Islamic world, its few proponents, although they understood the
true relationship between Muhammad and Aristotle, faced serious problems in asserting their own authority—an authority
that is based on the priority of philosophy to religion.

Ideally, since every religion is philosophical in origin, the
philosophers, according to al-Farabi, ought to be employed to
monitor how well each particular religion complies with its theoretical source. The philosophers should comprehend the practical applications of reason and should possess an ability to analyze religious discourse at all levels. Does this also mean that
philosophers should have the capacity for making religions?
Several passages in al-Farabi's writings suggest this requirement.
The ultimate philosopher is one who fully comprehends, not

just theoretical knowledge, but all practical applications of it as well. The philosopher can judge the value and success of any given religious expression in terms both of how well or accurately it imitates theoretical reality and of how well it functions in promoting its practical goal. Further, al-Farabi seems to claim that the philosopher possesses this ability in part because a philosopher can perform the role of legislator if need be. Philosophers—at least true, consummate philosophers—are, therefore, prophets and lawgivers; they are masters of practical as well as theoretical reason and hence could provide the human community with a new religion if they deem it necessary.

Al-Farabi's view of religion as practical reason might thus be seen as his way of resolving a problem that arose in the Islamic context. Muhammad's religion, in this view, began prior to philosophy. When, subsequently, philosophy arrived, it commenced a struggle for recognition, which for several reasons it had not previously achieved. Nevertheless, even though Islam contains no explicit role for philosophers, it is all the more vital for the continued health of this religion that Aristotle assume his proper place or that a new Aristotle be found within the Islamic realm. In fact there ought to be a series of Islamic Aristotles. Here it is essential to remember that al-Farabi never spoke of Islam or of Muhammad. Instead, without doubt, he saw this need for philosophers as generic; since almost any religion might be seen as *prior to philosophy,* in the sense just posited for Islam, then all religions may be measured without prejudice by philosophy. All examples of practical reason are reflections of theoretical knowledge, and the need for a new Aristotle is constant in each and every tradition.

V. The Place of Practical Reason

At this point it appears as though al-Farabi's real concern is the advancement of philosophy's claim to superiority over religion. The dominion of Aristotle ultimately rules that of Muhammad, or at least ought to, he says. Demonstrative knowledge produces the only valid standard; all other modes of thought or discourse must be judged against it. Therefore, a professional class of philosophers of religion should form a privy council to regulate and control the way that the masses think and act and to modulate religious beliefs according to the capacity of the masses for absorbing abstract concepts. One could easily conclude, therefore, that a false optimism about the ultimate certainty of theoretical truth has lured al-Farabi into a form of philosophical imperialism and an attempt to colonize religion intellectually.

That, however, is almost certainly to misunderstand what al-Farabi actually said and, most critically, did not say. To be sure, a share of al-Farabi's disciples, such as Avicenna and possibly Averroes, may be guilty of wanting or expecting exactly this result. Yet it was no misdirection that, in his refutation of philosophy's primacy, al-Ghazzali did not direct his attack at the words of al-Farabi but rather at those of Avicenna.[35] A closer review of al-Farabi's writings reveals why this is so. As noted earlier, for each of the many major steps that al-Farabi's investigations reached, the final step—its purported conclusion—remained open rather than closed, ambiguous and tentative rather than final and fixed. Despite an outward appearance to the contrary, there was, for him, no closure of the argument, no precise conclusion, no definitive solution, and what is most important, no claim of absolute certainty. A most telling realization of this occurs at the end of al-Farabi's summary of Aristotle.[36] His account of Aristotle's philosophy takes us only to a realization that the master of theoretical reasoning was unable to complete metaphysics and that he was forced, as a consequence, to retrace his path and to reconstruct anew the edifice of philosophy in an unfinished quest for this final achievement. Al-Farabi, likewise, leaves both us and his Aristotle shy of that goal. His concluding statement, after noting that "we have no metaphysical science," is that "therefore philosophy must necessarily come into being in every man in the way possible for him."[37]

Those who would demand a seamless definitude will never find it in the teachings of al-Farabi. Instead, seams abound, as do paradoxes and contradictions. Each treatise (and often each section of a given treatise) comes to its end with an unexpected twist, usually an ambiguity that requires starting all over again.

Many critics then and now have simply given up on al-Farabi; consequently they disdain his notion of philosophy and the role he envisioned for it, and they argue that if philosophy does not yield the certainty that philosophers claim for it, then that certainty must exist elsewhere. They abandoned al-Farabi (and also his Aristotle) for this latter search. As a consequence, many of the later philosophers within Islam, as well as the main religious parties, rejected or ignored him. Only a small number—the professional philosophers—continued to express their regard.

The problem is that al-Farabi did not hold that philosophy can represent certainty or even that it can provide an ultimate truth. Philosophy is not certainty itself but rather the science of certainty. It is an investigation of the ways to truth—and the method of judging truth—rather than being absolute truth itself.

The problem of the religious lawgiver is an important example of one of al-Farabi's incomplete conclusions and of an ambiguous result that, never resolved, always perplexes and urges upon us new interpretations. The material given in the previous sections reflects what al-Farabi had to say about this matter, including especially the puzzle of who the consummate lawgiver actually might be. Although we have chosen Muhammad as a paradigm of the lawgiver, we readily admitted that on the surface Muhammad hardly qualifies as al-Farabi's philosopher-prophet—without, that is, boldly asserting an unknown fact that he was a proper philosopher in addition to being a prophet. The true, ultimate combination of philosopher and prophet would, of course, have to be both. If, on the other hand, Aristotle perfected philosophy by reaching an understanding of demonstration, as al-Farabi certainly asserted, another question arises: Is there, or was there ever, a religion actually based on his results? One answer to both of these questions is to claim that al-Farabi speaks only of an ideal: the perfect amalgamation of theoretical and practical reason in a single person is something that either does not truly exist (and never has?) or is God Himself and God alone.

Thus, in this second and more cautious reading, al-Farabi's Aristotle begins to lose his high status. His unqualified superi-

ority evaporates in a cloud of doubt—doubt that al-Farabi himself both engendered and fostered. Realizing that this was purposeful on al-Farabi's part and that theoretical perfection was,
for him, an elusive ideal at last sets philosophy in its real place.
Hence it becomes necessary to accord due respect, separately
and in proper proportion, both to Aristotle and to Muhammad.
Perfect theoretical reason and perfect practical reason are not
the same, and therefore their personification in two different
individuals or two separate agents (or perhaps two personali-
ties of one agent) is an enduring requirement—and a fact that
demands recognition both in philosophy and in religion.

As master of the practical application of reason, a lawgiver
may operate in a variety of cultural spheres and employ a range
of means to achieve a goal. (Broadly speaking, these means are
characterized by the arts of poetry and rhetoric.) But if this is so,
then the category of lawgivers may include anyone from an
ordinary poet to a Muhammad. However, the creator of a major
religion, a prophet *par excellence,* is also as rare as a Muhammad,
a Jesus, or a Moses, existing but once in a millennium. It would
seem that Aristotles are much easier to come by; they can, in
fact, be made in each generation by propagating and encouraging the study of his books. Reading Aristotle with the requisite
mental acuity reproduces an Aristotle. Reading the Quran, no
matter how intelligently, does not replicate Muhammad. As with
the Quran itself, he does not have his like. Nevertheless, his
uniqueness is not in and of itself a sign of his superiority over
others. Relative merit is still to be determined, and it requires a
universal standard of comparison which is not self-evident in
each particular case of prophecy.

What al-Farabi intended with all this speculation about lawgivers and philosopher-prophets, I believe, was to force those
who understand this dilemma back to its roots, back to the
uncertain relationship between the theoretical and the practical,
between the universal and the particular, and between logic
and grammar. One key is his contention that discourse is, in
essence, practical. It is a facet of action and is not *per se* the
equivalent of thought. One should not speak of discourse (either as language or discursive reflection) and abstract thought

as if they are exactly the same. Therefore, while discourse is properly a vehicle of what he would see as practical reason—though it is not necessarily that reason itself—theoretical reason really has no vehicle because if it did or if it does come to have one it becomes practical.

But, on the other hand, what actually *is* this practical reason? Is it prudence, deliberation over particulars, the basis of volition or choice, or discursive as opposed to deductive thinking? This is still a real problem for al-Farabi. He has recognized a distinction between theoretical knowledge and practice and then has identified something he understands as practical reasoning, which is the mental component of the latter. Finally, he asserts a connection between theoretical and practical reason in order to establish a philosophical interest in the latter, even though there remains some mystery as to what that connection really is. Nevertheless, because he allows the prophet, as the creator of religion, to stand as the master of practical reasoning, he confesses also the lofty, though perhaps not exactly comprehensible, position which practical reason holds when it functions with consummate perfection.

Al-Farabi thus insists on a distinction between discourse and true theory. Of course the practical applications of any theory are not solely confined to discourse, but discourse is the primary field wherein what begins as theory turns into practice. Since all practice requires action, it must always be particular. Comparison, moreover, must be comparison of discourse, not theory, although it will focus on theory as its standard because without a standard no comparison is possible. Particulars, insofar as they are particular, are unique and thus do not compare. Practical reason alone, therefore, will not, by itself, permit genuine comparing, since it is always isolated in its practicality. Only by deriving from them what is theoretically common to several particulars can a comparison actually exist.

In his investigation of discourse as practice, al-Farabi preferred to view discourse through the Aristotelian organon (adding rhetoric and poetics), even though strictly as a discursive vehicle it is not itself logic. Seen this way poetry and rhetoric are far more effective—they are more practical—than either dialectic or demonstration, which are closer to theoretical reason and therefore less practical. As modes of reasoning, however, each logical art yields a degree of theoretical knowledge, poetry lowest, and demonstration highest. As discourse, poetry and rhetoric belong to a given culture and tradition. In dialectic, discourse moves away from its natural base, and in demonstration it becomes universal without (at least ideally) a reference to ordinary languages. For al-Farabi, in terms of theory, the opposite obtains, because for him there must exist a universal that is independent of the language or discourse that might be used to express it. It is this that is common to all discourse and all reasoning. Comparing examples of practical reasoning or its results, whether poetic or otherwise, without a standard of analysis and comparison, tends to produce gibberish. In the study of poetry, for example, poets are limited insofar as they rely solely on their own personal, poetic gift. That is why the academic study of poetry, as well as study of the other practical arts—including religion—is done by doctors of philosophy.

Notes

1. Abu Bakr Muhammad b. Zakariya' al-Razi (Rhazes), d. 925 A.D.

2. For Maimonides and for Averroes this judgement encompasses Avicenna who, from their vantage point, is among those between themselves and Aristotle. No one in the long stretch from the thirteenth century A.D. back to Aristotle ranks in importance with al-Farabi.

3. Modern admiration for al-Farabi's political philosophy occurs in part because he attracted considerable attention from Leo Strauss and his students, particularly Muhsin Mahdi. Both men were drawn to al-Farabi primarily for this aspect of his thought. See, for example, Strauss's "Farabi's Plato" in *Louis Ginzberg: Jubilee Volume* (New York: American Academy for Jewish Research, 1945), 357–93, and Mahdi's introductions to the revised edition of the *Philosophy of Plato and Aristotle* (Ithaca: Cornell University Press, 1969), xi–xxv, 3–10. See also Mahdi's study "Alfarabi" in *History of Political Philosophy*, ed. L. Strauss and J. Cropsey (Ithaca: Cornell University Press, 1963), as well as the following articles by him: "Al-Farabi and the Foundation of Islamic Philoso-

phy," *Islamic Philosophy and Mysticism* (Delmar: Caravan, 1981), 3–21; "Alfarabi on Philosophy and Religion," *Philosophical Forum* 4, no. 1 (1972): 5–25; "Remarks on Alfarabi's *Attainment of Happiness*," *Essays on Islamic Philosophy and Science* (Albany: State University of New York Press, 1975), 47–66; "Science, Philosophy and Religion in Alfarabi's Enumeration of the Sciences," *The Cultural Context of Medieval Learning* (Dordrecht: D. Reidel, 1975), 113–45; and "Al-Farabi's Imperfect State," *Journal of the American Oriental Society* 110 (1990): 691–726.

4. Significantly, politics and religion are all but interchangeable in al-Farabi's theory of practical philosophy. The term *city (madīna)* appears in one of his works in the same context where another uses *religion (dīn)*. In his introduction to al-Farabi's *Book of Religion (Kitab al-milla)*, Mahdi, for example, remarks that, "Alfarabi employs the phrase *al-milla* in *Al-Fusul* in many instances in which he uses the phrase *al-madina* in the book on *Al-Madina al-Fadila*" (p. 30 of Arabic introduction).

5. In addition to the highly important articles by Muhsin Mahdi cited previously, two substantial studies of al-Farabi have appeared only recently. They are Miriam Galston, *Politics and Excellence: The Political Philosophy of Alfarabi* (Princeton: Princeton University Press, 1990) and Deborah L. Black, *Logic and Aristotle's Rhetoric and Poetics in Medieval Arabic Philosophy* (Leiden: E. J. Brill, 1990).

6. A complete list of al-Farabi's writings, although not itself extensive, would serve no purpose here. These works are the principal references in what follows: *Alfarabi's Book of Letters (Kitab al-Huruf)*, ed. M. Mahdi (Beirut: Dar el-Machreq, 1970); *Alfarabi's Book of Religion and Related Texts (Kitab al-Milla wa-Nusus Ukhra)*, ed. M. Mahdi (Beirut, Dar el-Machraq, 1968); *Al-Farabi on the Perfect State: Abu Nasr al-Farabi's Mabadi' Ara' Ahl al-Madina al-Fadila*, ed. and trans. R. Walzer (Oxford: Clarendon Press, 1985); *Kitab al-Siyasa al-Madaniya (The Political Regime)*, ed. F. Najjar (Beirut: Imprimerie Catholique, 1964); partial English trans. of the same in *Medieval Political Philosophy: A Sourcebook*, ed. Lerner and Mahdi (Ithaca: Cornell University Press, 1963); *Tahsil al-Sa`ada (The Attainment of Happiness)*, ed. J. Al-Yasin (Beirut: Al-Andaloss, 1981); English trans. by M. Mahdi in *The Philosophy of Plato and Aristotle* (Ithaca: Cornell University Press, 1969); *Falsafat Aflatun (The Philosophy of Plato)*, ed. F. Rosenthal and R. Walzer (London: Warburg Institute, 1943); English trans. M. Mahdi in the work of the same name; *Kitab al-Jam` Bayna Ra'yay al-Hakimayn Aflatun al-Ilahi wa Aristutalis*, ed. F. Dieterici (Leiden: n.p., 1890); *Ihsa' al-`Ulum (The Enumeration of the Sciences)*, ed. Angel Gonzalez Palencia (Madrid: n.p., 1953); partial English trans. in *Medieval Political Philosophy*, 24–30.

7. In his *al-Talwihat,* ed. H. Corbin, *Opera Metaphysica et Mystica* 1 (Istanbul: Maarif Matbaasi, 1945) 70–74. See also Hossein Ziai, *Knowledge and Illumination* (Atlanta: Scholars Press, 1990), 145–47.

8. Ibn Tufayl, *Hayy Ibn Yaqzan,* ed. Leon Gauthier, 2d ed. (Beirut: n.p., 1936). There are numerous translations of this famous work.

9. See, for example, al-Farabi's explanation of this distinction in his *Enumeration of the Sciences,* 35, discussed by Mahdi, "Enumeration," 119. For al-Farabi the science of language is of a particular language, whereas the treatment of what is common to the languages of all nations belongs to logic.

10. This is the claim al-Farabi makes at the end of his *Attainment* (Arabic, 96–97; English trans., 49 [para. 62]).

11. *Attainment,* Arabic, 92–93; trans., 46–47 (paras. 57, 58).

12. Ibid., Arabic, 92; trans., 26.

13. Ibid., Arabic, 93; trans., 47.

14. Al-Farabi does not use this term but rather the neutral *nāmūs* and *nawāmīs* (nomoi).

15. Galston, *Politics and Excellence,* 68 (citing *Fusul,* no. 7, 29:8–11; and *Siyasa,* 33:4–5).

16. On this see especially Miriam Galston, "Al-Farabi on Aristotle's Theory of Demonstration," in *Islamic Philosophy and Mysticism* (Delmar, N.Y., 1981), 23–34.

17. *Enumeration,* Arabic, 50.

18. "Happiness means that the human soul reaches a degree of perfection in existence where it is in no need of matter for its support, since it becomes one of the incorporeal things . . . and remains in that state continuously forever" (*Virtuous City,* 206–7).

19. *Attainment,* 13–14.

20. Ibid., Arabic, 61–62; trans., 22–23.

21. Ibid., Arabic, 64, trans., 25.

22. Or "deliberative faculty."

> Things of this sort are not covered by the theoretical sciences, which cover only the intelligibles that do not vary at all. Therefore

another faculty and another skill is required with which to discern the voluntary intelligibles, insofar as they possess these variable accidents: that is, the modes according to which they can be brought into actual existence by the will at a determined time, in a determined place, and when a determined event occurs. That is the deliberative faculty. (*Attainment,* Arabic, 68; trans., 27–28)

23. Ibid., Arabic, 90; trans., 44.

24. "Both comprise the same subjects and both give an account of the ultimate principles of the beings . . . an account of the ultimate end for the sake of which man is made. In everything of which philosophy gives an account based on intellectual perception or conception, religion gives an account based on imagination" (Ibid., Arabic, 90; trans., 44). This passage in the *Attainment* in its entirety is one of the clearest statements of al-Farabi's theoretical understanding of religion.

25. "It is this man who receives divine revelation." He is a "visionary prophet." "This man holds the most perfect rank of humanity and has reached the highest degree of happiness" (*Virtuous City,* 145). The same view occurs in the *Political Regime,* Arabic 79, trans., 36.

26. "It is possible to imitate these things for each group and each nation, using matters that are different in each case. Consequently, there may be a number of virtuous nations and virtuous cites whose religions are different, even though they all pursue the very same kind of happiness. For religion is but the impressions of these things or the impressions of their images, imprinted in the [individual] soul" (*Political Regime,* Arabic, 85–86; trans., 41).

27. "Once the conditions that render their actual existence possible are prescribed, the voluntary intelligibles are embodied in laws. Therefore the legislator is he who, by the excellence of his deliberation, has the capacity to find the conditions required for the actual existence of the voluntary intelligibles in such a way as to lead to the achievement of supreme happiness" (*Attainment,* Arabic, 91; trans., 45).

28. Ibid., Arabic, 94; trans., 47.

29. "Religion is defined as the totality of practical judgments and theoretical and practical teachings that a ruler transmits in his effort to lead a community to a specific goal or set of goals" (Galston, *Politics and Excellence,* 99, citing *Milla* 43:3–4, 44:14–46:10).

30. On the general problem encountered by the Arabic philosophers in explaining the expanded *organon,* see the excellent and extremely important study by Deborah Black cited earlier.

31. *Political Regime* (Siyasa), 79:15–17; Galston, *Politics and Excellence,* 67.

32. What follows here is based on al-Farabi's account of philosophy and religion as it occurs in the middle portion of his *Kitab al-Huruf* (131–61). In many ways his statement there is unique and without explicit parallel elsewhere, although he did not contradict what he said in this one instance. The only detailed analysis of this passage thus far is Mahdi's article "Alfarabi on Philosophy and Religion." The discussion which follows here owes much to Mahdi's summary of al-Farabi's argument.

33. *Huruf,* 153 (para. 147).

34. Mahdi, "On Philosophy and Religion," 15.

35. See, for example, the observations of Muhsin Mahdi, "Avicenna," *Encyclopaedia Iranica,* ed. E. Yarshater (London: Routledge and Kegan Paul, 1983–), 66.

36. This is the third and final section of his *The Philosophy of Plato and Aristotle.*

37. Arabic, 133; trans., 130.

References

Black, Deborah L. 1990. *Logic and Aristotle's Rhetoric and Poetics in Medieval Arabic Philosophy.* Leiden: E. J. Brill.

al-Fārābī, Abū Naṣr. 1890. *Kitāb al-Jamᶜ Bayna Ra'yay al-Ḥakīmayn Aflāṭūn al-Ilāhī wa Arisṭūṭālīs.* Edited by F. Dieterici. In *Alfarabi's philosophische Abhandlungen.* Leiden: n.p.

———. 1963. *Falsafat Aflāṭūn (The Philosophy of Plato).* Edited by F. Rosenthal and R. Walzer. London: Warburg Institute; English translation by M. Mahdi in *The Philosophy of Plato and Aristotle.*

————. 1953. *Iḥṣā' al-ʿUlūm (The Enumeration of the Sciences)*. Edited by Angel Gonzalez Palencia. Madrid: n.p.; partial English translation in *Medieval Political Philosophy*.

————. 1964. *Kitāb al-Siyāsa al-Madanīya (The Political Regime)*. Edited by F. Najjar. Beirut: Imprimerie Catholique; partial English translation of the same in *Medieval Political Philosophy: A Sourcebook*, edited by R. Lerner and M. Mahdi. Ithaca: Cornell University Press, 1963.

————. 1968. *Alfarabi's Book of Religion and Related Texts (Kitāb al-Milla wa-Nuṣūṣ Ukhrā)*. Edited by M. Mahdi. Beirut: Dar al-Machreq.

————. 1970. *Alfarabi's Book of Letters (Kitāb al-Ḥurūf)*. Edited by M. Mahdi. Beirut: Dar el-Machreq.

————. 1981. *Taḥṣīl al-Saʿāda (The Attainment of Happiness)*. Edited by J. Al-Yasin. Beirut: Al-Andaloss; English translation by M. Mahdi in *Philosophy of Plato and Aristotle*. Ithaca: Cornell University Press, 1969.

————. 1985. *Al-Farabi on the Perfect State: Abū Naṣr al-Fārābī's Mabādiʾ Arāʾ Ahl al-Madīna al-Fāḍila*. Edited with English translation by R. Walzer. Oxford: Clarendon Press.

Galston, Miriam. 1981. "Al-Fārābī on Aristotle's Theory of Demonstration." In *Islamic Philosophy and Mysticism*, edited by Parviz Morewedge. Delmar, N.Y.: Caravan Books.

————. 1990. *Politics and Excellence: The Political Philosophy of Alfarabi*. Princeton, New Jersey: Princeton University Press.

Ibn Tufayl. 1936. *Ḥayy Ibn Yaqẓān*. Edited by Leon Gauthier. 2nd edition, Beirut: n.p.

Lerner, R. and Muhsin Mahdi, eds. 1963. *Medieval Political Philosophy: A Sourcebook*. Ithaca: Cornell University Press.

Mahdi, Muhsin. 1963. "Alfarabi." In *History of Political Philosophy*, edited by Leo Strauss and Joseph Cropsey. Chicago: University of Chicago Press.

————. 1969. *Philosophy of Plato and Aristotle*. Ithaca: Cornell University Press.

————. 1972. "Alfarabi on Philosophy and Religion," *Philosophical Forum* N.S. 4, no. 1(1972):5–25.

————. 1975. "Remarks on Alfarabi's *Attainment of Happiness.*" In *Essays on Islamic Philosophy and Science,* edited by George F. Hourani, 47–66. Albany: State University of New York Press.

————. 1975. "Science, Philosophy and Religion in Alfarabi's *Enumeration of the Sciences.*" In *The Cultural Context of Medieval Learning,* edited by E. Murdoch and E. D. Sylla, 113–145. Dordrecht: D. Reidel Publishing Co.

————. 1981. "Al-Fārābī and the Foundation of Islamic Philosophy." In *Islamic Philosophy and Mysticism,* edited by Parviz Morewedge, 7–21. Delmar: Caravan Books.

————. 1983. "Avicenna." In *Encyclopaedia Iranica,* edited by E. Yarshater. London: Routledge and Kegan Paul.

————. 1990. "Al-Fārābī's Imperfect State," *Journal of the American Oriental Society* 110 (1990):691–726.

Strauss, Leo. 1945. "Farabi's Plato." In *Louis Ginzberg: Jubilee Volume,* 357–393. New York: American Academy for Jewish Research.

al-Suhrawardī. 1945. *al-Talwīḥāt.* Edited by H. Corbin. In *Opera Metaphysica et Mystica* I. Istanbul: Maarif Matbaasi.

Ziai, Hossein. 1990. *Knowledge and Illumination.* Atlanta: Scholars Press.

Chapter 4

In Defense of Rather Fragile and Local Achievement: Reflections on the Work of Gurulugomi

Charles Hallisey

Most, if not all, cultures have more than one theory by which the appearances of the world are ordered and understood. Although it remains unclear how many theories a culture may possibly or ideally preserve, there are always at least two different kinds of disciplined ways of thinking about the world, such as what we find in the contrastive visions of common sense and science in European and American cultures. The existence of multiple theories in a single culture and their relative valuation are empirical issues which have attracted the attention of sociologists, anthropologists, and historians for a long time.[1] They are also of considerable philosophical interest, and indeed the recognition of the possibility of multiple theories seems to be a necessary condition for philosophy itself.

It seems obvious as well that such theories, although often quite disparate, are usually integrated within a culture, their differences either minimized or explained. But as Lee Yearley

121

has pointed out, it also is evident that in spite of this integration, sophisticated thinkers in particular cultures can still contrast the available theories to become better aware of the potentials and limits of each.[2] Such thinkers are able rationally to combine different theories about the world "in a way that preserves the critical insights of those positions and also resolves internal problems in them and fills their lacunae."[3] The combination and integration of multiple theories about the world seem to be necessary conditions for culture itself, but such combinations are also of considerable interest to philosophers.

This chapter takes up a third issue which follows clearly from these two. The combination of, say, two different theories about the world presupposes the possibility of simultaneously holding different relations between them. This is because the very existence of different theories indicates a continuing separation and contrast between them even as their combination and integration suggest otherwise. The possibility that two theories could be simultaneously separated and combined raises the question of whether it is also possible to combine multiple *ways of relating* different theories about the world "in a way," as Yearly says about combining different theories themselves, "that preserves the critical insights of those positions and also resolves internal problems in them and fills their lacunae."

This, like the first two observations, is above all an empirical issue, and we must consider whether or not we see any evidence that sophisticated thinkers do simultaneously use multiple schemata or structures for relating different theories about the world and, if they do, under what circumstances or for what purposes. But like the other two, this issue is also of broad philosophical interest. It may be that, in addition to accepting the co-existence of different theories in a culture, considering the multiple relations between them as co-eval can help us to understand better the "realm where those details of contingent human life that we include in 'practice' actually *meet* the sorts of disciplined thinking we mean by theory."[4]

This chapter aims to contribute to our understanding of the meeting of practice and theory with the aid of some material taken from a twelfth-century Buddhist commentator and philosopher named Gurulugomi (Guruḷugōmī). This material provides initially an empirical focus for our considerations, but it also provides a catalyst for a particular kind of philosophical reflection. This can be handily distinguished, as P. F. Strawson has recently done, from another common approach to philosophy by analogies to grammar and therapy.[5] Philosophical work that is analogous to grammar—understanding grammar as the laying bare of what we do when we use language—builds on the expectation that we can "add to our practical mastery something like a theoretical understanding of what we are doing when we exercise that mastery," while philosophy, which is more analogous to therapy, is pursued to liberate ourselves from "confusions and perplexities" in which we already find ourselves.[6] As viewed with this latter analogy, "the philosopher explains nothing except, perhaps, the source of our confusions."[7] At the same time these two kinds of philosophy are not completely unrelated. Philosophy on the analogy of therapy can prepare the ground for future "grammatical" philosophical work, and that is what I will try to do here by using Gurulugomi to highlight the value of distinguishing between action, justification, and education when we think about the meeting between practice and theory.

Careful consideration of Gurulugomi's example as a philosopher can enhance our vision of comparative philosophy of religion as an intellectual practice, and I will take up these possibilities at the end of this chapter.[8] It is important at least to note at the outset that the converse is also true: careful consideration of philosophical questions which are of contemporary concern to us, and about which we seek clarification, can enhance our historical understanding of Gurulugomi as a Buddhist thinker. In historical studies, studying a thinker in a way that assumes the sense and coherence of the subject's ideas is ironically an effective check on the biases of the historian, as R. G. Collingwood recognized when he recommended it as the ideal historical method.[9] By explicitly asking philosophical questions—by identifying, rethinking, and evaluating the schemata which Gurulugomi uses to connect theory and practice—we ideally will better grasp in our own vocabulary the meanings and purposes which Gurulugomi assumed and conveyed in the conventions familiar to him.

≈✦≈

It is likely that Gurulugomi was originally from the Andhra region of south India, but he was active as an author in Sri Lanka. He wrote two books, both in Sinhala. One, *Amāvatura,* is a devotional biography of the Buddha (Gurulugomi himself calls it a *Buddhacarita* or "life of the Buddha") while the other, *Dharmapradīpikā* is a doctrinal work arranged as a commentary on the Pali *Mahābodhivaṃsa* (Gurulugomi calls this work a *parikathā,* an "explanation,"[10] but he also calls it a work on *Buddhadharma*[11]). Much of the religious writing of medieval Sri Lanka, from the twelfth to the fourteenth centuries, belongs to these two genres of writing—devotional works on the life and virtues of the Buddha and doctrinal expositions—and thus Gurulugomi's work may be representative of intellectual practices which were widespread in his historical context.

A popular tradition about Gurulugomi's life, however, renders the fact that he authored both of these books problematic. According to this tradition, Gurulugomi gave a copy of *Amāvatura* to his older sister who commented after reading it, "My brother still has the smell of milk in his mouth," a figure of speech connoting immaturity, and Gurulugomi is said to have written his other work, *Dharmapradīpikā,* after having heard his sister's comment. It is a pleasing anecdote, gentle in the way it integrates different orders of knowledge about the world, but historically it is not true. We are quite certain that *Amāvatura* was written after *Dharmapradīpikā* because the former text refers to the latter by name.[12] But even if this story is not true with respect to literary history, adding it to the fact that Gurulugomi wrote two very different books presents a problem which we should not ignore. It is a general task for any historical interpretation of Gurulugomi's career as an author to establish (a) whether there is a deeper connection between his two works, such that the concerns of his doctrinal work help us to understand him as the author of a devotional text, and vice versa, or (b) whether his two books only exemplify his virtuosity as a writer, able to compose classics in the two genres of religious literature which were most popular in his day.

This small example reminds us that the distinction and relation between the comparative philosophy of religion and the historical study of religion are analogous to those between the history of philosophy and the history of ideas with philosophical material as the subject:[13] "The history of ideas is history before it is philosophy, while with the history of philosophy it is the other way round. In any worthwhile work of either sort, *both concerns are likely to be represented,* but there is a genuine distinction."[14]

These two concerns—one more historical, the other opening out into the nature of comparative philosophy itself—permeate the following discussion of the material taken from Gurulugomi as part of a consideration of how "those details of contingent human life . . . actually *meet* the sorts of disciplined thinking we mean by 'theory.' " Our aim is to move toward a more informed understanding of how, with respect to practice and theory, "excellence in one is linked to excellence in, or an understanding of, the other."[15] If we can accomplish this we will not only know Gurulugomi better, but at the same time we will be able to add reflexively to our knowledge about our own intellectual practices.

The focus of this chapter is a single passage from *Dharmapradīpikā* whose contents are directly relevant to our larger subject—the meeting between practice and theory. The present section will introduce the passage and attempt to give some measure of its richness, while in the next section we will use it as a vantage point for clarifying some perplexities that can arise when we think about the meeting of practice and theory.

As stated above, *Dharmapradīpikā* is ostensibly a Sinhala-language commentary on the *Mahābodhivaṃsa,* a historical work written in Pali about the Bodhi tree, but its purposes actually seem more doctrinal than exegetical. The exegetical character is so minimal, in fact, that "readers hardly notice that the work is a commentary of the *Mahābodhivaṃsa*."[16] Gurulugomi says that his method is to select words from the Pali text and to explain them,[17] although with this method he probably could have achieved his doctrinal goals even if he had chosen another work to comment on.[18] It has been suggested that the connection between the *Mahābodhivaṃsa* and *Dharmapradīpikā*, while not integral, was still purposeful: "The *Mahābodhivaṃsa* was a textbook used by students . . . and the association of the *Pradipika* with this work gave it the chance of reaching a greater number of readers."[19]

In context, the passage explains a phrase from the *Mahābodhivaṃsa*, "*manokulaṃ dhammaṃ desento*," which can be roughly translated "teaching a truth that is channeled according to mind":

This phrase means that the teaching of the Buddha is twofold. It is conventional teaching *(samvṛttideśana)* and teaching in an absolute sense *(paramārtha-deśana)*.

"This is a person *(pudgala)*, this is a being *(sattva)*, this is a woman, this is a man, this is a one of the *kṣatriya* caste, this is a brahman, this is a god, this is a Mara." Such things are customary teaching.

"This is impermanent *(anitya)*, this is suffering *(duḥkha)*, this is not-self *(anātman)*, this is an aggregate *(skandha)*, this is an element *(dhātu)*, this is a sensory sphere *(āyatana)*." Such things are teaching in an absolute sense.

If a person will make a special attainment *(viśeṣādhigama)* having comprehended what is heard in a teaching in the conventional way, then he [i.e., the Buddha] teaches the conventional way. If a person will make a special attainment having comprehended what was heard in a teaching that is teaching in an absolute sense, then he [the Buddha] makes a teaching in an absolute sense.

Furthermore, the Buddha makes a conventional teaching for eight reasons: In order to show modesty and shame *(hiri-otap)*, to show the individual's force of *karma*, to show separate human natures *(pṛthak puruṣākāra)*, to show deeds with unending consequences, to show the *brahmavihāras*, to show previous existences, to show the purity of what is being given, and in order not to discard the established practice of the world.

When he says, "aggregates, elements, sensory spheres bear shame," people do not understand and are confused. They say, "What is this? How do aggregates, elements, sensory spheres have shame?" When he says that "people, ksatriyas, brahmans, gods, Maras have shame," they understand. They are not confused. For that reason, in order to show shame and modesty, the Buddha teaches with the conventions of the world.

When he says, "aggregates experience *karma*," it is in the same way. . . . When he says, "Great monasteries like the one at Veluvana are built by aggregates, by elements, by sensory spheres," it's the same. . . . When he says aggregates murder their mother or father, or a noble person, or cause the Buddha's blood to flow, or cause a division in the Sangha," it's the same, and for this reason, in order to show deeds with unending consequences, he teaches with a conventional teaching.

Aggregates practice lovingkindness . . . it is the same. When he says, "Aggregates remember their previous lives," it's the same. When he says, "Aggregates accept alms, elements and sensory spheres accept alms," people do not understand. They are confused. They draw towards others and say, "How is it that aggregates, elements, and sensory spheres accept alms?" "Persons accept, virtuous ones accept," when he speaks thus, they know. They do not turn away. For that reason, the Buddha, in order to show the purity of what is given, teaches with a conventional teaching.

The Buddha does not discard what is customary in the world. He teaches with the nomenclature of the world, with the idiom of the world, with a worldly way of speaking. For all those reasons, the Buddha teaches a conventional teaching *(samvṛittideśana)* in order not to discard the custom of the world.[20]

Those who are familiar with Buddhist thought may immediately feel that they know the point of this passage as soon as
the categories of conventional and absolute teaching are mentioned. It is well known that various Buddhist schools distinguished between the conventional and the absolute, and it is
equally well known that all schools also ranked these theories
of the world hierarchically and commonly at the expense of the
conventional. When we look more closely at the various uses of
this pair in Buddhist literature, however, we begin to suspect
that we have overestimated the significance of the hierarchy
itself: its place in contemporary scholarship is due more to the
considerable attention it has received than to its intrinsic relevance to understanding Buddhist usage. This overestimation
has encouraged us to mistake one interpretation of the distinction for the distinction itself, and it has consequently prevented
us from noting other interpretations which are found in the
different Buddhist traditions.

We cannot ignore these interpretations. There is no doubt
that Gurulugomi was well acquainted with the intellectual resources of the Theravadin scriptural and commentarial heritage.
Indeed, the passage's contents themselves give ample evidence
of Gurulugomi's familiarity with the Pali commentaries which
were authoritative in the Theravada tradition. He is clearly using in this passage ideas found in Buddhaghosa, whose own
commentaries provided a standard of orthodoxy for much of
Theravadin thought, although we cannot be sure if Gurulugomi
has taken this passage from Buddhaghosa directly or from some
other oral or written source.[21]

It is heuristically valuable for us—insofar as we may expect ranking to be an intrinsic part of any use of the conven-
tional-ultimate pair, and insofar as we may also feel that our
expectations are justified because they apparently receive cor-
roboration from the labels themselves—to examine first a use of
these labels which considers the conventional and absolute not
as hierarchically ranked, but only as separate and contrasted.
This can be seen in a discussion of kinds of truth (sacca) found
in the commentary to the Katthāvatthu, also attributed to

Buddhaghosa. These truths are formally different and contrasted, without specifying any positive relation between them: "The Perfectly Enlightened One, the best of teachers, spoke two truths, that is, the customary and the absolute—one does not come across a third; a customary statement is true because of convention and an absolute statement is true since it is about the real characteristics of things."[22]

The commentary to the *Katthāvatthu* further emphasizes that the conventional and the absolute are both true, saying that "whether [Buddhas] use conventional speech or absolute speech, they speak what is true, what is factual, and not false."[23] But the conventional and the absolute are different kinds of truth because they have different truth conditions. Absolute truth assumes a set of realist truth conditions, its terms representing what really exists, while conventional truth is true on nonrealist grounds, the extension of its terms fixed by custom rather than by the way things are. The *Atthasālinī*, Buddhaghosa's commentary to the *Dhammasangaṇi*, a canonical *abhidhamma* text, says that customary teaching *(vohāra)* is that which is acceptable insofar as it is in accordance with established meanings *(attha)*.[24]

The acceptance of different kinds of truth, distinguished by their truth conditions, is not particularly Buddhist or South Asian. All of us in the twentieth century pragmatically accept different kinds of truth when we discuss, for example, a star as a cloud of glowing gas or as a component of a constellation.[25] It would probably strike most of us as beside the point to try to evaluate these two conceptions of a star by a single standard, or to try to rank them abstractly, without regard to circumstances of use. The same reluctance would apply to this particular formulation of the conventional-absolute distinction as only separated and contrasted.

The two kinds of truth could be ranked hierarchically if they shared some property. None is identified here, although we can assume a minimal similarity insofar as each is a description of the world. Rather than being integrated in any more substantial way, they are portrayed only as different in kind, and it is thus easy to draw the conclusion that knowledge of one is not necessary for knowledge or mastery of the other, nor will changes in one require changes in the other.[26]

This contrastive treatment of conventional and absolute truth does not, however, preclude a hierarchical ordering. It leaves open the possibility that conventional and absolute teaching could be integrated in a hierarchy. In the Theravada commentarial tradition, such a hierarchical integration is illustrated analogically by a parallel dichotomy between texts which have a direct meaning *(nītārtha/nītattha)* and those which have an indirect meaning that needs to be specified further *(neyārtha/ neyyattha)*. This interlocking of the two dichotomies can be seen in the following discussion, also from Buddhaghosa:

> A sutta of the form "there is one individual, O monks," "there are two individuals, O monks." "there are three individuals, O monks," . . . etc. is a sutta of indirect meaning. Here although the Perfectly Enlightened One speaks of "there is one person, O monks," etc. its sense has to be inferred since there is no individual in the absolute sense *(paramāttho)*. But a person because of his folly may take this as a sutta of direct meaning and would argue that the Tathagata would not have said "there is one individual, O monks" etc. unless a person existed in the absolute sense. Accepting the fact that since he has said so there must be a person in the absolute sense, he represents a sutta of indirect meaning as a sutta of direct meaning. One should speak of a sutta of direct meaning (as of the form), "this is impermanent, sorrowful and devoid of substance."[27]

Although Buddhaghosa accepts both indirect and direct teaching as valid, he emphasizes here the danger of taking indirect teaching independently from direct teaching. This could result in a confusion of the two, with conventional teaching wrongly taken as an equal to absolute teaching. With this as a possibility, it is inadequate only to separate and contrast the conventional and the absolute. Once they are connected, absolute teaching may serve as a constraint, and if necessary a corrective, against the confusion which the conventional itself is unable to check.

Thus knowledge of absolute teaching contributes to knowledge and mastery of the conventional, but not vice versa.

When Buddhaghosa insists that the meaning of an indirect teaching—that is, a conventional teaching—is to be inferred only on the basis of what is known from a teaching whose meaning is more direct, it is easy to see that the application of the indirect-direct pairing to the conventional-absolute dichotomy changes the relation between the absolute and the conventional from a difference in kind to a difference in degree, with the relative adequacy of each to be judged by the degree to which what really exists is accurately represented. Both kinds of teaching ultimately utilize a single set of truth conditions.

While conventional and absolute teaching can be considered as forming one field, it is still possible to separate and contrast them, but this will be done on different grounds than in the previous interpretation. When conventional teaching forms a single field with absolute teaching about the world, it loses any claim to give access to a meaning established by its own truth conditions to the same degree that it gains validity as a means for knowing what is otherwise displayed by absolute teaching. It is accordingly reduced to being a false, if convenient, way of speaking about that which is only truly described by absolute teaching. The conventional and the absolute become implicitly separated and contrasted as the true and the false, whereas in the earlier instance they were contrasted and separated as different kinds of truth.

A third interpretation of the customary and absolute distinction also tends to establish relations between them so that together they appear simultaneously as both the same and different, but it does this in yet another way. This interpretation utilizes analogically the distinction between *pariyāya* and *nippariyāya*,[28] a dichotomy which itself permits various relations between its two elements.

A contrast between *pariyāya* and *nippariyāya* is suggested by their grammar; the prefix *ni(r)* in *nippariyāya* denotes "without, away from." The pair is found, beginning in canonical literature, as a description of different ways that the Buddha

taught.[29] *Nippariyāya* is defined as a demonstration which "is
not by a particular instance."[30] It is a discourse which radically
decontextualizes its subjects; thus it also has connotations of
states of affairs which are unchanging.[31] For example, a
nippariyāya discussion of suffering *(dukkha)* displays suffering
generically (that is, suffering per se—*dukkhadukkha*), while
pariyāya discussions of suffering approach it as "earache, tooth-
ache, fever born of lust, fever born of hate, etc."[32] In such instances, there is an assumption of a relation between *pariyāya*
and *nippariyāya* like that between genus and species, or between the abstract and the concrete, in which the particular is
derived from the general. In a manner similar to what we saw
with the indirect meaning–direct meaning pair, *pariyāya-
nippariyāya* modes of teaching, while contrasted and separated,
can also form a single field. This is because a definitive aspect of
any phenomenon described as *pariyāya* is only deducible from
what is displayed by *nippariyāya*. In this understanding,
pariyāya-nippariyāya seems to refer to contrasts and relations
like those between the particular and the general.

These same labels are used in commentarial literature as
descriptions of texts, the names extended to the pedagogical
methods which typically employ concrete or abstract modes of
expression. The texts of the *Suttapiṭaka,* the Buddha's own sermons, are described as *pariyāya,* while Abhidhamma literature
is described as *nippariyāya*.[33] Teaching in the *pariyāya* mode,
textured by "thick terms" and rich with illustrations and applications, is aptly called *ad hominem,* because it is always directed *to somebody*.[34] We can thus distinguish *pariyāya* and
nippariyāya as modes of teaching separated and contrasted in
terms of both contents and audience. The contrast, however, is
relative: Abhidhamma, the defining illustration of *nippariyāya,*
can be addressed to a particular person in appropriate circumstances, and it then becomes a *pariyāya,* alongside other particularistic and *ad hominem* accounts, such as the *jātaka*.[35]

This relativity provides a qualification that is important
for understanding the relations between the two modes of
teaching. It suggests that in an important way, *pariyāya* and

nippariyāya are as much equivalents as opposites, as can be seen in the following passage, again from Buddhaghosa; note too that it illustrates the *pariyāya* method itself, even as its contents address the relation between the Buddha's modes of teaching: "Just as if there were a teacher, who explains the meaning of the Three Vedas and is versed in the regional languages *(desabhāsakusalo);* to one who would understand the meaning if he spoke in the Tamil language, he explains it in the Tamil language and to another who would understand (if he spoke in) the Andhra language, he speaks in that language."[36]

Buddhaghosa then says that *both* the conventional and the absolute teachings of the Buddha are like the languages used by the teacher to convey the meaning of the Vedas.[37] This formulation puts the conventional and the absolute within a larger framework that gives value to both, rather than combining them, as we saw above, within a single field in which one element consistently gives value to the other.

As with all metaphors, it is unclear just how far we should push the application. We can see that the simile clearly implies that both the conventional and the absolute modes of teaching are capable of expressing the same thing, but the simile leaves unclear just what they are capable of expressing. Should we take "the meaning of the Vedas" as referring to reality, which is described by the ultimate manner of teaching? Or should we take it as referring to a truth which is more characteristic of conventional truth, its truth conditions established by the rules of a system and not by reality itself? Such questions, important as they are, seem to fall outside the insight afforded by the metaphor.

If the image does not provide clear answers to every question we have, it does suggest a relation between conventional and absolute teaching that we have not previously considered. It relates the conventional and the absolute in a way that allows us to perceive them as mutually independent and mutually opposed—separate and contrasted—as well as equivalent and alternative within a larger framework. While different languages can be contrasted with each other by sound and grammar, they are interchangeable with each other as means of communication. Their proper use is determined by the audience addressed, rather than by judgements about their respective value as representations of reality. The metaphor, in contrast to the more descriptivist understandings of conventional-absolute teaching which we saw in the previous two examples, seems to suggest that the Buddha's choice of conventional or absolute teaching acknowledges but is not constrained by the force of specific truth conditions attached to each. A larger framework instead relativizes any fixed hierarchy between conventional and absolute teaching which might be established by utilizing truth conditions. The conventional and the absolute are displayed in the metaphor as related to each other coevally within a larger framework which also suggests the conditions for their proper use.

Within the methods of historical interpretation, we cannot insist that only one of these three schema is relevant for determining the meaning of Gurulugomi's explanation of the phrase "teaching a truth channelled according to mind." It is possible to see some allusion to all three interpretations in the passage. The two opening paragraphs treat the conventional and absolute as separate and contrasted, and from the examples provided, we can conclude that this distinction is made on pluralist and descriptivist principles which allow one to accept different conceptions of truth with different truth conditions. The third paragraph takes them as equivalent and alternative, the choice of either determined pragmatically by reference to the particular audience and to long-range goals.

The rest of the passage defends conventional teaching as an alternative to absolute teaching. In contrast to what we saw above, here conventional teaching is more valued than teaching in an absolute mode because of its impact on people. Moreover, when Gurulugomi gives eight reasons for using conventional teaching, we might take this as a suggestion that conventional teaching is more suitable than absolute teaching for displaying important aspects of the world, aspects which are both factual and valuational, and we might conclude that

Gurulugomi would endorse Martha Nussbaum's statement that "there may be some views of the world and how one should live in it . . . that cannot be fully and adequately stated in the language of conventional philosophical prose, a style remarkably flat and lacking in wonder, but only in a language and in forms themselves more complex, more allusive, more attentive to particulars."[38] Gurulugomi, however, does not rule out the possibility of showing "separate human natures" in the view of the world conveyed by absolute teaching. He only suggests that it would not be attractive or convincing to some, if not most, people. Thus although Gurulugomi ranks the conventional above the absolute, he does this, in contrast to Nussbaum, only on nondescriptive grounds. Conventional teaching is more effective in some circumstances as a means to an end defined by Buddhist soteriology.

This soteriological framework itself implies yet another hierarchy insofar as it posits a set of gradualist relations between conventional and absolute teaching. Gurulugomi explains that the Buddha teaches in an absolute manner to a person who is able to "make an attainment" religiously from hearing such a teaching. Within the framework of Buddhist soteriology, one would only have such capabilities because of the previous performance of other actions, such as the giving of alms to monks or the donation of a monastery. That is, practice motivated and guided by conventional teaching leads gradually, but inevitably, to conditions in which practice can be motivated and guided by absolute teaching. In a profound sense, conventional teaching creates the conditions for absolute teaching.

In the end, Gurulugomi does not combine these different relations into one systematic whole.[39] Instead, he leaves the firm impression that since one cannot dispense practically with either conventional or absolute teaching, they are best understood theoretically as coeval. We may find this unsatisfactory as a theoretical position, especially if we take systematic coherence—the inter-relation between ideas so that they provide each other with mutual support to the maximal degree possible—to be a mark of rational method in a thinker.[40]

We may appreciate more the apparent absence of theoretical integration in the passage from *Dharmapradīpikā* if we consider it in connection to our more general concern about the meeting of theory and practice. We should not make the common mistake, however, of equating absolute teaching with theory and conventional teaching with practice. Gurulugomi makes clear in his initial distinction between conventional and absolute teaching that both are theories about the world. Instead, we would do better to note that this passage structures the meeting between practice and theory with two models: one treats theory outside of practice as an action guide, while the other includes theory within practice as a constitutive part of a process of character formation and moral education.

We can sharpen our understanding of these two models, left largely unarticulated by Gurulugomi, by turning to Paul Griffiths' article "Denaturalizing Discourse: Ābhidhārmikas, Propositionalists, and the Comparative Philosophy of Religion" and to Lee Yearley's book, *Mencius and Aquinas: Theories of Virtue and Conceptions of Courage.*[41] As we make these somewhat distant comparisons, however, we end up turning the tables, with Gurulugomi becoming as much a tool of analysis as an object for analysis. He helps us to become aware that a source of our own confusions about the practical applications of theory is that our categories make it easy to conflate *reasons* for action with *dispositions* for action. And he also helps us to see that the expectation that theory functions pre-eminently as an action guide, which justifies and thus helps us to select proper practices, may blind us to the very different expectations we should bring to theory when it is utilized in contexts of training and education.

We will turn to Paul Griffiths first. In his article, he does two things. First, he proposes that 'denaturalized discourse,' a notion which developed in contemporary analytic philosophy, could usefully serve as a descriptive category for cross-cultural study, and second, he tries to develop deductively the thesis that the comparative philosophy of religion is itself best pursued in the fashion of denaturalized discourse as he describes it. For our purposes here, the first proposal is of greater interest.

Griffiths defines denaturalized discourse and clarifies its characteristics with a "series of contrasts," using a method which, as we shall see below, fits well with his understanding of its relation to naturalized discourse:[42]

> Polysemy, multivalence, the stuff of poetry and the language of love: these are not values for a user of denaturalized discourse. This is usually because the contexts within which such discourses are developed and applied are judged to be unreal, consisting in apparent or constructed objects rather than real ones. The *lebenswelt*, the constructed world of lived experience in which we have our being is, of course, exceedingly messy. We always say more than we mean and less than we hope; we use language to evoke sentiment, to inspire to action, to manipulate, and to mediate.
>
> All of this is discourse in context, naturalized discourse that glories in specificity, growing from and shaping particular human needs in particular cultural contexts.
>
> Denaturalizing discourse is everything that this is not. It is normative and universalizable in its claims, formal and abstract in its style, concerned to disambiguate and make possible precise description of or reference to what there really is. . . .
>
> In sum, formally, a denaturalized discourse is one that, in its ideal-typical form, shows no evidence of rooting in any sociocultural context; exhibits no essential connections with any natural language, and is completely unambiguous. Functionally, a denaturalized discourse is aimed primarily at making available to its users what really exists, a function that from the viewpoint of a user of such discourse, cannot be performed by ordinary, non-denaturalized, discourse.[43]

This formal and functional definition makes it plain that denaturalized discourse is theory *par excellence*. Stanley Fish has noted that theory attempts to stand outside of practice in order to govern it. Like all theory, denaturalized discourse's claim to govern practice seems to derive from the claim that it is able "to *reform* practice by neutralizing interest, by substituting for the parochial perspective of some local or partisan point of view the perspective of a general rationality to which the individual subordinates his contextually conditioned opinions and beliefs." The apparent success of this reform justifies, in turn, a second claim, that it is able "to *guide* practice from a position above or outside it."[44]

Denaturalized discourse, as Griffiths describes it, also corresponds quite closely to the first understanding of absolute teaching we saw above. When he says that denaturalized discourse is functionally "aimed primarily at making available to its users what really exists," we may immediately recall Buddhaghosa's statement that "absolute truth is true because it is about the real characteristics of things."[45] This correspondence is perhaps not so surprising since Griffiths, a specialist in Buddhist philosophy, uses Abhidharma in his article as the major example to demonstrate the usefulness of denaturalized discourse for cross-cultural studies, and we may assume that his knowledge of the Buddhist traditions contributed to his characterization of the descriptive category.[46]

Griffiths' depiction of the relation between denaturalized and naturalized discourse corresponds only partially to what we saw in *Dharmapradīpikā*. Griffiths argues for "a radical disjunction"[47] between naturalized and denaturalized discourse in much the same way that Buddhaghosa and Gurulugomi separate and contrast conventional and absolute truth. But although Griffiths explicitly theorizes denaturalized and naturalized discourse as radically disjunctive, he actually treats them as related in other ways.[48] The unacknowledged relations are similar to those which we have already seen used by Gurulugomi with respect to conventional and absolute teaching. For example, when Griffiths says that "denaturalized discourse is almost always (perhaps always) linked with an attempt to clean up the messy ambiguity of ordinary language used in ordinary contexts,"[49] the imagery of "cleaning up" implies a hierarchy between naturalized and denaturalized discourse similar to what we saw in the pairing of indirect teaching and direct teaching; in both cases, the higher element in the hierarchy reforms the lower. These hierarchical relations between naturalized and denaturalized discourse would seem to be critical for a proper understanding of the latter's connection to practice for another reason. Denaturalized discourse is able to *influence* (taking influence in its original sense from astrology, of the stars affecting human behavior) practice through its hierarchical relation to naturalized discourse, but because it remains separated from and contrasted to naturalized discourse, and thus by definition unrooted in particular cultural contexts, denaturalized discourse is able to remain quite apart from practice and to retain its claim to govern practice from outside.[50]

A critical aspect of Griffiths' argument is that denaturalized discourse is able to "make attractive" directly, without the mediation of any naturalized discourse, the intellectual practices of a community to those outside it.[51] It is "perhaps the only possible practice when the goal in mind is not simply to make a statement of the universalizable facts and norms espoused by the community, but also, in making that statement, to make it evident to those outside the community that these facts and norms do have universal applicability."[52] While this aspect of Griffiths' account seems to me to be descriptively plausible, the conclusions—both descriptive and normative—that he draws are wrong. He mistakes what occurs in a particular kind of competitive context for an essential property of denaturalized discourse deriving from its own inner logic.[53] Significantly, this aspect is something which Gurulugomi would probably deny. We saw in the passage from *Dharmapradīpikā* that many people—although notably not all—are not attracted to the Buddha's teaching when it is expressed in the manner of absolute teaching; instead they are confused, and they turn away. Gurulugomi thus usefully draws our attention to motivation as a basic issue in the meeting of practice and theory.

Griffiths offers no evidence that denaturalized discourse has any power to attract across communal boundaries,[54] although with respect to facts about the physical world or epistemology, we can readily admit its plausibility under some circumstances. With respect to practical affairs, things get a bit more sticky, and, on the basis of ordinary experience, it would seem, at the very least, that in this sphere a power to attract cannot be taken for granted. Motivation usually occurs when there is a clear relevance of theory to explaining or resolving a practical problem. A link between theory and practice is thus established through human motivation in circumstances where desire and belief overlap. This would seem to be impossible for denaturalized discourse, which ideally shows no connection to particular problems.[55] The two expectations that we have of theory—that it stand outside of practice and that it govern practice—pull in opposite directions. The recognition of this tension has made the issue of motivation of central significance in contemporary philosophy, and it is generally admitted that "accounts of moral judgement which do not explain its special power to motivate are unsatisfactory."[56]

One way of addressing this tension is to consider the nature of moral facts. If they are like other facts, apprehended theoretically and best described with a language approximating denaturalized discourse, then when one accepts a proper judgement about a fact, correspondingly one will be motivated to action in accordance with it. If this is not the case, then it is not clear in what sense they are facts.[57] Moreover, if motivation to action depends on something outside of factual knowledge—something like desire, will, or character—then it remains obscure how denaturalized discourse, characterized by rationality, can claim to govern practice without being able to control this nonrational element.

Faced with these perplexities, some modern philosophers have argued that it can be frankly admitted that theory, as a rational description of fact, has no connection to practice. Moreover, practical discourse is misunderstood if it is taken as a statement of fact. It is, according to some who have taken this position, only an expression of a speaker's feelings, or, according to others, an attempt to influence other people's behavior. These views, usually known as "subjectivism" or "emotivism," were put forward earlier in this century, and few today would accept them as theoretically adequate descriptions of practice, because they allow no place for reason in ethics or for a concern for what really exists, and this is clearly false; it is worth noting that the shadows of subjectivism and emotivism mix with Griffiths' characterization of naturalized discourse.[58]

Recently some philosophers have sought to bypass the difficulties of explaining how facts motivate action by a completely different route. They have argued that the whole idea of seeing the meeting of theory and practice in terms of action guides was misconceived. These philosophers have returned to the notion of virtue as it was first developed in ancient Greece and have argued that questions about practice are better addressed by attention to character and images of the good life within particular traditions than by rules and action guides directed to particular problems. This approach, generally known as "virtue theory," has been interested in wide varieties of practice—in marrying, having children, choosing where to work and play—as long as they are areas of life which form character; this interest has often resulted in an apparent preference for the local and particular over the universal. In these local images of "human flourishing," the boundaries between facts and values are blurred and the question of how action is motivated tends more to be simply de-emphasized than clarified.[59]

Instead of focusing on motivation as a connection between theory and practice, virtue theorists tend to conceptualize the issue in terms of dispositions as components of character. As a result, virtue theory has had to be interested in moral education and character formation; this route appears closer to Gurulugomi's interest in the manner of the Buddha's *teaching*.

Lee Yearley's book *Mencius and Aquinas: Theories of Virtue and Conceptions of Courage* is firmly within this stream of philosophy. As the title indicates, the specific purposes of Yearley's book are to compare Mencius' and Aquinas' accounts of virtue, but in the course of his inquiry, he develops a number of "general ideas on how best to compare what seem to be radically different discourses on human excellence."[60] Yearly thus makes some important proposals about the nature of the comparative philosophy of religion, but we will not take them up, just as we did not discuss Griffiths' strong thesis about the best way to pursue the comparative philosophy of religion.

Yearley's most general argument was alluded to at the beginning of this chapter: "sophisticated thinkers about human flourishing" often employ in a rational fashion different kinds of theories about the world.[61] In developing this proposal, Yearley distinguishes between different kinds of theories about the world. Beginning with a classification of two kinds of theory—primary and secondary—developed by anthropologist Robin Horton, Yearley adds a third of his own:

> *Primary* theories, concerning subjects like water's effect on the growth of plants, provide explanations that allow people to predict, plan, and cope with normal problems the world presents. Such theories appear evidentially true to most in a culture and often have a universal character. *Secondary* theories, which differ from culture to culture, usually are built from primary theories to explain peculiar or distressing occurrences, such as why water suddenly kills not nurtures plants. They utilize ideas about a class of beings (such as malevolent spirits) that differ from visible phenomena and therefore appear even to those in the culture to mix the familiar and the strange. *Practical* theories often work on the ideas primary theory produces and can link with notions in secondary theory. But practical theory presents a more theoretical account than primary theory and stays closer to normal phenomena than secondary theory. Moreover, the aim is to guide people toward full actualization and therefore concepts like virtue, obligation, and disposition are utilized. Much of practical theory, then concerns what we call ethics.[62]

Yearley compares practical theory to the knowledge of informed observers of a game of basketball; this example makes it evident that Yearley's notion of practical theory is similar to what we saw above in our discussion of denaturalized discourse as an example of theory. "Practical theory . . . generates a form of explanation, prediction, and control" from the outside.[63] It is perhaps as true to say that practical theory includes an attempt to create action guides that are generated from within practice itself. In contrast to primary theory or secondary theory, which both attempt to guide practice by reference to states of affairs outside of practice, practical theory presupposes an intimate knowledge of the practice that it seeks to guide.[64] Yearley sees in Mencius a model example of this attempt to guide practice from within:

> He conceives of ethical reasoning as a process that depends on perceiving clearly and then identifying correspondences or affinities. He especially opposes the idea . . . that ethical reasoning mainly involves the application of rules or principles. The view he opposes need not embrace a simple or mechanical idea about how people know and apply rules. Rules, for instance, may become apparent to people either only after careful reflection or only in situations where duress forces them to make a thorough assessment. But a style of thinking that operates from rules differs from one that moves from concrete cases where the perception of salient characteristics is clear to other concrete cases where it is not clear.
>
> The most significant difference between the two points of view probably lies in the importance given to the true description of a situation, and thus to the intelligent awareness that produces the description. To gather a situation under a rule, a person must describe the situation. If I am to decide whether rules apply I must know the person before me is a brother rather than a friend or a distant acquaintance. But such descriptions are hardly as textured as those that occur when I try to see if correspondences or affinities fit. . . .
>
> Ethical thinking that relies on resemblances or affinities demands what John Henry Newman calls real apprehension, a contact with complex particulars, rather than just notional apprehension, an abstract understanding of something's general character.[65]

Yearley's notion of a practical theory seems to do justice to the complexities of Gurulugomi's comment on the phrase "teaching a truth channelled according to mind." As Yearley notes, practical theory "sits between primary and secondary theory,"[66] and this allows someone guided by it to acknowledge close connections between secondary theory and practice, but at the

same time, to inculcate practices that seem at odds with secondary theory.[67] We should keep in mind, however, that Gurulugomi
does not articulate the kind of practical theory envisioned by
Yearley in this passage. We should especially avoid any tendency to equate practical theory with conventional teaching.
Instead, practical theory should be reserved for the attempt to
justify the use of conventional teaching. But Gurulugomi's statements do seem to presuppose a style of ethical reasoning similar to the practical theories which Yearley discusses, especially
in the insistence on analogical predication.

While Yearley can help us to flesh out what it is that
Gurulugomi is doing, it is also the case that Gurulugomi brings
an important question to Yearley's description of practical theories. Gurulugomi's justification of conventional teaching is not
connected to any theoretical concerns, but to the practical considerations of education and character formation. This practical
context makes it hard for us to go behind the actions and reflect
theoretically on what may lie behind them. Should we say that
the Buddha teaches with conventional teaching because of his
acceptance of a certain style of ethical reasoning or because he is
able to inform others about aspects of the world which cannot
be conveyed by absolute teaching? Or should we follow the
lead of the passage and say that the choice of absolute and
conventional teaching is relative, determined by the Buddha's
insight into the circumstances at hand? This second option invites us to consider further the use of theory within the practices of education.

Two important consequences follow if we use a model of
education to structure our vision of the meeting of practice and
theory. First, the example of conventional teaching and absolute
teaching suggests that different theories, although distinguished
by the degree to which they are abstract and distant from practice, can function as alternative and overlapping rhetorical strategies within an educational context. Both, depending on the
audience, can be used to ground and to motivate actions that
are felt to bring about the success of a community or of its
individual members.[68] This would apply as well to practical
theory. Second, within the model of education, there will be

occasions when theories which are distant from practice—and which in other circumstances would be valuable as action guides—must be checked so that they do not become obstacles to education. Parents and teachers are well aware of the many instances in which an objectively accurate explanation prevents mastery of the subject and thus prevents complete understanding at a later date. But for those who are in a position to understand it, then a more accurate, if recondite, account can be given. Checking the impulse to abstraction which is inherent in theory will also be necessary in those circumstances where analogical predication is employed to cultivate dispositions and to motivate practice. Thus it appears necessary for anyone theorizing— especially theorizing in a way that is intended to be universal, disengaged, and an absolute conception of the world—to acknowledge the achievement of local perspectives in the process of education and consequently to accept the necessity of defending these local perspectives which at the same time appear rather fragile and imperfect before the competition of theoretical reflection.

Perhaps we are able to see at this point that Gurulugomi's understanding of the relations between conventional and absolute teaching within a process of character formation provides a coherent rationale for his writing a devotional work such as *Amāvatura.* Using the categories and assumptions of conventional teaching, *Amāvatura* is part of the same effort as *Dharmapradīpikā;* that is, the effort to ensure that absolute teaching and what it can accomplish will have a place in the world. By Gurulugomi's own implied practical theory, the correct estimation of a devotional work like *Amāvatura* cannot be made independently of the perspective of absolute teaching, and we thus would expect Gurulugomi to turn to issues of absolute teaching first, as in fact he did in *Dharmapradīpikā.*

We might also say that Gurulugomi's activities as an author mirrored what he saw in the Buddha's teaching. Just as the Buddha taught in conventional and absolute modes, ultimately for a single purpose, so Gurulugomi wrote a doctrinal and a devotional work, each in contrast to the other, but each mutually constituting the other's worth, enabling each to be effective toward a shared end.

cᴧ◉rɔ

In *Dharmapradīpikā,* Gurulugomi says that one reason for the Buddha's making a conventional teaching is "in order not to discard the established practice of the world." This is to be expected given what we have seen of the critical role that conventional teaching can play in character formation within a Buddhist framework, but perhaps there is also another lesson for us here about the nature of the comparative philosophy of religion and about the formation of our own characters as practitioners of it.

Although programmatic statements about the comparative philosophy of religion tend to depict it as a critical reflection on the claims made by or about religions, we can also see in the essays included in this series of volumes that comparative philosophy of religion is a name for a kind of philosophy that uses the resources of a religious tradition that is not the author's "own" to address interpretive issues of his or her own milieu. Both of these understandings of comparative philosophy of religion, however, raise difficult questions about our standpoint vis-à-vis the material we interpret.

Wilhelm Halbfass has said about comparative philosophy more generally that "we have to be aware that there is a problem concerning the standpoint of the observer. Its neutrality cannot simply be declared."[69] This problem reappears in every methodological issue encountered by those involved in doing philosophy of religion comparatively, but especially with respect to such broad issues as the nature of the comparative enterprise itself and what we can expect to learn from the discourse of intellectuals from cultures other than the Western academic (Will they help us with questions that are already significant to us or will they teach us about different questions that we will recognize as equally significant?).[70] Moreover, Halbfass reminds us specifically that the " 'comparative method,' as an explicit project, has its roots in certain specific constellations of modern western thought [which raises doubts about] its freedom from Hegelian premises."[71] Such large questions seem to be present even in our most innocent vocabulary, such as when we use the first person possessive pronoun.[72] Halbfass has noted that references to "our own past" often accompany a

> strong, if not pervasive tendency in the European historiography of philosophy to relegate [the] thought [of other cultures] in toto to the past or even to the prehistory of European philosophy. This tendency, which has precedents in Greek thought and doxography, has found its most powerful and provocative expression in the system of Hegel. In a less obvious fashion, the retrospective and subordinating perspective is still widespread in the post-Hegelian approaches to non-Western traditions. In a sense, it pervades the whole enterprise of "understanding" not just the past, but also all foreign traditions; that is, the attempt to explore what they really mean, to reveal their implied structures, premises, and intentions. Implicitly or explicitly, this entails the idea of a privileged viewpoint, a higher level or more comprehensive horizon of awareness and reflection. We cannot simply discard this perspective; to some extent, it has become factually unavoidable. But we have to be aware of its background and historical ramifications.

This subordinating perspective is, of course, assumed in claims for comparative philosophy of religion as a discipline whose proper object is the evaluative analysis of the systematic thought of particular religious communities. The assumption of a more comprehensive perspective is also implicit in suggestions that an equally proper object for comparative philosophy of religion is the construction of normative claims about the nature of religion generically.

As Halbfass's references to the history of philosophy suggest, the problems with this kind of historical subordination are not superficial, but rather go to the heart of modern philosophy itself. Others have recognized this too and have suggested alternative understandings of what philosophy ideally should do. There have been voices within the various communities of Western philosophy in the twentieth century which have challenged the many claims of philosophical progress and even the very idea of philosophical progress. These challengers, like Heidegger and Wittgenstein, have argued that "keeping a conversation going [is] a sufficient aim of philosophy."[73] This view acknowledges that although we may have many doubts about the philosophical topics which we inherit, and indeed we may not be able to see them as consistent or even meaningful, we are not in a position to discard our inheritance without severe loss. These challengers point out that even though we know that we inherit philosophical topics from "our past" with all sorts of difficulties and confusions, without them we would not be able to engage in philosophy at all. This kind of awareness is evident in the following statement from Halbfass's introduction to his account of ontology in Indian intellectual history:

> Over the years, my methodological positions and philosophical allegiances have changed. The result has been a certain eclecticism and growing doubts concerning the meaning and relevance of the topic itself. We do not know whether the "question of being" is a meaningful question. But once this question is gone, or reduced to certain linguistic, semantic, or logical technicalities, what else could provide us with a comparable sense of philosophical wonder and perplexity? What would happen to philosophy itself?[74]

Up to now, advocates of this philosophical position have spoken about "continuing a conversation" that somehow is already "our own." Thus it may be that the most novel aspect of the collective project of any comparative philosophy, including the comparative philosophy of religion, will be to create contexts in which we can learn how to "continue conversations" that are not "our own" (or at least not yet our own) in the light of the invented traditions within which we habitually do philosophy today. If we begin to conceive of comparative philosophy of religion in this way, we will come to see it as an educational process in its own right, and we will take as one of our proper tasks the preservation of the intellectual resources that we receive from different traditions. We will become instruments for the transmission of ideas which we may only dimly understand, and we will resist our tendency to turn those ideas into instruments for our own judgements or constructions. Preservation, by listening to another and by rethinking alongside, as we tried to do in this chapter with Gurulugomi, would become a primary philosophical activity.

We can find some inspiration in the Theravada Buddhist tradition for taking preservation as a proper aim of a comparative philosophy of religion. Buddhaghosa distinguishes three kinds of learning:

> [There is] study after the manner of one catching a snake, study for the purpose of salvation, and study as of a treasurer. Of these, that study which is badly acquired out of a desire to be vexatious to others, etc., is like catching a snake. Concerning which it is said: "Just as, bhikkhus, a person desirous of catching a snake goes out in search of one. He sees a big snake and catches it either by the body or the tail. And the snake turning back bites him on the hand, the arm, or any other part of the body big or small. On that account he dies or suffers pain approaching death. And why? Because, bhikkhus, in the religion some good-for-nothing persons improperly study the doctrine in its various branches.... These people study the doctrine for the purpose of annoying others or of freeing themselves from the criticism or scoffing of others.... [But] that study, which is well acquired by one desirous of fulfilling a body of precepts, etc., and not for the sake of annoying others is for the sake of salvation.... Finally, [there is] the saint, who has acquired a complete knowledge of the aggregates, got rid of the corruptions, developed the Path, penetrated the Fruition of Arahantship ... [and who] studies merely for the purpose of preserving the tradition, and of guarding the lineage of the doctrine. This is the study as of the treasurer."[75]

There is real danger, already realized, that those of us interested in comparative philosophy of religion can become examples of what Buddhaghosa calls those who "study after the manner of one catching a snake," especially when the evaluative dimensions of philosophical inquiry are stressed at the expense of efforts to listen and think alongside. Even though I would expect none of those who have engaged or will engage in comparative philosophy of religion to be a "saint" in Buddhaghosa's sense, perhaps we might take an orientation for our collective project from his idea of "study as of a treasurer." If we did, we might then feel a need to acknowledge that if we are willing to use, for our own purposes, the intellectual resources of a religious tradition which we may not call our own, we also have a responsibility to preserve that tradition in some manner.

The image of philosophy "as of a treasurer" reminds us that our responsibilities are not only to ourselves, but to past and future generations, and it also reminds us that these responsibilities impress on us certain expectations for how we should approach our expanding intellectual inheritance. As we have learned with respect to those Western philosophical traditions which we already call "our own," we have a responsibility to listen and to "continue the conversation" of tradition, even when it leaves us confused and even when we are confident that our reflections have "discovered" conceptual inadequacies within it. Our responsibility is to preserve what we use—and to preserve in the process of use—without making the resources of a culturally distant tradition "grist for our mill."[76]

This incitement to preservation is inherent in the very nature of philosophical understanding, in which ideas and problems received from the past have an autonomous interest beyond what can be explained by reference to their previous historical contexts. This is because philosophical understanding always constructs a future for ideas. As Heidegger says, in his own unique style:

> Listening to . . . is Dasein's existential way of Being-open as Being-with for Others. Indeed, hearing constitutes the primary and authentic way in which Dasein is open for its ownmost potentiality-for-Being—as in hearing the voice of the friend whom every Dasein carries with it. Dasein hears, because it understands. As a Being-in-the world with Others, a Being which understands, Dasein is "in thrall" to Dasein-with and to itself; and in this thraldom it "belongs" to these. Being-with develops in listening to one another.[77]

The key idea here is found in the statement that "Dasein hears, because it understands." If we recall that Heidegger's notion of understanding *(verstehen)* has a connotation of projection into the future *(vorstehen)*, we can paraphrase this sentence in the following way: "You are open to yourself and others when you realize that what others say has a place in your future." That is, we only understand something when we are able to project both it and ourselves into the future; when we view it from this vantage point in the future, standing alongside it, we consequently wake up to it in the present.[78] In this view, understanding is inevitably coincident with the incitement to preservation as well as with character formation, with becoming open to our own potential.[79] Thus it seems proper, if not imperative, to ask whether comparative philosophy of religion is worth doing without such an understanding; for it is precisely this understanding which creates dispositions within us to preserve, and if necessary to defend, the rather fragile and local achievements it presumes to examine; and whether it is worth doing outside of a "thraldom (in which) it belongs to these." If our answer is that it is not worth doing apart from such an understanding, then the comparative philosophy of religion which we create should include a kind of practical theory in its own right.

Notes

1. The issue can be approached in dramatically different ways. See, for examples, Robin Horton, "Tradition and Modernity Revisited," in *Rationality and Relativism,* ed. M. Hollis and S. Lukes (Cambridge, Mass.: MIT Press, 1982), 201–60; Marshall Sahlins, *Culture and Practical Reason* (Chicago: University of Chicago Press, 1976); Steven Lukes, "Some Problems about Rationality," in *Rationality,* ed. Bryan Wilson (Oxford: Basil Blackwell, 1970), 214–20, especially 216; and Paul Griffiths, "Denaturalizing Discourse: Ābhidhārmikas, Propositionalists, and the Comparative Philosophy of Religion," in *Myth and Philosophy,* ed. Frank Reynolds and David Tracy (Albany: State University of New York Press, 1990), 57–91.

2. See Lee H. Yearley, *Mencius and Aquinas: Theories of Virtue and Conceptions of Courage* (Albany: State University of New York Press, 1990), 177; see also Horton, 235.

3. Yearley, 182.

4. Sally Gressens, "Conference Summary," (1 July 1992), 2.

5. P. F. Strawson, *Analysis and Metaphysics: An Introduction to Philosophy* (Oxford: Oxford University Press, 1992).

6. Ibid., 9.

7. Ibid.

8. Careful consideration of Gurulugomi also has some broad implications for our historical understanding of the Theravada as a religious tradition as well. As a lay intellectual who knew Pali and Sanskrit and was familiar with the doctrinal and scholastic literature written in those languages, he is difficult to fit into the received sociological generalizations of Theravada Buddhism that emphasize a distinction between monks and laymen. Careful study of Gurulugomi would contribute to a revision of the sociology of knowledge that is conventionally assumed by those engaged in the intellectual history of Theravada Buddhism.

9. R. G. Collingwood, *The Idea of History* (Oxford: Clarendon Press, 1946), especially 231–46, 282–302.

10. Gurulugomi, *Dharmapradīpikā,* ed. Baddegama Vimalavamsa Thera (Colombo; Gunasena, 1967), 346.

11. Gurulugomi, *Amāvatura,* ed. Kodagoda Ñanaloka Thera (Colombo: Gunasena, 1967), 142.

12. *Amāvatura,* 142.

13. For a brief but helpful discussion of these fields and their relation, see Bernard Williams, *Descartes* (Harmondsworth, England: Penguin, 1978), 9–10.

14. Williams, 9 (italics added).

15. Gressens, "Conference Summary."

16. C. E. Godakumbura, *Sinhalese Literature* (Colombo: Colombo Apothecaries, Co., 1955), 47.

17. *Dharmapradīpikā,* 346.

18. Godakumbura, 47.

19. Ibid.

20. *Dharmapradīpikā,* 258–59.

21. Compare, however, this passage with MA I.137–39; see also AA I.94–95. Abbreviations of the titles of texts are those used by the *Pali Text Society Dictionary;* texts are cited from Pali Text Society Editions.

22. KvuA 34.

23. Ibid.

24. DhsA 40.

25. For a useful discussion of this example in connection to the "irrealism" of Nelson Goodman, see Hilary Putnam, *Renewing Philosophy* (Cambridge, Mass.: Harvard University Press, 1992), 111–15.

26. This is obvious in our example of different ways of thinking about a star; knowledge about gases does not mean that one will be able to navigate by constellations, nor will developments in the scientific description of stars change our perception of the Big Dipper.

27. AA 2:118.

28. For a general discussion of the interpretation of this pairing throughout the Buddhist traditions, see Genjun Sasaki, "Pariyāya und Nippariyāya" in *Wiener Zeitschrift für die Kunde Sud-und Ostasiens* 6 (1962): 47–59.

29. A 4:450–56.

30. AA 4:206.

31. See Miln 113, 123.

32. VbhA 94; Vism 499.

33. DhsA 154, 222, 289, 308.

34. *Pali Text Society Dictionary,* ed. T. W. Rhys Davids and William Stede, s.v. *pariyaya.*

35. DhsA 63, 77, 224.

36. MA 1:137–38. Translation from K. N. Jayatilleke, *Early Buddhist Theory of Knowledge* (Delhi: Motilal Banarsidass, 1980), 364–65.

37. MA 1:138.

38. Martha Nussbaum, *Love's Knowledge* (New York: Oxford University Press, 1990), 3.

39. An illuminating comparison and contrast with Gurulugomi can be found in Lee Yearley's book on Aquinas and Mencius when he outlines the forma-

tion of emotion by reason. Although in themselves, judgement and emotion are not at all analogous to conventional and absolute teaching, Yearley employs a set of connecting relations which is identical with what we have just seen in Gurulugomi. First, there are contexts when judgement and emotion "severely conflict," making it difficult to decide upon and to accomplish virtuous acts; a second pattern emerges when virtuous actions are accomplished, but they are only judged to be virtuous after the fact, rather than actually generated by virtue; a third connection between the two is also possible when there is no conflict between emotion and judgement and actions proceed from the virtuous character that encompasses both. When we compare these three relations between judgement and emotion with Gurulugomi, we see that Yearley's first possibility is similar to the idea of conventional and absolute truth as separate and contrasted; in both cases, severe conflicts are to be expected. In the second case, there is a hierarchy between judgement and emotion which works to salvage some actions motivated by the latter and allows us to perceive their worth as virtuous and commendable, just as we saw in the hierarchy of indirect and direct teaching. The third pattern displays both emotion and judgement as unified within the larger framework of a virtuous character without conflict between them. In the same way, there is no possible conflict between conventional and absolute teaching when the Buddha uses them to instruct individuals in particular contexts.

Despite this similarity, there is a very significant difference between Yearley's discussion and Gurulugomi's. Yearley portrays the possible relations between judgement and emotion as a series of *ascending* stages with the third stage representing the goal which gives value to the other two stages. He thus constructs an encompassing and sequential hierarchy for the three *relations* between judgement and emotion for which we see no counterpart in Gurulugomi. Instead, Gurulugomi avoids any final integration of the three relations between conventional and absolute teaching in a theory but rather leaves them separate at the end of his discussion (103).

40. See T. L. S. Sprigge, *The Rational Foundation of Ethics* (London: Routledge, 1988), 3.

41. See nn. 1 and 2.

42. Griffiths, 64.

43. Ibid., 65.

44. Stanley Fish, "Consequences," in *Against Theory,* ed. W. J. T. Mitchell (Chicago: University of Chicago Press, 1989), 110.

45. Kvu 34.

46. Despite the close correspondence between denaturalized discourse and absolute teaching, we still need to be careful about taking the pairing of denaturalized and naturalized discourse as corresponding to the pairing of absolute and conventional teaching. Griffiths' account of naturalized discourse seems less than adequate as a description of conventional teaching, although admittedly it is outside of his interests and we only learn about it contrastively from denaturalized discourse; there is no formal and functional definition of naturalized discourse comparable to what we are given for denaturalized discourse. Moreover, in the course of his article, Griffiths lumps together as examples of naturalized discourse the "descriptive-historical discourse" of historians, the conceptual and value systems embodied by natural languages, and contingent human life as a whole, thus making naturalized discourse into a residual category which groups together disparate phenomena which only have in common that they can be contrasted to denaturalized discourse.

47. Griffiths, 60.

48. The tendency to theorize reductively to such a degree that we distort what we also intend to describe is so common in theoretical reflection that many have argued that we should reject theory altogether with respect to human practices; see, for example, Bernard Williams, *Ethics and the Limits of Philosophy* (London: Fontana Paperbacks, 1985).

49. Griffiths, 64.

50. Some, like Stanley Fish, have argued that this claim to influence and also to remain apart is illusory. "The argument *against* theory is simply that this substitution of the general for the local has never been and will never be achieved. Theory is an impossible project which will never succeed. It will never succeed simply because the primary data and formal laws necessary to its success will always be spied or picked out from within the contextual circumstances of which they are supposedly independent" (Fish, 110).

51. Griffiths, 81.

52. Ibid., 80.

53. See Horton, 244–46, for a discussion of the impact that a shift to a competitive setting has on theory: "In the 'competitive' setting, the leading part in stimulating theoretical innovation is played, not by practically-significant experiences and problems, but by configurations of experience selected or devised specifically for purposes of inter-school warfare. As a result, we get a progressive divorce of secondary theory from practical life. Such a divorce has been a major feature of the development of Western 'modernism.' From the

beginning of the seventeenth century to the middle of the nineteenth, the great flowering of secondary theory owed little to practically-significant experience and had virtually no impact on practical life" (246). The Buddhist *abhidharma* which Griffiths describes also flourished in a similar competitive setting, but it seems unwarranted to generalize from these historically particular cases to all uses of denaturalized discourse.

54. Indeed, in an aside, Griffiths seems to suggest that achieved instances of denaturalized discourse may actually be attractive to no one; see Griffiths, 64.

55. Although perhaps a case could be made that denaturalized discourse does have continuity with and relevance to such a problem by giving more emphasis to Griffiths' comment that having access to what really exists "is a goal usually thought to have soteriological significance" (80).

56. Sprigge, 150.

57. Some examples can illustrate the issue: we cannot attribute logical consistency to a person who makes a declarative statement that "she was here yesterday, but I don't believe it," but we do not find it inconsistent that someone might say, "I ought to do it, but I have no inclination to."

58. For example, Griffiths, 64: "We use language to evoke sentiment, to inspire to action, to manipulate."

59. See Yearley, 100.

60. Ibid., 3.

61. Ibid., 177.

62. Ibid., 7.

63. Ibid., 178.

64. See Robert Louden, *Morality and Moral Theory* (Oxford: Oxford University Press, 1992), 140.

65. Yearley, 65–66.

66. Ibid., 178.

67. Ibid., 179.

68. See Matthew Kapstein, "Samantrabhadra and Rudra: Innate Enlightenment and Radical Evil in Tibetan Rnyang-ma-pa Buddhism," in *Discourse and Practice*, ed. Frank Reynolds and David Tracy (Albany: State University of New York Press, 1992), 54.

69. Wilhelm Halbfass, *On Being and What There Is* (Albany: State University of New York Press, 1992), 14.

70. Compare Griffiths, 57: "The enterprise of constructing a new intellectual discourse—the comparative philosophy of religion—must include some consideration of what is involved in bringing together the usually normative discipline of philosophy with the usually descriptive and analytic discipline of the history of religions. A number of theoretical issues arise here, including: the nature of the comparative enterprise; how philosophers use myth (more than they think); how historians of religion use normative philosophical discourse (not as self-consciously as they should); how important the institutional settings and cultural contexts of both (indeed all) intellectual practices are; what can be learned by looking at examples of the discourse of intellectuals from cultures other than the Western-academic; what the intellectual history of Western-academic culture reveals about the practices and values of those who want to engage in the discourse of the new discipline under consideration; and how the complex of categories derived from all this (myth, theory, narrative, practice, power) may best be clarified and used in the service of our own ends."

71. Halbfass, 14.

72. Note the use of first person pronouns in the following programatic statement by Griffiths: "Self-consciously engaging in [the comparative philosophy of religion] requires that we tell each other what we take to be important parts of the story of the complex cultural and intellectual history that has made us what we are, and that makes it seem worthwhile for us to engage in the comparative philosophy of religion. It is a small part of that story that I wish to tell in this paper. It begins inevitably with Aristotle. . . . This part of *our own* (Western-academic) intentional world is far too important to be left in tacit limbo" (58, italics added).

73. Richard Rorty, *Philosophy and the Mirror of Nature* (Princeton: Princeton University Press, 1979), 378. On philosophy as a kind of conversation, rather than a search for objective truth, see Rorty, 365–79; Wittgenstein, *On Certainty* (Oxford: Basil Blackwell, 1969), 18c–21c; and Martin Heidegger, *Being and Time* (Oxford: Basil Blackwell, 1962), 206–7. I wish to thank John McCarthy for bringing these passages to my attention.

74. Halbfass, vii.

75. *The Expositor (Atthasālinī),* trans. Maung Tin (London: Pali Text Society, 1920), 1:29–30.

76. See Kapstein, 55.

77. Heidegger, 206–7.

78. Bernard Williams gives another name for this kind of understanding when he speaks of "the relativism of distance" (*Ethics and the Limits of Philosophy,* 162). For a useful critique of Williams, see Putnam, 103–7.

79. This, of course, does not preclude change. See Kapstein, 55: "Against our implicit (and often explicit) retention of the familiar dichotomy between theory-philosophy, on the one hand, and that which theory-philosophy seeks to explain-interpret, on the other, we require a vision of human culture-forming discourse in which historical, philosophical, mythic, poetic, and other specific discourse genres may be seen to interact as possibly coequal conversation partners. In such culture-forming discourse conservation is indeed equivalent to creation, so that the conception is one of a dynamic system that is necessarily extended in time, subject to continuous change, generating itself, anew in each cultural-historical instant."

References

Buddhaghosa. 1920. *The Expositor (Aṭṭhasālinī).* Translated by Maung Tin. London: Pali Text Society.

Collingwood, R. G. 1946. *The Idea of History.* Oxford: Clarendon Press.

Fish, Stanley. 1989. "Consequences." In *Against Theory,* edited by W. J. T. Mitchell. Chicago: University of Chicago Press.

Godakumbura, Charles. 1955. *Sinhalese Literature.* Colombo: Colombo Apothecaries, Co.

Gressens, Sally. 1992. "Conference Summary." unpublished.

Griffiths, Paul. 1990. "Denaturalizing Discourse: Ābhidhārmikas, Propositionalists, and the Comparative Philosophy of Religion." In *Myth and Philosophy,* edited by Frank Reynolds and David Tracy, 57–91. Albany: State University of New York Press.

Guruḷugōmi. 1967. *Amāyatura.* Edited by Kodagoda Ñanaloka Thera. Colombo: Gunasena.

———. 1967. *Dharmapradīpikā.* Edited by Baddegama Vimalavamsa Thera. Colombo: Gunasena.

Halbfass, Wilhelm. 1992. *On Being and What There Is.* Albany: State University of New York Press.

Heidegger, Martin. 1962. *Being and Time.* Oxford: Basil Blackwell.

Horton, Robin. 1982. "Tradition and Modernity Revisited." In *Rationality and Relativism,* edited by Martin Hollis and Steven Lukes, 201–60. Cambridge, Mass.: MIT Press.

Jayatilleke, K. N. 1980. *Early Buddhist Theory of Knowledge.* Delhi: Motilal Banarsidass.

Kapstein, Matthew. 1992. "Samantrabhadra and Rudra: Innate Enlightenment and Radical Evil in Tibetan Rnyang-ma-pa Buddhism." In *Discourse and Practice,* edited by Frank Reynolds and David Tracy, 51–82. Albany: State University of New York Press.

Louden, Robert. 1992. *Morality and Moral Theory.* Oxford: Oxford University Press.

Lukes, Steven. 1970. "Some Problems about Rationality." In *Rationality,* edited by Bryan Wilson, 201–60. Oxford: Basil Blackwell.

Nussbaum, Martha. 1990. *Love's Knowledge.* New York: Oxford University Press.

Putnam, Hilary. 1992. *Renewing Philosophy.* Cambridge: Harvard University Press.

Rorty, Richard. 1979. *Philosophy and the Mirror of Nature.* Princeton: Princeton University Press.

Sahlins, Marshall. 1976. *Culture and Practical Reason.* Chicago: University of Chicago Press.

Sasaki, Genjun. 1962. "Pariyāya und Nippariyāya." *Wiener Zeitschrift fur die Kunde Sud-und Ostasiens* VI, 47–59.

Sprigge, T. L. S. 1988. *The Rational Foundation of Ethics.* London: Routledge.

Strawson, P. F. 1992. *Analysis and Metaphysics: An Introduction to Philosophy.* Oxford: Oxford University Press.

Williams, Bernard. 1978. *Descartes.* Harmondsworth: Penguin.

———. 1985. *Ethics and the Limits of Philosophy.* London: Fontana Paperbacks.

Wittgenstein, Ludwig. 1969. *On Certainty.* Oxford: Basil Blackwell.

Yearley, Lee H. 1990. *Mencius and Aquinas: Theories of Virtue and Conceptions of Courage.* Albany: State University of New York Press.

Part III

Practical Reason and the Flow of Time

Chapter 5

Chronophagous Discourse: A Study of Clerico-Legal Appropriation of the World in an Islamic Tradition

Aziz Al-Azmeh

Amongst* all religious traditions, Islamic civilization has produced what is perhaps the most deliberately sustained concern with, and profuse body of writing on, history. The concern with the past is manifest in all genres of Arabic *Schrifttum:* poetry was classicized with the establishment of anterior texts and modes; pietistic and legal works established a knowledge of early Muslim practice as *Fürstenspiegel* and valorized salutary and deleterious acts of kings and sages from many histories; Koranic exegesis required monumental knowledge of Muslim precedents and linguistic usages of yore; dynasties, times, and biographies were meticulously chronicled and recorded;

* I am particularly indebted to Sheryl Burkhalter and Martha Mundy for their roles in the genesis of this study. I should also like to thank the conferees at Chicago in May 1992 for their stimulation and comment. I am grateful to Osman Tatan for preparing the bibliography.

universal histories were composed on a massive scale.[1] The entire range of engagements with the past is in evidence, from the officiously technical record of dates and events to the wholesale appropriation of past events by myth. Of these engagements, salvation history is one which was the mainstay of the Muslim clerical establishment. Clearly, this view of history, shared with other monotheisms, was subjected to very individual inflections. One of these is the legal, and it is the purpose of this essay to sketch some lineaments of Islamic views of salvation history and to describe their fundamental structures, before proceeding to study one possible consequence of the salvation historical outlook, namely the inscription within its structures of the theoretical techniques utilized by Islamic legal theory *(uṣūl al-fiqh)* for reducing legal judgements to arguments from authority. These techniques betoken the all-too-human proclivity to apperceive the world in terms of myths of origin. In the Muslim context, this was the means by which the clerical gaze appropriated the world for itself and made this world at once the validation of the clerical metanarrative and the field of clerical action and authority. It was, of course, simultaneously the means by which other voices and perspectives were marginalized. Analysis of these processes in Islamic tradition will allow for elements of a general theory of dogmatic discourse.

1

Islamic civilization shares an almost universal concern with origins and beginnings, of the world, of social order, as of particular artifacts and customs. The cultures of antiquity cultivated this interest in origins[2] no less than modern industrial civilization, which with its theories of social contract and its evolutionism is alone in claiming descent from savages and even from lowlier creatures rather than from gods and heroes.[3] This pursuit of origins provided, among other perhaps more important things, explanations for the *status quo* of a historical type based upon a conception of generic continuity over time. Chinese literature knew a distinct literary genre of "techno-historical dictionaries" concerned with the first occurrences of things, systematized in the third century BCE.[4] Arabic literature has likewise left a rich patrimony on *awā'il* (first occurrences),[5] whose main purpose seemed to have been to provide gems of recherché knowledge of an unusual and exotic character, a knowledge that formed part of courtly urbanity.

This register of "firsts" is a record of archetypes;[6] it indicates single acts of foundation which figure as legendary charters of consequence for perpetuity and in perpetuity. Thus, for example, Arabic historical traditions indicated the archetypal act, which somehow subsumes all later instances in which women used a viscous sugar solution for the removal of body hair, to be King Solomon's desire to see the hair removed from the queen of Sheba's legs. Similarly, the use by kings of astrologers started with Zoroaster, and the manufacture of shields goes back to King David.[7] Royal sovereignty had its beginning with Lucifer, who was the first to be granted a dominion by God,[8] and the self-same Lucifer was the first to introduce the concept of measure when, in the primal act of disobedience, he measured himself against Adam.[9] And though it was often recognized that much of this record of beginnings was spurious,[10] it nevertheless seemed to provide discrete elements which wove together tightly what was known of the world. The relationship between inaugural events and their present simulacra is one in which the foundation is also the accomplishment, and in which subsequent calques constitute a string of successive instants identical to each other as to the inaugural event.

This schema, in which a series of generically connected events consists of identical moments of foundation and of re-enactment, produces temporal series: instances of kingship whose time is inaugurated with Lucifer, instances of astrological consultation dating from the activities of Zoroaster, and so forth. These consist in reality of an archetypal event, which founds a paradigm that is then repeated in a syntagmatic series. The diachronic flow of this series is arhythmic, for these events do not occur at regular intervals. The time of each of these series of events, like the time of myth, is one with neither perpetual duration nor regular succession, but one which results in configurations of identical content, divided by boundaries akin in their mode of division to musical bars.[11] Succession in this sense yields identity, and all imputations of causality or of implication within this type of succession yield only "amplified and unfolded forms of an enriched identity."[12] It is thus that astrological consultation once inaugurated remains changeless in perpetuity and is merely repeated again and again. And it is thus that a dynasty remains itself, an identity which, in Arabic as in other historical narratives, is reinforced by the signaling of historical and certain dynastic beginnings with new calendars.

Identical successive elements of this type are particularly enriched and amplified when their temporal flow is punctuated and amplified by rhythms dictated by the sacred. It is herein that we encounter the more consequential tempo, rhythmic and otherwise, of amplifications resulting from what has been called "great time." Great time casts its foundations as a sort of sacral *awā'il*. It is a reservoir of durable and momentous foundations and triumphs. It is time of ritual value, a great time which, in rituals and rites, crosses the ordinary time of continuous flow; it marks the divisions of ordinary time with its own signs, and thus appropriates it. The intensity, durability, and necessity of repetition of great time far outweigh the regular and continuous rhythms of ordinary time.[13]

Ordinary chronometric time, when set against this great time, the time of the sacred and of ritual and its associated myth, is a qualitative vacancy, an ontological sham which receives quality only when marked by what has been described as the "accents" which divide the times of the sacred, as they do the spaces of the sacred.[14] The succession of these accents marking the time of the sacred—the periodic rituals of cultic memory, the irregular rhythms of salvation history which culminate in an end repeating the beginning in all its amplitude—is fully an "amplified and unfolded" form of an "enriched identity." This structure of succession and re-enactment accounts for salvation history, whose construction of a particular attitude to religious origins is by no means peculiar to Islam, but could be regarded as the very *differentia* of monotheistic confessions.[15]

Be that as it may, it has been rightly maintained that in the Muslim conception, creation is a sign of the end,[16] so that history consists of a great cycle which closes in upon itself, joining beginning with end, each the reality of the other, history being the trajectory traversed in the process of this closure. It must be stressed that the type of Islam under discussion is majoritarian Sunnism in the particular inflection it attained in its clerical Shar ͨist complexion; Isma ͨili and other esotericist sects which adopted a theory of seven cycles of history, each ending with a recommencement, and culminating in a final cycle which ends without recommencement will not be discussed, although the structures of divine temporality herein are identical with those found in other varieties of Islam.[17]

We have seen that the vacuous syntagm of ordinary time is the instrument of a finalist paradigm whose instances punctuate the course of this flow at certain loci of accentuation that enclose values of sacredness, lending the sense of sacredness to historical succession. These values are, primarily, an integrality of divine order which reigned with the creation of Adam, the imperative of its complete restoration in paradise, and the intermittent attempts to calque this order in the history of prophecy, culminating in the definitive and final establishment of prophecy with the Muḥammadan order, itself to be re-established on the eve of the Apocalypse. Subsumed under this great cycle are others of smaller magnitude, which partake nevertheless of its sacred substance. As in Christianity, where the Fall justifies the existence of historical time,[18] history in Islamic tradition is "a decisive time of probation"[19] in which God's presence takes the form of revelation to a string of prophets that culminates in Muḥammad.[20]

Thus the first object created by God was the pen, which was commanded to write "everything," and thus inscribed the entire future course of creation[21] as a register of archetypes and re-enactments. Adam was known by names that betoken his archetypal character. He was called Abū Turāb, the Father of Earth, out of which humanity is fashioned and to which it returns; he was also known as Abū Al-Bashar, Father of Humankind, and Abū Muḥammad, the primeval Muḥammadan appearance.[22] God taught Adam the entire human lexicon from its most sublime to its most vulgar words, with its verbs and nouns, its superlatives and diminutives.[23] Thus the linguistic order assuring human life was established, as were the skills of agriculture and metalwork,[24] for perpetuity and in definitive generic form. In the same way, the punishments meted out to Eve marked the lot of womankind for all perpetuity, albeit with a misogynist impulse that almost pales into insignificance compared to medieval Christian writing on women: the pains of conception and menstruation, a lengthy pregnancy, inferiority to men, and so forth.[25]

Matters of greater consequence, more germane to the realm of the sacred, were likewise delineated at the beginning. Among them are elements of cultic memory, one of the most notable of which is pilgrimage rites to Mecca. Adam was the first to perform the pilgrimage at a spot where his son Seth later built the Ka ʿba; he performed it according to the rite of circumambulation (clockwise) which the angels are sometimes said to have performed two thousand years before him.[26] The founding moments of the said pilgrimage rites are also attributed to Abraham, Hagar, and Ishmael.[27] But the diversity of attribution is inconsequential. It occurs in the same sources, and it betokens no conflict, as the phylogenetic line is continuous and its elements substantively indistinct, from Adam through Abraham on to Muḥammad: the primeval character attributed to the first is equally attributable to the second and culminates in the third. In all cases, we are speaking of a single truth revealed at different times, without differentiation. In these as in many other locations along the line of prophecy, it is understood that that which is revealed is the singular, primeval, and perpetual truth, which is Islam.

The sole creed available to Adam was *tawḥīd,* an archetypal monotheism, and to him were revealed the fundamental interdictions on eating pork, blood, and carrion.[28] Abraham was the primeval and timeless Muslim *par excellence* and received what are variously thought to be unnamed fundamental generic institutes of the faith or certain exemplary attributes of the faithful, particularly those concerning purity, such as circumcision and the removal of body hair. He also received and instituted cultic rituals, and most specifically the pilgrimage rites at Mecca.[29] These different articulations of the primeval religion—Islam— at different times and in different settings are ones in which the posterior event recapitulates the anterior. When modifications occur, these do not, in Muslim writing, imply invalidation of that which was subject to modification. They are modifications which can be characterized as no other than consummation in generic continuity, an *Aufhebung* of Hegelian import, a phylogenesis. The specific instances of ritual, as of prophecy, are calques of an invariant beginning completely in keeping with the structures of temporality addressed above. Such calques find completion and closure when profanity is wiped off the face of the earth in the history of the future: this occurs when a series of cataclysms will herald the coming of the Mahdī (the Messiah) and the restoration of the Adamic order in prepara- tion for the day of judgement, a day which consigns profanity to the absurdity of Hell and recommences the Edenic order in Paradise.[30]

Following the antinomian signs of the Hour and its sub- versions of Order—the rise of the sun from the west, the un- leashing of the destructive force of the Gog and Magog upon the world, the reign of the Dajjāl, the Antichrist, and other events that occur in the history of the future[31]—the decks are cleared for the recommencement of the Adamic order, much as they were with the Deluge. The Messiah is called "Muḥammad Ibn ʿAbd Allāh": he is the Prophet's namesake and clansman; in other religious traditions he might well have been considered his avatar. The armies ranged against the Dajjāl are commanded by Jesus, son of Mary, who consummates his primeval reality by overcoming the pre-Muḥammadan historical specificity which rendered him inconsummate and shedding the vestiges of erst- while imperfections following his initial appearances: he breaks the Cross and kills all pigs; he abrogates the toleration canoni- cally extended to non-Muslim Peoples of the Book—Christians, Jews, Sabeans, and Zoroastrians—and accepts no further con- versions to Islam, but rather kills all the unconverted. The cos- mic counterpart of this recapitulation of the purity of the Adamic order is a similar recapitulation of the precreation order in preparation for the recommencement of all origins: at the coming of the Hour, God commands the angels to die, before they and the rest of creation are resurrected; until then, nothing remains but the Divine Face (Koran, 28:88 and 55:26–7).[32]

Each instance of prophecy, therefore, is a "realization of eschatology,"[33] a regeneration of the time of divinity, much as time was regenerated annually in the ancient Near East, by kings and with the Adonisian myth. The detailed rhythms of these recapitulations in their turn recapitulate numerical and chronological accents of the archetype. The number of men who fought alongside Muḥammad at the battle of Badr against the Meccans in A.D. 624 was the same as that of the Israelites who fought Goliath.[34] The day of ʿAshura, the tenth day of the Muslim month of Muḥarram on which the Passion of Ḥusain is commemorated, is the equivalent of the Jewish day of atonement, and is believed by Shīʿīte Muslims to be the day on which God forgave Adam and the day Noah's ark landed.[35] In the month of Ramaḍān was revealed the Torah, no less than the initial verses of the Koran.[36] And much as Christians invested a particular accent in Sunday, being the Lord's day following the cosmic week and also the day of resurrection,[37] Friday for Muslims is the day on which Adam was created and died and the day of the resurrection.[38] Friday was so acutely accented that it is said of some persons of exceptional piety that they had a particular preference for sexual intercourse on Fridays.[39] Al-Masʿūdī in the tenth century quoted contemporary Arab Christians as believing the day on which Christ was crucified corresponds to the day Adam was ejected from heaven and the day he died.[40]

Typological interpretation[41] serves as the hermeneutical complement and the mode of apprehension of this serial recursivity, according to which the history of the sacred is conceived as theodicy. Just as the historical appearance of Jesus in early and, to some extent, in Patristic Christianity, was a proleptic eschatology[42] so are all historical appearances of divine significance prefigurations of the end or recapitulations of the beginning. Moses could be and was read as *figura Christi,* Noah's ark as *praefiguratio ecclesiae,*[43] indeed, medieval European kingship was read as *Christomimesis* and as the crowned *typus Christi*.[44] The relationship that obtains in this reading is far more substantive than one of allegory.[45] Both figure and event, as we have seen, are ranged in a sequence outside that of the mere flow of time as accents of intensity that betoken a form of rather erratic immanence. Just as Muḥammad and Abraham are removed from chronometric time and transposed to the perspective of epiphany, and just as the Battle of Badr referred to above is removed from its local character of a raid in customary ancient Arabian style and textually read as *jihād* and therefore as an element in theodicy,[46] so too, according to the hermeneutics of *Heilsgeschichte,* are all significant events removed from concreteness and, to use Auerbach's phrase, "transpose[d] . . . into the perspective of eternity."[47] Thus, Muslim clerics regarded both the Old and the New Testaments to contain a necessary prefiguration of the appearance of Muḥammad; any denial of such prefiguration by Christians could only be the result of *taḥrīf,* the corruption of the biblical text.[48] The church fathers had already leveled against Jews the charge that their refusal of allegorical interpretation was motivated by their unwillingness to discover Jesus in the Old Testament.[49]

For this typological interpretation to be possible, time needs to be conceived according to a particular physiognomy, some elements of which have already been discussed. Substantive time has to be made specific to the series of events inscribed in the writ of theodicy and restricted to this sequence of moments. In the context of this qualification of time, chronometry is appropriated by the narrative of providence as a mere mode of discursive organization, as are indeed other modes of organization in historical writing, such as kingship in medieval Arabic historical literature.[50] The chronophagous discourses of salvation history appropriate time by the reduction of certain moments of history to a privileged assimilation to an eternity, to the great time under such philosophical names as Providence or Destiny, or without such elaboration, as signs, types, prefigurations, and cognate notions.[51] Thus chronological time is a continuum external to the sequence of providential moments and does not have a corresponding rhythm. It is the mere count of unqualified instants and has no substantial or immanentist function, for immanence is a substance which is communicated from one moment of theodicy to its subsequent recapitulation across spaces of qualitative discontinuity notwithstanding their chronometric continuity. It is thus with the constitution of the series commencing with archetype and closing the circle of time by the definitive regeneration of this archetype.

The primacy of narrative over process in this type of historical discourse has been noted;[52] the narrative of epiphanic and providential succession with its successions of calques—as types, prefigurations, and accomplishments—constitutes the time of the sacred as a space of narrative. In order to comprehend continuity over time, succession has to be represented by a spatial paradigm of contiguity regardless of a discontinuity which, being merely chronological, is only virtual. From the time of Parmenides, space has been considered the first condition of possibility for plurality; plurality in time, which is the very plurality required by succession—even the succession of identities, as in this case—makes of time a "supernumerary spatial dimension," an extension.[53] Chronometric or "vulgar" time, the Aristotelian time as measure of movement, is, indeed, itself spacing, a relation of space to itself.[54]

Homogeneity over time can only be assured, as Bergson insisted following a long tradition, with a spatialization that quantifies events bereft of quality and with their arrangement along a continuum.[55] This dequalification is intended in the Bergsonian analysis for events that occur in the natural sciences and indicates elements in "continuous multiplicities" whose measure is outside themselves. The discontinuity of instances in the time of theodicy with inaugurations, re-enactments, types, prefigurations, and accomplishments divided by oceans of chronometry does not, however, produce a bald atemporality; it is itself a connected multiplicity, hence a space and therefore a time. It constitutes a "discrete multiplicity" or a discrete manifold in the sense Riemannean geometry gives to multiples that carry their measure within themselves and whose units are numerical only in a determinate virtual sense.[56] This is a conception grounded in the twin assumptions that space is not homogeneous and that geometry is a doctrine of relations and not of measure. In a discrete rather than a continuous manifold, such as the one under consideration, therefore, measure (spacing) is contained within it rather than coming from an extrinsic axis of continuity.[57]

With providential events, whose measure is within, it is their archetypical substance which provides the substrate of their specific temporality and the principle of their spacing, being the only element in their rhythm. Yet this string of essentially atemporal events, founded, re-enacted, and consummated, is written in terms of the inferior medium of the merely chronological string of moments. There is no tension between the two strings: the latter simply expresses by profane beats the occurrence of the former and its timing; the manner of writing is merely virtual with respect to the ontological weight of sacred history, whose rhythms are expressed in terms of the chronometric moments accented and amplified by sacred history. Yet the moments of sacred time are related to one another by ties similar to those that join the moments of chronology. They are both connected by succession, a relation of space to itself. It is thus possible that the two movements can be posited in correspondence, and it is to this task that Hegel applied himself when synchronizing the movement of the Geist with that of nature.

But whereas the time of chronology is bereft of quality, being the succession of instances with no specific densities, the time of providence is fully laden with amplitude which carries not only significance, but also consequence. For in the assembly of succession, the series inaugurated by an act of potency proves so singular as fully to describe the nature of the series, epiphanic or ritual, and to render subsequent moments re-enactments of the archetypal occurrence.

The space of providential time as a space of re-enactments therefore can be construed as a genealogical space of filiation, one of whose main properties is the confirmation of identity by conceiving priority as prefiguration and posteriority as recommencement and accomplishment. The chronophagous proclivity of the discourse on providential history—as of every other genealogical history—is one which dissipates the density of the event rendered providential by depriving it of the specific gravity deriving from its conditions of emergence in its own time. The time of the divine in its spatial representation thus corresponds to the time of myth. It tends to confirm one contention of Lévi-Strauss' theory of myth: myth is structured asemantically, musically, allowing the narrative of myth—or the unfolding of providence in its different tellings and redactions or epiphanies—to be likened to a cylindrical form with an invariant structure *(langue)*, alongside an open dimension, its *parole.* In this analysis, the content-specific tellings of the myth (or specific events in the string of salvation) are not anterior to the myth; rather, as Lévi-Strauss notes, it is "the myth [that] moves towards a particular content through the attraction of its specific gravity."[58] The invariant is the schema, not its content.

Thus ontogenesis is fully assimilated to phylogenesis; the space of the narrative, like the space of historical time in its sacred telling, is divided by bars akin to those that organize the space of the argument and the space of logic.

2

The generic determination and generic closure thus far encountered are not confined to salvation history or cultic memory. The remit of archetypal explanation is very wide. For one thing, the archetypal construal of the past was of decided educational import. Myth is not only "exemplary history."[59] Archetypal events in every field are served up as a body of *exempla* for the guidance of action, and these stretch from the "Homeric encyclopedia"[60] across the entire field of historical formations whose cultures are pronouncedly oral. The Cathars of Longuedoc adopted the *exemplum* as a primary educational instrument,[61] and the genre of *Fürstenspiegel* functions along lines of the same order. In medieval Arab-Islamic culture the *Fürstenspiegel* genre and prophetic example were united with the educative intent of historical writing in the performance of this task, which was the provision of a body of archetypal examples of political, ethical, and pietist technology.

In all cases, there is in the operation of archetypal reading a notion of time discussed above, premised as it is on the twin moments of foundation and of accentuation along the continuum of chronology. This space is a space not only of succession, but of genealogy, of fecundation; it is one which fixes a position under the auspices of a name. In the discourse of archetype, the distinction between temporal primacy and demiurgical potency remains virtual, as does the space of chronology, subject as it is to the ontological weight of epiphanic or ritual moments. The Philonic transformation of the argument for providence into an argument for creation[62] and the assonance of temporal, ontological, and normative primacy in medieval Islamic thought[63] are elaborate philosophical formulations of a prior conceptual trope which equally underlies talismanic and sympathetic magic. Priority is spermatically weighted.

This ontological primacy of the archetype, its explicit or implicit demiurgical modality, applies to more than re-enactments already accomplished; such primacy is not confined to the modality of accomplishment of events inscribed in the eschatalogical history of the future—the future anterior, as it were—nor in the models of wise political behavior contained in *Fürstenspiegel* and in chronicles. This primacy extends equally to re-enactments yet to come that do not have the deterministic certainty of eschatology. Among the many consequences of this almost universal genealogical notion of time is one of particular relevance to medieval Islamic legalism which bases itself upon variants of arguments from scriptural authority. Narratives of archetypal foundation take on the modality of performative statements, and these are contained in the Koran and other texts of canonical status. These texts are, for legal as for pietistic purposes, registers of archetypal acts to be repeated and calqued. Their imperative and normatively complete character is reducible, when actualized, to the serene ontology of identity which we have seen to be the pillar of the time of archetypes and re-enactments. The indeterminate actuality or probability of these commands and prohibitions, these recommendations and warnings, can by no means dent this ontology of identity;

discordance and dissonance are, in this perspective, mere aberrations and correspond ontologically to privation.

Arguments from authority fully recapitulate this structure. They are premised on the virtual notion of temporality consequent upon an ontology of identity. In them, the authoritarian writ is the unique substantive action to be re-enacted. The at-once primitivist and finalist character of re-enactments that occur in salvation history and in cultic memory are similarly constitutive of the relation between formative precedent and legislative consequent in Islamic jurisprudence (as in other systems of law).

Medieval Muslim jurisprudents were perfectly aware of the problems, some immediately apparent, that accompany any attempt to relate the mutable manifold of daily life to the finalist writ of archetypes contained in the Muslim canon of legal consequence—the text of the Koran, ḥadīth (the body of narratives relating to acts and sayings of Muḥammad and some of his immediate companions), and, later, the body of legal precedents consecrated as consensus (ijmāʿ—akin to what was later to be called the *opinio communis doctorum* of the Christian Schoolmen). Indeed, the Muslim science of jurisprudence *(uṣūl al-fiqh)* is the body of hermeneutical and logical concepts and procedures which aim at the husbandry of the infinite manifold of the world within the bounds of a body of archetypes contained in the Principles *(uṣūl)* which together constitute the nomothetic text. In modern jurisprudential terms, the main concern of Muslim legal theory is the much-debated question of *lacunae* in law. The highly elaborate deliberation of medieval Muslim jurisprudents is premised on the assumption that their prime concern is one with *lacunae,* for Muslim legal thinking rests on a radical assumption of incompleteness: there can never be enough archetypes, rendering the adequation of reality to archetype the primary concern. Modern discussions of the problem of *lacunae* in law seem rather primitive in comparison.[64]

The good order of the world did not await the accomplishment of the monotheistic project with the Muḥammadan message. Neither were the archetypal foundations contained in the Muslim nomothetic canon the sole founts of order. For order, no matter how uncertain and imperfect, did reign before Muḥammad. God had, after all, instructed Adam in the principles of good order.[65] Humanity had always, albeit imperfectly and unsystematically, used the faculty of reason to maintain forms of order in conformity with human interest. The advent of the *sharīʿa* with Muḥammad—and it must be stressed that this oft-misunderstood term is a general sign for order, not unlike *nomos* or *dharma,* and does not have in itself unqualified specific determinations—reorganizes and systematizes proclivities of human nature in the service of divine intent expressed in the nomothetic text; this in such a way that the human interest served by nomothetic commands, and the iniquity stalled by nomothetic prohibition, serve to prepare mundane life for the hereafter.[66]

In a sense, the transition from the natural to this *sharʿist* regulation of order is akin to that made in natural right theories between *ius gentium* and *ius civile.* This is paralleled by a transition from purely vernacular rational calculation which ascertains human interest, to legal prescriptions which channel and constrain human interest in conformity with the meta-legal requirements of the *sharīʿa.* In other words, legal discourse displaces the lexical sense of terms, along with the purely *zweckrational* procedures of human order, to a discursive space where primacy is given to the technical sense of terms in the context of jurisprudential discourse and to the jurisprudential rather than to positive natural considerations of causality and of the finality of acts. This procedure, akin to the displacement of meaning in which terms are transferred from a literal to a figurative sense,[67] is premised on a medieval Arab semantic theory essential to jurisprudence, which divides sense into the lexical, the conventional, and the legal.[68] An influential modern statement similarly refers to the legal foundation which allows for the objective validity of a legal order as one analogous to the Kantian transcendental conditions of knowledge.[69]

A legal judgement, therefore, is delimited in distinction from nature and the causality of nature or of society (although not against nature, as one modern scholar claimed in an excess of zeal).[70] Such judgement functions as legal causality according to the "principle of importation."[71] Thus it is not a matter of natural causality that is invoked in legal judgement, but of strictly legal *shar ͨist* causality.[72] And although this *shar ͨist* legal causality is ultimately connected to religious and moral considerations, these remain in the meta-legal domain, like considerations of human nature and interest. The religious subject and the legal subject are not identical.[73]

Thus abstracted from nature, and strictly speaking, even from religious ends, Muslim law inscribes its instances of realization within relations of beginning and repetition, archetype and re-enactment, which are specific to it and to its discourse, producing effects of accentuation and bars of division similar to those encountered above in the discussion of cultic and epiphanic great times. This sectoral specificity is signaled, guaranteed, and processed by the technical means deployed for it, the initial one of which is the technical specification of univocity that has been mentioned. But more important and consequential is the technical means of relating precedent and consequent, that is, the fixing of a modality relating archetypal imperatives and acts to come.

This relation can be construed either between unmediated terms, where the precedent and the consequent share explicitly identical conditions, or between these two terms mediated by some consideration of causality. The precedent, the archetype, finds articulation in the body of discrete statements that exist in the nomothetic discourse. This body is collectively known as *uṣūl* (sg. *aṣl;* literally, roots) while the consequent is a judgement, *ḥukm,* the body of which is collectively known as *furū ͨ* (sg. *far ͨ;* literally, branches). Both terms are particularly apt for genealogical arguments, but I shall term them henceforth as "principal" and "consequent" respectively. A principal is a statement containing within it a judgement that is transitive.[75] It is a principal the judgement within which is ascertainable directly,[76] almost by self-evidence, it being a function of the authoritative nature of the text (the Koran which is the utterance of God, and *ḥadīth,* the salutary example and command of a near-impeccable Prophet). A judgement is standardly defined as "nomothetic discourse when specific to the actions"[77] undertaken or yet to be performed by persons of legal capacity. The relationship between the two is unmediated when the principal is unambiguous and not open to interpretation *(naṣṣ)* such as the prohibition on the consumption of pork, carrion, and blood. There is also a class of what might be called virtual unambiguity: this is *naskh,* textual abrogation, which occurs when a Koranic verse is thought to have been revealed to Muḥammad later than one it contradicts. Examples of such abrogation are the praise of wine and its prohibition by a "later" verse and the legality of temporary marriage *(mutʿa)* in one verse and its prohibition in another. It will readily be noted that the notion of abrogation active here is identical to that with which Islam is related to previous monotheistic revelations, most specifically, to the Old and New Testaments: abolishing the import and force, but not the letter, of many of their statements.

Apart from *naṣṣ* and *naskh,* which encompass few facets of life, the infinity of the world is transformed into instances that are rendered instants of the principal by the interpretation of the text. Indeed, the science of jurisprudence, *uṣūl al-fiqh,* is essentially a body of hermeneutical procedures for the interpretation of texts and for making this interpretation of the canon transitive with respect to the infinite manifold of the mutable world. One could, *mutatis mutandis,* express this in terms of a certain terminological protocol and state that the purpose of the principles of jurisprudence is to transform secondary into primary rationality. It is through procedures of extraordinary formalist and interpretive dexterity that legislation acquires secondary principles of substantively wider input than those contained in the primary text. For the indicators *(adilla)* of judicial necessity comprise not only the *aṣl,* but also the *maʿqūl al-aṣl,* the ensemble of extra-textual elaborations upon the sense of the text.[77]

Filiation, the insertion of a given instance into the orbit of the text, here takes the form of an inferential sequence between principle and instance, for what *maʿqūl al-aṣl* amounts to is an assertion of causality behind the judgement contained in the text. It is a matter which becomes relevant after the two initial procedures for establishing filiation *(taʾṣīl)* are exhausted or con-

sidered inappropriate: these are exegesis, that is, lexical investigation *(tafsīr)*, and semantico-historical interpretation *(ta'wīl)*,
which comprises synecdoche (generalization and particulariza-
tion), implication, metaphorization, and similar considerations
as applied both to single words and to statements. Together,
these lead to the recapitulation of the archetype by its iconic
representation. These procedures attempt to close any gaps and
to clear any uncertainties in the line of filiation and of generic,
pseudo-causal connection. This is accomplished by no other
means than the assumption of an Ur-text, the recovery of the
original intention embodied in the statement. Things, including
statements, are recoverable not through history, but through
their original act of positing.

Once this original intention is unravelled, it is posited by
the jurist as the ground *('illa, pl. 'ilal)* of the judgement; it is
upon the *'illa* that the all-important notion of analogy, *qiyās*, is
based. And with *qiyās* we come to the fourth procedure of legislation—the other three being, as mentioned, reclamation of
the Koran, the *ḥadīth,* and consensus. But before proceeding
any further with the discussion of *qiyās,* it must be stressed that
the *'ilal* are neither naturalistic nor rational, but rather strictly
legal, being posited as legal causes by the nomothete (God or,
peripherally, the Prophet) regardless of whether or not they
correspond to any natural or rational exigency. The Mu'tazilites
took issue with this claim in asserting a quite different thesis of
theodicy: God's decree was invariably correlated to human interest, so it therefore cannot prescribe unreasonably and cor-
relatively; human reason is capable of legislating by its capacity
to apprehend good and evil.[78] This thesis, however, remained a
position unattractive to the majority of Sunni Muslim clerics,
who generally regarded it as a presumption upon the omnipotence of God, understood as an absolute that could not exclude
arbitrariness and unpredictability; the Judaeo-Muslim God is
essentially an amoral being who cannot be bound by the moral
imperatives he dictates to his creatures. There is therefore no
sense in talking of legal judgements proper, as distinct from the
natural or rational, before the Muḥammadan nomothesis.[79] So,
for example, although the effect of inebriation is judicially des-

ignated as the ground (*ʿilla*) for the prohibition of alcoholic beverages, this natural causality is incidental to the real ground of prohibition (God's interdiction contained in the Koran). Indeed, inebriation does not positively indicate a natural necessity for prohibition, otherwise alcoholic beverages would have been universally prohibited.[80] Such seemingly natural causes are posited as an indication of divine beneficence, making the comprehension of law more accessible to minds that are merely human, without positively ascertaining "causality" as conceived by the nomothete,[81] which remains ineffable.

Legal causes, *ʿilal,* are therefore and by almost universal consensus indices (*amārāt,* sg. *amāra*) which, as one medieval scholar stated, are "termed 'causes' only figuratively, for a cause is what causes that which is caused, by virtue of itself."[82] The potency of the *ʿilla* is therefore nominal, and the ascription of effectivity to it is akin to saying that blackness is the ground for asserting the blackness of that which is black.[83] The clearest demonstration of this is of course the precise order of rituals: there is no indication of why it is that prayers should take place five times a day; neither is it possible to produce an explanation of pilgrimage rituals or, indeed, of ritual cleanliness prescriptions or divorce procedures.[84] What renders these actions necessary is the command of nomothetic discourse, which prescribes fasting at the sighting of the new moon which initiates the month of Ramaḍān—and not another month. If illicit sexual intercourse by a married person, when attested to by four independent male witnesses who had witnessed the act directly, is punishable by stoning to death, this is not because adultery in itself requires stoning.[85] Stoning is merely the index recoverable as the necessary correlate of a particular form of sexual delinquency attended by certain determinate conditions according to an example set by early Islamic history (the rule is of extra-Koranic provenance).

In this context is inserted the analogical reasoning based on these "causes," indicative signs. Unmediated "causality" is indicated, as we have seen, by the text. For the rest, there are available in Muslim jurisprudence a variety of methods for ascertaining "causality": some methods derived from inductivist notions, some based on similitude, others based on concomitance, and yet others appealing to human interest.[86] In all cases, however, stress is laid on the strictly indexical character of "causality" thus revealed. Its various descriptions have been reduced to nominal variations dependent upon terminological and other conventions.[87]

The literature which treats this material is not always consistent, nor well concatenated, and appears to have resulted from two distinct movements which converged: a scholastic register of retrospective conceptual ratification of legal imperatives already in place, and the ideological elaboration of classical Islamism that will be discussed below. These movements together constituted the *uṣūl al-fiqh* in its scholastic form in the eleventh to the thirteenth centuries. It would not be productive for our purposes to retrace its course or to pursue the matter of its systematicity.[88] Of primary interest here is that the axial notion of *ʿilla* underlying analogical operations is not one which reveals a *ratio legis,* but rather a notion connecting precedent and consequent according to other principles.

The "causal" imperative linking consequent with precedent is based on certainty regarding the appropriateness of a judgement, without this certainty entailing any epistemological consequence. For it is one of practical conclusiveness (*qatʿ*—not *yaqīn,* certainty of an epistemological sort), with this practical conclusiveness indicated by "causes." An analogy, or an indicative demonstration of judicial consequence, is an inference which leads to a judgement by a particular interpreter and actor, the juris-consult; the analogy is not based on some objective or metaphysical ground, but on the basis of indices of correlation as interpreted by him.[89] The indices of correlation acquire force by virtue of being affirmed by particular actors speaking for a particular interpretative strategy. Such is the force of tradition. The force of legal authority is not one which has its main impulse in the weight of epistemology and its certainties; rather it is constituted by an aesthetic of filiation. Thus the force of the archetype becomes the inferential force of the *qiyās,* grafting a para-logical procedure onto the argument of authority and transferring the action of contiguity in the former, by analogy, to an action of contiguity in the latter. Ultimately, this force is derived from an ontology of identity that we have already encountered.

But before this last point can be properly explored, some further comments on the modality of connection between precedent and consequent are in order. It is manifest that the attribution of similarity is virtual and required by the authority of precedence posited by the interpreting and legislating authority. This similarity is posited within the bounds of a relationship, the invariant element of which is the schema of positing a relative potency, hence of inferential force. The intertwining of these two authorities, indeed their identification or at least their capacity for mutual displacement, is a hallmark of genealogical reason, with its identification of seniority, potency, and creativity in continuity and within a medium of identity. It is precisely this modality of relation that Ghazālī (d. 1111) so succinctly encapsulated, when describing the relation of the instance to the principal as one of submission or compliance *(idh ʿān)*.[90] For in order for what is in fact a syntagmatic series of elements divided by blank spaces of chronometric time to be taken for a paradigmatic series in which successive instants are identified and homogenized by a single act of foundation, a certain violence must intervene. From this results the submission of which Ghazālī spoke: a compliance to a particular instant taken, by clerico-juristic authority, for an invariant model which generically marks the relationship as one of filiation and as an argument from authority. The accentuations of mythical and divine great time are here affected by the denaturing of the instance and its ejection from the realm of the lexical to that of the technical legal sense, with the rhythm of the law taking over from the steady flow of the chronometer.

Yet as in great time discussed in the first part of this chapter, the rhythm of law is not discontinuous, but copies the structures of ordinary time. The main feature of this time, as we have seen, is a spatialized structure of pure succession, in which the magnitude of spaces dividing instants is irrelevant for structural and diagrammatic purposes alike, as for the imputation of imperative seriality and of consequence. In view of this irrelevance, it is unsurprising that there was a concerted attempt to represent legal analogies in syllogistic form.[91] This not only carries the rational authority of Aristotle; of greater importance for

the present argument, this seriality arranges precedent and consequent in an unambiguous structure of spatial succession and
linear order. Certainly Ghazālī and other legal theorists felt that
the Aristotelian syllogism produced certainty of a higher, opti-
mal order than inferences based on indices of similarity, including metaphors *(tamthīl)*; but, as we have seen, the science
of jurisprudence produces a practical certainty based upon an
epistemological probabilism which is nonetheless conclusive.[92]
A distinctly forced element clearly emerges in this procedure,
especially in the attempt to transform the judgement contained
in the principal to a major premise, to construe the ʿilla as a
minor premise, and to build analogies of similitude along the
BARBARA, i.e., universal affirmative or "first" mood of the
Aristotelian syllogism.

Both proponents and opponents of legal hermeneutics
clearly recognized that this syllogistic transformation had no
epistemological force. Avicenna for one strongly repudiated this
presumption upon syllogistic logic and with his unflinching rigor
anatomized its vacuity, insisting that a syllogism cannot be built
upon mere indices of correlation. He further argued that legal
analogies are less akin to the logic of Aristotle than to the inferences of phrenology.[93] At the opposite end of the spectrum lay
the relentless empiricism of Ibn Taymīya (d. 1327), an opponent
of Aristotelian logic on grounds of a radically sensualist epistemology and of a notion of the innate nature of logical inference.
The thrust of his criticism was the reducibility of syllogisms to
hermeneutical operations based on notions of similarity, on the
assumption that similarity is the sole means of building gener-
alities.[94] The starting point is always the particular.

Indeed, even the hearty advocates of syllogistic form in
jurisprudence emphasized that their inferences were based on
treating a particularity as if it were a generality.[95] An analogy is
the transference of certain features of a particularity to another
by the subsumption of the instance under the sway of the principal, treated as a generality.[96] The main feature of an analogical
relationship, as we have seen, is commonality of index. This
index might be iconic, metaphorical, or metonymical, so that, as

a major medieval Arabic rhetorician noted, "it is permissible to imagine the one to be the other."[97] It is difficult to constrain analogical operations evident in Islamic jurisprudence to the substantial and the formal (which include the purely nominal, hence metaphorical) evident in legal reasoning in general.[98] It is equally insufficient simply to classify its tropes in terms of arguments *a simili, a fortiori,* and *a contrario* which are as common in legal reasoning generally as they were in medieval scholasticism.[99] Nor is it quite useful to perform the task of distributing its modes of operation among metaphor, metonymy, and synecdoche, not least because these terms have been variously defined as rather lifeless models through the classical tradition until the present time.[100]

The tropes of Islamic legal hermeneutics can be seen to include all the above rhetorical figures in all the definitions given to each. More germane to the present argument, however, is a matter that has already been brought up more than once, namely, the conditions of efficacity of the legal inference under discussion. These are conditioned by the fact that the formalism of legal reasoning is virtual, for the logic of argumentation, including legal argumentation, can in the reality of its practice only be nonformal, and always contains a surplus.[101] Judicial reasoning, in opposition to the formal, is rarely correct or incorrect,[102] as Muslim jurists discovered a millennium ago. Legal hermeneutics can only be unraveled when we regard the mutual convertibility of metonymic, metaphorical, and synecdochal forms—which one almost always encounters in discursive practice—as the subtle interplay of, and transferrence among, formal and semantic operations whose effect is the addition and suppression of referential elements.[103] All this allows us to recapitulate matters discussed in the first part of this chapter, and to re-enter a world in which it is possible linguistically to convert subjects and objects, words and things. Here, as Frye notes, the "sense of verbal magic is sublimated into a quasi-magic inherent in sequence or linear ordering. Hence the medieval fascination with the syllogism and the great medieval dream of deducing all knowledge from the premises of revelation."[104] Virtual formalism is a dream whose reality can only be sustained by extra-formal means: in our case, by the authority of the clerico-legal institution whose particular passion and vocation it was.

3

It is the quest for similarity which invests in events a legal sense, bereft of nature, as it apportions to events an identity freed from chronometric distance; it is this quest which removes from events any "primary" rationality they may have and inserts them into the "secondary" universality of legal discourse. With this denaturalization of discourse, we have the positing of successive instances of identity, the one represented as history, the other represented by its diagrammatic analogue, inference. In all cases, we have a metaphysic of identity represented as an epistemology of correspondence that characterized the entire space of medieval Arab-Islamic scientific (Wissenschaftlich) discourse, including the science of jurisprudence—a situation not dissimilar to that which prevailed in premodern European thought, in which representation was "posited as a form of repetition," a situation in which the world speaks in signatures that are legible by means of analogy.[105] In the arena of Arab-Islamic civilization, the quest for historical origins and the interpretation of events as re-enactments—of wise dealings, of divine intervention and guidance, of righteous acts according to legalistic criteria—was a privileged field for the work of similarities and the legibility of signatures.

Yet we have seen the inferences from the past in the field of fiqh to be epistemologically only virtual. Its quasi-propositional structure is overdetermined by the argumentative desire of the clerico-legal institution (the ʿulamā), a matter only a faint glimmer of which has reached the register of standard scholarship on the matter of analogy in Islamic thought.[106] This matter is also connected to factors such as the characteristics—and consequent discursive effects—of Muslim judicial organization.[107] Moreover, it is well known that the science of legal theory, uṣūl al-fiqh, is not really a methodology of law but a legal epistemology whose construction postdates that of positive judicial doctrine, a doctrine whose efficacy was guaranteed and empowered by authority.[108]

Of direct interest here, however, is another matter, one which pertains to the authority of evidently spurious lines of argumentation and the adoption of the genealogical logic of filiation as the main mode of inference. This logic was not confined to traditional sciences, but was also evident in the rational sciences of the time. One of the most rigorous and highly mathematically formalized of these rational sciences, alchemy, depended for its workings on *a priori* numerical and other proportions of a magical nature; it appears that the demonstrative mode remained, above all, a topical feature, a mode for organizing traditional material to which the logical moment is subordinate.[109] Islamic Peripateticism itself—not unlike other Peripateticisms—appears constituted on the *presumption* of propositional and inferential rigor.[110] It constructed for itself, moreover, a legendary history of authority, proposing itself as *philosophia perennis* since its establishment, in definitive form and usually through divine inspiration, by Idrīs-Hermes, the first of all prophets, who received (from Gabriel in some sources) the arts of writing, arithmetic, astronomy, and philosophy.[111] The history of philosophy is that of the transmission of an invariant knowledge from impeccable origins, along a line that weaves together philosophical and prophetic genealogy through several moments—including such wisdom as was imparted to King Solomon by the Chthonian spirits *(jinn)* and culminating with Aristotle's appearance in a dream of the Caliph Al-Ma'mūn (r. 813–833), which caused Aristotle to be translated into Arabic and initiate the Islamic re-enactment of Aristotelianism.[112] One thing that facilitated this legendary account of origins is the aphoristic and anecdotal style of Islamic histories of philosophy, which among other (structural) things, served to keep doctrinal content at bay[113] and thus rendered possible the construction of quasi-historical filiations by binding events abstracted from their conditions of emergence to the continuum of a particular time, the time of the history of philosophy. Facilitating this process, as in the case of constructing legal facts, is the authority of the "mytho-logical drift *(dérive)*" described by one recent study of legal discourse as the articulation of *"ideaux logiciens"* and myths of origin.[114]

The material on which this "drift" works is, as in the case of the history of philosophy just mentioned, a body of discrete precedents. For after all, each narrative of Muslim tradition of legal consequence is a singular "judicial oracle,"[115] and oracular logos is invariably encrypted. Muslim juristic theory is a legal semiotics which regards the open book of nomothetic discourse—whose natural form is opened by metaphor, implication, generalization, etc.—with eyes set on the possibility of its closure, indeed on the necessity of its closure by specific interpretation.[116] For if, as Lotman asserts, "indeterminacy is the measure of information,"[117] closure is the measure of determinacy, of sense, of conclusiveness and, consequently, of practice. Just as Christian canon law construed determinacy by tracing a logical path that approaches the sacred text in asymptotic fashion, with constant reference to textual fragments out of which the inferential itinerary is made to proofs *pro et contra*,[118] and just as Jewish scholars used single texts to demonstrate contrary points as part of their training,[119] it is likewise here the closure of the text of the principal to chronometric time and to historical conditions of emergence which constitutes the axial feature of its interpretation as principal. Closure betokens a vertical connection to archetype, not an intra-textual or historical filiation. Thus the fragmentary nature of biblical stories strengthens their vertical connection, and indeed Old Testament figures embody moments of this vertical connection,[120] and Christian exegesis thus controls polysemy by its affirmation of biblical unity.[121] The fragments of principal that make up the body of Muslim texts of legal relevance and consequence and the exclusively topical structure of the works of *ḥadīth* and of law,[122] are likewise vertically disciplined by the control of polysemy—indeed, by the closure to polysemy with each act of interpretation-legislation—and by a vertical connection to a higher order, a metalegal order which affords the substance of similarity that arranges succession according to its own time, the time of identity.

This metalegal order, along with the relation of consequent and precedent it superintends, is one whose construction, elaboration, maintenance, and integrity must be managed and invigilated over time and across space. It must be institutionalized, paradigmatically and sociopolitically, as a habitus of the spirit based on repetition and constant ratification. The violence it does to history and reality, its manifest arbitrariness (in the sense this term came to carry in structural linguistics), is the hallmark of its efficacy and is strongly institutionalized both socially and intellectually.[123] In the psychoanalytic terms used by one analysis of similar procedures in medieval Christian Scholasticism, this violence to nature is guaranteed by it constituting a "cultural super-ego."[124]

The inferential sequences contained in Islamic law—as in Christian canon law and indeed, in law *tout court*—is an enunciation whose obsessional repetition of the textual repertoire announces the enunciating authority; this authority is the institution which makes the inference a location for its presence and for the effect of its potency. It is the power to prescribe action which makes possible the arbitrary enunciation and which guarantees its own credibility, veracity, and inferential truth. It is the same authority which carves out a region of the imaginary, renders it sequentially systematic, and affirms its denatured specificity by what, in the context of defining the elaboration of the religious field, has *mutatis mutandis* been termed as "autarchic self-reference."[125]

Inference is effected, therefore, by the sheer affirmation of inference, and consequence is likewise effected by the affirmation of sequence, provided the affirmation is that of a specific authority whose task it is to affirm these matters. That which empowers the institutional enunciation and endows it with veracity is its ceremonial performance, "of a clearly pronounced obsessional character"[126] of reading the text of the principal, and reading the instance as a moment of the principal. Although Islamic logolatry does not have the dramatic procedural elements of canon law that was systematically developed in medieval Europe,[127] it does share with it as a primary mechanism passage through "le lieu mythique."[128]

The inferential celebration is, in anthropological terms, a ritual. It is characterized by the repetition and routinization of

the finalist model of singular sense closed to interpretation. It is
a ritual celebration of a myth of identification by origin. Like all
other situations attested in ethnographical literature, ritual and
myth interact in a complex of subtle forms,[129] the difference
being that although it is theoretically possible to construe the
narratives of Muslim tradition and of the Koran as a constellation of connected and sequential series, it is in fact individual
motifemes that enter into each inferential ritual.[130] These individual motifemes—the principals, narratives of action or of acts
of command and of nomothetic enunciation—are the occasion
for the ritual of inference, the end of which is primarily classificatory. Consequent upon this function is the heavy inclination
toward metaphorization and cognate operations in analogies
and other *shar 'ist* procedures, for these can be seen as primarily
classificatory.[131] Inclusion in a string of inferential filiation, which
we have seen to be the primary operation of legal theorizing, is
a taxonomic act; its parent medium, the metaphysic of similarity and the succession of identities, affords the vast space of
filiation.

Within this space, we have what is in fact a nominal attribution of inclusion, and, concomitant with this attribution, indices of correlation serve as tokens of inclusion within a space—a
time sequence—as defined by its origins. In this process, as in
legal proofs in a very different setting, the signifier tends to
absorb the signified.[132] This signifier—the principal and that
which it wholly realizes in each instance, Islam—mediates the
different spheres of the semiosis and mediates semiotic with
nonsemiotic reality.[133] This mediation in the context of this discussion—of the semiotic and the nonsemiotic, of the denatured
and the natural, of the secondary and the primary—appears
based on integrating the one with the other and reducing them
mutually to one another; this mutuality, however, rests on the
assumption of a hierarchy which betokens the generation of
temporal precedence along a continuum of similitude.[134] This
defines a situation in which identified units are co-extensive as
well as co-intensive, changing into one another, thus perform-
ing one of the tasks assumed by Lévi-Strauss' totemic opera-
tors.[135] It is invariably thus that trans-historical collectivities are

posited. In the historical context relevant here, Islamdom is thus generated, but it is a name representing collectivities assimilable to the ambit of the name "Islam" only because it is so posited by the authority of the clerico-legal institution. Thus, in a certain sense, it is the imaginary, denoting nothing and connoting everything, that is the operative condition of representations such as these—the representation of Islam as the operative truth of every judgement made in its name by the institution whose task it is to conjure up the universality of the name "Islam." A similar situation is indicated in an analysis of Roman law which gives primacy to the conceptual over the historical reality that attempted to realize it, thus showing that "the 'divine' origins of institutions were, under their mythical cloak, much truer" than modern views.[136]

It is by semiotic means such as those described above that the world is first rendered into legal form, its fragments then assimilated to a protoplasm of substantive similitude and temporal continuity and thus rendered generically Islamic. It is thus that positive law becomes Islamic, that a history becomes Islamic, that a society becomes Islamic. All these trans-historical entities fall under the classificatory potency of a name which connotes everything and denotes nothing; it is a name that husbands difference and diversity, over space and in time, and causes it to mutate into singularity, similitude, and indistinctness.

The science of legal theory, *uṣūl al-fiqh*, was one means by which the Muslim clerico-legal institution caused the world to lose its bearings in time and space and become Islamic. It is a discursive formation, by which the institutes formally governing human intercourse could be read as Islamic signatures by the clerico-legal gaze which seeks fully to appropriate the world. But this was by no means a process which knew definitive closure. For one thing, the world was imperfect, and many institutes and customs that were condoned by the clerico-legal institution, the *ʿulamā* or Muslim priesthood,[137] were usually regarded as extra-legal. One main category of such rulings is *istiḥsān* and *istiṣḥāb,* legal preference on the basis of equity, custom, or the public weal which might contradict judgements arrived at by analogy.[138] It is a procedure which was much execrated, but nevertheless widely used in an implicit sense or without the use of the technical term. Another manner of assimilating imperfection to the *shar'ist* world was the procedure of *ḥiyal*, legal stratagems, which employed legal means for achieving extra-legal or even illegal ends (such as the prohibition of usury), or using analogies in a purely nominal, indexical sense (here used as a criticism rather than positive description of legal reality).[139] There were even *ḥiyal* regarded as salutary, and there is a vast body of these which, together with *istiḥsān*, provided the corpus of rulings governing sharecropping and rents, most comprehensively expressed in Ḥanafī commercial law; the last became the most complete and universal merchant's law in the medieval Near East and beyond.[140]

But there was a totalizing internal dynamic within the science of *uṣūl al-fiqh* which was not content to coexist with legal redundancy or with social realities not comprehended by the legal definition. As early as the eleventh century, Bājī (d. 1081) declared the formal proofs of law to comprise not only textual principals and their rational elaboration (analogy broadly considered), but *istiṣḥāb* as well.[141] It was left to Shāṭibī (d. 1388) to produce the most prodigiously sustained and comprehensive attempt to deploy the vast legacy generated by half a millennium of legal and metalegal thinking he had at his disposal, and create a synthesis which totalized order *tout court*, under the Islamic signature within the ambit of the *sharī'a*.

The strategy adopted for this totalization by Shāṭibī was to transform legal judgements into inferential certainties bereft of the probabilism discussed above, thus strengthening and absolutizing the quasi-propositional form of legal deduction,[142] and simultaneously to widen the ambit of the *sharī'a* to encompass all devotional and secular human activity. The latter task was accomplished by reviving and amplifying the unpopular, though potent, idea of the necessary concordance between divine command and human interest. Shāṭibī thus put into effect an implicit notion of natural law and deployed a notion of the index of correlation between principal and instance (*'illa*) which is given a directly utilitarian turn, the *'illa* indicating implicit or explicit interests served by a command or a prohibition.[143] All such indices are derivable from the axial notion of nomothetic intent in which Shāṭibī grounds his enterprise. This comprehends five categories of human interest: divine intent sets out to preserve religion, life, sanity, progeny, and wealth.[144] Thus custom is raised to the orbit of principals,[145] and *istiḥsān* becomes a consideration necessary for the validation of every judgement without exception.[146] The final stroke of this systematic closure is the direct reduction of human reason to divine inspiration.[147]

The enterprise undertaken by Shāṭibī, with its combination of lawyers' realism and the scholasticism of jurist theologians, was one which sutured—in a manner so tight as to render their texture seamless—the topics that have been addressed in the course of this and the preceding section of this essay. In other words, the totality of human action is divided between the merely natural and the nomothetic. This primary classification gives immense force to the vertical hinging of all rational human activity—rational by means of the correspondence between reason and the primal nature of right human action revealed in nomothetic discourse—and connects this activity directly and ineluctably with its archetypes. We have seen this to be a virtual connection premised on the elision of chronometric history and the construction of a generic history of the legal fact as re-enactment of its origin. With Shāṭibī we have the impeccable and integral statement of the legislative process as a ritual reading of a myth of origin and of repeated identity, of legal reason as mytho-logical practical reason, of the Muslim legist as mythologue. Shāṭibī thus affords the definitive statement of legal reason rendered a genealogical practical reason with a finalist charter, the practical reason of genealogy read backwards, a reason invested with the capacity for construing all human action as regenerative of its primeval innocence. The myths of origin thus break away from the usual setting of myth, the setting of stories. Instead the clerico-legal gaze here reads origins as if inscribed within the very texture of daily life. It is thus that Shāṭibī definitively closes, in the world under his supervision and that of his corporation, the gap between the two modes of divine will, the providential will *(irāda qadarīya)* manifested in creation, and the commanded will *(irāda amrīya)* manifested in nomothetic discourse.[148] This imaginary concordance is possible only when ratified by the ʿulamā, for only they are capable of turning sequence into consequence, the virtual into the actual, and of making practical reason out of canonical discourse. In this they are much like the sorcerer, described as basing his art on three errors: "He first mistakes the metaphoric symbol (i.e., the verbal label 'this is the hair of X') for a metonymic sign. He then goes on to treat the imputed sign as if it were a natural index, and finally he interprets the supposed natural index as a signal capable of triggering off automatic consequences at a distance."[149]

Notes

1. No adequate general account of Arabic historical writing exists. Dated as they may be, the following are serviceable when used with care: H. A. R. Gibb, 'Taʿrīkh' in idem., *Studies in the Civilization of Islam*, ed. S. J. Shaw and W. R. Polk (Boston, 1962), 108–37, and F. Rosenthal, *A History of Muslim Historiography* (Leiden: E. J. Brill, 1968).

2. See, for instance, Arthur O. Lovejoy and George Boas, eds., *Primitivism and Related Ideas in Antiquity* (Baltimore: Johns Hopkins University Press, 1935).

3. Cf. Marshall Sahlins, *Culture and Practical Reason* (Chicago: University of Chicago Press, 1976), 52–53.

4. Joseph Needham, "Time and Eastern Man," in idem., *The Grand Titration* (London: George Allen and Unwin, 1969), 267–68.

5. Editors' introduction to Abu Hilāl al-ʿAskarī, *Al-Awāʾil*, ed. M. Miṣrī and W. Qaṣṣāb (Damascus: Wazārat al-Thaqāfa, 1975), 1:13.

6. Mircea Eliade, *The Myth of Eternal Return*, trans. W. R. Trask (London: Routledge and Kegan Paul, 1955), 105.

7. Ibn Al-Athīr, *Al-Kāmil fiʾt-Tārīkh*, ed. C. J. Tornberg (Beirut: Dār Ṣādir, 1965–66), 1:223, 237, 273.

8. Al-Ṭabarī, *Tārīkh al-rusul waʾl-mūlūk*, ed. M. J. de Goeje (Leiden: E. J. Brill, 1879), 1:78–80.

9. Ibn al-Athīr, *Al-Kāmil*, 1:72.

10. For instance, Miskawayh and Abū Ḥayyān al-Tawḥīdī, *Al-Hawāmil waʾl-Shawāmil*, ed. A. Amīn and A. Ṣaqr (Cairo: Lajnat al-Taʾlīf waʾt-tarjama waʾl-nashr, 1951), 122.

11. Ernst Cassirer, *The Philosophy of Symbolic Forms,* trans. R. Manheim (New Haven and London: Yale University Press, 1955), 2:108.

12. Cornelius Castoriadis, *The Imaginary Institution of Society,* trans. K. Blamey (Cambridge, Mass.: MIT Press, 1987), 183.

13. Georges Dumézil, "Temps et mythes," *Recherches Philosophiques* 5 (1935/ 36): 240–42, 245.

14. Cassirer, *Symbolic Forms,* 2:118–19.

15. John Wansbrough, *The Sectarian Milieu: Content and Composition of Islamic Salvation History* (Oxford: Oxford University Press, 1978; London Oriental Series, no. 34), ix.

16. Y. Moubarac, *Abraham dans le Coran* (Paris: Vrin, 1958), 130.

17. On the cyclism of the Isma ʿili notion of history, see among others, P. Walker, "Eternal Cosmos and the Womb of History: Time in Early Islamic Thought," *International Journal of Middle East Studies,* 9/3 (1978):355–66.

18. Karl Löwith, *Meaning in History* (Chicago: University of Chicago Press, 1955), 181.

19. Ibid.

20. Moubarac, *Abraham dans le Coran,* 131–32.

21. Ṭabarī, *Tārīkh,* 1:29–30.

22. Ibn Kathīr, *Al-Bidāya waʾn-Nihāya* (Cairo, 1932):97; Maqdisī, *Kitāb al-Badʾ waʾt-Tārīkh,* ed. C. Huart (attributed to Balkhi) (Paris, 1899 ff.), 3:10.

23. Ṭabarī, *Tārīkh,* 1:95–96; Ibn Kathīr, *Bidāya,* 1:71.

24. Ṭabarī, *Tārīkh,* 1:128–31.

25. Masʿūdī, *Akhbār al-Zamān wa man abādahu al-ḥidthān,* ed. A. Ṣāwī (Beirut: Dār Al-Andalus, 1980), 74.

26. Ibn al-Athīr, *Kāmil,* 1:38, 40; Masʿūdī, *Akhbār al-Zamān,* 73; Ibn Qutayba, *Al-Maʿārif,* ed. Th. ʿUkāsha, 2nd ed. (Cairo: Dār al-Maʿārif, 1969), 20; Yaʿqūbī, *Tārīkh* (Beirut: Dār Ṣādir, 1960), 1:6.

27. Yaʿqūbī, *Tārīkh,* 1:27; Ibn Kathīr, *Bidāya,* 1:155; Ibn al-Athīr, *Kāmil,* 1:103, 107.

28. Maqdisī, *Al-Badʾ waʾt-Tārīkh,* 3:10.

29. Ṭabarī, *Tārīkh,* 1:309 ff.

30. Aziz Al-Azmeh, *Al-Kitāba al-Tārīkhīya wa'l-ma ʿrifa at-tārīkhīyya,* ch. 3, passim.

31. "Dadjdjāl" and "Hour," in J. Wensinck, *Handbook of Early Muhammadan Tradition* (Leiden: E. J. Brill, 1960); A. Al-Azmeh, "Barbarians in Arab Eyes," *Past and Present* 134 (1992), 15 ff.

32. Ibn Kathīr, *Nihāyat al-Bidāya wa'n-Nihāya,* ed. M. F. Abū ʿUbayya (Riyādh: Maktabat al-Naṣr al-Ḥadītha, 1968), 1:171–72, 176, 247; Ṭabarī, *Tārīkh,* 1:55.

33. This term is borrowed from Löwith, *Meaning in History,* 188.

34. Ibn al-Athīr, *Kāmil,* 1:219.

35. Eitan Kohlberg, "Some Shiʿi Views on the Antediluvian World," *Studia Islamica* 52 (1980), 57.

36. Yaʿqūbī, *Tārīkh,* 2:34.

37. Gilles Quispel, "Time and History in Patristic Christianity," in *Man and Time: Papers from the Eranos Yearbooks, 3,* ed. Joseph Campbell (Princeton: Princeton University Press, 1957; Bollingen Series, 30.3), 91.

38. Ibn Kathīr, *Nihāya,* 1:278–79. See the sceptical criticism of Ibn al-Athīr, *Kāmil,* 1:20.

39. Ibn Qutaiba, text in *Al-Jins ʿind al-ʿArab* (Köln: Al-Kamel Verlag, 1991), 1:7.

40. Masʿūdī, *Kitāb al-Tanbīh wa'l-Ishrāf,* ed. M. J. de Goeje (Leiden: E. J. Brill, 1894), 125.

41. For a particularly succinct account of this matter, see Tzvetan Todorov, *Symbolisme et interpretation* (Paris: Seuil, 1978), 110 ff.

42. Quispel, "Time and History," 87 ff.

43. Of the vast literature on this matter, the reader is particularly referred to the crystalline account of Erich Auerbach, "Figura," in idem., *Scenes from the Drama of European Literature* (Manchester: Manchester University Press, 1984), 38.

44. E. H. Kantorowicz, *The King's Two Bodies: A Study in Mediaeval Political Theology* (Princeton: Princeton University Press, 1957), 88–89 and passim.

45. On the distinction between allegory and typology, see J. N. D. Kelly, *Early Christian Doctrines,* 5th ed. (London: Adam & Charles Black, 1977), 69 ff., and Auerbach, "Figura," 54.

46. On this transformation, see Wansbrough, *The Sectarian Milieu,* 25–27.

47. Auerbach, "Figura," 42.

48. Ibn Kathīr, *Bidāya*, 2:147 ff. For such a typological interpretation of the Old Testament, see Ibn Qayyim al-Jawzīya, *Hidāyat al-ḥayārā fi ajwibat al-Yahūd wa'n-Naṣāra* (Beirut, n.d.), 51 ff. See also Al-Azmeh, *Al-Kitāba al-tārīkhīya*, 32–34, and idem., *Arabic Thought and Islamic Societies* (London: Croom Helm, 1986), 111.

49. Harry Austryn Wolfson, *Philosophy of the Church Fathers*, 2nd ed. (Cambridge, Mass.: Harvard University Press, 1964), 74.

50. Aziz Al-Azmeh, "Histoire et narration dans l'historiographie arabe," *Annales Économies, Sociétés, Civilisations* (March-April, 1986):411–31; and cf. Roland Barthes, "Introduction to the Structural Analysis of Narratives," in idem., *Image-Music-Text,* trans. S. Heath (London: Fontana, 1977), 99.

51. Dumézil, "Temps et mythes," 245.

52. Wansbrough, *The Sectarian Milieu,* 91.

53. Castoriadis, *The Imaginary Institution,* 191–92, 200.

54. Jacques Derrida, *Margins of Philosophy,* trans. Alan Bass (Brighton: The Harvester Press, 1982), 43.

55. Henri Bergson, *Time and Free Will: An Essay on the Immediate Data of Consciousness,* trans. F. L. Pogson (London: George Allen & Unwin and New York: Macmillan, 1910), 98–99, 107–8. See the comments on this tradition by Derrida, *Margins,* 35–37, 40–44. The reader is advised that the present author tends more towards the epistemological interpretation of Bergson as in Gilles Deleuze, *Le Bergsonisme* (Paris: Presses Universitaires de France, 1966), than towards the psychologistic interpretation often proposed as, for instance and with respect to matters germane to the topic under discussion, by Maurice Halbwachs, *Les cadres sociaux de de la mémoire* (Paris-La Haye: Mouton, 1976), esp. ch. 7.

56. Deleuze, *Le Bergsonisme,* 31–32, 36.

57. Cf. Ernst Cassirer, *Substance and Function and Einstein's Theory of Relativity,* trans. William Curtis Swabey and Marie Collins Swabey (New York: Dover Publications, 1953), 440 f.

58. Claude Lévi-Strauss, *The Naked Man: Introduction to a Science of Mythology: 4,* trans. John and Doreen Weightman (London: Jonathan Cape, 1984), 633, 629; and cf. Yuri M. Lotman, *Universe of the Mind: A Semiotic Theory of Culture,* trans. Ann Shukman (London and New York: I. B. Tauris, 1990), 34.

59. Mircea Eliade, *Traité d'histoire des religions* (Paris: Payot, 1949), 366–67; and cf. ch. 11, passim.

60. Eric A. Havelock, *Preface to Plato* (Oxford: Basil Blackwell, 1963), ch. 4, passim.

61. Emmannuel Le Roy Ladurie, *Montaillou: Cathars and Catholics in a French Village, 1294–1324,* trans. Barbara Bray (Harmondsworth: Penguin Books, 1980), 344.

62. Harry Anstryn Wolfson, *Philo: Foundations of Religious Philosophy in Judaism, Christianity, and Islam* (Cambridge, Mass.: Harvard University Press, 1968), 1:298.

63. Al-Azmeh, *Arabic Thought and Islamic Societies,* 1 ff.

64. There is a textbook treatment of the Muslim science of jurisprudence in English: Mohammad Hashim Kamali, *Principles of Islamic Jurisprudence,* rev. ed. (Cambridge: Islamic Texts Society, 1991).

65. Shāṭibī, *Al-I ʿtiṣām,* ed. Muḥammad Rashīd Riḍā (Cairo, A. H. 1332 [1914]), 1:46.

66. For instance, Shāṭibī, *Al-Muwāfaqāt fī uṣūl al-aḥkām,* ed. Muḥammad Munīr (Cairo, A. H. 1341 [1922]), 2:27–28, 255–56, 3:7, 88.

67. Pazdawī, *Kanz al-wuṣūl,* published on the margins of Bukhārī, *Kashf al-asrār* (Istanbul: Maktabat al-Ṣanāʾiʿ, A.H.1301 [1884]), 1014.

68. Ghazālī, *Al-Mustaṣfā min ʿilm uṣūl al-fiqh* (Cairo 1356/1937), 1:322 ff.; Shawkānī, *Irshād al-fuḥūl ilā taḥqīq al-ḥaqq min ʿilm al-uṣūl* (Cairo: Muṣṭafā al-Bābī al-Ḥalabī, 1937), 21–22. In fact, semiosis in medieval Arab-Islamic thought is not confined to a tripartite theory of signification, but was multipartite. See Al-Azmeh, *Arabic Thought and Islamic Societies,* 106 ff., 115 ff.

69. Hans Kelsen, *Pure Theory of Law,* trans. Max Knight (Berkeley and Los Angeles: University of California Press, 1967), para. 3, 16, 34d.

70. Ibid., para. 17.

71. Ibid., para. 18.

72. Āmidī, *Al-Iḥkām fī uṣūl al-aḥkām* (Cairo, 1914), 1:182.

73. Baber Johansen, "Staat, Recht und Religion im Sunnitischen Islam," in *Essener Gespräche zum Thema Staat und Kirche (20),* ed. H. Marré and J. Stütig (Münster, 1986), 17; idem., "Die Sündige, gesunde Amme. Moral und gesetzliche Bestimmung (ḥukm) im islamischen Recht," *Die Welt des Islams*

28 (1988):271–73, 278–79; Chafik Chehata, "La religion et les fondements du droit en Islam," *Archives de Philosophie de Droit* 18 (1973):19–21. Cf. Kelsen, *Pure Theory of Law*, para. 18.

74. Ibn ʿAqīl, "Kitāb al-jadal ʿalā ṭarīqat al-fuqahāʾ," ed. George Makdisi, *Bulletin d'Etudes Orientales* 20 (1967), para. 48.

75. Baiḍāwī, *Minhāj al-wuṣūl ilā ʿilm al-uṣūl* (Cairo, A.H. 1326 [1908]), 94.

76. Ghazālī, *Mustaṣfā*, 1:35.

77. Al-Bājī, *Kitāb al-minhāj fi tartīb al-ḥijāj*, ed. A. Turki (Paris: Maisonneuve et Larose, 1978 [Publications du Département d'Islamologie de l'Université de Paris-Sorbonne, 7), paras. 19, 300 ff; Āmidī, *Iḥkām*, 1:227.

78. See Al-Azmeh, *Arabic Thought and Islamic Societies*, 82, 88 ff.

79. For a classic statement, see Ghazālī, *Mustaṣfā*, 1:8, 55 ff. For particularly pronounced and acute statements which contain a denial of any notion of causality, however metaphorical: Ibn Ḥazm, *Al-Iḥkām fī uṣūl al-aḥkām*, ed. Aḥmad Shākir (Cairo: Maṭbaʿat al-Imām, n.d.), 1127–31.

80. Ibn Rushd (al-Jadd), *Al-Muqaddimāt al-mumahhidāt* (Cairo: n.p., n.d.), 23.

81. Pazdawī, *Kanz al-wuṣūl*, 661, 663.

82. Ibn ʿAqīl, 'Kitāb al-Jadal', 42.

83. Al-Baṣrī, *Kitāb al-muʿtamad fī uṣūl al-fiqh*, ed. Muḥammad Ḥamīd Allāh et al. (Damascus: Institut Français d'Etudes Arabes, 1964–65), 704.

84. Ibn Jinnī, *Khaṣāʾis*, ed. Muḥammad ʿAlī Najjār (Cairo: Dār Al-Kutub al-Miṣrīya, 1952–56), 1:48; Shāṭibī, *Iʿtiṣām*, 2:129.

85. Ghazālī, *Mustaṣfā*, 1:93.

86. Convenient overviews can be sought in Shawkānī, *Irshād*, 210 ff., and Baidāwī, *Minhāj*, 83 ff.

87. Shawkānī, *Irshād*, 206–7; Bājī, *Minhāj*, paras. 47–48. See ʿĀdil Fākhūrī, *Al-Risāla al-ramziya fī uṣūl al-fiqh* (Beirut: Dār al-Ṭalīʿa, 1978), 29–30.

88. The reader is referred to the rigorous work of Hammū Naqārī, *Al-Manhajīya al-uṣūlīya wa'l manṭiq al-Yūnānī min khilāl Abī Ḥāmid al-Ghazālī wa Taqī al-Dīn Ibn Taimīya* (Casablanca: Dār an-Nashr al-Maghribīya Wallāda, 1991), ch. 4. For a detailed account of ʿilla, see Sālim Yafūt, *Ḥafrīyāt al-maʿrifa al-ʿArabīya al-ʿIslāmīya. Al-Taʿlīl al-fiqhī* (Beirut: Dār al-Ṭalīʿa, 1990).

89. Āmidī, *Iḥkām*, 1:7–8; Baiḍāwī, *Minhāj*, 78, 82–83; Ibn Rushd, *Al-Muqaddimāt al-mumahhidāt*, 24.

90. Ghazālī, *Miḥakk al-naẓar fi'l-manṭiq*, ed. Badr al-Dān Naᶜsānī and Muṣṭafā Qabbāni (Cairo: Al-Matbaᶜa al-Adabīya, n.d.), 33.

91. See particularly, Naqāri, *Al-Manhajīya al-uṣūlīya*, 177 ff., 187–89, 206 ff., and Wael B. Hallaq, "Logic, Formal Arguments and Formalization of Arguments in Sunni Jurisprudence," *Arabica* 37 (1990):315–58. For Ghazālī's terminological transformation of Aristotelian logic for legal purposes, see Ghāzalī, *Miḥakk*, 31 ff., and idem., *Miᶜyār al-ᶜilm*, ed. Sulaymān Dunyā (Cairo: Dār al-Maᶜārif, 1961), 243 ff. The most systematic such transformation is of course that of Ibn Ḥazm, *Al-Taqrīb li-ḥadd al-manṭiq bi-l alfāẓ al-ᶜāmmīya wa'l-amthila al-fiqhīya*, ed. Iḥsān ᶜAbbās (Beirut: Dar al-Ḥayāt, 1959).

92. Ghazālī, *Miᶜyār*, 161, 163, 193 ff; Naqārī, *Al-Manhajīya al-uṣūlīya*, 181–83.

93. Ibn Sīnā, *Al-Shifa': Al-Manṭiq, 4 (Al-Qiyās)*, ed. Saᶜīd Ziyāda (Cairo: Wizārat al-Thaqāfa, 1964), 575–77, 579.

94. Ibn Taymīya, *Naqḍ al-manṭiq*, ed. Muḥammad Ḥamza and Muḥammad al-Fiqī (Cairo: Al-Matbaᶜa al-Salafīya, 1951), 165–66, 200–1; idem., *Al-Radd ᶜalā al-manṭiqīyīn* (Lahore: Idarat Tanjuman al-Sunna, 1978), 115–20. See also Naqārī, *Al-Manhajīya al-uṣūlīya*, 197–99, 200–5, 223.

95. Ghazālī, *Miᶜyār*, 170–73, 202; idem., *Maqāṣid al-falāsifa*, ed. Sulaymān Dunyā (Cairo: Dār al-Maᶜārif, 1961), 90, 91 ff; Khwarizmī, *Mafātīh al-ᶜulūm*, ed. G. van Vloten (Leiden: E. J. Brill, 1968), 9.

96. There is a tendency in modern New Rhetoric to infer logic itself from analogy. See W. Sacksteder, "Analogy: Justification for Logic," *Philosophy and Rhetoric* 12 (1979):27–29 and passim.

97. Al-Jurjānī, *Asrār al-balāgha*, ed. Muḥammad Rashīd Riḍā (Beirut: Dār al-Maᶜrifa, 1978), 79–80.

98. M.-J. Borel, J.-B. Grize, and D. Miéville, *Essai de logique naturelle* (Bern: Peter Lang, 1983 [Sciences pour la Communication: 4]), 154–55.

99. Ch. Perelman, *Logique juridique: Nouvelle rhétorique:* (Paris: Dalloz, 1976), para. 8.

100. Of the vast literature, the reader is particularly referred to the fine analyses of Peter Schofer and Donald Rice, "Metaphor, Metonymy and Synechdoche Revis(it)ed," *Semiotica* 21/1-2 (1977):121–49.

101. Borel, et al., *Logique naturelle,* 20, 25, and ch. 1, passim.

102. Perelman, *Logique juridique,* para. 6.

103. Cf. Schofer and Rice, "Metaphor," 130–31, a propos Groupe μ and Genette.

104. Northrop Frye, *The Great Code: The Bible and Literature* (London: Routledge and Kegan Paul, 1982), 11.

105. Michel Foucault, *The Order of Things: Archaeology of the Human Sciences* (London: Tavistock Publications, 1974), 17, 21, 25 ff. This is a rigorous reading of the unreflected and impressionistic comments often made on the "symbolist attitude" prevalent in the European middle ages: for instance, Jan Huizinga, *The Waning of the Middle Ages,* trans. F. Hopman (Harmondsworth: Penguin Books, 1972), 195, and Aaron Gurevich, "The Representation of Property during the High Middle Ages," *Economy and Society* 6 (1977):11.

106. For example, Louis Gardet, "La dialectique en morphologie et logique arabes," in Jacques Berque, et al., *L'ambivalence dans la culture arabe* (Paris: Éditions Anthropos, 1967), 131.

107. Robert Brunschvig, "Le système de la preuve en droit musulman," *Recueils de la Société Jean Bodin* 18 (1963):170, 173, 175.

108. For instance: Chafik Chehata, "Logique juridique et droit musulman," *Studia Islamica* 23 (1965):16–17; idem., "L'Ikhtilaf et la conception musulmane du droit," in Berque, et al., *L'ambivalence dans la culture arabe,* 259–63; Al-Azmeh, *Arabic Thought and Islamic Societies,* 171–77.

109. Al-Azmeh, *Arabic Thought and Islamic Societies,* 25–28, 152.

110. Ibid., 152, 160–61.

111. Ibn al-Athīr, *Kāmil,* 1:59; Mas ʿūdī, *Akhbar,* 78; Qifṭī, *Tārīkh al-ḥukamā',* ed. J. Lippert (Leipzig, 1903), 1; Mubashshir Ibn Fātik, *Mukhtār al-ḥikam wa maḥāsin al-kalim,* ed. ʿAbd al-Raḥmān Badawī (Beirut: Al-Mu'assasa al-ʿArabīya, 1980), 10; Wahb Ibn Munabbih, *Kitāb al-Tījān fī mulūk Ḥimyar* (Sanaa: Markaz al-dirāsāt wa'l-abḥāth al-Yamanīya, 1979), 29–30.

112. Al-Azmeh, *Arabic Thought and Islamic Societies,* 159–60; Roger Arnaldez, "L'Histoire de la pensée grecque vue par les Arabes," *Bulletin de la Société française de Philosophie* 72/3 (1978):117–68; Jean Jolivet, "L'idée de la sagesse et sa fonction dans la philosophie des 4ᵉ et 5ᵉ siècles," *Arab Sciences and Philosophy* 1 (1991):31–65; Qifṭī, *Tārīkh,* 29; Nadīm, *Al-Fihrist,* ed. Riḍā Tajaddud (Beirut [1971]), 303–4.

113. Jolivet, "L'idée de la sagesse," 61–62.

114. Jacques Lenoble and François Ost, *Droit, mythe et raison: Essai sur la dérive mytho-logique de la rationalité juridique* (Bruxelles: Facultés Universitaires Saint-Louis, 1980), 5, 173–76, 218.

115. Jacques Berque, *Essai sur le méthode juridique maghrébine* (Rabat, 1944), 21.

116. Naqārī, *Al-Manhajīya al-uṣūlīya*, 10, 29–31.

117. Lotman, *Universe of the Mind*, 227.

118. Pierre Legendre, *L'amour du censeur: Essai sur l'ordre dogmatique* (Paris: Éd. du Seuil, 1974), 109, and cf. 82, 86–87, 90.

119. Howard Eilberg-Schwarz, "Myth, Inference, and the Relativism of Reason: An Argument from the History of Judaism," in Frank Reynolds and David Tracy eds., *Myth and Philosophy* (Albany: State University of New York Press, 1990), 251 ff.

120. Erich Auerbach, *Mimesis: The Representation of Reality in Western Literature*, trans. W. R. Trask (Princeton: Princeton University Press, 1968), 17.

121. Todorov, *Symbolisme et interpretation*, 104.

122. See Al-Azmeh, *Arabic Thought and Islamic Societies*, 150 ff.

123. Cf. Pierre Bourdieu and Jean-Claude Passeron, *Reproduction in Education, Society and Culture*, trans. Richard Nice (London and Beverley Hills: Sage Publications, 1977), para. 3, gloss. 2. For these institutional underpinnings in Arab-Islamic culture, see Al-Azmeh, *Arabic Thought and Islamic Societies*, 155 ff., 223 ff.

124. Legendere, *L'amour du censeur*, 34–36.

125. Pierre Bourdieu, "Genèse et structure du champ religieux," *Revue Française de Sociologie* 12 (1971):302–3.

126. Legendre, *L'amour du censeur*, 109.

127. Ibid., 111–16.

128. Ibid., 78; Lenoble and Ost, *Droit, mythe et raison*, 230.

129. I regard the dispute over the primacy of the one over the other to be meaningless, as was shown half a century ago: Clyde Kluckhohn, "Myths and Rituals: A General Theory," *Harvard Theological Review* 35 (1942):45–56.

130. Cf. Walter Burkert, *Structure and History in Greek Mythology and Ritual* (Berkeley and Los Angeles: University of California Press, 1979), 6. For some elementary possibilities open to students of early Islamic narratives, see

Albrecht Noth, *Quellenkritische Studien zu Themen, Formen and Tendenzen frühislamischer Geschichtsüberlieferung* (Bonn: Bonner Orientalische Studien, 1973). See al-Azmeh, *Al-Kitāba al-tārīkhīya,* ch. 2.

131. Hedwig Konrad, *Etude sur la métaphore* (Paris, 1939) 91, quoted in Paul Ricoeur, *The Order of Metaphor,* trans. R. Czerny, et al. (London: Routledge, 1978), 107.

132. Louis Gernet, *The Anthropology of Ancient Greece,* trans. John Hamilton and Blaise Nagy (Baltimore: Johns Hopkins University Press, 1981), 225–26.

133. Cf. Lotman, *Universe of the Mind,* 101, 104, 111.

134. Thus it is unjustified to regard seriality and "participation" as excluding one another, as with Ch. Perelman and L. Olbrechts-Tyteca, *The New Rhetoric: A Treatise on Argumentation,* trans. John Wilkinson and Purcell Weaver (Notre Dame and London: University of Notre Dame Press, 1969), 331–33.

135. Cf. Claude Lévi-Strauss, *The Savage Mind* (London: Weidenfeld and Nicolson, 1966), 20–21.

136. Castoriadis, *The Imaginary Institution,* 121–28, 131, 142, 148. I do not adhere to the author's apparent contentions concerning the full primacy of fantasy.

137. On this institution—the denial of whose existence, albeit sociologically absurd, is one constant trope in modern scholarship—see Al-Azmeh, *Arabic Thought and Islamic Societies,* 211 ff.

138. See Aziz Al-Azmeh, "Islamic Legal Theory and the Appropriation of Reality," in *Islamic Law: Social and Historical Contexts,* ed. Aziz Al-Azmeh (London: Routledge, 1988), 258–60. For a particularly clear general exposition, see Ibn Qayyim al-Jawzīya, *Iʿlām al-muwaqqiʿīn ʿan rabb al-ʿālamīn',* ed. Ṭāhā Saʿd (Beirut: Dār al-Jīl, n.d.), 1:339–42.

139. For some outrageous, presumably hypothetical examples: Ibn Qayyim al-Jawzīya, *Iʿlām,* 3:175.

140. Ibid., 335–36, and Avram L. Udovitch, *Partnership and Profit in Medieval Islam* (Princeton: Princeton University Press, 1970), 251–54, 258. See also Maxime Rodinson, *Islam et capitalisme* (Paris, 1966).

141. Bājī *Al-Minhā* para. 19, 58 ff., 500 ff.

142. Shāṭibī, *Muwāfaqāt,* 1:1–17, 43–45, 3:78–84.

143. Ibid., 1:185.

144. Ibid., 2:4–6 and passim. This formulation is first attested in Ghazālī *Mustaṣfā,* 1:286.

145. Shāṭibī, *Muwāfaqāt,* 2:220–21.

146. Ibid., 4:134–38, and idem., *I ʿtiṣān,* 2:136–39.

147. Shāṭibī *I ʿtiṣām,* 1:46.

148. Shāṭibī *Muwāfaqāt,* 3:81–82.

149. Edmund Leach, *Culture and Communication, the Logic by which Symbols Are Connected: An Introduction to the Use of Structuralist Analysis in Social Anthropology* (Cambridge: Cambridge University Press, 1976), 31.

References

Āmidī. 1914. *al-Iḥkām fī Uṣūl al-Aḥkām.* Cairo: n.p.

Arnaldez, Roger. 1978. "L'Histoire de la pensée grecque vue par les Arabes." *Bulletin de la Société française de Philosophie,* 72:3.

ʿAskarī, Abū Hilāl al-'. 1975. *al-Awāʾil.* Edited by M. Miṣrī and W. Qaṣṣāb. Damascus: Wazarāt al-Thaqāfa.

Auerbach, Erich. 1968. *Mimesis: The Representation of Reality in Western Literature.* Translated by W. R. Trask. Princeton: Princeton University Press.

———. 1984. "Figura." In *Scenes from the Drama of European Literature,* by Erich Auerbach. Manchester: Manchester University Press.

Al-Azmeh, A. 1983. *al-Kitāba al-Tārīkhiyya wa al-Maʾrifa al-Tārīkhiyya.* Beirut: Dār al-Ṭalīʿa.

———. 1986. "Historie et narration dans l'historiographie arabe." *Annales Économies, Sociétés, Civilisations* (March-April).

———. 1986. *Arabic Thought and Islamic Societies.* London: Croom Helm.

———. 1988. "Islamic Legal Theory and the Appropriation of Reality." In *Islamic Law: Social and Historical Contexts,* edited by Aziz Al-Azmeh. London: Routledge.

———. 1992. "Barbarians in Arab Eyes." *Past and Present,* 134.

Baiḍāwī. 1326 A.H. [1908]. *Minhāj al-Wuṣūl ilā 'Ilm al-Uṣūl*. Cairo: n.p.

al-Bājī. 1978. *Kitāb al-Minhāj fī Tartīb al-Ḥijāj*. Edited by A. Turki. Paris: Maisonneuve et Larose (Publications du Département d'Islamologie de l'Université de Paris-Sorbonne, VII).

Barthes, Roland. 1977. "Introduction to the Structural Analysis of Narratives." In *Image-Music-Text*, by Roland Barthes, translated by S. Heath. London: Fontana.

al-Baṣrī. 1964–65. *Kitāb al-Mu'tamad fi Uṣūl al-Fiqh*. Edited by Muḥammad Ḥamidullāh, et al. Damascus: Institut Français d'Etudes Arabes.

Bergson, Henry. 1910. *Time and Free Will: An Essay on the Immediate Data of Consciousness*. Translated by F. L. Pogson. London: George Alan & Unwin; New York: Macmillan.

Berque, Jacque. 1944. *Essai sur le méthode juridique maghrébine*. Rabat: n.p.

Borel, M.-J., J.-B. Grize, and D. Miéville. 1983. *Essai de logique naturelle*. Bern: Peter Lang (Sciences pour la Communication: 4).

Bourdieu, Pierre. 1971. "Géenese et structure du champ religieux." *Revue Française de Sciologie* 12.

Bourdieu, Pierre, and Jean-Claude Passeron. 1977. *Reproduction in Education, Society and Culture*. Translated by Richard Nice. London and Beverley Hills: Sage Publications.

Brunschvig, Robert. 1963. "Le systeme de la preuve en droit musulman." *Recueils de la Société Jean Bodin* 18.

Burkert, Walter. 1979. *Structure and History in Greek Mythology and Ritual*. Berkeley and Los Angeles: University of California Press.

Cassirer, Ernst. 1953. *Substance and Function and Einstein's Theory of Relativity*. Translated by William Curtis Swabey and Marie Collins Swabey. New York: Dover Publications.

———. 1955. *The Philosophy of Symbolic Forms*. Translated by R. Manheim. New Haven and London: Yale University Press.

Castoriadis, Cornelius. 1987. *The Imaginary Institution of Society*. Translated by K. Blamey. Cambridge, Mass.: MIT Press.

Chehata, Chafik. 1965. "Logique juridique et droit musulman." *Studia Islamica* 23.

————. 1967. "L'Ikhtilaf et la conception musulmane du droit." In *L'ambivalence dans la culture arabe*, by Berque, et al. Paris: Anthropos.

————. 1973. "La religion et les fondements du droit en Islam." *Archives de Philosophie de Droit* 18.

Deleuze, Gilles. 1966. *Le Bergsonisme*. Paris: Presses Universitaires de France.

Derrida, Jacques. 1982. *Margins of Philosophy*. Translated by Alan Bass. Brighton: The Harvester Press.

Dumézil, George. 1935–36. "Temps et Mythes." *Recherches Philosophiques* 5.

Eilberg-Schwarz, Howard. 1990. "Myth, Inference, and the Relativism of Reason: An Argument from the History of Judaism." *Myth and Philosophy*, edited by Frank Reynolds and David Tracy. Albany: State University of New York Press.

Eliade, Mircea. 1949. *Traité d'histoire des religions*. Paris: Payot.

————. 1955. *The Myth of Eternal Return*. Translated by W. R. Trask. London: Routledge and Kegan Paul.

Fākhūrī, ʿĀdil. 1978. *al-Risāla al-Ramzīyya fī Uṣūl al-Fiqh*. Beirut: Dār al-Ṭalīʿa.

Foucault, Michel. 1974. *The Order of Things: Archeology of the Human Sciences*. London: Tavistock Publications.

Frye, Northrop. 1982. *The Great Code: The Bible and Literature*. London: Routledge and Kegan Paul.

Gardet, Louis. 1967. "La dialectique en morphologie et logique arabes." In *L'ambivalence dans la culture arabe*, by Jacques Berque et al. Paris: Éditions Anthropos.

Gernet, Louis. 1981. *The Anthropology of Ancient Greece*. Translated by John Hamilton and Blaise Nagy. Baltimore: Johns Hopkins University Press.

Ghazālī. 1356/1937. *al-Mustaṣfā Min ʿIlm Uṣūl al-Fiqh*. Cairo: n.p.

————. 1961. *Maqāṣid al-Falāsifa*. Edited by Sulaymān Dunyā. Cairo: Dār al-Maʿārif.

————. 1961. *Miʿyār al-ʿIlm*. Edited by Sulaymān Dunyā. Cairo: Dār al-Maʿārif.

————. n.d. *Miḥaqq al-Naẓar fi al-Mantiq*. Edited by Badr al-Dīn al-Naʿsānī and Muṣṭafā Qabbāni. Cairo: al-Maṭbaʿa al-Adabīyya.

Gibb, H. A. R. 1962. "Tarikh." In *Studies in the Civilization of Islam*, by H. A. R. Gibb, edited by S. J. Shaw and W. R. Polk. Boston: n.p.

Gurevich, Aoran. 1977. "The Representation of Property during the High Middle Ages." *Economy and Society* 6.

Halbwachs, Maurice. 1976. *Les cadres sociaux de de la mémoire (1925)*. Paris–La Haye: Mouton.

Hallaq, Wael B. 1990. "Logic, Formal Arguments and Formalizations of Arguments in Sunni Jurisprudence." *Arabica* 37.

Havelock, Eric A. 1963. *Preface to Plato*. Oxford: Basil Blackwell.

Huizinga, Jan. 1972. *The Waning of the Middle Ages*. Translated by F. Hopman. Harmondsworth: Penguin Books.

Ibn ʿAqīl. 1968. "Kitāb al-Jadal ʿalā Ṭarīqat al-Fuqahā'." Edited by George Maqdisi. *Bulletin d'Études Orientales* 20.

Ibn al-Athīr. 1965–66. *al-Kāmil fi al-Tārīkh*. Edited by C. J. Tornberg. Beirut: Dar Sadir.

Ibn Fātiq, Mubashshir. 1980. *Mukhtār al-Ḥikam wa Maḥāsin al-Kalim*. Edited by ʿAbd al-Raḥmān Badawī. Beirut: al-Mu'assasa al-ʿArabiyya.

Ibn Ḥazm. 1959. *al-Taqrīb li Ḥadd al-Mantiq bi al-Alfāẓ al-ʿAmmīyya wa al-Amthila al-Fiqhiyya*. Edited by Iḥsān ʿAbbās. Beirut: Dār al-Ḥayāt.

————. n.d. *al-Iḥkām fī Uṣūl al-Aḥkām*. Edited by Aḥmad Shākir. Cairo: Maṭbaʿat al-Imām.

Ibn Jinnī. 1952–56. *Khaṣā'iṣ*. Edited by Muḥammad ʿAli Najjār. Cairo: Dār al-Kutub al-Miṣriyya.

Ibn Kathīr. 1932. *al-Bidāya wa al-Nihāya*. Cairo: n.p.

————. 1968. *Nihāyat al-Bidāya wa al-Nihāya*. Edited by M. F. Abū ʿUbayya. Riyaḍ: Maktabat al-Naṣr al-Ḥadītha.

Ibn Munabbih, Wahb. 1979. *Kitāb al-Tījān fī Mulūk Ḥimyar*. Sanaa: Markaz al-Dirāsāt wa al-Abḥāth al-Yamaniyya.

Ibn Qayyim al-Jawziyya. n.d. *Hidāyat al-Ḥayāra fī ajwibat al-Yahūd wa al-Naṣāra*. Beirut: Dār al-Kutub al-ʿIlmiyya.

————. n.d. *I ʿlām al-Muwaqqi ʿīn ʿan Rabb al- ʿĀlamīn*. Edited by Ṭāhā Sa ʿd. Beirut: Dār al-Jīl.

Ibn Qutayba. 1969. *al-Ma ʿārif*. Edited by Th. ʿUkāsha. Cairo: Dār al-Ma ʿārif.

Ibn Rushd (al-Jadd). n.d. *al-Muqaddimāt al-Mumahhidāt*. Cairo: n.p.

Ibn Sīnā. 1964. *al-Shifāʾ: al-Manṭiq, 4(al-Qiyās)*. Edited by Sa ʿīd Ziyāda. Cairo: Wizārat al-Thaqāfa.

Ibn Taymiyya. 1951. *Naqd al-Manṭiq*. Edited by Muḥammad Ḥamza and Muḥammad al-Fiqī. Cairo: al-Maṭba ʿa al-Salafiyya.

————. 1978. *al-Radd ʿalā al-Manṭiqiyyīn*. Lahore: Idarat Tarjuman al-Sunna.

————. 1991. *al-Jins ʿInd al- ʿArab*. Köln: Al-Kamel Verlag.

Johansen, Baber. 1986. "Staat, Recht und Religion im Sunnitischen Islam." In *Essener Gespräche zum Thema Staat und Kirche (20)*. Edited by H. Marré and J. Stütig. Münster: n.p.

————. 1988. "Die Sündige, Gesunde Amme: Moral und Gesetzliche Bestimmung (ḥukm) im islamischen Recht." *Die Welt des Islams* 28.

Jolivet, Jean. 1991. "L'idée de la sagesse et sa fonction dans la philosophie des 4e et 5e siécles." *Arab Sciences and Philosophy* 1.

al-Jurjānī. 1978. *Asrār al-Balāgha*. Edited by Muḥammad Rashīd Riḍā. Beirut: Dār al-Ma ʿrifa.

Kamali, Mohammad Hashim. 1991. *Principles of Islamic Jurisprudence*. Rev. ed. Cambridge: Islamic Texts Society.

Kantorowicz, E. H. 1957. *The King's Two Bodies: A Study in Medieval Political Theology*. Princeton: Princeton University Press.

Kelly, J. N. D. 1977. *Early Christian Doctrines*. 5th ed. London: Adam and Charles Black.

Kelsen, Hans. 1967. *Pure Theory of Law*. Translated by Max Knight. Berkeley and Los Angeles: University of California Press.

Khawārizmī. 1968. *Mafātīḥ al- ʿUlūm*. Edited by G. Van Vloten. Leiden: E. J. Brill.

Kluckhohn, Clyde. 1942. "Myths and Rituals: A General Theory." *Harvard Theological Review* 35.

Kohlberg, Eitan. 1980. "Some Shiʿi Views on the Antediluvian World." *Studia Islamica* 52.

Konrad, Hedwig. 1939. *Etude sur la métaphore*. Paris: n.p.

Ladurie, Emmanuel Le Roy. 1980. *Montaillou: Cathars and Catholics in a French Village, 1294–1324*. Translated by Barbara Bray. Harmondsworth: Penguin Books.

Leach, Edmund. 1976. *Culture and Communication, the Logic by Which Symbols are Connected: An Introduction to the Use of Structuralist Analysis in Social Anthropology*. Cambridge: Cambridge University Press.

Legendre, Pierre. 1974. *L'amour du censeur: Essai sur l'ordre dogmatique*. Paris: Éd. du Seuil.

Lenoble, Jacques, and François Ost. 1980. *Droit, mythe et raison: Essai sur la dérive mythologique de la rationalité juridique*. Bruxelles: Facultés Universitaires Saint-Louis.

Lévi-Strauss, Claude. 1966. *The Savage Mind*. London: Weidenfeld and Nicolson.

———. 1981. *The Naked Man: Introduction to a Science of Mythology: 4*. Translated by John and Doreen Weightman. London: Jonathan Cape.

Lotman, Yuri M. 1990. *Universe of the Mind: A Semiotic Theory of Culture*. Translated by Ann Shukman. London and New York: I. B. Tauris.

Lovejoy, Arthur O., and George Boas, eds. 1935. *Primitivism and Related Ideas in Antiquity*. Baltimore: Johns Hopkins University Press.

Löwith, Karl. 1955. *Meaning in History*. Chicago: University of Chicago Press.

al-Maqdisī. 1899 ff. *Kitāb al-Bad' wa al-Tārīkh*. Edited by C. Huart (attributed to Balkhi). Paris: Leroux.

Masʿūdī. 1894. *Kitāb al-Tanbīh wa al-Ishrāf*. Edited by M. J. de Goeje. Leiden: E. J. Brill.

———. 1980. *Akhbār al-Zamān wa man Abādahu al-Ḥidthān*. Edited by A. Ṣāwī. Beirut: Dār al-Andalus.

Miskawayh and Abū Ḥayyān al-Tawḥīdī. 1951. *al-Hawāmil wa al-Shawāmil.* Edited by A. Amīn and A. Ṣaqr. Cairo: Lajnat al-Ta'līf wa al-Tarjama wa al-Nashr.

Moubarac, Y. 1958. *Abraham dans le Coran.* Paris: Vrin.

Nadīm. [1971]. *al-Fihrist.* Edited by Rida Tajaddud. Beirut: n.p.

Naqārī, Hammū. 1991. *al-Manhajiyya al-Usūliyya wa al-Manṭiq al-Yūnānī Min Khilāl Abī Ḥāmid al-Ghazālī wa Taqī al-Dīn Ibn Taimiyya.* Casablanca: Dār al-Nashr al-Maghribiyya Wallāda.

Needham, Joseph. 1969. "Time and Eastern Man." In *The Grand Titration,* by Joseph Needham. London: George Alan and Unwin.

Noth, Albrecht. 1973. *Quellenkritische Studien zu Themen, Formen und Tendenzen frühislamischer Geschichtsüberlieferung.* Bonn: Bonner Orientalische Studien.

Pazdawī. 1307 A.H. [1889–90]. *Kanz al-Wuṣūl,* published on the margins of Bukhārī, *Kasf al-Asrār.* [Istanbul]: Maktab al-Ṣanāyiᶜ.

Perelman, Ch. 1976. *Logique juridique: Nouvelle rhétorique.* Paris: Dalloz.

Perelman, Ch., and L. Olbrechts-Tyteca. 1969. *The New Rhetoric: A Treatise on Argumentation.* Translated by John Wilkinson and Purcell Weaver. Notre Dame and London: University of Notre Dame Press.

Qiftī. 1903. *Tārīkh al-Ḥukamā.* Edited by J. Lippert. Leipzig: n.p.

Quispel, Gilles. 1957. "Time and History in Patristic Christianity." In *Man and Time: Papers from the Eranos Yearbooks, 3,* edited by Joseph Campbell. Princeton: Princeton University Press (Bollingen Series, 30.3).

Ricoeur, Paul. 1978. *The Order of Metaphor.* Translated by R. Czerny, et al. London: Routledge.

Rodinson, Maxime. 1966. *Islam et Capitalisme.* Paris: Éditions du Seuil.

Rosenthal, F. 1968. *A History of Muslim Historiography.* Leiden: E. J. Brill.

Sacksteder, W. 1979. "Analogy: Justification for Logic." *Philosophy and Rhetoric* 12.

Sahlins, Marshall. 1976. *Culture and Practical Reason.* Chicago: University of Chicago Press.

Schofer, Peter, and Donald Rice. 1977. "Metaphor, Metonymy and Synechdoche Revis(it)ed." *Semiotica,* 21:1–2.

Shāṭibī. 1332 A.H. [1914]. *al-'Iʿtiṣām.* Edited by Muḥammad Rashīd Riḍā. Cairo: n.p.

———. 1341 A.H. [1922]. *al-Muwāfaqāt fī Uṣūl al-Aḥkām.* Edited by Muḥammad Munīr. Cairo: n.p.

Shawkānī. 1937. *Irshād al-Fuḥūl ilā Taḥqīq al-Ḥaqq Min ʿIlm al-Uṣūl.* Cairo: Muṣtafā al-Bābī al-Ḥalabī.

al-Ṭabarī. 1879 ff. *Tārīkh al-Rusul wa al-Mulūk.* Edited by M. J. Goeje. Leiden: E. J. Brill.

Todorov, Tzvetan. 1978. *Symbolisme et interpretation.* Paris: Seuil.

Udovitch, Avram L. 1970. *Partnership and Profit in Medieval Islam.* Princeton: Princeton University Press.

Walker, P. 1978. "Eternal Corners and the Womb of History: Time in Early Islamic Thought." *International Journal of Middle East Studies* 9:3.

Wansbrough, John. 1978. *The Sectarian Milieu: Content and Composition of Islamic Salvation History.* Oxford: Oxford University Press (London Oriental Series, no. 34).

Wensinck, J. 1960. *Handbook of Early Muhammadan Tradition.* Leiden: E. J. Brill.

Wolfson, Austryn Harry. 1968. *Philo: Foundations of Religious Philosophy in Judaism, Christianity, and Islam.* Cambridge, Mass.: Harvard University Press.

———. 1964. *Philosophy of the Church Fathers.* 2d ed. Cambridge, Mass.: Harvard University Press.

Yaʿqūbī. 1960. *Tārīkh.* Beirut: Dār Ṣādir.

Yafūt, Sālim. 1990. *Hafrīyāt al-Maʿrifa al-ʿArabiyya al-Islāmiyya: al-Taʿlīl al-Fiqhī.* Beirut: Dār al-Ṭalīʿa.

Chapter 6

Dis-solving a Debate: Toward a Practical Theory of Myth,[1] with a Case Study in Vedic Mythology

Laurie L. Patton

Introduction: Theories of Myth

The theory of myth has fallen on hard times. The historical critique of recent philosophies of myth, in all of its manifestations, is well known. Among others, Geo. Widengren,[2] R. D. Baird,[3] Guilford Dudley,[4] J. Z. Smith,[5] Ivan Strenski,[6] Gregory Alles,[7] and Ariel Glucklich[8] have shown the ways in which an exclusively theoretical approach to myth risks being profoundly ahistorical, subordinating historical events in the development of religious traditions to the larger pattern of myth in which these events are said to participate. Moreover, such philosophies cannot account for social change, but merely give a template for "discovering" the same patterns or axioms in a variety of divergent phenomena worldwide. Since philosophy's impetus is thus toward universalization and transcendentalization, a philosophy of myth risks rendering symbols empty containers wherein objects reside because they represent, through shared characteristics, a certain abstract aspect of the world.[9]

If culture is to be respected, and historical inquiry is to maintain its own rigor and identity as a discipline, myth must refer not to some larger, transcendent symbol such as the "Center," but back to the historical and cultural circumstances from which it came. J. Z. Smith, in his recent work criticizing the Eliadean notion of the "Center," puts it eloquently:

> Without examining each and every instance, it cannot be claimed that the pattern of the "Center" is a fantasy, but it is clearly far from a universal (or even dominant) pattern of symbolization. At the very least, the burden of proof has shifted to those who will claim that a particular cultural construction represents a "Center." The "Center" is not a secure pattern to which data may be brought as illustrative; it is a dubious notion that will have to be established anew on the basis of detailed comparative endeavors.[10]

As Smith asserts, the impetus of theory itself may be precisely what prevents the historical variety of the mythic form from receiving its full exposure.

Yet a philosophy of myth is equally unsatisfactory from the philosophical point of view itself. Ivan Strenski[11] remarks that theorists are working from constructed concepts of myth which are often at cross purposes with each other, resulting in theoretical chaos. Ernst Cassirer sees myth as a symbolic form based in language; Claude Lévi-Strauss defines it as "strongly structured stories"; Bronislaw Malinowski views myths as "pragmatic narratives"; and Mircea Eliade focuses on myths as "creation stories." All of this chaos is exacerbated by the imperialistic tone that has dominated most attempts to philosophize about myth. Theorists do not invite readers to see myth in one way or another, but rather strive to tell them what it is.[12]

The rift between historians and philosophers of myth might profitably be understood in the light of Lee Yearley's work on primary, secondary, and practical theories, found in his book,

Mencius and Aquinas: Theories of Virtue and Conceptions of Courage.[13] Building on the work of Robin Horton,[14] Yearley explains how primary theory involves a kind of everyday logic, whereby the events of normal life are negotiated, regulated, and calculated according to experience. These theories will vary from culture to culture insofar as they are affected by particular exigencies of climate, social organization, etc. However, many primary theories, such as the changes of seasons or the measures of weights, remain shared universally. Secondary theories are those which are developed from primary theories to explain singular, extraordinary, or troubling occurrences; such theories differ widely from culture to culture. Such secondary theories often involve spirits, deities, and other supernatural phenomena to account for those occurrences with which primary theories cannot cope. While these two levels of theory may be adequate to explain certain cultural phenomena, Yearley claims the need for an intermediate category, that of practical theory, which is concerned with ethics and the place of human action. For Yearley, practical theory aims at a more concise organization of human experience than does primary theory, but stays far closer to the peculiar, particular messes of human life than does secondary theory. Practical theories aim to guide appreciation and action, to explain human activities, and to shape people's practices. Practical theories, writes Yearley, generate forms of explanation, prediction, and control.[15]

Whatever one might think of these categories as descriptions of cultural thought, they are illuminating when applied to theories of myth. The secondary theorists (philosophers) and the primary theorists (historians) of myth are at war. For the secondary theorists, myth itself is a unique and extraordinary occurrence. To them, myth must have its own form of being and its own laws because it is so radically distinct from normal everyday life; myth is, to use a telling truism, an irruption of the extraordinary sacred into the everyday profane world. The primary theorists, the historians, accuse the secondary theorists, the philosophers, of creating an illusory, overly transcendent category, "myth," to explain phenomena which only *seem* unique and extraordinary. The primary theorists argue that all such phenomena can and must be located in the realm of everyday logic, as part of the normal human struggles for power and position called "history." What is missing, and what could help resolve this conflict, is a practical theory of myth. Such a theory stays close to the historical "ground" of human experience yet attempts to make a more concise organization of myth in order to understand the ways in which myth has guided human action. Put more specifically, a practical theory of myth involves the discernment of myth's relationship to human flourishing throughout history—when myth contributes to such flourishing, and when myth precludes the possibility for such flourishing altogether.

In what follows I will abandon the attempt to establish either a primary (historical) or a secondary (philosophical) theory of myth and proceed instead with the practical theory—an invitation to see myth in the ways outlined above. I make one important addendum to Yearley's formulation: a practical theory of myth involves an intellectual operation distinct from strictly philosophical or historical thought—an operation that I have come to call a "practice of reading." A practice of reading is an intellectual operation which, while axiomatic, does not have the construction of a series of axioms as its primary end.[16] A secondary theory of myth must rest with a singular claim or series of claims about a "thing" called myth, and a primary theory tends to reduce myth to a number of other sociohistorical functions. A practice of reading, however, hypothesizes a number of possibilities that the mythic form might take in its use by myth makers throughout history. Yet reading delays "applying" such hypotheses; it delays "demonstrating" a regular, transcendent pattern. Whereas a secondary theory must subsume facts into patterns and exceptions to such patterns, a practice of reading is more easily interrupted by new information and is liable to change its focus entirely.

Moreover, such a practice of reading emphasizes that myth, like all of human activity, can *itself* be a kind of practical theory. Provisionally and quite generally, I define the term *myth* as the process by which a cultural form can be transcendentalized, thus guiding and regularizing human behavior. Such a process can take a number of different forms—whether it be the creation narrative of the Hainuwele, studied by Adolf Jensen and others[17] as the archetype of the dying and rising god of vegetation; the image of the black Frenchman saluting the flag, thought by Roland Barthes to be the appropriation and distortion of a historical moment;[18] or the commodities of nineteenth-century Paris, thought by Karl Marx,[19] Theodor Adorno,[20] Walter Benjamin,[21] and others to be "mythical fetishes" that falsely promise a social utopia. A practice of reading looks for the process by which an object is made transcendent, becoming a sanctioned norm or explanation for human behavior. And a practice of reading allows such a process to arise in various modalities of cultural knowledge, including texts, commodities, and icons. Finally, a practice of reading admits that myths, as kinds of practical theories, may contribute to or hinder human flourishing. While mythic forms may remove the historical contingency of a religious tradition, they can also act to resist and to relativize the claims to transcendence that a religious tradition makes.

In my emphasis upon a practical theory of myth based upon a practice of reading, I will move the discussion of myth away from the usual cast of characters and place it temporarily in the context of the work, especially the later work, of another highly complex and problematic thinker—Walter Benjamin. Benjamin's discussion of myth sits simultaneously, and rather uncomfortably, on both sides of the debate between philosophers and historians. As a historical materialist he refuses to engage any theory of myth that does not simultaneously concern itself with the vicissitudes of history, while as a philosophically and theologically informed thinker, he does not relinquish the possibility of the transformative power of the image and the word—two of the most powerful vehicles for producing that form of cultural knowledge traditionally called "myth."

The first part of this essay will consist of a survey and critique of Walter Benjamin's attitude toward myth, focusing particularly on his later works. The survey will show that for Benjamin, the mythic image participates in both the obfuscation and the liberation of possibilities for change. While myth is a kind of doom from which modern humanity must break free, its images partake of a materiality which must be remembered, and in being remembered, also suggest emancipation. The critique will show that Benjamin's analysis of mythical image depends upon the dichotomy between the archaic and the modern, and, in an uncriticized form, shares many of the difficulties presented by a hermeneutics of nostalgia.

In the second part of this essay I will provide a particular example of this kind of practice of reading myth—the Ṛg Vedic hymn to Soma, characterized as a "worldly working song" about the production of wealth in Vedic India. More particularly, I will show that Benjamin's ideas can and should be incorporated into the reading of so-called "archaic" images. By tracing the history of the image of wealth-producing labor in early Indian religious texts, I will show how such imagery is used to "mythologize," to assert the transcendentally sanctioned priority of the brahmin-controlled Vedic sacrifice over all other forms of the production of wealth. I will also show, however, that the very images used to transcendentalize privilege also suggest possibilities for change and can be used accordingly. Thus, my discussion will provide one small example of the ways in which myths can be read with a view to their use for *and* against social change.

Benjamin

It must be said at the outset that it would be highly problematic simply to view Benjamin's thought, developed sporadically throughout the teens, twenties, and thirties of this century, as a new "alternative method" in the study of religions. As Hannah Arendt comments,

> To describe adequately his work and him as an author within our usual framework of reference, one would have to make a great many negative statements, such as: his erudition was great, but he was no scholar; his subject matter comprised texts and their interpretation, but he was no phi-

lologist; he was greatly attracted not by religion but by theology and the theological type of interpretation for which the text itself is sacred, but he was no theologian and he was not particularly interested in the Bible; he was a born writer, but his greatest ambition was to produce a work consisting entirely of quotations; . . . he reviewed books and wrote a number of essays on living and dead writers, but he was no literary critic; he wrote a book about the German baroque and left behind a huge unfinished study of the French nineteenth century, but he was no historian, literary or otherwise; I shall try to show that he thought poetically, but he was neither a poet nor a philosopher.[22]

Given Benjamin's refusal to plant himself firmly in any one particular intellectual mold, one would be hasty in crediting him with uniting the fields of philosophy and history, which have been at such cross purposes for so long.[23] However, Benjamin at least begins to show some ways in which historical thought and philosophical thought might be reconfigured in relation to each other. Benjamin's relevance lies precisely in the fact that he lends an analysis of experience *(Erfahrung)* to historical materialism.[24] Such an inquiry into experience is precisely where the question of myth enters in.

Dissolving Philosophy: History and Image

A discussion of Benjamin's view of myth must be placed within the larger framework of his project for philosophy. Not surprisingly, Benjamin has early roots in Husserlian phenomenology, placing great faith in the philosophical gesture that freezes the animate.[25] It is ironic that, like historians of religion Henri Corbin[26] and Mircea Eliade,[27] whose larger morphological projects he would abhor, Benjamin is largely philosophical in orientation. Much like Henri Corbin, he wanted to reform philosophy and free it from the "frozen wasteland of abstraction."[28]

For Benjamin, philosophy can be rendered tangible through the momentary contemplation of an image. Far from being static and escapist, such contemplation is dialectical in that it contradicts ingrained assumptions of "human progress" and reminds the contemplative of the often violent and untold history of those who have been left out of the record. Traces of the past stand in juxtaposition to the present, interrupting the progress of history asserted by the victors. Through the dialectical image, Benjamin is, in his words, "putting to the test as to what extent you can be concrete in historico-philosophical contexts."[29]

In earlier essays, and later in his notes for an uncompleted work, *Passagenwerk,* a description of the Paris arcades, Benjamin attempts to describe as directly as possible nineteenth-century urban phenomena in all their ugliness and all their obsolescence. As he puts it in his essay, "One Way Street," while describing a fan in a back-alleyway, "the faculty of imagination is the gift of interpolating into the infinitely small, of inventing, for every intensity, an extensiveness to contain its new, compressed fullness, in short, of receiving each image as if it were that of the folded fan. Which only in spreading draws breath and flourishes, in its new expanse, the beloved features within it."[30]

Instead of locating his discussion in the realm of the archaic, Benjamin relentlessly seeks to find such power in the images of recent history. He finds particular power in surrealistic emphasis on the image of the dream. Just as images of empirical reality and their "rational" organization became contents of a dream in surrealism, so too the empirical realities of history are likened to the unconscious actions of the dreaming individual. For Benjamin, empirical history is dreamlike "insofar as history is man-made, yet without consciousness or design."[31]

The historical image is intimately related to Benjamin's concept of experience *(Erfahrung).* Through contemplation of history he attempts to "explode the limitations set by Kant and regain that fullness of the concept of experience held by earlier philosophers"—in short, to restore the experience of theology.[32] Yet theology as such is out of the question; Benjamin shares with the surrealists an intense revolt against the reign of Catholicism in his day. Benjamin's deeper and more complex relationship to Jewish messianic theology, however, is central to his thinking. He was engaged in a lifelong effort to merge Jewish philosophy and Marxist, materialist perspectives; his long time friend Gershom Scholem despaired that one of the foremost Jewish theologians of the twentieth century had been lost to an unfortunate case of intellectual crossbreeding.[33]

For Benjamin, the only way to restore the intensity of such theological experiences is by "profane" illumination:

> It is a cardinal error to believe that, of surrealist experience, we know only the religious ecstasies, or the ecstasies of drugs . . . but the true, creative overcoming of religious illumination certainly does not lie in narcotics. It resides in a *profane illumination,* a materialistic, anthropological inspiration to which hashish, opium, or whatever else can give a preliminary lesson.[34]

In short, such illumination is Benjamin's project of translating into the secular all that had been claimed for religious experience.

These material realities suggested by profane illumination are the stuff of remembrance *(Eingedenken),* a term adapted from Proust's concept of *mémoire involontaire.* Remembrance is made up of those traces of perception long trodden down by the habits of daily life. In his essay, "Some Motifs on Baudelaire," Benjamin asserts that remembrance can be inspired by some material object. Proust encounters remembrance in the taste of a pastry called *madeleine,* which transported him back to the realities of his childhood. As Benjamin puts it, such an experience is not open to the "promptings of memory which obey the call of attentiveness."[35] On the contrary, such a memory takes one by surprise, interrupting the flow of daily life.

In his essay "On the Mimetic Faculty,"[36] Benjamin explores further the relationship between image and experience. He asserts that archaic humanity possessed a mimetic faculty which is now lost. The mimetic capacity consisted of a sensuous, qualitative type of behavior toward things, a gift of producing similarities which preceded the capacity for language. In positing this faculty, Benjamin develops the idea that palpable knowledge can be a means of cognition, "not only nurtured by what appears sensorily before the eyes, but which is also able to assimilate mere knowledge, even dead facts as if they had been lived and experienced."[37] Remembrance can thus be wrested from the private world of Proust and used as a means of writing history.

For Benjamin, any historical epoch is a dream filled with alienated objects—a dream from which one must awaken. The dialectical image inspires such an awakening and allows one to interpret history. Benjamin develops this idea of the liberating power of the image "frozen in the present," in the sixteenth "Thesis on the Philosophy of History": "A historical materialist cannot do without the notion of a present which is not in transition, but in which time stands still and has come to a stop. For this notion defines the present in which he himself is writing history. Historicism gives the "eternal" image of the past; historical materialism supplies a unique experience with the past."[38] Even more specifically, historical chronology—the very thing which morphologists such as Mircea Eliade and Henri Corbin vehemently reject—is for Benjamin a harbinger of, even a contributor to, the power of the lived image. The image is not history's implacable enemy. He writes: "A chronicler who recites events without distinguishing between major and minor ones acts in accordance with the following truth: nothing that has ever happened should be regarded as lost for history."[39]

Benjamin has escaped the antithesis of the eternal and the historical through the micrological technique of concentration on the minute, through which historical movement is halted and settled into an image—hence his notion of "dialectics at a standstill."[40] For Benjamin, dialectical image and historical event imply each other; the image becomes a means of awakening history, turning historical facts into "something that just happened to us."[41]

Benjamin's defense of the chronicle finds its fullest expression in his essay "The Storyteller."[42] Benjamin praises storyteller Johannes Hebel for his handling of the passage of time in his stories. In one of Hebel's stories, a bride learns that her husband has died in a mine; as an old woman, she discovers his body preserved in iron vitriol at the bottom of the mine. Hebel deals with the time intervening as a chronicle:

In the meantime the city of Lisbon was destroyed by an earthquake, and the Seven Years' War came and went, and Emperor Francis I died, and the Jesuit Order was abolished, and Poland was partitioned, and Empress Maria Theresa died.... America became independent, and the united French and Spanish forces were unable to capture Gibraltar.... Napoleon captured Prussia and the English bombarded Copenhagen, and the peasants sowed and harvested. The millers ground, the smiths hammered, and the miners dug for veins of ore in their underground workshops. But when in 1809 the miners at Falun [uncovered a body] . . .

Benjamin comments that "never has a story teller embedded his report deeper in natural history than Hebel manages to do in this chronology. Read it carefully. Death appears in it with the same regularity as the Reaper does in the processions that pass around the cathedral clock at noon."[43]

For Benjamin, the chronicler has an eschatological orientation; he must make a simple recording of all the facts which, as he later was to write, is illumined both by its irreversibility and the inevitable redemption of humanity.[44] Contrasting the historian with the chronicler (who, one would hazard a guess, may well be the forerunner of the historical materialist), he writes that the historian must explain the happenings with which he deals, whereas the chronicler can content himself with displaying events as models of the course of the world.[45] Basing their historical tales on a divine plan of salvation, chroniclers are exempt from the burden of explanation, and chronicled events can simply shine as the predecessors of Benjamin's dialectical images. The storyteller deals with experiences which have not been subject to psychologization,[46] but which instead reveal the minute particulars of material circumstances—the *mémoire involontaire* politicized and written into history.

Thus Benjamin fuses the overtly theological motivation of his earlier works with a historical materialist coloring. Although equally teleological in its overtones, Benjamin's justification of the chronicle is never identified with industrial progress and continuity; ironically, faith in such continuity is what he condemns as historicism. His immersion in the simple narrative about things material is not the same as a cult of materiality, but rather the disenchantment of that cult of materiality.[47]

Benjamin's turn to material objects never became wholly secularized, however. His later work is construed by some scholars as a theology of interruption, or a kind of messianic materialism. For instance, James McBride[48] takes issue with deconstructionists such as Paul DeMan,[49] Carol Jacobs,[50] and others,[51] who have appropriated Benjamin precisely because he remains "undecided" between Marxism and messianic Jewish philosophy and therefore anticipates the deconstructionist claim of the elusiveness of truth and meaning.[52] McBride argues that Benjamin is not remaining undecided, but rather attempting to fuse the two elements into an entirely new one. In Benjamin's thinking, the sudden experience of profane illumination found in material objects corresponds to the Kabbalistic understanding of divine language as immanent in the world. Even in his later work, "Theses on the Philosophy of History," messianic power and revolution are never far apart:

> Thinking involves not only the flow of thoughts, but their arrest as well. Where thinking suddenly stops in a configuration pregnant with tensions, it gives that configuration a shock, by which it crystallizes into a monad. A historical materialist approaches a historical subject only when he encounters it as a monad. In this structure he recognizes the sign of a Messianic cessation of happening, or, put differently, a revolutionary chance in the fight for the oppressed past.[53]

Thus one can see the similarities between Benjamin's work and what Yearley calls a "practical theory." Benjamin refuses to transcendentalize image, to take it outside of history, but at the same time he imbues it with profound significance for revolutionary human activity in the world. Benjamin's image—the arrest of the flow of thought—stays close to the ground of historical human experience, while at the same time it explains human activity, particularly that which has been lost to conscious memory, in order to guide people's action for social change.

Benjamin on Myth

Benjamin's dissolution of philosophy into image and history lays the groundwork for his discussion of myth—a discussion which will help to develop a practical theory of myth. Not surprisingly Benjamin's notions of myth do not coalesce into a single, unified philosophy.[54] As he was suspicious of philosophy's reification of lived historical experience, Benjamin did not place any faith in the Romantic agenda of the "new mythology," its ability to endow the world with meaning and synthesize a variety of disparate elements. Nor, however, did he participate in the Enlightenment thinkers' negative valuation of myth as "poor reasoning" or a "distortion of truth."[55] From his earliest writings, Benjamin maintained that the essence of all mythical occurrence is recurrence, and in that aspect, myth partakes of futility.[56] In his resolute commitment to translation into the secular, Benjamin typifies the "modern man" whom Eliade had in mind when he wrote that the spiritually impoverished modern man could only perceive archaic man as "doomed," as caught in a stagnating cycle of the repetition of myth. For Benjamin, myth's temporal mode is the doom of "eternal recurrence," of "all the same."[57]

Yet, as evident above, Benjamin's project is not imbued with the myopia of modernity; on the contrary, it is engaged in a critique of modernity. Benjamin is consciously trying to remove himself from all theories of myth that he views as indifferent to a philosophy of history—a move which distinguishes him from other theorists. Indeed, he attacks several of his contemporary theorists. To Benjamin, Ernst Cassirer demonstrates an overly aesthetic, ahistorical view of myth. When Cassirer does address the question of history, he lapses into an evolutionary schema whereby myth is only the stepping stone to proper religion and, ultimately, to theoretical knowledge.[58] Moreover, in a proposal for the arcades project for the New Institute, Benjamin planned to write vehemently against the works of C. G. Jung and Ludwig Klages, in an attempt to distinguish his own theory of collective "wish-images" from theirs.[59] Relatedly,

Adorno also comments on the antithetical relationship between Benjamin and yet another version of a philosophy of myth, *philosophia perennis:* "Benjamin's images do not present invariant archetypes that are to be extracted from history; rather they shoot together by means of the force of history, directed toward the historical in direct opposition to *philosophia perennis.* His philosophical interest was indifferent to the ahistorical, and focuses primarily on the temporally determinate, the irreversible."[60]

Also unlike many philosophers of myth, in his earlier writings Benjamin rejects myth as a source from which to draw knowledge and illumination. In precisely inverse relation to humanity's rejection of repetition, seen as disastrous by Eliade, Benjamin writes of a *redemptive* breakthrough from repetition in his analysis of the tragic hero in German drama. In *The Origin of German Tragic Drama,* the tragic hero overcomes the mythical laws of expiation and guilt; by undermining a dated body of laws he liberates himself from a world wherein every mythical retribution produces a new guilt. The hero enters upon a new time in which the power of repetition over existence comes to an end.[61]

Benjamin's suspicion of myth is further developed in his critique of Creuzer's *Symbolik und Mythologie der alten Völker.* Interestingly, the debate centers on the question of allegory, and the allegorical aspects of the German tragic drama. For both Creuzer and Benjamin, the temporal form of the symbol is "momentary totality," while the temporal form of allegory is "progression in a series of moments"—that is, chronological. Yet Benjamin disagrees with Creuzer that allegory can be a form of myth. Given Benjamin's historical emphasis, one can see the way in which he might turn Creuzer's definition upon its head. For Benjamin, symbol relates to both magic and myth, and yet allegory figures in the dismantling of myth. As he puts it in *The Origin of German Tragic Drama,*

> Whereas in the symbol destruction is idealized and the transfigured face of nature is fleetingly revealed in the light of redemption, in allegory, the observer is confronted with the

facie hippocratica of history as a petrified, primordial landscape. . . . And although such a thing lacks all symbolic freedom of expression, all classical proportions, all humanity—
nevertheless it significantly gives rise not only to the
enigmatic question of the nature of human existence as such,
but also of the biographical historicity of the individual.[62]

Similar to the chronicle, allegory thus is anti-mythical—
antithetical to the mystical, totalitarian momentousness of the
symbol in that it allows for chronology, and thus, by implication, for decay and death.[63] For philosophers such as Henri
Corbin, allegory is an attempt to conceal "what is real."[64] For
Benjamin, allegory's historical form is more truthful to the irreversibility of the historical human situation. And thus, unlike
many of his earlier counterparts, he does not drag the past into
the mythological, but on the contrary "dissolves" mythology in
the historical.[65]

In his later work, however, Benjamin's attitude toward myth
develops in a different direction. Myth does not remain a single,
fateful time structure in his thinking, but becomes a multiplicity
of various limited mythologies.[66] Myth moves from being an all-
captivating force to a loose framework which informs much of
modern life. Particularly in the arcades project, Benjamin attempts to show how correspondences were at work between
the modern technical world and the archaic symbol world,[67]
specifically architecture and language as the modern forms of
mythology.

In *Passagenwerk,* Benjamin's writing on myth corresponds
to Marx's idea that capitalism presents itself as a kind of "second nature."[68] Benjamin takes the movement of mythic process
out of the realm of nature and into the modern world of commodities. Buildings, architecture, and even street names replace
the stuff of nature, becoming the cultural landscape to be "read"
by the historical materialist critic. Thus Benjamin describes his
studies of Paris as "a metaphysics of places."[69] The Paris arcades, and their successors, the world expositions, are the shrines
of this landscape—"the original temple[s] of commodity capitalism,"[70] displaying commodities like "icons in niches."[71] In the

context of the arcades project, Benjamin also embarks upon a careful study of Paris street names with this idea of myth in mind and comments that there are fantasies "hidden within the names of corporations."[72] Thus, Benjamin's mythic forms are first and foremost "wish-images" of urban life; the expositions are the hallways of the "*ur*-forms" of the phantasmagoria of progress, that false consciousness of nineteenth-century capitalism.

Benjamin's development of the relationship between myth and modernity in his later work places a good deal of emphasis on the archaic. First, it must be remembered that the particular configuration of Benjamin's ideas does not arise from the classical study of sacred narratives transposed onto modern life. On the contrary, his analyses of myth are formed within the context of a theory and a critique of capitalism and take up the question of the archaic within the course of such theoretical deliberations. Thus, in an inversion of morphological thought, Benjamin, like Eliade, builds upon the Goethean concept of *"Ur-phänomen"* but attempts to translate it from the realm of nature to that of history: "I am also involved in fathoming origin. That is to say, I am pursuing the origin of the construction and transformation of the Paris arcades from their rise to their fall, and am laying hold of this origin through economic facts."[73]

More specifically, the mythology of technical and cultural objects constitutes the category of "commodity fetishism" in Benjamin's work. The full-scale commodity production of the nineteenth century signified a reversion to the great myth—the reproduction of "always the same" (the fact of alienated and dominated labor) under the semblance of the "perpetually new" (the illusion of industrial progress).[74]

There is, however, even more to Benjamin's mythical wish-images than an analysis of commodity fetishism. These ideas also contain an element of utopian idealism. The collective mythic wish-images have a double movement, stepping back into the past while projecting out into the future. Benjamin writes: "To the form of the new means of production that in the beginning is still dominated by the old one (Marx), there correspond in the societal superstructure wish-images in which the new is intermingled with the old in fantastic ways."[75] Benjamin is referring to Marx's assertions that, at its newest stage, technology still reverts to recently outmoded, but nonetheless still conventional, forms. As Marx also remarked, the earliest experimental locomotive had its origin in an animal image: it had two feet that it raised up alternatingly like a horse.[76]

Benjamin pushes this idea even further, asserting that the wish-images of modern capitalist life do not simply preserve the new technology in outmoded forms. These images also reach back to mythical forms precisely in order to sever their ties with the conventional. Thus, Benjamin writes of the intermingling of the old mythology and the new technology:

> This intermingling owes its fantastic character above all to the fact that in the course of social development, the old never sets itself off sharply from the new; rather, the latter, striving to set itself apart from the recently outmoded, renews archaic, *ur*-temporal elements. The utopian images that accompany the emergence of the new always concurrently reach back to the *ur*-past. In the dream in which every epoch sees in images before the eyes the one that follows it, the images appear wedded to elements of *ur*-history.[77]

When mass-produced food appears miraculously on the shelf as if dropped from the sky, for example, the end of material scarcity and exploitation seems to be at hand. And while the consuming public does not understand the false, dreamlike quality of that promise, those utopian wish-images would be redeemed as utopian inspirations toward a revolutionized humanity if society should ever awaken. As Susan Buck-Morss puts it, "Paradoxically, collective imagination mobilizes its powers for a revolutionary break from the recent past by evoking a cultural memory reservoir of myths and utopian symbols from a more distant *ur*-past."[78]

Thus, in the dialectical image, humanity's capacity for a mimetic relationship to things is again utilized as a means of illumining that historical "thing-world," *(Dinglichkeit)*—the world of alienated objects. While surrealist mythology puts objects at a distance, and keeps them in the realm of the dream, the Benjaminian notion of a materialistic mythology illuminates the realm of dreams, the collective image-making capacity, in order to awaken the sleeper.[79]

The Practice of Reading and the Ambiguity of Myth

Benjamin's theory of the dialectical image, outlined above, implies that the social world of things *(Dinglichkeit)* should be transformed into meaningful images. Although myth as "ever the same" and "eternally recurring" is to be blasted apart by allegory and an emphasis upon historical form, at the same time, myth contains the element of imagery which is so crucial to profane illumination.[80] On the one hand, the dialectical image interrupts the mythical power of images *(Bildkraft)* by means of the dialectic of knowledge, and on the other hand, it implies that the authentic knowledge itself is, at least in part, "based on images and thereby on myth."[81] Benjamin distinguishes experience, with its link to mythical forms of meaning, from abstract knowledge; here Benjamin presents a dialectic in his breaking apart *and,* at the same time, rescuing myth in its formation of experience.[82]

Benjamin's portrayal of myth has important implications for the practice of reading discussed above. The multiple movement of myth implies no culminating philosophy of myth, but rather the dissolution of theory[83] into the act of reading. A few words on Benjamin's idea of the act of reading, an idea on which I draw in formulating my practice of reading, are necessary at this point. Commenting on Benjamin's idea of history, Ian Balfour has remarked that what Benjamin presents in the guise of a theory of history is really a monogram, a sketch, or an outline for the reading, writing, and acting of history. The models that Benjamin adopts for history—philology, citation, translation, and critique—take the form of a reading. In his relentless juxtaposition of quotations and images, in his love for montage, he constructs an encounter of one text with another, of one language with another. Thus historical knowledge is integral to the practice of reading, but not to the construction of philosophical theory.[84]

As mentioned above, the same practice of reading is relevant to the practical theory of myth. Benjamin's idea of myth is such that he demands that no philosophy (secondary theory) of myth be written, and, further, that the history (primary theory) of myth should be rewritten with an eye toward the possibility of radical human transformation. For Benjamin, the mythic process must be read in the texts of storytellers, the street names of Europe, the names of corporations, on the exhibit halls of the expositions, and in the architecture of the arcades. This process of reading is not simply scholarly amusement. For Benjamin, what prompts a person to read is the same thing that prompts him or her to practical, revolutionary action and social change. In the moment of contemplation, the world is brought forth to "readability" *(Lesbarkeit)* and helps the contemplative to discern possibilities for change.[85]

Even more specifically, potentials for meaning found in the cultural products of earlier, traditional societies contain a promise of change. While (as many of Benjamin's critics have pointed out)[86] the dialectical image alone can do nothing, if it is accompanied by action it can catalyze revolution. As Benjamin writes, "The past carries with it a temporal index by which it is referred to redemption. There is a secret agreement between past and present—messianic power to which the past has a claim."[87] History, or primary theory, is irrelevant unless it guides human action; philosophy, or secondary theory, is only relevant insofar as it is grounded in the concrete minutiae of experience—especially that experience left behind by the "progress" of history.

Critique of Benjamin

There is, however, a catch to Benjamin's attempt to fuse messianism with materialist history, to "read" the world theologically through traces of a deserted past. This catch has significant implications for a practical theory of myth. To be sure, Benjamin's investigation of the traditional or communal basis of experience should be credited with narrowing the abyss that separates the modern from the traditional world.[88] However, his connections between the archaic and the modern still depend upon an uncritical view of tradition and an uncritical view of the past. This view of the past takes both subtle and obvious forms. In "The Storyteller," cited above, Benjamin juxtaposes past-present and tradition-modernity in an idealized fashion. For example, Benjamin argues that with the onslaught of modernity and the control of the middle class, the art of storytelling lapses into the realm of the archaic; the era in which that "old co-ordination of hand, eye and soul" was possible has been replaced by the era of "information." As he puts it, such tale telling is a craft antithetical to the modern dissemination of information; storytellers such as Hebel "faced the technology of industrialization as a stranger."[89] There is no room for maneuvering across the hard lines Benjamin draws between utopian old and decadent new.

In his later essays, Benjamin does not juxtapose the utopian past with the decadent present in quite so obvious a fashion.[90] However, the realm of the "archaic" remains intact in these essays as well. In "Some Motifs in Baudelaire," Benjamin still views the past as redemptive and remote, or better, redemptive because remote. He asserts that it is the "data of prehistory" that restores Baudelaire; as Benjamin writes, "What makes festival days significant [for Baudelaire] is an encounter with an earlier life."[91] And, in a similar vein, Benjamin writes, "The further a wish reaches out in time, the greater its hopes for fulfillment."[92] Significance goes hand in hand with remoteness in time.

Given Benjamin's view of the past, one must wonder whether it is *only* the past which can possess these redemptive potentials. Is the present, modern age doomed never to receive the deposits of the promises of transcendence in Benjamin's mind? If that is the case, then Benjamin is reduced, like Eliade, to a hermeneutics of nostalgia.[93] Like many a Romantic and a neo-Romantic, his work becomes less a demystification of ideology than a rescuing of "failed semantic potentials" from the past in an attempt at redemptive critique. Benjamin knows that the present becomes the past, yet he does not grapple with the problem that then faces him: what does one make of the mythical wish-images *of the present* that will constitute the "memory" of the future?[94]

In view of this critique, a modification of Benjamin's approach to myth is necessary. The relationship between past and present needs to be reconfigured. The present is not the only time which must be criticized for forgetting; the past too consists of a number of former presents, themselves the agents of forgetting and erasure. Those worlds of the past—traditional societies—must not be privileged because of their remoteness. Like the present, they must be "read" with critical perspective. One must discern those forms of knowledge which claim transcendence; one must read for the mythologizations of language and imagery.

To put it in the terms set out in the introduction, a practical theory of myth must be fully grounded in all periods of human history; it must discern myth's relationship to human flourishing not only in the context of a critique of modernity, but also in terms of a critique of the so-called archaic. The mythic process, with its double movements of stagnation and change, has existed in other forms and in other contexts than that of the transition from the archaic to the modern. Each moment posits its own past, its own transitions, which erases and remembers just as vividly as those moments caught in the clutches of the present. With this view in mind, the mythic processes of "antiquity" can be subject to the same readings as the Paris arcades. Thus practical theory's aim to guide appreciation and action can be deepened.

The Myth of Various Callings: A Case Study

In the light of this analysis of Benjamin, one can derive a number of significant practices of reading which contribute to a practical theory of myth.[95] By focusing on the changes in the mythic process throughout history, one can avoid the danger of reifying myth into a "thing." As mentioned above, reading for a mythic process involves discerning the various strategies by which an object is made transcendent, becoming a sanctioned norm or explanation for human behavior. While this practice of reading can and should include social and political forms of culture, it can also focus on textual forms—the mythic process as it appears through textual conversations. Since Benjamin presents a dialectic in his breaking apart *and,* at the same time, rescuing myth in its formation of experience, one can configure the practice of reading myths in some new ways. Following Benjamin, one can break apart the transcendence of myth by linking mythical and socioeconomic concerns; without "reducing" myth to money or money to myth, one can show the ways in which both are bound up in promises of utopia and abundance. On the other side of the dialectic, Benjamin's concentration on the concrete minutiae of experience allows the reader to recover the material quality of myth. Through this recovery, one can discern myth's capacity to relativize transcendent claims and suggest social change.

In what follows I will give an example of this kind of practice of reading myth, showing the vicissitudes of the mythic process in its attitude toward social change. However, in order to underscore the necessity of breaking down Benjamin's problematic distinction between the modern and the archaic, I have chosen a remote textual tradition, that of the *Ṛg-Veda* (RV; c. 1200 BCE) and its related commentaries. I will show how one particular hymn contained within the *Ṛg-Veda,* a hymn to Soma, undergoes a process of transcendentalization in the evolution of Vedic commentary. I will go on to discuss how one of the main images used in that process—the motif of the drought—is used in other, later texts to complicate that transcendence. While all of the texts I will examine are highly brahminical in their outlook, one can read the process of erasure while the history of the victors is composed, as well as read intimations of social change that relativize that history.

Transcendentalizing Brahmins' Work: Myths of the Drought I

Before discussing the Ṛg-Vedic hymn in detail, a word about Vedic sacrifice is in order. As has been exhaustively demonstrated, for the Vedic Aryan, sacrifice is the primary means of producing knowledge in the form of an eloquent and efficacious *mantra,* or verse. Such knowledge, when uttered in an appropriately performed ritual, in turn produced wealth—in the form of cows, gold, rain, fertility, and long life. As J. C. Heesterman puts it, "Vedic ritual, as transcendent injunction, can only be devoted to the maintenance of a static, unchanging order of the universe. . . . It should keep up a constant, uninterrupted circulation between men and gods, earth and heaven. The burnt offering goes upward to heaven whence it comes down again in the form of rain."[96] Transcendent injunction is that knowledge which automatically produces wealth, or wealth-giving elements, such as rain, in an "unbroken order based on automatic reciprocity."

Thus, in the light of a Benjamin-derived practice of reading myth, one might say that the myths which give the sacrifice its means of claiming transcendence are directly related to practical, economic concerns. The assertion of the supreme efficacy of the sacrifice is also seen to be the means of producing wealth; if one sacrifices, one gains wealth in the forms of gold, cattle, and sons. Even more basically, an explicit link is made between the transcendent power of the sacrifice and the social prestige of those who perform it, the brahmin priests. While the sacrifice itself may not remain the only form of transcendent power in Indian religions, the link between brahmin status and transcendence remains intact, becoming solidified and codified over the next millennium.

The Ṛg-Vedic hymn to Soma celebrates the various means of producing the Vedic wealth referred to above. The hymn is from the ninth book of the *Ṛg-Veda,* a comparatively late book, whose hymns are thought by most scholars to have been gathered for ritual reasons at a time when the sacrificial cult was well solidified. Its verses compare the brahmin priest who crushes the Soma, the intoxicating source of wisdom and eloquence in the Vedic sacrifice, to a number of other kinds of wealth seekers:

> Our thoughts bring us to various callings, setting people apart: the carpenter seeks what is broken, the physician a fracture; and the Brahmin priest seeks one who presses

Soma. O, Drop of Soma, flow for Indra. With his dried
twigs, with feathers of large birds, and with stones, the
smith seeks all his days a man with gold. O drop of Soma,
flow for Indra. I am a poet; my Dad is a physician and
Mum a miller with grinding stones. With diverse thoughts,
we all strive for wealth, pursuing it like cattle. O drop of
Soma, flow for Indra. The harnessed horse longs for a light
cart; seducers long for a woman's smile; the penis for two
hairy lips, and the frog for water. O drop of Soma, flow for
Indra. (RV 9.112)[97]

As many Vedic scholars have remarked, the hymn is both
worldly and ironic, suggesting that amongst all the diverse oc-
cupations in early India, wealth is always the object. Just as the
harnessed horse longs for a light cart and the frog for water, so
too the smith seeks all his days for a man with gold and the
sacrificer longs for a generous patron.

As it appears above, this song is not a full-fledged narrative; its mythic aspects reside in the means by which the images of Soma are invested with extraordinary power. Some
have interpreted the hymn as a "working song" for those who
are pressing and crushing the Soma to prepare it as a drink in
the sacrifice. More specifically, it belongs to a group of hymns
dedicated to Soma Pavamana, or "Soma in the process of clarification." Most likely, these songs were sung during a rudi-
mentary form of the *agniṣṭoma,* the basic Soma ritual. While
the hymns themselves give little indication as to what the actual procedure must have been, the Sutra literature gives us a
detailed description of the later form of such rites.[98] After the
sacrificer was consecrated, the stalks of Soma were ceremoni-
ously bought and conveyed to the sacrificial arena; the juice
was then pressed from the Soma, offered to the fire, and consumed by the officiants at the ritual. These ritual acts were
repeated in the morning, at midday, and in the evening. Longer
Soma rituals were usually reserved for rare occasions, such as
the royal consecration *(rājasūya)* and the horse sacrifice
(aśvamedha). (The sexual connotations of the third verse of
RV 9.112 may well be a reference to the ritual copulation that
accompanied the *aśvamedha,* a sacrifice also well known for

its power to demonstrate the prestige and political power of its patron.)

Despite the hymn's deep embeddedness within the *agniṣṭoma* tradition, however, the poets of *RV* 9.112 and other Soma Pavamana hymns are not primarily concerned with the ritual details of pressing; instead they revel in describing the physical act of pressing the stalks. Such hymns reveal what Benjamin might call the material quality of the mythic image— the physical changes of the Soma stalk as it is being crushed, the comparison between the sound of the mortar and the kettle-drum, and so on. Like Benjamin's micrological technique of concentration on the minute, the Vedic poets illuminate the simple process of crushing a plant by a series of detailed descriptions and metaphors.

The descriptions used in *RV* 9.112 are not only suggestive of the kind of material imagination that Benjamin discusses. Like much of Benjamin's description of nineteenth-century phantasmagoria, the hymn also uses images which call to mind the labor that produced the object. The carpenter searching for what is broken, the physician looking for a fracture, and even the seducer seeking a woman's smile are all forms of work. On at least one level, the hymn seems to celebrate all forms of human labor, not ranking them in a hierarchical fashion but juxtaposing them creatively. Indeed, in much of early Vedic literature the practice of the poets is compared to the specialized skill of the artisans or manual laborers, such as cartwrights, weavers, and carpenters.[99]

While such a reading is tempting, and quite consonant with Benjamin's material imagination, it would not tell the whole story. Despite *RV* 9.112's delightful celebration of diversity, the hymn is not recovering the memory of those vanquished by history. On the contrary, the song is engaged in claiming transcendence. According to the practice of reading outlined above, one can see how the hymn assumes a kind of practical theory, whereby human action is guided toward the goal of material abundance, achieved by participation in the transcendent sphere of the sacrifice. In this hymn, the pounding of the Soma, the production of knowledge about the sacrifice, and the production of wealth are all inextricably connected. Pounded Soma causes an intoxicated state of mind that gives eloquence to the *mantras,* or verses, spoken in the sacrifice. In turn, the eloquent *mantra,* with the help of the intoxicating Soma, allows for the smooth execution of the sacrifice. The properly performed sacrifice will lead to the god Indra's satisfaction and subsequently to the production of wealth, usually in the form of gold and cattle.

Moreover, as Benjamin observes of the diverse commodities of the Paris arcades, utopian wish-imagery often masks the division and alienation of labor. Utopian wish-imagery of wealth is clearly present in these sacrificial *mantras,* and indeed the sacrifice also involves the division and alienation of labor. While *Ṛg-Veda* 9.112 explicitly celebrates the fact that the crushing of Soma promises a perfect abundance of wealth, the first verse is equally unambiguous: the various means of producing wealth "set people apart" *(nānānam jananām).* Implicitly, the priests' crushing of Soma is seen to be the most appropriate and effective means of gaining gold and cattle, "set apart" from other means. The implication is that the priestly *varṇa* (social class) produces more and better abundance.

Thus, in true Benjaminian form, the mythic images of *Ṛg-Veda* 9.112 are quite ambiguous. While the hymn ostensibly keeps the sacrifical system of priestly privilege in place, such claims are relativized by the comparisons between forms of labor. The Soma crushing, with all of its wealth-giving potential, is consistently compared to other means of the production of wealth-giving knowledge, such as that of the smith, the carpenter, and the physician. Even more explicitly, the priestly poet's parents are a miller and a doctor—people who make a living quite differently from the traditional brahminical roles. Thus, the hymn has a double thrust. The practice of reading suggests that while *Ṛg-Veda* 9.112 is imbued with elitist claims about the transcendence of sacrificial labor, its images also contain a suggestive materiality, comparing the sacrifice to other, less elite forms of productivity.

This reading of *Ṛg-Veda* 9.112 is not simply the product of a twentieth-century author with a taste for ambiguity. A practice of reading such as the one above assumes that a myth has its own history and that the history itself is quite revealing. Vedic commentators picked up on such a double message seven and eight hundred years after the hymn was probably composed, precisely during the period in which brahminical norms were being consolidated and codified.[100] Because of its hinting at the admixture of *varṇas* in certain forms of labor, this hymn made such later commentators exceedingly nervous.

Thus Yāska, the author of the *Nirukta,* a brahminical etymological dictionary of the fifth century BCE, introduces the hymn with the following scenario: "Indra asked the seers, 'How does one live in famine?' One of them answered, 'Nine are the means of livelihood in famine: a cart, a field, cows, agriculture, still water, a wood, the sea, a mountain, a king; so we live.' This verse is explained by the mere reading of it."[101] This introduction of the conversation between the god Indra and the poets entirely changes the meaning of *Ṛg-Veda* 9.112. The list of objects that the seers give in response to Indra's question are presumably metonymic symbols for the means of labor themselves— "a cart" implying some kind of marketing; "a field" meaning some form of farming; "the sea" involving some kind of fishing; "a king" connoting the acceptance of gifts from royalty, and so on. These various means of making a living are listed as comparable to, and indeed an introduction for, the various means that are encountered in the hymn itself.

More important, the practical theory implied in *Ṛg-Veda* 9.112 is made even more explicit. The added scenario implies that it is not simply diversity that accounts for the various ways in which human beings long for wealth—famine must be the attenuating circumstance in which priests would choose a way of making a living other than their appropriate brahminical role. If famine is present, then those other means of earning a living are justified. In Yāska's view, the hymn intimates that even priestly seers might live in ways which are appropriate only to other *varṇas*; thus, Indra's question must be inserted in order to justify such possible comparisons. For Yāska, the "miller mother" and the "physician father" are understandable only in the context of famine.[102] Thus, in the light of a practice of reading, one can see the process of erasure at work. In this new interpretation of the hymn, all of the hymn's suggestive materiality is forgotten. The diversity of labor, the common production of wealth, and the direct relationship suggested between priests and members of lesser *varṇa*s are all ignored for the sake of the establishment of brahminical purity.

Several hundred years later (first to fifth centuries CE), the commentary of the *Bṛhaddevatā* embarks upon a more elaborate treatment of the same theme. It introduces *Ṛg-Veda* 9.112 with a story of a drought—an emergency situation likely to produce famine. Indra asks the same question, and the same answer is given by the seers. However, the scenario serves an additional function; it explains how the entire ninth book of the *Ṛg-Veda*, the *maṇḍala* to Pāvamāna, or Soma,[103] was composed:

> While a drought was occurring, the Lord of Śaci [Indra] asked the *ṛṣis*, "In this great time of distress, by what action do you live?" "A cart, a field, cows, agriculture, still water, a wood, the sea, a mountain, a king; thus we live." Praising thus, the seer Śiśu, son of Aṅgiras, declared and recited to him with the hymn, *"Our thoughts bring us to various callings, setting people apart: the carpenter seeks what is broken, the physician a fracture; and the Brahmin priest seeks one who presses Soma. O, Drop of Soma, flow for Indra. With his dried twigs, with feathers of large birds, and with stones, the smith seeks all his days a man with gold. O drop of Soma, flow for Indra. I am a poet; my Dad is a physician and Mum a miller with grinding stones. With diverse thoughts we all strive for wealth, going after it like cattle. O drop of Soma, flow for Indra. The harnessed horse longs for a light cart; seducers long for a woman's smile; the penis for two hairy lips, and the frog for water. O drop of Soma, flow for Indra,"* (RV 9.112) in the presence of the *ṛṣis*. Indra said to all of them, "Perform great *tapas*. This distress cannot be removed without penance." Then all of them performed *tapas*, wanting to win heaven. Then, as a result of the *tapas*, they spoke verses belonging to Pāvamāna. (*BD* 6.137–46)[104]

While the *Bṛhaddevatā*'s insertion of an introduction is similar to the *Nirukta*'s,[105] the brahminical agenda—its practical theory—is even clearer in this commentary than its earlier counterpart in the *Nirukta*. The drought causes the seers, the brahmin priests, to "live in various ways" and thereby pollute themselves. At the end of the hymn Indra commands them to perform great *tapas*, or asceticism. The *tapas* leads them to recite the "*mantra*s to Pāvamāna"—the purificatory *mantra*s that rid them of the uncleanliness brought on by the actions they were forced to perform due to the drought. The *Bṛhaddevatā* is thus engaged in an even more thorough process of erasure and forgetting than the earlier text, the *Nirukta*. Benjamin's reading of myth as the "doom of eternal recurrence" is intact; brahmins will always remain pure, and in this case, the Vedic seers as brahmins are even given the means to do so by virtue of their purificatory *tapas*.

These brief passages from the *Bṛhaddevatā* and the *Nirukta* are short meditations upon what was later to be termed *apad dharma*—the *dharma* of emergencies. The myth of the drought, prevalent since even the earliest times, is used to justify the offensive variety of the means of labor. The extreme aspect of this mythic process can be seen in *The Laws of Manu*, where ways of making a living in such extremities are not merely suggested, but rigidly codified. Challenged by orthodox renouncers in their own tradition, as well as Buddhists and Jains gaining political patronage, the authors of *Manu*, compiling in the first few centuries BCE, can leave no room for ambiguity:

> If priests who are Vedic graduates are fainting [with hunger] for want of base metals or money, they should ask the king, and if he does not want to give anything he should be rejected. Accepting an untilled field is not as much a fault as accepting a tilled one; a cow, a goat, a sheep, gold, grain and cooked food—each is less of a fault to accept than the one that follows it. There are seven ways of obtaining property in accordance with the law: inheriting, finding, buying, conquering, investing, working and accepting from good people. Sharing knowledge, handicrafts, working for wages, service, tending livestock, marketing, farming, being supported, begging for alms, and lending money are ten ways of making a living. (10.116)[106]

As the commentators on this text put it, these ten ways of making a living are understood to be appropriate only in times of distress. The commentators further specify that the knowledge imparted by brahmins during this time might not always be Vedic, but includes logic, exorcisms, magic spells, etc.[107] Thus, diverse labor is not a hypothetical possibility in the case of distress but is strictly delineated as the only allowable means of making a living in the time of distress. Brahmins have become eternally pure, their speculative musings replaced by strict rules of exigency. *The Laws of Manu* are practical theories made into an elaborate science.

Relativizing Brahmins' Work: Myths of the Drought II

There is another aspect to this mythic process; myths, acting as practical theories, can challenge exclusive claims to transcendence as well as support them. The Ṛg Vedic notion of "various means of making a living" may well have been rendered acceptable by the prevailing brahminical ideology, through the addition of the myth of "exigency"—drought, famine, or other disaster. Yet the very conditions of "exigency" give rise to another possibility as well—that of relativizing established social relationships. Indeed, in many of the epics and the *Purāṇas* of later, classical Hinduism, the myths of drought provide occasions for the contemplation of a social order other than that which has been claimed as transcendent.

Like *The Laws of Manu,* the *Mahābhārata* epic organizes itself around a system not of sacrifice, but of social *dharma.* While it is in conformity with the growing brahminical ideology, it is unlike the Vedic commentaries in that it is less closely interwoven with the ideal ritual practice and learning of the Vedic tradition. Also unlike the Vedic tradition, during the time of the epic's compilation (c. fourth century BCE to fourth century CE), folklore tended to find its way into the text more freely than occurred with previous texts.

It is in all likelihood due to this fluidity that the *Mahābhārata* tells a different kind of myth of the drought. An example from the *Mahābhārata* (12.139.13–92) illustrates this clearly:

> Once there was a twelve year drought, when Indra sent no
> rain. All *dharma* was destroyed and people ate one an-
> other. The great sage Viśvamitra came to a place inhabited
> by outcastes who ate dogs; seeing a dead dog, he tried to
> steal it, reasoning that theft was permissible in time of ex-
> tremity. An outcaste tried to stop him from committing the
> sin of eating a dog, but in vain. Viśvamitra ate the rump of
> the dog and burned away his sin by performing asceticism,
> and eventually Indra sent rain.

Some reversal of social role is evident here, where the sage is
being instructed by the outcaste. And, in the light of Benjamin's
analysis above, it is no accident that it is in the sensual, bodily
act of eating that such a reversal of roles takes place. True to the
spirit of Benjamin's concept of *Eingedenken,* it is the physical
act of eating that "calls to mind" the one who is traditionally
forgotten—the outcaste. While untouchables play absolutely no
role in the texts of the Vedic commentators except as the subject
of passing references, here they possess a voice, albeit one dis-
torted by the twice-born ideology of the *Mahābhārata.*

Another example of such relativization occurs in the
Mahābhārata story of Arundhatī, the perfect wife.[108] During a
drought, the seven sages depart to perform asceticism in order to
procure rain. Siva, in the shape of a brahmin, revealed himself to
Arundhatī and begged for food. As she had no food but jujube
fruit, she cooked that for him for twelve years. Finally the rain
came and the seven sages returned. Siva revealed his true identity and declared Arundhatī's powers of asceticism to be stronger
than the sages' and rewarded her accordingly. While this story is
a classical epic story about the perfect wife, its point is made by
relativizing the power of the ascetic. The domestic wife in the
kitchen is seen to be more powerful than the seven sages, the
esteemed and venerable founders of the Vedic tradition.

It is important to be very clear here. It would be highly
inaccurate to claim that, because the untouchable has entered
the picture, the text becomes the stuff of revolution. Indeed,
such myths of reversal often end by perpetuating the ideology
of caste exclusion. As David White has argued of the story of
Viśvamitra and the untouchable told above, the orthodox ideol-

ogy ultimately reasserts itself by making the untouchable wrong even when he is right and the brahmin right even when he is wrong. It is the brahmin, and not the untouchable, who procures rain by burning away his sin by asceticism. So, too, the story of Arundhatī is one among many in the *Mahābhārata* that extols the virtues of the women who uphold *dharma* at great expense to themselves. But here again the social order is upheld even in a narrative whose expressed purpose is to relativize that order.[109]

Yet even while revolution remains an improbable category within such stories, the process of relativization nonetheless remains. The social order presented in such texts is certainly less transcendent than in myths where it is unequivocally asserted. Moreover, one finds myths of drought where it is quite unclear as to whether the brahmin is always right and the untouchable wrong. The Purāṇic texts go even farther than the epics in this regard. As is well known, the *Purāṇas* make more extensive use of the *bhakti* motif, whereby salvation is often a function of the power of devotion rather than of social status, making a less ambivalent relativization of social hierarchy possible.

One mythic episode, told in various versions[110] in the *Viṣṇu, Brahma* and *Devībhāgavāta Purāṇas,* provides an example. The comparatively late text of the *Devībhāgavāta Purāṇa* (c. 800–1100 CE)[111] tells the following story: In the midst of a drought, Triśanku asks the brahmin sage Vasiṣṭha to send him bodily to heaven, where he can dwell with the nymphs and hear the sweet songs of the gods. When Vasiṣṭha refuses, Triśanku declares that he will find a priest who will help him. Vasiṣṭha loses his temper and curses the king to become an untouchable dog cooker. Triśanku is transformed immediately into an untouchable and, knowing his foul-smelling body to be repulsive, remains on the banks of the Ganges apart from his family. Meanwhile, the brahmin sage Viśvamitra, Vasiṣṭha's age-old rival, comes in hunger and asks Triśanku the untouchable to feed him some dog's flesh. The untouchable reminds him of the *dharma* of a brahmin not to eat meat, and at that moment Indra sends rain. This small episode in a much larger story relativizes the social order even less equivocally than the epic tale of the dog cooker. Unlike the *Mahābhārata* version, in which the asceticism of the brahmin has the power to put an end to the drought, here the untouchable himself, by means of his admonition, forces Indra to send rain.

In sum, this study of the mythic process has taken some intriguing new directions, showing the process of transcendentalization and relativization at work. While *Ṛg-Veda* 9.112 comprises a celebration of the elite, Vedic sacrifice, its metaphorical language is suggestive enough of the mixture of social classes that the hymn must be reinterpreted in the context of a drought. The uncomfortable, socially disruptive suggestions are erased. This erasure is fully completed in the *Laws of Manu,* where options have become rules. The mythic process, whereby brahmins remain the transcendent, unsullied caretakers and producers of knowledge, remains intact. All suggestion of aberrant brahminical behavior is explained and codified. And yet the very fact of having to make a living, having to find food in the midst of exigency, contains the seeds for transformation of social relationships. This situation gives rise to the other side of the mythic process of relativization. One can see this process at work in a series of other, less brahminically oriented myths that play upon new possibilities for social relationship. The untouchable takes a place at the center of the story.

Conclusions

With the help of Benjamin's ideas, one can read the mythic process at work. In the specific context of early India, the images of drought and famine help to solidify transcendent claims about the sacrifice and brahminical power. The possibilities for human labor to extend across classes are erased. Yet in other texts, from the epics and *Purāṇas,* such claims become relativized by the same situation of drought and hunger that these earlier, concrete images presented. In such cases, authority is given to those untouchables and women whose labor is not traditionally valued. The mythic process involves suggestion and erasure in a number of different configurations. If one can read such a process in these texts, which are primarily the product of the Indian elite—the varṇas of brahmin and warrior—how much more might one read such a movement of myth in cultural forms produced by more radical socioreligious perspectives.[112]

More generally, in the practical theory of myth exemplified above, the reader of myth must acknowledge the ambiguity of the mythic process; myths can involve practical theories that are both reactionary and radical in nature. The mythic process has a double capacity to participate in the "history of the victors" as well as to draw upon material experience to relativize that history. A scholar's responsibility is to trace the points of liberation and repression in the historical life of any given mythical process. The practice of reading does not solve the debate between historians and philosophers of myth, but rather dis-solves it into a series of interpretive acts. The practical theorist of myth might act both as critic and as advocate, normatively and descriptively, without engaging in an increasingly uninteresting polemic against history, philosophy, or both.

Notes

1. I wish to thank Frank Reynolds, Francis X. Clooney, Joel Kovel, Gregory Alles, Ariel Glucklich, Wendy Doniger, Gary Ebersole, and Anthony Yu for their thoughtful comments on an earlier draft of this chapter.

2. For the more historical articulation of this view, see G. Widengren, "La méthode comparative: entre philologie et phénomènologie," *Numen* 18 (1971):161–72. See also "Some Remarks on the Methods of the Phenomenology of Religions," in *Acta Universitatis Upsaliensis* 17; Universitetet och Forskingen, 250–60.

3. R. D. Baird, *Category Formation and the History of Religions* (The Hague: Mouton, 1971), and his *Methodological Issues in the Study of Religion* (Chico, Calif.: New Horizons Press, 1975).

4. See Guilford Dudley, "Mircea Eliade: Anti-Historian of Religions," *Journal of the American Academy of Religion* 44 (1976):345–59.

5. See J. Z. Smith, *Imagining Religion* (Chicago: University of Chicago Press, 1982), and also his *To Take Place* (Chicago: University of Chicago Press, 1987).

6. Ivan Strenski, *Four Theories of Myth in the Twentieth Century* (Iowa City: University of Iowa Press, 1987).

7. Gregory Alles, "Wach, Eliade, and the Critique from Totality" *Numen* 35 (1988):108–38.

8. Ariel Glucklich, "Images and Symbols in the Phenomenology of *Dharma*," *History of Religions*, 29:3 (1990):259–85.

9. Ibid., 267.

10. J. Z. Smith, *To Take Place*, 17.

11. Strenski, *Four Theories*, 6–7.

12. Ibid., 2.

13. State University of New York Press, 1990. See particularly his discussion on pp. 175–82.

14. Robin Horton, "Tradition and Modernity Revisited," in M. Hollis and S. Lukes, eds., *Rationality and Relativism* (Cambridge, Mass.: MIT Press, 1982), 201–60.

15. Ibid., 178.

16. I must say at the outset that the intellectual practice of theory which does aim to construct a series of simple axioms is not one to be disparaged. Paul Griffiths in his essay, "Denaturalizing Discourse," provides a good example of how such theory works to benefit the study of religion.

17. A. Jensen, *Myth and Cult Among Primitive Peoples*.

18. Barthes, *Mythologies*, 117–21.

19. See Karl Marx, *Das Capital*, ch. 1; "Die 18te Brumaire des Louis Napoleon," *Die Revolution*, 1852.

20. Letter, Adorno to Benjamin, 2 August 1935, in Benjamin, *Gesammelte Schriften*. *(GS)* 6 vols., ed. Rolf Tiedemann and Hermann Schweppenhauser (Frankfurt: Suhrkamp, 1972–1988) 5:1128 ff.

21. Walter Benjamin, *GS* 5:213 ff.

22. Hannah Arendt, introduction to Benjamin's *Illuminations*, trans. Harry Zohn (New York: Schlocken Books, 1968), 34.

23. See Jurgen Habermas, "Walter Benjamin: Consciousness-Raising or Rescuing Critique," in Gary Smith, ed., *On Walter Benjamin* (Cambridge, Mass.: MIT Press, 1988), 90–128. For an evaluation of Habermas' attempt to integrate Benjamin's work into a progressive critique of society, see also Philip Brewster and Carl Buchner, "Language and Critique: Jurgen Habermas on Walter Benjamin," *New German Critique* 17 (Spring, 1979):15–29. Richard Wolin's work, *Walter Benjamin: An Aesthetics of Redemption,* adds that in addition to a theory of experience, Benjamin should be credited with rescuing an appreciation of tradition in the midst of a vociferous critique of industrialist culture (New York: Columbia University Press, 1982, 213 ff.).

24. Ibid.

25. In fact, although Benjamin was very close to Husserl in this regard, he objected to his transcendentalist leanings and was fond of claiming that he didn't understand him. (See Adorno, "An Introduction to Benjamin's Schriften," in *On Walter Benjamin* [Cambridge, Mass.: MIT Press, 1988], 7.)

26. See Henri Corbin, *Histoire de la Philosophie islamique* (Gallimard, 1964); *Creative Imagination in the Sufism of Ibn Arabi,* trans. Ralph Manheim (Princeton: Princeton University Press, 1969); *The Man of Light in Iranian Sufism* (Boulder and London: Shambala, 1979); *La Philosophie Iranienne Islamique aux XVII et XVIII siecles* (Paris: Buchet Chastel, 1981). Corbin's most articulate arguments against historicism are contained in later works, such as *The Concept of Comparative Philosophy,* trans. Peter Russell (Ipswich: Golgonooza Press, 1981); *Cyclical Time and Ismaili Gnosis* (London: Kegan Paul, 1983); *Temple and Contemplation,* trans. Philip Sherrard (London: Kegan Paul, 1986).

27. See Mircea Eliade, *Cosmos and History,* trans. Willard Trask (Princeton University Press, 1954); *Patterns in Comparative Religion,* trans. Rosemary Sheed (London and New York: Sheed and Ward, 1958); "Structures and Changes in the History of Religion," in *City Invincible* (Chicago: University of Chicago Press, 1960), 351–66; *Images and Symbols,* trans. Philip Mairet (Sheed, Andrews, and McMeel, 1961); "The New Humanism," in *The Quest* (Chicago: University of Chicago Press, 1975).

28. As mentioned by Adorno in "Introduction to Benjamin's Schriften," 1988, 6.

29. *GS* V:1086. For a full treatment of the dialectical image see Tiedemann, "Dialectics at a Standstill," in *On Walter Benjamin* (Cambridge, Mass.: MIT Press, 1988), 286. Also Irving Wolfarth, "Walter Benjamin's Image of Interpretation," *New German Critique* 17:70–98; Ackbar Abbas, "On Fascination: Walter Benjamin's Images," *New German Critique* 48 (1989):43–62; and, perhaps most

important, Susan Buck-Morss, *The Dialectics of Seeing: Walter Benjamin and the Arcades Project* (Cambridge, Mass.: MIT Press, 1989).

30. *Illuminations,* 83.

31. See Rolf Tiedemann, "Dialectics at a Standstill," in Gary Smith, *On Walter Benjamin,* 268.

32. This citation originates from an early fragment, "Uber die Wahrnehmung" (6:33–38); trans. Tiedemann (1989), 269.

33. *Briefe,* ed. Gershom Scholem and Theodor Adorno, vols. 1 and 2 (Frankfurt am Main: Suhrkamp Verlag), 526. For a full discussion of this central matter of Benjamin's Jewish philosophy, see James McBride, "Marooned in the Realm of the Profane: Walter Benjamin's Synthesis of Kabbalah and Communism," *JAAR* 57.2 (1989):241–66.

34. Benjamin, "Surrealism," in *Reflections,* trans. Edmund Jephcott, ed. Peter Demetz (New York: Schocken Books, 1978), 179.

35. Benjamin, *Illuminations,* 158.

36. In Benjamin, *Reflections,* 333–36.

37. *GS* 5:1053.

38. Benjamin, *Illuminations,* 262.

39. Ibid., 254.

40. Adorno, "Introduction," 12.

41. *GS* 5:490. This way of thinking might well be in line with Gregory Alles' (1988) recent criticisms of the Chicago School. Alles makes a case for a critical, extraverted, and historical methodology, with "event" as a "category that neither idolizes meaning nor dissolves it into that which it is not" (1988:25). Similar to "event" in Alles' work, the prudent and renovated use of "image" might move beyond the introversion of previous theorists—Wach's "flight from conflict" and Eliade's "meager comments on society."

42. Benjamin, *Illuminations,* 83–109.

43. Ibid., 95.

44. Ibid., 263–64.

45. Benjamin's ideas move in the opposite direction to other notions about the difference between chronicle and historical narrative. For example, Arthur Danto writes that "the chronicler cannot make use of such terms as *climax,*

crisis, turning point, he cannot use language like *anticipates;* he cannot mention first and last things (the "winter's heaviest snowfall" is an allowable
description only if it occurs on the last day of winter, a description which
incidentally does not make a claim on the future). A chronicle has the structure, finally, of a list, and though it is possible to find a degenerate set of
descriptions which do make reference to events which occur later than a given
extent—and hence still yields something little distinguishable from a list—we
would want narrative to make inter-referential connections of the sort we find
in stories" (1982:26).

46. Ibid., 91.

47. See Adorno, "Introduction," 11. Here, there is little risk of the category of
the "sacred" reifying and theologizing the study of myth.

48. See McBride, "Marooned," 247 ff.

49. Paul DeMan, *Allegories of Reading* (New Haven: Yale University Press,
1979), 78.

50. Carol Jacobs, *The Dissimulating Harmony: The Image of Interpretation in
Nietzsche, Rilke, Artaud, and Benjamin* (Baltimore: Johns Hopkins University
Press, 1978), 101 ff.

51. Cf. John Fekete, "Benjamin's Ambivalence," *Telos* 14.3, no. 49 (1978); Susan
Sontag, "The Last Intellectual," *New York Review of Books,* October 12, 1978.

52. As McBride also notes, the focus on the "mute, noumenal world of material reality" disrupts the teleological rhythms of progress with a constant pausing for breath. Benjamin compares this epistemological pausing to yoga, in
which the practitioner breathes in accordance with holy syllables. Such practice lifts the world of maya—defined in the context of modernist capitalism as
the world of the bourgeois philosopher. (See *One-Way Street and Other Writings,* trans. Edmund Jephcott and Kinglsey Shorter [New York: New Left
Books, 1970], 75; McBride, "Marooned," 248.)

53. Benjamin, *Illuminations,* 263.

54. See Winfried Menninghaus, "Walter Benjamin's Theory of Myth," in *On
Walter Benjamin* (Cambridge, Mass.: MIT Press, 1988), 292–325. See also his
Walter Benjamins Theorie der Sprachmagie (Frankfurt am Main: Suhrkamp
Verlag, 1980).

55. Benjamin writes of myth as having a wholly indifferent attitude toward
truth—not in the sense of detracting from it, as the Enlightenment perspective
might have it, but in the sense of having absolutely nothing to do with truth.

(See *GS* 1:162; Menninghaus, 296.) In his earlier essays, in fact, he writes of god and religion as being the critical antipodes of myth, whereas in later writings, such as the Elective Affinities Essay, the elements of myth on the one hand, and god and religion on the other, become less contrasted.

56. *GS* 5:178.

57. *GS* 1:137.

58. Benjamin, *Briefe*, ed. Gershom Scholem and Theodor Adorno (Frankfurt am Main: Suhrkamp Verlag, 1966), 407.

59. *GS* 1:1157.

60. Adorno, "Introduction," 7.

61. Benjamin, *The Origin of German Tragic Drama*, trans. John Osborne (London: New Left Books, 1977), 115. For a full discussion of the relationship of myth to modernity, see Samuel Weber, "Genealogy of Modernity: History, Myth and Allegory in Benjamin's *Origin of the German Mourning Play*," *Modern Language Notes* 106.3 (1991):465–500; Rainer Nagele, "Das Beben des Barock in der Moderne: Walter Benjamin's Monadologie," *ibid.*, 501–27.

62. Benjamin, *Origin*, 166.

63. Here, Benjamin directly contradicts Cassirer's transcendentalism found in his theory of symbolic forms. For both Creuzer and Benjamin, the symbol's temporal form is "momentary totality" and the temporal form of allegory is "progression in a series of moments," that is, chronological. Yet Benjamin disagrees with Creuzer that allegory can be a form of myth. Given Benjamin's historical emphasis, we can see the way in which he might turn Creuzer's definition upon its head.

64. For Corbin, allegory is an inferior form of symbolic discourse, a concealment of the interior by the exterior. It is surpassed by the hierophanic *Imago Templi*, because there spirit and body internally manifest themselves. Although the images might be different in *Ezekiel*, Philo, and the *Qmran*, they all lead to authentic interiority, whereby the logos as high priest in the spiritual macrocosm corresponds to the true man reborn in the soul. (See his *Temple*, 308.)

65. *GS* 5:1014.

66. In particular, see his "Berliner," "One-Way Street," and "Passagenwerk."

67. *GS* 5:576.

68. Menninghaus, "Theory of Myth," 323.

69. *GS* 5:134.

70. *GS* 5:86. For a full description and analysis of Benjamin's work on the arcades, see Susan Buck-Morss, *Dialectics,* ch. 4, "Mythic History: Fetish."

71. Buck-Morss, *Dialectics,* 83.

72. *GS* 5:645.

73. "N [Theories of Knowledge, Theories of Progress]," trans. Leigh Hafrey and Richard Sieburth, *The Philosophical Forum* 15:1–2 (1983):1–40, sheafs 2a, 4. Cited in Tiedemann, "Dialectics," 280.

74. See Wolin, *Walter Benjamin,* 174.

75. 5:1224–25; translated by Buck-Morss, *Dialectics,* 115.

76. Benjamin cited Marx's *Capital* in *GS* 5:217.

77. *GS* 5:139.

78. Buck-Morss, *Dialectics,* 117.

79. *GS* 5:998. Unlike recent theorists who blame visual "freezing" of the colonized "other" for all present ills in the study of religion, for Benjamin, contemplation as such, the visual image as such, is not a politically suspect means of interpretation. It is the ultimate interruption of the so-called continuum and progress of the history of the victors (or colonizers); it is capable of blasting open the belief in the "ongoing progress" of history (*Illuminations,* 253). In the light of Benjamin's remarks, Fabian and others are mistaken in equating "eternity" with "image" and with "imperialism." Fabian's otherwise subtle thought seems like a misguided attempt to find a single "key" to the problem of Western anthropological complicity in oppression of the other; it blames one "sense"— the visual—for all political ills. In the light of the above, Benjamin offers to students of religion a more historically and experientially grounded view of the term image. To begin with, his notion of "profane illumination" challenges recent critiques of the overly visual emphases in the study of religion as well as in anthropology. Anthropological writers such as Fabian (1983), Schivelbusch (1979), Tyler (1986), and others have launched various theoretical attacks on the notion of visual "freezing" as the basis for all anthropological imperialism in particular, and political and intellectual control in general. Fabian, for example, asserts that, beginning with the medieval writer Ramus, spatial metaphors have been the "frames" with which the West can encounter and control the "other," the "archaic world," the world of the primitive. He writes, "As long as anthro-

pology presents its object primarily as *seen*, [emphasis mine] as long as ethnographic knowledge is conceived primarily as observation and/or representation (in terms of models, symbol systems, and so forth), it is likely to persist in denying coevalness to its Other" (1983:151–52).

80. The same double thrust obtains for Benjamin's later ideas on the work of art. Wolin remarks that, in Benjamin's later works, such as "The Storyteller," "The Image of Proust," "The Mimetic Faculty," and "Some Motifs in Baudelaire," works of art receive full due as phenomena which are at once mediated and autonomous sources of knowledge in their own rights. As such they not only mirror ongoing social processes, but reorganized diffuse features of social life into an intelligible whole, and thereby present at the same time an independent perspective, polemically at the same matrix of social relations from which they organized (Wolin, *Walter Benjamin,* 215–16).

81. Menninghaus, *Theory of Myth,* 315.

82. Even the "aesthetic" or "formal" connotations of the term "image" need not be construed as ahistorical. As Terry Eagleton writes in his *Ideology of the Aesthetic,* "The aesthetic is at once . . . the very secret prototype of human subjectivity in early capitalist society, and a vision of human energies as radical ends in themselves which is the implacable enemy of all dominative or instrumentalist thought. It signifies a creative turn to the sensuous body, as well as an inscribing of that body with a subtly oppressive law; it represents on the one hand a liberatory concern with concrete particularity, and on the other hand a specious form of universalism. . . . Any account of this amphibious concept which either uncritically celebrates or unequivocally denounces it is thus likely to overlook its real historical complexity" ([Oxford: Basil Blackwell, 1989], 9). The same could be said of the term *myth* in the study of religions.

83. As Adorno puts it, disappointment is inevitable if one seeks results from Benjamin's thought; it satisfies only one who broods over it long enough to find out what inheres in it; " 'Then one night, it comes alive' as in George's Tapestry" (Introduction, 13). Cf. Stefan George, "The Tapestry of Life," in *The Works of Stefan George,* trans. O. Marx and E. Morwitz (Chapel Hill: University of North Carolina Press, 1974), 185.

84. Ian Balfour, "Reversal, Quotation (Benjamin's History)," *Modern Language Notes* 106.3 (1991):622–47. As Balfour also comments, this assertion is not to say that Benjamin reduces the acting and writing of history to reading, because no reduction is involved, except for those who think language is trivial (647). Analogous to reading, Benjamin writes of a kind of meditation: "The themes which monastic discipline assigned to friars for meditation were

designed to turn them away from the world and its affairs. The thoughts which we are developing here develop from similar considerations" (*Illuminations,* 258). When the politicians turn away from the world, that is to say, from their stubborn faith in progress, they will encounter a history other than that of the victors.

85. See McBride's discussion, in "Marooned," 262–63.

86. Rolf Tiedemann's critique: the "method" of the dialectical image cannot find a crack and extend beyond the immanent context of society in which it originates; it cannot transcend the standstill of society. It must instead critically reflect on its own position in a coercively organized society. Adorno feels that dialectical images are fine for redeeming forgotten or misunderstood literary texts, but not for the sphere of social life itself. Because dialectical images are not social products, but constellations in which the social situation represents itself, no ideological or social accomplishment can ever be expected of dialectical image (see Wolin, 182).

87. Benjamin, *Illuminations,* 254.

88. Wolin, *Walter Benjamin,* 217.

89. Benjamin, *Illuminations,* 92.

90. Wolin, *Walter Benjamin,* 226.

91. Ibid., 182.

92. Ibid., 179.

93. See Frederic Jameson, *Marxism and Form* (Princeton: Princeton University Press, 1971), 60 ff.

94. In a related way, Benjamin's idea of the "collective image-making capacity" also turns out to be problematic. Most probably, Benjamin adopts this category in order to transcend the individualistic bias of the surrealists. To him, placing the image within the collective subject would politicize the image even further. However, as Adorno comments, by positing a mythical collective subject, one masks the actual historical relations of inequality and suffering which lead to commodity fetishism. Jung and Klages succumb to the mythologization of history through an appeal to ultimately illusory archetypal images of the archaic past. Through Benjamin's ideas of a "cultural memory reservoir" and a "collective imagination" which can serve to awaken the modern world from its mythical fetishes, he too posits a pristine collective ego which is ultimately illusory. See Wolin's discussion in *Walter Benjamin,* 180.

95. A number of other practices of reading are also implied here. Benjamin's thought can also add a historical dimension to recent cognitivist theories of religious imagery. Cognitive scientists such as George Lakoff (*Women, Fire and Dangerous Things* [University of Chicago Press, 1987]), Mark Johnson (*Metaphors We Live By* [University of Chicago Press, 1980]); *The Body in the Mind* [University of Chicago Press, 1988]), Eleanor Rosch ("Human Categorization," 1977; "Principles of Categorization," 1978), and others claim that much of human language is grounded in the concrete experience of the body. Basic-level metaphors, called "image schemata" (in/out, up/down, etc.) derive from such bodily perceptions. These "image schemata" provide the structure of much of language's more sophisticated metaphorical forms. While the cognitivist emphasis on bodily experience is an important new direction in the analysis of culturally and religiously significant images, Benjamin also demonstrates that images can be used not only to illuminate the cognitive states of the individual, but also to examine the dynamics of social change. To be sure, the straightforward claim that religious images should be analyzed according to their social and historical connotations is not new. Among others, J. Z. Smith, in his essay, "The Effect of Symbols upon Social Change" (1978), makes a similar point. Implicit in such work is the idea that images have a great deal to do with social perspectives and could indeed contribute to the work of history—the tracing of events. In an essay in the same volume, "Birth Upside Down or Right Side Up?" (122–147), Smith goes on to demonstrate a particular case, examining the ways in which the image of upside-down posture has signified both an "unnatural" state of affairs and a deliberate reversal of the social order in the *Acts of Peter.*

96. J. C. Heesterman, *The Inner Conflict of Tradition* (Chicago: University of Chicago Press, 1985), 88.

97. Wendy O'Flaherty, *The Rig Veda* (Harmondsworth: Penguin, 1981), 235, translation modified.

98. See W. Caland and V. Henry, *L'agnistoma,* and Jan Gonda, *The Ritual Sutras,* 468–69.

99. See *RV* 5.2.11; 1.61.4; 1.130.6; 3.38.1, etc. Also see Gonda, *Vedic Literature,* 73.

100. See Sheldon Pollock's "Mīmāṃsa and the Problem of History in India," *Journal of the America Oriental Society* 109.4 (1989):603–10.

101. *Nirukta* 6.5. See *The Nighaṇṭu and the Nirukta: The Oldest Indian Treatise on Etymology, Philology, and Semantics, Critically Edited from Original Manuscripts and Translated by Lakshman Sarup* (London and New York: Oxford University Press, 1920–27).

102. A later commentator on this text, Durga does not comment on the question of Indra to the ṛṣis, but he does comment on another hymn, *RV* 1.70.1. He considers the following phrase from that hymn: "another is not to be introduced." He explains that "another" must mean a low-caste man, who lives *in various ways* and is not to be brought into the assembly of the good. Presumably, these who "live in various ways" are offensive in the same way that the unmodified Ṛg-Vedic verse is.

103. Many scholars have noticed its obviously "un-Vedic" character. Cf. Geldner, *Indische Studien* 2:158, *Manu* 10.116, and *Yajñavalkyah* 3.42.

104. See *The Bṛhaddevatā*, ed. and trans. Arthur Anthony Macdonell, 2 vols., Harvard Oriental Series (Cambridge, Mass.: Harvard University Press, 1904), 2:145. The translation is my own.

105. Scholars have debated whether this introduction is a slightly later interpolation in the cases of both texts, due to the fact that Indra's question is omitted by many manuscripts and it has more in common with passages from *Manu* 10.116 *(daśajīvanahetavaḥ)* and *Yajñavalkya* 3.42 *(āpattau jīvanāni)*. Even if one ascribes a later date to the passage, placing it contemporary with *Manu,* the process of transcendentalization is still clear.

106. See *Laws of Manu,* trans. Wendy Doniger with Brian K. Smith (New York: Penguin, 1991), 249, translation modified. Also see L. Sternbach, *Mānavadharmaśāstra* (Varanasi: All India Kashiraj Trust, 1974).

107. Ibid.

108. *Mahābhārata* 9.47.37–51.

109. David White, *Myths of the Dog-Man* (Chicago: University of Chicago Press, 1991), 78.

110. *DBh* 10.1–58; 7.11.1–53; 12.1–64; 7.13.1–62; 7.14.1–23; Cf. *Visnu* 4.3.14 and *Harivamśa* 9–10. In the *Viṣṇu,* Triśanku is cursed to become an outcaste. He nonetheless provides the flesh of a deer for the sage Viśvamitra, spreading the food on the branches of trees by the banks of the Ganges so that the sage will not have to undergo the indignity of accepting food from an untouchable.

111. See Ludo Rocher, *The Purāṇas* (Wiesbaden: Otto Harrassowitz, 1986), 166, for a discussion of the date of the *Devībhāgavata*. Rocher thinks that the final form of the text was probably no later than the eleventh century CE.

112. Indeed, the next stage in this project would be to trace the usage of the drought motif in the literature of such movements throughout Indian history, such as *bhakti* and religiously based resistance movements.

References

Selected Sanskrit Texts

Brahma Purāṇa. 1895. Edited by H. N. Apte. Ānandāśrama Sanskrit Series 28. Poona: Ānandāśrama.

Bṛhaddevatā. 1893. Edited by Rajendralala Mitra. Bibliotheca Indica Sanskrit Series, nos. 722, 760, 794, and 819 (new series). Calcutta: Baptist Mission Press.

———. 1904. Edited and translated by Arthur Anthony Macdonell. 2 vols. Harvard Oriental Series. Cambridge: Harvard University Press.

The Mahābhārata. 1933–60. Edited by Visnu S. Sukthankar. 19 vols. Poona: Bhandarkar Oriental Research Institute.

———. 1973–78. Edited and translated by J. A. B. Van Buitenen. 3 vols. Chicago: University of Chicago Press.

Manu Smṛti. 1886. Translated by George Bühler. *Sacred Books of the East.* Oxford: Clarendon Press; reprint ed., New York: Dover Publications, 1969.

———. 1972–82. Edited by J. H. Dave. 5 vols. Bhāraitīya Vidyā Series. Bombay: Bhāratīya Vidyā Bhavan.

———. 1991. Translated by Wendy Doniger with Brian Smith. New York: Penguin.

Yāska's Nirukta *with Durga's Commentary.* 1918. Edited by H. M. Bhadkamkar. 2 vols. Bombay Sanskrit and Prakrit Series, nos. 73 and 85. Bombay: Government Central Press.

The Nighaṇṭu and the Nirukta. 1920–27. Edited from Original Manuscripts and Translated by Lakṣman Sarup. London and New York: Oxford University Press.

Ṛg Veda Samhitā, together with the Commentary of Sāyana Āchārya. 1966. Edited by F. Max Müller. 4 vols. Varanasi: Chowkhamba Sanskrit Series.

Sarvānumkramaṇī, with Commentary of Ṣaḍguruśiṣya. 1886. Edited by Arthur Anthony Macdonell. Oxford: Clarendon Press.

Viṣṇu Purāṇa. 1840. Translated by H. H. Wilson. London: Oriental Translation Fund Committee; rep. Calcutta, 1972.

————. 1967. Bombay: Veṅkateśvara Press.

Secondary Sources

Abbas, Ackbar. 1989. "On Fascination: Walter Benjamin's Images." *New German Critique* 48:43–62.

Adorno, Theodor W. 1988. "An Introduction to Benjamin's Schriften." In *On Walter Benjamin.* Cambridge, Mass.: MIT Press.

Alles, Gregory. 1985. " 'When Men Revile You and Persecute You': Advice, Conflict, and Grace in Shinran and Luther." *History of Religions* 25.2:148–62.

————. 1988. "Wach, Eliade, and the Critique from Totality" *Numen* 35:108–38.

Baird, R. D. 1971. *Category Formation and the History of Religions.* The Hague: Mouton.

————. 1975. *Methodological Issues in the Study of Religion.* Chico, Calif.: New Horizons Press.

Balfour, Ian. 1991. "Reversal, Quotation (Benjamin's History)." *Modern Language Notes* 106.3:622–47.

Barthes, Roland. 1972. *Mythologies.* Translated by Jonathan Cape, Ltd. New York: Noonday Press.

Benjamin, Walter. 1968. *Reflections.* Translated by Edmund Jephcott. New York: Schlocken Books.

————. 1970. *One Way Street and Other Writings.* Translated by Edmund Jephcott and Kingsley Shorter. London: New Left Books.

————. 1972–88. *Gesammelte Schriften.* 6 vols. Edited by Rolf Tiedemann and Hermann Schweppenhauser. Frankfurt: Suhrkamp.

————. 1977. *The Origin of German Tragic Drama.* Translated by John Osborne. London: New Left Books.

————. 1978. *Illuminations.* Translated by Harry Zohn. New York: Schlocken Books.

————. 1979. "Doctrine of the Similar." Translated by Knut Tarnowski. *New German Critique* 17:65–69.

Berger, Adriana. 1986. "Cultural Hermeneutics: The Concept of Imagination in the Phenomenological Approaches of Henry Corbin and Mircea Eliade." *Journal of Religion.* 66:141–56.

Buck-Morss, Susan. 1989. *The Dialectics of Seeing: Walter Benjamin and the Arcades Project.* Cambridge, Mass.: MIT Press.

Corbin, Henri. 1981. *The Concept of Comparative Philosophy.* Translated from the French by Peter Russell. Ipswich: Golgonooza Press.

———. 1986. *Temple and Contemplation.* Translated by Philip Sherrard. London: Kegan Paul.

Dange, Sadavshiv. 1969. *Legends in the* Mahābhārata, *With a Brief Survey of Folktales.* Delhi: Motilal Banarsidass.

Danto, Arthur. 1982. "Narration and Knowledge." *Philosophy and Literature* 6:17–33.

DeMan, Paul. 1979. *Allegories of Reading: Figural Language in Rousseau, Nietzsche, Rilke, and Proust.* New Haven: Yale University Press.

Doniger, Wendy, trans. 1991. *Laws of Manu.* New York: Penguin.

Dudley, Guilford. 1976. "Mircea Eliade: Anti-Historian of Religions." *Journal of the American Academy of Religion* 44:345–59.

Eagleton, Terry. 1981. *Walter Benjamin or Towards a New Criticism.* London: Verso and New Left Books.

———. 1989. *The Ideaology of Aesthetic.* Oxford: Basil Blackwell.

Eliade, Mircea. 1954. *Cosmos and History.* Translated by Willard Trask. Princeton: Princeton University Press.

———. 1958. *Patterns in Comparative Religion.* Translated by Rosemary Sheed. London and New York: Sheed and Ward.

———. 1975. "The New Humanism." In *The Quest.* Chicago and London: University of Chicago Press.

Fabian, Johannes. 1983. *Time and the Other.* New York: Columbia University Press.

Fekete, John. 1978. "Benjamin's Ambivalence." *Telos* 11.1, no. 35.

George, Stefan. 1974. "The Tapestry of Life." In *The Works of Stefan George,* translated by O. Marx and E. Morwitz. Chapel Hill: University of North Carolina Press.

Glucklich, Ariel. 1990. "Images and Symbols in the Phenomenology of *Dharma.*" *History of Religions* 29:3.259–85.

Gonda, Jan. 1977. *A History of Indian Literature.* Vol. 1, fasc. 2, *The Ritual Sūtras.* Wiesbaden: Otto Harrassowitz.

———. 1975. *A History of Indian Literature.* Vol. 1, fasc. 1, *Vedic Literature (Saṃhitās and Brāhmanas).* Wiesbaden: Otto Harrassowitz.

Habermas, Jurgen. 1979. "Consciousness Raising or Redemptive Criticism?" *New German Critique* 17:30–79.

Hultkrantz, Ake. 1974. "Über Religionsethnologische Methoden." In *Selbstverständnis und Wesen der Religionswissenschaft,* edited by G. Darmstadt, 360–93.

Jacobs, Carol. 1978. *The Dissimulating Harmony: The Image of Interpretation in Nietzsche, Rilke, Artuad, and Benjamin.* Baltimore: Johns Hopkins University Press.

Kitagawa, Joseph. 1985. *History of Religions: Retrospect and Prospect.* New York: Macmillan.

Kittsteiner, H. D. 1986. "Walter Benjamin's Historicism." *New German Critique* 39:179–218.

Lakoff, George. 1987. *Women, Fire and Dangerous Things.* Chicago: University of Chicago Press.

Lakoff, George and Mark Johnson. 1980. *Metaphors We Live By.* Chicago: University of Chicago Press.

McBride, James. 1989. "Marooned in the Realm of the Profane: Walter Benjamin's Synthesis of the Kabbalah and Communism." *Journal of the American Academy of Religion* 57.2:241–66.

Menninghaus, Winfried. 1982. *Walter Benjamins Theorie der Sprächmagie.* Frankfurt am Main: Suhrkamp Verlag.

———. 1988. "Walter Benjamin's Theory of Myth." In *On Walter Benjamin.* Cambridge, Mass.: MIT Press.

Nagele, Rainer. 1991. "Das Beben des Barock in der Moderne: Walter Benjamins Monadologie." *Modern Language Notes* 106.3:501–27.

O'Flaherty, Wendy. 1976. *Origins of Evil in Hindu Mythology.* Berkeley: University of California at Los Angeles Press.

———. 1981. *The Rig Veda.* Harmondsworth: Penguin Books, 1981.

Patton, Laurie. 1989. "Summary Report VI." In *Deconstructing/Reconstructing the Philosophy of Religions,* edited by Francisca C. Bantly. Chicago: The University of Chicago Divinity School.

Poole, Fitz John Porter. 1987. "Metaphors and Maps: Toward Comparison in the Anthropology of Religion." *Journal of the American Academy of Religion* 14:3.411–57.

Rabinbach, Anson. 1985. "Benjamin, Bloch, and Modern Jewish Messianism." *New German Critique* 34:78–124.

Rudolph, Kurt. 1973. "Das Problem der Autonomie und Integrität der Religionswissenschaft." *Nederlands Theologisch Tijdschrift* 27:105–31.

———. 1981. "Basic Positions of Religionswissenschaft." *Religion* 11:97–107.

Scholem, Gershom. 1981. *Walter Benjamin: The Story of a Friendship.* Translated from the German by Harry Zohn. Philadelphia: The Jewish Publication Society of America.

Sharpe, E. J. 1971. *Comparative Religion: A History.* London: Open Court.

Smith, Gary, ed. 1988. *On Walter Benjamin.* Cambridge, Mass.: MIT Press.

Smith, J. Z. 1982. *Imagining Religion.* Chicago: University of Chicago Press.

Sontag, Susan. 1978. "The Last Intellectual." *New York Review of Books,* October 12.

Strenski, Ivan. 1987. *Four Theories of Myth in the Twentieth Century.* Iowa: Iowa University Press.

Tiedemann, Rolf. 1988. "Dialectics at a Standstill." In *On Walter Benjamin.* Cambridge, Mass.: MIT Press.

Tokunaga, Muneo. 1981. "On the Recensions of the *Bṛhaddevatā.*" *Journal of the American Oriental Society* 101.3:275–86.

———. 1979. "The Text and Legends of the *Bṛhaddevatā.*" Ph.D. dissertation, Harvard University.

Weber, Samuel. 1991. "Genealogy of Modernity: History, Myth, and Allegory in Benjamin's Origin of the German Mourning Play." *Modern Language Notes* 106.3:465–500.

White, David Gordon. 1991. *Myths of the Dog-Man,* with a Foreword by Wendy Doniger. Chicago: University of Chicago Press, 1991.

Widengren, Geo. 1971. "La méthode comparative: entre philologie et phénomènologie." *Numen* 18:161–72.

Wohlfarth, Irving. 1979. "Walter Benjamin's Image of Interpretation." *New German Critique* 17:70–98.

———. 1986. "Refusing Theology: Benjamin's Arcades Project." *New German Critique* 39:3–24.

Wolin, Richard. 1982. *Walter Benjamin: An Aesthetic of Redemption.* New York: Columbia University Press.

Zuesse, Evan. 1985. "The Role of Intentionality in the Phenomenology of Religions." *Journal of the American Academy of Religion* 13:51–71.

Chapter 7

The Reason of Myth and the Rationality of History: The Logic of the Mythic in Bimin-Kuskusmin "Modes of Thought"

Fitz John Porter Poole

In the time of the great Afek[1] and the first ancestors,[2] and before the coming of suffering and death,[3] the 'center-place' *(abiip mutuuk)*[4] was a 'sacred time-place' *(aneng aiyem)* . . . joined to . . . the spine of . . . the ancestral underworld. . . . Men could then [more clearly] 'understand' *(khaim'khraak'khaanamin)*[5] . . . the 'sacred things' *(kokuu aiyem,* in reference to their concealed, secret meanings) that were revealed . . . in the sacred myths . . . , [for] these now secret and hidden and unknown things were then ordinary and everywhere . . . , on the surface of the center-place, . . . a part of everyday experience. . . . With the advent of suffering and death . . . , something 'unprecedented' *(kamaa'iniim nakaamiit*—literally, 'first winds from a new source') began to appear on the land, in the center-place. . . . Historical events began to appear like occasional earthquakes and landslides . . . , coming unexpectedly, changing the shape of long familiar things . . . , sometimes things that were 'sacred' *(aiyem)*. . . . Sometimes they left enduring scars on the bones of the center-place . . . ,[6] and then were known to be sacred. . . . Sometimes they were quickly enfolded by forest and garden, and no trace remained. . . . In the time of the first ancestors, the canopy of the sky—Afek's mantle—enveloped [both] the center-place and the ancestral underworld. . . .[7] Storms were gentle and short-lived . . . , bringing rain to forest, garden, and river . . . , bringing the roar of waterfalls and the radiance of rainbows. . . . Spider webs in the forest reflected the glow of phosphorus in secluded glades and the fire [mirrored] in the crystals of cult houses, lighting the spirit paths along which the ancestors traveled. . . .[8] Then came the first great time of darkness and the first appearance of the elder brother of the sun, and soon suffering and death. . . .[9] For a long, long time, the gradual weakening of the *finiik* 'spirit or life-force' of the ancestors did not severely erode the power of narrations of myth and performances of ritual. . . . , and the center-place was strong. . . . Then, in the terrible time of the great destruction, elaborate divinations revealed that the sacred strength was ebbing from the center-place . . . and from the spine of the ritual region. . . .[10] The ritual elders of all of the original clans of the center-place assembled to understand these divinations . . . , and then to shield the 'sacred things' (*muufak aiyem,* in reference to their embodiment as material *sacrae*) from further harm. . . . [11] Ever since that time . . . , we have tried to see the new winds . . . [that] now blow fiercely over the land with the wisdom, . . . through the eyes, . . . with the understanding, . . . of our great ancestors.

    —Trumeng, paramount ritual elder of the Imoranmin patrician and Kuskusmin ritual moiety

⚬⊙⚬

This chapter explores the nexus of 'sacred myth' *(aiyem sang)* and 'historical events' *(khaa'tebemaam)* as these phenomena are culturally constituted and socially instantiated in a genre of interpretive practice among the Bimin-Kuskusmin of the West Sepik interior of Papua New Guinea.[12] The analytic endeavor is centered on the explication of a mosaic of Bimin-Kuskusmin concepts in the context of such *praxis,* how that *praxis* and its conceptual frameworks are understood, and how they are subject to transformation in some re-imagination of the possibilities of both myth-centered interpretive and event-centered historical change.[13] Through such analysis, the immediate intent of the essay is to illuminate some of the shifting contours and foci of a folk model of the character and interpretive use of ideas of *history* and of *myth* in a particular non-Western, nonliterate, "traditional" society of Melanesia.[14] Thus, the emphasis of the essay is directed toward explicating Bimin-Kuskusmin perspectives on the character of the historical and the mythic.

The more fundamental concern, however, is to provoke attention to certain general problems of comparative analysis in the anthropology of religion(s) and in comparative and historical religious studies.[15] These problems of comparison focus not only on how some senses of *myth, history, reason,* and *praxis* are culturally framed and socially instantiated in particular interpretive efforts with respect to the notion of a "past" in a *religious tradition,* but also on how such seemingly enduring and often tacit cultural constructs and the conventions governing their social use—ultimately embedded in fundamental notions of mythic-ritual efficacy and, thus, of self, person, and agency[16]—are subjected, under certain circumstances, to self-conscious recognition, foregrounding, appraisal, criticism, and change.[17] Although largely in the background of the ethnographic focus, this comparative concern is implicit throughout the essay.

In an earlier analysis,[18] I sought to unravel something of the cultural character, ritual embeddedness, and social force of Bimin-Kuskusmin *mythologiques* in attending to certain qualities of sacredness, wisdom, sacred speech, ritual knowledge, interpretation, and meaning that variously inform how sacred myth is conceptualized in making sense of historical change. In this context, it was suggested that sacred myth is understood both as a portrait of ancestral designs in the shapes of enduring "tradition" and as a hermeneutic framework for comprehending certain orders of phenomena in relation to such traditional designs and, thus, is brought to bear upon the decipherment of historical events. Special attention was devoted to the complex role of metaphor and "analogical imagination" (in Tracy's phrase)[19] in the discourse and in the underlying cultural logic of Bimin-Kuskusmin mythic interpretations—both in general and in making local sense of selected aspects of the coming of the European to their region.[20] In this analysis, it was also noted that Bimin-Kuskusmin have recently developed a remarkably elaborate and ever-expanding corpus of exegesis on their *praxis* of mythic interpretation to an extent rare in Melanesia and exceptional even in the surrounding Mountain-Ok region, which is famed for its intricate exegetical traditions in most communities.[21] It was argued that this consensual effort to enhance and, in the process of enhancing, to reshape mythico-historical understanding—however still enfolded by enduring sociocultural beliefs about the imaginable trajectories of understanding such matters may be—constituted at least the rudiments of a significantly "philosophical" stance—at once critical, analytic, and synthetic in different respects.

In this complementary essay, however, I probe the nature of certain fundamental changes that are recognized by Bimin-Kuskusmin to have occurred relatively recently in Bimin-Kuskusmin history—changes that have significant entailments and consequences for transformations of a local perspective on the "epistemology" and "metaphysics" of sacred myth as constituting an interpretive framework for understanding historical events.[22] These changes, and local reactions to them, may underlie, at least in part, the marked efflorescence of Bimin-Kuskusmin interpretive endeavors and commentaries upon these efforts in recent times. The Bimin-Kuskusmin *praxis* of mythic interpretation appears to have confronted a moment of major crisis—the 'time of the great destruction' *(aneng daraata'koruun miitan)*—in the recent past. As a consequence, certain existential and epistemological assumptions are perceived by ritual elders of the community to have been fundamentally challenged, and a new vision of how best to interpret and otherwise to respond to the crisis is said to have begun to emerge. The self-conscious engagement with this crisis provoked a significant skepticism about past understandings of certain phenomena of the "human condition" (as locally construed) and a reconceptualization of the nature and relationship of sacred myth and historical events. Thus, the present essay focuses on a historical reconstruction of an ethno-historical account of changing conceptualizations of sacred myth and historical events—an analytically constructed history of an ethno-history of historical events perceived through the refocusing lenses of sacred myth.[23] The essay also attends to the ideological stakes and political maneuvers underlying and giving shape to these interpretive endeavors.[24]

The analysis is guided by a fundamental concern to expose not only something of the ways in which certain aspects of the conceptualizations—mostly esoteric and often tacit—of *myth, history, reason,* and *praxis* are revealed in a local tradition and are subject to various modes of cultural constitution and transformation and social expression. It also explores some of the senses in which Bimin-Kuskusmin have begun to develop a self-conscious, abstract *logos* in subtle relationship to their traditional understandings of the interpretive power of *mythos* as historical events of certain orders in recent times have increasingly impinged more forcefully on their apprehensions of place, time, agency, person, self, community, and cosmos. It is this self-conscious stance, however much it may be encompassed and constrained by yet more fundamental cultural understandings neither recognized and foregrounded nor challenged, that is a focus of special analytic attention. The character of such perceived changes in mythico-historical interpretation that are now locally recognized is deemed to have had profound consequences not only for a fundamental change in understandings of tradition, but also for an accommodation of the dramatic events of the modern era increasingly sweeping over the region.

The Bimin-Kuskusmin *praxis* of the mythic interpretation of historical events provokes a consideration of the character and shape of practical reason in a community beyond the socio-cultural pale of those philosophical traditions usually at issue in scholarly contemplation of such matters. In this regard, the present concern is the nexus between the cultural forms of theory and their entailments and consequences for the social contours of practice. In any sociocultural context, there is invariably some kind and degree of connection between certain orders of cultural or folk theory and certain forms of social practice, and, thus, practical theory—here taken as an interest in how cultural or folk theory is brought to bear upon and informs social practice in making sense of particular events—and its concomitant modes of reasoning inform and shape activities (practices) in the context of the socioculturally contingent understandings of a community and also provide a rationale for and legitimation of such practices. Yet, practical theory and practical reasoning here must be understood in the context of Bimin-Kuskusmin culture and society, in general, and of this genre of cultural (mythic) interpretation as it is socially exercised, in particular. In this instance, the cultural understandings of mythic interpretation shape interpretive acts under certain circumstances, with particular kinds of significance, and with recognized implications for the performance of mythically prescribed ritual acts. In seeking the character, cause, and consequence of historical events as the foundation of warrants for and guides to rational, remedial action, mythic interpretations are primarily intended to map, circumscribe, and identify the pragmatic implications of historical events in eroding, permuting, transforming, or destroying some critical sense of tradition—especially in its ritual forms.

The Bimin-Kuskusmin use of myth to make sense of historical occurrences is a theoretical undertaking with profound pragmatic consequences for social action—especially for ritual action. On the one hand, mythology is significantly a theory of tradition—the cultural marking, interpretation, and explanation of essential, enduring, significant, and sacred patterns of ancestral design in the midst of the ebb and flow of historical contingencies and exigencies. On the other hand, historical events, as perceived and reconstituted through the lenses of myth, are variously seen as distinctive, peculiar, and potentially insignificant, as significant and sacred, or as threatening phenomena. Such events may be seen to be only superficial and inconsequential, or to be omens or signs of some positive change emanating from the ancestral underworld with respect to which community submission and support is appropriate. In the latter case, mythic interpretation is seen to have disclosed some heretofore unrecognized aspect of ancestrally ordained tradition. In turn, however, such events may threaten those ancestral designs of tradition that should encompass and limit imaginable change, and their effects, if deemed threatening, may then require some manner of ritual effacement, containment, control, or accommodation.

In Horton's sense, the mythic theory of the ancestral design of Bimin-Kuskusmin tradition is a secondary theory.[25] Thus, it is peculiar in its content to Bimin-Kuskusmin culture and society, although it makes claims of universality within the traditionally known world of the Bimin-Kuskusmin. It deals with deciphering in a structured manner the ambiguous, anomalous, and invisible in the apparently ordinary but perhaps extraordinary. It is intended to identify, interpret, and explain evidence of the nonevident—of the distinctive, peculiar, extraordinary, and often threatening phenomena, the most significant characteristics of which are not self-evident or explicable by ordinary means. The interpretive instantiation, by analogy, of myth-in-history and history-in-myth involves an activity which is predicated on imagining that any historical event is intrinsically inchoate in certain of its manifestations and often experientially somewhat chaotic, that it has both apparent and hidden qualities, that its fundamental significance is bound up with its ordinarily invisible characteristics, and that its significant design(s)—hidden and invisible—can be discerned through the lenses of myth. Mythic lenses are said to have the capacity to illuminate those characteristics of historical events that are only incidental or either conform to or violate and threaten ancestral designs of tradition, and to ignore or render insignificant those that are ordinary and without consequence for the sacred qualities of ancestral tradition. The deployment of myth as a culturally constituted interpretive framework, in turn, involves local canons of analogy and inference and of imagination legitimately used only by those ritually entitled to engage in mythic interpretations.

I begin this exploration by focusing upon the Bimin-Kuskusmin notion of 'imagination' (gaangan'nuuriin), for it is certain transformations of a traditional sense of the imagination of sacred myth and of historical events, and of their foci and boundaries and contexts and relationships, that are central to understanding the development of the (mythico-)historical consciousness of Bimin-Kuskusmin during a particular period in the history of their community. Indeed, during this period of the "time of the great destruction" and its aftermath, the very notion of historical events may have become culturally marked, distinguished, and elaborated in a new way and provoked a reconceptualization of the character of sacred myth and its role in understanding not only the 'winds of the first ancestors' (*iniim khyrkhymin,* referring to an enduring sense of tradition), but also the 'first winds from a new source' (*kamaa'iniim nakaamiit,* referring to fundamental change potentially reshaping or threatening that sense of tradition).

The ambiguous concept of the imagination is notably problematic both in philosophy and in psychology. It is often reminiscent of a long discredited "faculty psychology," cast in inchoate poetic images that resist analytic scrutiny, harboring vague allusions to some confluence of creativity, emotion, fantasy, introspection, imagery, and the like. It has generally been conceptualized as a reflective and reflexive quality of "apprehension" (roughly in Whitehead's sense of the term)[26] that is highly intuitive, synthetic, and aesthetic, yet it also suggests some manner of insight that has (or may have) the capacity to advance (analytic) understanding. As Engell notes, the Western notion of imagination, in its many historical senses, importantly became an explicit focus of literary and philosophical concern and explication in the eighteenth century, and that legacy still infuses much exploration of the matter.[27]

It is generally agreed, however, that the imagination, in its synthesizing qualities of apperception or apprehension, is often bound up with the representation of what is no longer present, is nonexistent, and is only possible or potential, although the relations of imaginary representations to those of the "present" and the "real" commonly remain obscure in these portraits of the phenomenon.[28] Yet, it is often associated with the rudiments of a critical elaboration of traditional concepts in new and insightful ways by innovative transgressions of ordinary boundaries, bridgings of once segregated domains, recastings of privileged understandings, foregrounding illuminations of the ordinarily tacit and inchoate, and other extensions and transformations of an accepted order of comprehension.[29] However these insights may come to be cast in conceptual form,[30] they seem to proceed from nonconceptual "images," visual and otherwise,[31] and their conceptual articulation may be seen as problematic in the ambiguities of the translation from image to concept. Wittgenstein often uses the term *imagine* in his attempts to extend philosophical insights, to *imagine* situations or conditions which lie beyond ordinary modes of thought and experience.[32] Indeed, for Wittgenstein *imagine* is clearly an "odd job word," suggesting the rich and diverse meanings it has had for Brentano, Coleridge, Collingwood, Hume, Husserl, Kant, Sartre, Wordsworth, and others, and the "family resemblances" among them.[33]

The focus on this multifaceted and ambiguous, yet somehow powerful notion in this essay is motivated by a concern not only to make sense of particular Bimin-Kuskusmin ideas about apperception, apprehension, and interpretation that seem to be both similar to and different from certain Western ideas about imagination in their concerns, but also to attend to the elaborately metaphoric character of their mythico-historical interpretations that fundamentally implicate their sense of imagination.[34] As Verbrugge and McCarrell suggest, "metaphor invites pretending, imagining, reasoning by analogy; in its more powerful forms, it requests a perception of resemblances by means of an unconventional reshaping of identities."[35] In turn, Johnson notes that images and "image-schematic structures . . . can be metaphorically extended to structure our network of meanings and, thereby, to direct and constrain our reasoning," while allowing new insights to be illuminated.[36] Indeed, according to Johnson, the imagination generally refers to a metaphoric (or metonymic) "capacity to organize mental representations (especially percepts, images, and image schemata) into meaningful, coherent unities . . . [that] generate novel order," that enable an envisioning of similarity-in-difference and difference-in-similarity in ways which may lead to new conceptual formulations of puzzling phenomena so apprehended.[37]

Despite considerable emphasis on the unconstrained nature of the possibilities of imaginative innovation, Turner aptly notes that, "imagination is not unfettered; it is governed by principles" of the construction of images and metaphors in a sociocultural tradition.[38] Yet, on occasion, the images and metaphors of the cultural imagination may be somewhat loosened from the moorings of these constraints, enlarge or transform a vision of "possible worlds," and then be brought to bear upon a self-conscious *praxis* of interpretation in reflecting upon the apparent entailments and consequences of this new vision vis-à-vis aspects of the tradition from which they arise.[39] In regard to this imaginative interpreting, extending, and recasting of symbolic constructions and of the exegetical traditions that encompass them, Wagner suggests, "The necessity to innovate is . . . characteristic of all cultural activity. It [usually] amounts to the cultural necessity . . . to formulate . . . meaning in terms of already known referents or contexts. The metaphor may be one that has been repeated . . . before, or it may be a *completely original creation,* but in either case it achieves its expressive force through the contrast that it presents and the analogy that this contrast elicits" (italics mine).[40] Indeed, although such creativity may be characteristic to some extent of a culture at any moment, imaginative innovation in a time of crisis seems to have transformed certain Bimin-Kuskusmin notions of *myth*[41] and *history*[42] and brought a new understanding of the shape and force of tradition to the center-place.

From an analytic perspective, the Bimin-Kuskusmin sense of the imagination may refer to almost any act of interpretation deemed consequential for the community, its descent and residential categories and groups, and the encompassing center-place. Only fully initiated men (including male ritual elders) and female ritual elders, however, are endowed with the kind and degree of *finiik* 'spirit or life-force'—constituting sociomoral personhood and, thus, "thinking/feeling" and agential capacity—to engage in such consequential acts of interpretation. Of the seventeen forms of cognitive-affective thinking/feeling capacity discriminated by Bimin-Kuskusmin, however, it is only senior male ritual elders who may be possessed of *kuurkhaaraniin* ('being in the same time-place with'). This unique capacity is the basis of an especially powerful, insightful form of 'understanding' *(khaim'khraak'khaan'naam)* of 'sacred meanings' *(aiyem'khaa)* and the foundation of esoteric ritual knowledge and the image *par excellence* of the imagination in its most elaborate forms. Thus, uniquely endowed with this imaginative capacity, it is senior male ritual elders alone who possess the entitlements to engage in mythic interpretations.

This distinctive form of thinking/feeling—connoting an exceptional quality of insightfulness and an ability to induce 'images' *(takhaak,* a term with particular reference to reflections and shadows)—enables the ability to 'locate oneself within a sacred myth' *(uum khraan aiyem sang mutuuk ker duuranginamiin),* within the sacred time-place of ritual and the ancestral underworld. The image-laden experience of dreams, visions, certain forms of spirit possession, exposure to the cognitive-emotional intensity of ritual performances and mythic narrations, and a special class of 'sacred illnesses' *(mufaagoriinok aiyem)* which befall those in constant and close proximity to sacred phenomena, all enhance the imaginative capacity to locate oneself within a sacred myth.[43] Thus, the imagination is focused most forcefully on the interpretive *praxis* of utilizing sacred myth as a lens—as a "crystal" in the local idiom—for 'bringing to the eye within' *(kiin mutuuk daakhaaraan)* strange and puzzling phenomena in the world.

Indeed, divinations, which are often both prelude and accompaniment to mythic interpretations and which are deemed similar in interpretive form to the latter,[44] sometimes involve literally using large ritual crystals to reflect images of unknown phenomena.[45] The divinations are focused both on the object of curiosity and on the crystal that manifests its image(s). Ritual crystals, specially consecrated, are believed to be both animate and sentient and to be endowed with a powerful *finiik* 'spirit or life-force' and, thus, a capacity for agency, which is revealed in

their ability to reflect and refract various forms of both visible
and invisible light in the shadows and reflections cast by hidden images. Crystals are said to capture simultaneously reflections and shadows from other phenomena, from themselves (mirrored in other phenomena and among their myriad facets), and
from the 'unseen' *(kiin'ba)* of the sacred time-place of ritual
performances, of the ancestral underworld, and of the primordial era of the first ancestors. In some mysterious ways, they
can detect and fuse the totality of all images—not only visual,
but also auditory, gustatory, olfactory, tactile, and the special
quality of being in the same time-place with—of phenomena, as
could the eyes of the first and omniscent ancestors with which
they are associated.

Thus, the most important divinations, accompanied by sacrificial rites to invoke 'ancestral wisdom' *(agetnaam kusem),*
focus not only on the reflective, refractive, and otherwise illumi-
native qualities of crystals, but also on a ritually consecrated
milieu that is the locus of the crystals. That ritual context is
distinguished by acts of drumming in the resonant chamber of a
cavern of crystals, partaking of the meat and fat of sacrificial
animals (notably the cassowary and the echidna associated with
Afek and Yomnok), inhaling the smoke of sacrifice, rubbing the
crystal with human and wild boar semen, and otherwise sym-
bolically bounding or marking the sacred time-place of the
divinatory rite. The most auspicious contexts for mythic interpretations of historical events are held to be these vast caverns,
which often extend for many miles. The caverns are believed to
be connected ultimately to the ancestral underworld. They are
festooned with arrays of stalactites, stalagmites, fossils, and crystals, serve as ossuaries for human skulls and the skulls of cassowaries and echidnas, and contain enormous sacrificial
hearths.[46] Here, mythic interpretation and divination are brought
together, yielding 'images of varied light' *(takhaak iraag'daanam
kanuum,* evoking the reflective qualities of crystals), into the
most powerful forms of imaginative understanding.

The most elaborate and powerful forms of mythic interpretation, invariably conducted by paramount male ritual elders in

these remote caverns and accompanied by intricate divinatory rites, seem to focus on those historical events that are revealed— by preliminary divination, by traditional omen, or by some other form of interpreted 'sign' *(faariik)*—to have left (or, eventually, are destined to leave) an indelible scar on the 'spine of the center-place' *(abiip mutuuk daang kuun)*. These forms of mythic interpretation are known as the 'voice of divinatory rites' *(weeng'kwaar ben'kwiintok)*, for they are cast in the archaic genre of ritual speech associated with the first ancestors and portrayed as 'images encased in words' *(kamiin feibaaklinan duu weeng)* and 'condensed, congealed speech' *(weeng waarak)*.[47] This highly figurative speech is also associated with various altered states of thinking/feeling produced through ingestion of hallucinogenic substances; forgoing food, drink, and sleep; ritual ordeals and illnesses; forms of spirit possession; dreaming; and other modes of imagining the sacred time-place.[48] This metaphoric mythic-ritual speech is believed to approximate the fundamental but often hidden images of those historical events deemed worthy of the imaginative effort of the combined *praxis* of divination and mythic interpretation, for mythic-ritual speech is itself crystalline in certain respects and enables creative linguistic representations of nonlinguistic images in mysterious but illuminating ways.

The Bimin-Kuskusmin recognize, nevertheless, that the phenomena of the world may project appearances that are 'illusions' *(kiin'kwanaak)*, which are inevitably a part of merely the external 'surface' *(bangep'khaan magaang)* of such phenomena. Such a surface is hard and opaque, casting no proper or significant reflections of its own. Only sacred things—once recognized as such, ritually sanctified, and enclosed in ritual settings—do not possess this illusory quality, although their 'meaning' *(miit maagamiin)* is nonetheless never fully comprehended. Yet, some phenomena that are sacred, but are not recognized, sanctified, and enclosed, still bear the nonreflective 'dry dust of ordinary things' *(iip'kuukor kuup)*, which contains the illusory qualities of external surfaces.[49] Indeed, it is often a puzzlement for elders in their divinations whether some phenomenon is sacred or not, for all things possess hidden and ambiguous aspects that are not apparent at their first appearance. If those hidden and ambiguous aspects should also be secret, which is a distinctive mark of the association of 'ancestral power' *(kusem kuuran)* and the sacred, then the phenomenon possesses a power, influence, potency, or efficacy to bring fundamental change to—to have a 'great effect' *(kuur'taan kuuser)* on or to produce a 'scar' *(guur)* in—the center-place. This potential for effecting significant change is the acknowledged threat of all manner of experientially unknown things, for their source remains obscure and is assumed to be beyond the center-place. It was the mythic and divinatory interpretation of such problematic events that intrude upon the center-place that became the focus of anxious and concerted attention in the time of the great destruction.

At first glance, the Bimin-Kuskusmin *seem* to represent almost a classic instance of what Lévi-Strauss describes as the character of "cold" societies without any effective sense of history, in which events of the past are collapsed, transformed, obscured, or ignored vis-à-vis pervading and enduring cultural structures and sociofunctional configurations that constitute a timeless sense of tradition.[50] Yet, before the establishment of a European presence in their region and the proselytizing efforts of missions, the Bimin-Kuskusmin had complex modes of conceptualizing time and attending to the "past" both within and beyond the reaches of living memory, and their interest in the "past" (in several senses) was not altogether encompassed by the sacred myths that narratively enshrined their sense of tradition. Indeed, they seem long to have imagined a tension between both the 'time of ordinary things' *(tem'khaan ken kuup)* and the 'everyday experience of living' *(kwan utaamamiin)*, which constitute most historical events, and the sacred time-place, which encompasses sacred myth, ritual, the ancestral underworld, and the time of the first ancestors. Through acts of imaginative interpretation, of mythic decipherment and divinatory revelation, which are known together as 'revealing crystal images' *(weng tuum takhaak dagaamaniim)*, it is thought to be essential, when early divinations, omens, and other signs suggest the potential presence of an indelible scar on the center-place, to attempt to perceive paths, bridges, strings, or roots interconnecting these two time frames, to probe the boundaries and interconnections between *history* and *myth*,[51] and, thus, to disclose whether or not a historical event is possesssed of sacred qualities.

Beyond (and, in some senses, between) these two time frames that encase the enduring patterns of the primordial era, the sacred time-place of ritual performance and mythic narration, and the ancestral underworld, on the one hand, and the remembered, experienced, and often transitory flow and flux of recent and present events, on the other, Bimin-Kuskusmin recognize a number of other modes of temporality which are only partially, if at all, articulated in everyday discourse. In myth, however, ordinarily discrete time frames may be interconnected in special ways that mark the sacred and reflect the fusing of times in the sacred time-place. Diurnal and nocturnal reckonings are finely calibrated with respect not only to astral, lunar, and solar positions, but also to the changing rhythms of birdsongs, tree frog trills, wind, rain, temperature, and the qualities of light and shadow. Astral, lunar, and solar cycles, however, also mark longer spans of time that sometimes have cosmological significance and punctuate the social calendar of ritual events in the community. It is within these longer temporal cycles that the sudden appearances of comets, meteors, and solar eclipses are seen as sacred punctuations of ordinary time and potential harbingers of significant changes to come upon the center-place.

In turn, the ritual and social life of the community traces its seasonal oscillations in accordance with an ecological sense of time, which focuses upon changes in rainfall, wind, and temperature, in the maturation and propagation cycles of myriad faunae and florae, and in more subtle variations of sound, light, color, growth, and decay. Invariably, however, these ecological time reckonings are articulated with the temporality of social activities ordained and calendrically positioned by mythic images and ritual actions. Many important rites attend to the interlinkage of fertility and fecundity in humans and in numerous plants and animals of special importance and believed to be endowed with *finiik* 'spirit or life-force.' Sometimes the emphasis of reckoning is reversed as the social-ritual calendar punctuates the ordinary sense of ecological temporality in special ways. Such reversals are often said to mark a recognition of some usually hidden temporal rhythm of the ancestral underworld that is never visible in the world of the living except in the special contexts of the mythic-ritual constitution of a sacred time-place.

In turn, temporal reckonings give shape to individual and social passages and cycles within the community. Distinguished by gender, individual life cycles are marked by conception, divinatory disclosure of destiny, birth, a series of intricate rites of passage, and several kinds of ancestorhood as personal names fade into lineage and clan identities and then suffer the fate of genealogical amnesia after four or five generations, at the rise of the most recent culture heroes. The continuous recycling of four age-grades in male initiation, putatively extending to the end of the time of the first ancestors, is loosely bound up not only with the marking of generations through men, but also with notions of the recycling of *finiik* within the boundaries of clans. Another axis reveals the complexities of genealogical time as it unfolds in the reckoning of descent, kinship, affinal relations, adoption, the incorporation of immigrants, *et cetera,* that bestow the criteria of social identity, and of the claims to rights and resources that can be made through genealogy. The developmental cycles of domestic and residential groups may be conceptualized in genealogical terms, but they are also marked by the various entailments and consequences of the life-cycle events of birth, marriage, divorce, temporary emigration or more permanent political realignment, and death.

These several senses of time are foregrounded or backgrounded, implicitly or explicitly, at different moments in the normal ebb and flow of Bimin-Kuskusmin community life, and one or more may occasionally and unexpectedly give shape to a passing scene usually conceptualized in other temporal terms when something unusual arises and is culturally marked by some genre of omen. Such temporal frames are often illuminated in various folktales portraying the male and female tricksters and the forest spirits at play with time in nontraditional ways. Indeed, unusual alignments or juxtapositions of ordinary time frames are commonly seen as omens of impending change and become a mythic vehicle for marking the fundamental nature and significance of historical events, interweaving their spatio-temporal dimensions with those of the sacred time-place and tracing the character of the analogies and dis-analogies revealed.

In conceptualizing these myriad time frames, as well as those of the time of ordinary things or everyday experience of living and of the sacred time-place, however, at least two other senses of time ordinarily or inevitably intrude upon and are refigured by the narrative representation of temporality.[52] In the first instance, any mode of temporal reckoning may be marked by an anatomically based system of counting in which the basic span of twenty-seven units is divided into halves (corresponding to the right and left sides of the body) and is centered on the midpoint of the skull (the nose). Each unit corresponds to an underlying bone which is classified as sacred or not, and the direction of anatomical counting may be right to left or left to right depending upon whether the context of counting is ordinary or sacred. Each of these discriminations, or several in combination, may be used to order any other temporal framework. In the second instance, the linguistic-discursive conventions of narratively describing time frames adds its own resources and constraints in terms of temporal profiles, processes, and predications characteristic of verb forms and their derived nominalizations, and all Mountain-Ok languages are known for their complexities in these regards.[53] Some of these linguistic characteristics are peculiar to the archaic forms of ancestral ritual speech of mythic discourse, which reveal their own unique resources for framing time.

The time reckoned in Bimin-Kuskusmin 'ancestor myths' *(kusem sang)* may be articulated with many other temporal modalities within the details of the narrative, but the plot of the mythic narrative as a whole unfolds within distinctive eras. As genealogical reckoning begins to fade at four or five ascending generations, the contours of mythic time begin to emerge in extending a sense of the "past" into the realm of ancestorhood. Beyond the names of ancestors known (by living memory or remembered account) to the eldest of the living and which are still the potential foci of descendants' sacrifices, there is a partitioning of the past into four eras, each of which is successively more distant from the present. The 'time of the culture heroes' *(anaak afaariik'so)*, when human strength and endurance were displayed in renown exploits of war, hunting, and wandering, gives way to the 'time of the forebears of the ritual elders' *(anaak ben'kusem aiyem)*, when the clan cult houses were rebuilt to renew the ritual strength of the center-place, and then to the 'time of the human founders of the clans' *(anaak fiitep on'takhaas)*, when "totemic" sacrifices were instituted to enhance ritual efficacy, and finally to the 'time of the great human ancestors' *(anaak maakmaak fiitep)*, when humans had first to contend with their newfound mortality and the loss of Afek's mantle enveloping and protecting the center-place. Beyond the mythic eras, the sacred time-place of the first ancestors—the time of the primordial ancestors Afek and Yomnok and all of their immediate and immortal progeny—becomes the primary focus of sacred myth.

The temporal frame of sacred myth, and especially of the ritually prominent 'sacred myths of Afek' *(afek sang aiyem)*, is that of an enduring sacred time-place which pervades not only the primordial epoch, but also the present ancestral underworld and contemporary ritual performances and mythic narrations. It is believed to represent, albeit opaquely, the core of the traditional foundations of Bimin-Kuskusmin culture and society which are distinctive and have remained somehow intact, but are more and more hidden and unknown with the increasing fragility of mortal human effort to perceive, understand, implement, and revitalize them through ritual performances and mythic narratives that attempt to construct bridges, paths, strings, and roots connecting the center-place to the sacred time-place.

The force of this special sense of temporal duration is marked not only in the narrations of myth and performances of ritual which are set apart from the ordinary spatial and temporal maps of the terrain of the center-place, but also in the myriad sacred places and discovered relics—primarily deliberately excavated artifacts (from old sites of habitation) and fossils (from caves) and other geological formations seen to be living and to change (notably stalactites and stalagmites)—that recast those maps in terms of the contours of the sacred time-place. The sacred time-place is also associated with profound images of androgyny, incest, twinship, deathless life, telepathic powers, the non-human loci of *finiik* 'spirit or life-force,' enduring time, floating 'bubbles' *(mot'motaan)* of space,[54] astral travel, and the like, that conflate and confound classificatory discriminations (including categories of time) otherwise assumed to be immutable and fundamental. The efforts of the imagination in mythic interpretation and ritual divination are directed toward encasing or sealing various new and potentially threatening phenomena within this time frame so that the images of their sacred and enduring qualities may be apprehended, ritually controlled, and harnessed to community interests.

The boundary between the time of sacred myth and that of the eras of ancestor myth is marked by several orders of cataclysm—notably drought, famine, illness, fire, and earthquake. The first 'great time of darkness' *(aneng irepkha temtaak mitiik'kuuran)* and the first appearance of the 'elder brother of the sun' *(ataan fiik),* however, are its most distinctive features (see note 9). These portraits of tephra fall and eclipse are believed to be omens of the coming of suffering and death and of their profound entailments and consequences for the increasing fragility of the human condition in the center-place. These images are seen to portray a reordering of relations of sun and moon, the first children of Afek, that would, in turn, transform the shape and force of myriad aspects of tradition on the Bimin-Kuskusmin landscape. Before these great catastrophes, there were no markings of significant change, no indelible scars on the center-place, following the establishment of the traditional foundations of the Bimin-Kuskusmin sociocultural order by Afek, and many of the classificatory distinctions among persons that are the framework for resentment and conflict were not recognized. All those who had ever lived remained together in harmony.

The eras of ancestor myth, in turn, are marked by events that variously tested and renewed the ever-waning strength of now-mortal humans. Each event is believed to have been fore-shadowed by an omen, usually in the form of a crushing earth-quake or a devastating fire originating in the ancestral under-world and issuing from the mouths of great caverns, that foretold of the tenuous reinstitutionalization of some long-lost, essential, but now only partially efficacious 'rite of strengthening' *(ben'kitiirnaamok)* to renew the waning power of the mortal human *finiik.* It was invariably the forms of sacred myth, which are believed to have survived intact from the primordial time in their archaic forms of ancestral speech but not in their once transparent 'meaning' *(miit maagamiin),* that became the path-ways or guides for these human endeavors to reduce the seem-ingly relentless weakening of the powers of *finiik.* Images of mythic interpretation (and ritual divination) are linked to an understanding of the cataclysmic omens and to the design of human effort in contending with their prophecies. The proximal boundary of ancestor myth, however, is marked by reference to a somewhat different order of catastrophe, the time of the great destruction.

In the eras of ancestor myth before the time of the great destruction, Bimin-Kuskusmin maintain that all historical events were initially viewed as unprecedented, unanticipated occur-rences that were located at their source beyond the pale of the sacred time-place that circumscribes ritual performances and mythic narrations. They might come to be seen as sacred, but what impact they had on the Bimin-Kuskusmin landscape lay outside of the realm of *sacrae.* Whatever indelible scars, if any, they were subsequently seen to have left on the center-place, these scars did not efface the ever-enduring forms of sacred myth and ritual and, thus, the essential core of tradition. In-deed, such effacement was apparently not imaginable in the times of the ancestor myths, for its very possibility seemed to erode the only means at human disposal for making sense of historical events. As one elder observes, "These historical events are like dust in the wind. . . . They are always there. . . . Sometimes you notice them, sometimes not. . . . In the past, we did not believe them to be separated from the wind itself."[55] They were deemed alien in the senses that they were only ambiguously and problematically related to the shapes of the land and the traditional foundations of local cultural and social forms and forces as manifested in the natural order and in certain institutional designs. Another elder notes that, "Sometimes historical events would occur . . . , and they would bring a death, an injury . . . , some kind of misfortune. . . . But the diviners would show that they left no scar . . . , only a wound that healed." Yet another elder suggests, "Leaves and branches fall regularly into rivers, but most are swept away—rotting into the river mud, disappearing on the current, not interrupting the flow of the current in any noticeable way. . . . The course of the river [itself] is not altered . . . , its banks are not eroded. . . . Sometimes, however, a leaf or branch will temporarily dam the river, dislodge a boulder . . . , or even cause the river to change course . . . , to overflow its channels in flood. . . . When a historical event has a great effect, it must be observed for signs of its importance."

Such historical events in the times of the ancestor myths bore no apparent relationship to the forces of ancestral powers or designs associated with the first ancestors unless divinations indicated that they were signs of ancestral interest, wrath, or intervention. But these ancestral concerns were believed always to be directed away from the ancestors' own insubstantial bodies, beyond the sacred time-place of myth and ritual. Thus, they were seen to have no direct affect on the realm of the sacred as embodied in the *sacrae* that pervade the center-place. At the moment of their appearance, they were not judged to have the capacity to influence even the familiar ebb and flow of community life in any but a more or less transient and inconsequential way, for they were conceived as only an interruption. Their traces did not apparently endure, but were borne away on the winds of the first ancestors.

The time of the great destruction, however, is said to have been borne by the first winds from a new source and to have been marked by a cataclysm of major and recent significance. In the mid-1940s, the Bimin-Kuskusmin perception of the occurrence of several disasterous historical events provoked a profound sense of crisis and a significant change in their view of the character of such events, of sacred myth, and of the interrelationships between these two genres of knowledge. Word came from the great ritual center at Telefolip far to the west that, during the course of one phase of the Telefolmin rites of male initiation, the novices had been secluded in a ritual structure which had burned to the ground, killing all the boys.[56] A group of senior Bimin-Kuskusmin ritual elders immediately journeyed to the Telefolmin ritual center, bringing powerful ritual crystals encased in sacred barkcloth to protect these *sacrae* when borne beyond the center-place, in order to view the remains of the catastrophe, to hold counsel with Telefolmin elders on its possible 'cause' *(maagamuut),* 'importance' *(miitaan'khaa),* and 'significance' *(miit maagamiin),* and to conduct divinations of their own of the charred vestiges of the ritual structure, of the *sacrae* within it, and of the bones of the boys.[57] From the Telefolmin elders, they learned that earlier divinations had revealed a hidden breach of the sanctity of the sacred time-place of the rite of initiation—an unknown fossil had appeared from the center of a ritually enshrined fossil that had cracked open in the fire. Using the ritual crystals that they had brought, the Bimin-Kuskusmin elders began their own divinations, which disclosed an aura of sheet lightning coursing amidst the remains of charred cassowary, echidna, and human skulls and of cracked ritual crystals.[58] Whether or not it might be the cause of the matter, however, remained obscure. These divinations also revealed the seemingly strange fossil from Telefolip to be one recognized as ritually inauspicious but already known in the center-place and, thus, of seemingly no special or major consequence among the charred *sacrae.*

Upon their return to the center-place, the elders launched sacrifices of the already burned remains brought from Telefolip in all of the cult houses of the original clans in order to 'bring them to ancestral eyes' *(kusem weng'kiin daakhaaraan)* and then held a long series of divinations focused on the sacrificially reburned, charred fragments of the tragedy and on their sacrificial smoke and on the myriad *sacrae* throughout the center-place which might have been desecrated in some way by the events at Telefolip. The combination of both sacrifice and divination of these different kinds of *sacrae* was deemed most unusual but was believed to yield more powerful, double images from reflections of the object and shadows and reflections of its sacrificial smoke. For the first time in living and mythic memory, these divinations revealed that the sacred time-place of the broader ritual region seemed to have sustained an indelible scar but that it apparently remained largely at the edge of the Bimin-Kuskusmin domain. This revelation was reinforced by subsequent reports from widespread areas within the Mountain-Ok region of torrential rains, flooding rivers, earthquakes, landslides, and raging fires that had destroyed or damaged important *sacrae* elsewhere, but such omens had not been detected in the center-place. Couriers were quickly sent to gather remnants of instances of this sudden defilement of sacred things throughout the area, and special truces were negotiated in areas of hostility to ensure that the collection of these remnants was rapid, methodical, and unimpeded.

When the elders had assembled damaged *sacrae* from ritual centers near and far, they subjected all of them to several powerful rites of purification and then arranged them in a great design on a ledge in their largest and most sacred cavern. The remains of the disaster at Telefolip were paired with similar phenomena from the Bimin-Kuskusmin elders' own ritual repertoire and arranged in a circle around a cluster of newly consecrated cassowary and echidna skulls which, in turn, enveloped an enormous crystal. Damaged *sacrae* from other, less important, ritual centers were arranged in concentric circles around this assemblage. The pattern of the design portrayed an accepted hierarchy, from the Bimin-Kuskusmin viewpoint, of key ritual centers throughout the Mountain-Ok region. Although there was no memory of or mythic-ritual charter for an assemblage of this kind, it was recognized that a concentric arrangement focused on a crystal might reveal something of the connections between the mysteries of the damaged *sacrae* and 'things known' *(kokuu'kanuum)*. The presence of the cassowary and echidna skulls—the emblems of Afek and Yomnok—was believed to enhance the power of the crystal under these seemingly unprecedented circumstances. Beneath the ledge, a new hearth was fashioned from small and fragmented crystals found scattered on the cavern floor and elsewhere, with the intent that they might enhance the ability to see the reflections and shadows cast by these assembled objects by amplifying and refracting the light of the fire. The dense, dark *taantaanak* wood, which is used in the construction of cult houses and exudes an oily substance when burned, was gathered for the fire, for its vaporizing sap would leave a residue on the crystals, enhancing their ability to capture images of unknown qualities hidden in the objects.

The paramount elder, Trumeng, who had led the expedition to Telefolip, spoke at length about what had been witnessed, the Telefolmin accounts and divinations of the disaster, and the uncertain images of their own divinations. Trumeng notes, "I told them all I could recall . . . , in great detail. . . . Many asked questions . . . , looked at the things brought back . . . and gathered elsewhere. . . . Others brought news heard at Kweram [to the southeast], Enkyaakam [to the southwest], Feramiinam [to the west], and elsewhere. . . . What was said was the same everywhere. . . . A wind from a new source. . . . All were troubled at the news." The elder Maakeng adds, "We were all very upset. . . . Some thought we should not approach these things . . . , things that were sacred elsewhere . . . and damaged in unheard of ways. . . . They were not sacred things we understood. . . . Did we know how to purify them? Would they pollute our sacred things? . . . Everyone was afraid." The charred skulls of ancestral humans, cassowaries, and echidnas and the shattered crystals provoked the most anxiety and fear, for these particular *sacrae* are held to be highly similar among all ritual centers despite local differences in the significance attributed to them.

Before proceeding with planned divinations, the elders summoned many fully initiated men to cut trees and then to build barriers in the recesses and at the mouth of the cavern so that whatever happened would not seep out into the forest or through the passages to the ancestral underworld. Bringing many provisions for their seclusion and certain ritual paraphernalia, the paramount elders of the sixteen original patriclans were sealed inside the cavern, and the barriers were adorned with myriad amulets and boar blood and also with the yellow funerary mud of mourning to ensure that all passages from the cavern were closed. The fire was lit in the new hearth, and traditional forms of praise to the first ancestors were chanted. Then, many days of divination, focused on each object in turn, were organized in elaborate detail. These divinations disclosed that there were indeed certain ominous qualities shared among the damaged *sacrae* which were not present among the more or less analogous ritual objects of the center-place. Everywhere among the damaged *sacrae* the unfathomable aura of sheet lightning appeared, reflected in the giant crystal. Although badly charred, the skulls of the cassowaries and echidnas seemed not to have been otherwise damaged, yet they were seen no longer to hold the sacred heat of the sacrificial fire as objects so sacred generally do. Not being 'ritually hot' *(kaarkaar),* they could no longer be viewed as powerful *sacrae* in any usual sense. The human skulls and the bones of the boys killed at Telefolip, however, exhibited an inexplicably shiny surface which reflected the firelight, and they crumbled to the touch, revealing that the intricate cavities and bony networks within them—the sites of traces of blood, semen, and marrow to which ancestral *finiik* adhere— had been destroyed. The presence of sheet lightning, the inability of sacred bones to retain ritual heat, and the shiny surfaces of the fragile, gutted skulls suggested that the damage to the Telefolmin *sacrae* was fundamental.

In all instances, it was suspected, something of consequence had happened to the *finiik* 'spirit or life-force' associated with

each object, utterly or largely obliterating its ritual efficacy. Furthermore, the *finiik* of the boys killed at Telefolip had disappeared from their bones, suggesting that it had become fragmented and lost forever from the Telefolmin corpus of *finiik*
and, thus, had permanently weakened the ritual power of the
great Telefolip shrine center. The mysterious and ominous presence of images of sheet lightning, soon emanating from the sky
above all ritual centers of the area in the immediate aftermath of
the Telefolip tragedy and both visible and otherwise apparent
in divinations, suggested that the threat of these historical events
was pervasive, and that threat had already been manifested in
myriad indelible scars of the most incredibly devastating kind
throughout most of the sacred centers of the entire ritual region.

These preliminary divinatory conclusions brought deep consternation, for the Bimin-Kuskusmin held the view that a delicate balance existed between the ritual centers at Telefolip and
the center-place. The efficacy of each depended on the strength
and integrity of the other. In addition, the Telefolmin had declared in the wake of this calamity that performances of the ill-
fated phase of their male initiation ritual cycle would never
again be held, thus further weakening this crucial ritual center.[59]
It was assumed that the historical events at Telefolip must have
profound consequences of some kind for the center-place, not
only because of the vital mythic, ritual, and political linkages
between Telefolip and the center-place, but also because the sky
from which the mysterious sheet lightning had come encompassed both ritual centers. Yet, the divinations revealed that the
Bimin-Kuskusmin *sacrae* were all still fully intact and reflected
none of the inauspicious signs associated with all ritual objects
from elsewhere. These historical events were clearly ones of
importance and great effect, but further divinations disclosed
nothing of their meaning in the center-place.

It was then decided after much debate that an attempt
should be made to encase the images revealed through divination in the forms of sacred myth. Given a long tradition of sharing and exchanging certain ritual *sacrae* (including mythic narratives) among elders of the entire region, however, it was

deemed necessary now to excise all remnants of borrowed myth from the corpus of sacred myths revealed to the Bimin-Kuskusmin first ancestors by Afek—to purify the corpus to its "sacred bone," its "marrow," its "spine," its "traditional foundations." If desecrations of *sacrae* beyond the center-place were widespread, the efficacy of sacred myth from abroad was also suspect. Those elements of sacred myth associated with its most obvious and least significant 'skin or husk' *(kaar aiyem)* and 'tail or stem' *(mongoom aiyem),* and often heard by elders from other ritual centers, also should be deleted because their very presence in now-weakened mythic-ritual traditions elsewhere might have eroded their efficacy in the center-place. But how best to proceed in this effort? The first step in living memory was taken as long conversations and debates among the elders consensually revealed mythic segments that were known to have come from elsewhere. The second step, based on common knowledge of the narrative structure of sacred myth and its distinguishable segments and levels, was to reclassify the skin or husk and tail or stem aspects of these myths as no longer sacred and, thus, not to be narrated in contexts associated with the sacred time-place. The third step, however, which was believed to be altogether unprecedented, was to subject each of the key foci of the cycle of sacred Afek myths, the very centerpiece of the corpus of sacred myths, to the scrutiny of divination.

The concentric design of diverse *sacrae* was first disassembled, and the damaged *sacrae* from other communities were carefully placed in deep holes in the walls of the cavern, which were then filled with stones and earth packed tightly and covered with funerary mud. Their Bimin-Kuskusmin analogues, however, were rearranged in rows along the back of the ledge and covered with protective sacred barkcloth, creating an opening in the assembled *sacrae* and exposing the large crystal to the full range of firelight. The then-young ritual elder, Trumeng (of the opening narration of this essay), who had recently succeeded his father as paramount elder of his clan, was selected for the narration on several grounds. His command of the repertoire of sacred myth was already legendary, and he had devoted more than a year to traveling through the ranges of mountains that encompass the center-place to visit the many hundreds of mythically marked sites which represent a path of successive episodes in the cycle of sacred Afek myths and operate as a mnemonic framework for guiding narrations. In recent weeks, he had experienced an elaborate dream of myth telling that was widely reported and met with much interest as some kind of omen. He had been especially prominent in the ultimately accepted interpretations of the preliminary divinatory images of the damaged *sacrae,* thus exhibiting a special talent for interpretive undertakings. He had tamed a wild cassowary chick in his youth so that it came to the edge of the forest to eat nuts and fruits at his feet—a remarkably auspicious sign of a special understanding of sacred things associated with Afek. And finally, the frequent and sometimes unusual sacrifices held in his cult house were deemed largely responsible for the exceptional garden harvests and forest hunts which had occurred since he had recently become the paramount ritual elder of the Imoranmin patriclan. In short, he was held to be a revered man of special prowess in the realms of myth, ritual, and the sacred time-place.

Trumeng was first ritually purified by the anointing of his torso with boar blood and fat in the recesses of the cavern; then he was seated facing the great crystal so that his 'speech would be a wind' *(ku'weeng iniim khaanuuk)* blowing toward the crystalline surface, giving voice to its reflected images, and encompassing interpretively the suspected first winds from a new source. Close to the sacrificial fire, he perspired profusely and rubbed the facets of the great crystal with his sweat so that his *finiik* and the *finiik* of the crystal would be joined together. For some four days, without sleep and with only cucumber (for moisture) and boar fat (for nourishment) to eat, Trumeng traced the course of the entire cycle of sacred Afek myths, pausing after each distinctive episode for other elders to consider the character of the shadows and reflections revealed in the great crystal. When he had completed the narration, several episodes of the Afek myths had been consensually identified as alien and divined as not sacred and were then marked for deletion from the corpus. As each such episode was identified, Trumeng was asked to repeat it in ordinary speech. When each repeated episode had ended, another ritual elder rubbed some of the sap residues produced in the smoke of the sacrificial fire from the clouded facets of the crystal, wrapped them in parcels of sacred barkcloth, and deposited them in holes in the same manner as had been done with the other alien and damaged *sacrae*. Then the fire was extinguished, the barriers were disassembled, the undamaged *sacrae* of the center-place were removed, and the elders departed from the cavern.

In the following several days, elders journeyed to the sites associated with the mythic episodes that had been excised from the corpus of sacred myth and desanctified each site in turn, destroying its movable relics, effacing its "natural" contexts in certain ways, and transforming some part of it into a tiny taro garden.[60] All gardening, hunting, trapping, and gathering in the mountain forests surrounding these sites was halted. All ceremonial activities were delayed, and all public disputes were held in abeyance. The fully initiated men of all of the original patriclans were asked to fast, and all women and children were removed from their normal hamlets of residence to a temporary camp on the eastern flank of the center-place near the Strickland Gorge. Continuous sacrifices were conducted in the hearths of all of the cult houses of the original clans. Once these preparations were complete, the elders reassembled in the cavern in order to institute a new form of mythic interpretation to be focused on the great destruction. Once again, Trumeng became the narrator, and all was in readiness for the launching of an unprecedented form of mythic interpretation of a seemingly unprecedented historical event.

In a manner now much recounted among elders, Trumeng began by announcing an extraordinary strategy of mythic interpretation. He noted that he had directly witnessed the aftermath of the great destruction at Telefolip and had participated in all the sacrifices, divinations, and narrations that had followed this historical event. He observed that nothing of this kind had happened in the time in which he had lived and that he had never heard of such happenings from the forebears whom he had known. There were, he maintained, some things hidden and unknown that were *neither* a part of everyday experience, *nor* an aspect of the sacred time-place. They were simply unprecedented in any recognizable context, for no one, living or dead, had ever seen them before. And some events, he argued, such as earthquakes, had been experienced many times but could not be anticipated because what they were—however enshrined in sacred myth—did not reveal the cause or root of why they occurred when they did. Also, he insisted, some historical events had to do simply with the 'fragile work of men' *(kunum ogaak'khaa beyt'an)*, who too often believed that everything could be understood in terms of sacred myth *alone* and without reference to their own activities, or with things of the forest that could be understood largely by watching the life of the forest.

In the course of these claims, he made repeated reference to the omnipresent signs of the ever-weakening state of the *finiik* as an indication that mortal and flawed human forces were at work in many historical events making them only partially interpretable by traditional means, and said that this weakened state also was impeding understanding gained through sacred myth, for such myths were revealed to the much more powerful first ancestors for them to use. He then declared that such historical events as the tragedy at Telefolip could *not* be understood *only* by the usual means of mythic interpretation, for many things existed beyond the present bounds of the sacred time-place that could nonetheless be significant for understandings of tradition in the center-place. In the time of the first ancestors, he claimed, any historical event could be encased in sacred myth, for the center-place was entirely encompassed by the sacred time-place. The great rituals were more powerful then, he stated, and the first ancestors too had greater strength then men do now. In the time of the great destruction, however, an understanding of such events was to be found in attending not only to sacred myth, but also to the ways of men and the ways of the forest and, perhaps, the coming of the European. Thus, one could not always expect, he suggested, that the winds from a new source always really came from the sacred time-place. In such statements, he provoked an image of a kind of ambiguity in significant historical events so that encasement in the forms of sacred myth could not be seen as always or only the best mode of interpretation. The profound skepticism that is attributed to Trumeng's preliminary remarks, which were at first met with some angered rejection and much heated debate, has since been largely accepted and much extended and embellished in many ways, especially since the advent of the presence of the European,[61] and has lent to the notion of historical event an epistemological status that is highly ambiguous and is apparently different, at least in these regards, from what preceded it.

Having stated these opinions, Trumeng proceeded nonetheless to launch a mythic interpretation focused exclusively on the known phenomena associated with the events at Telefolip, but, in a rather unorthodox way, he interlaced his interpretation with a commentary of his own, reinforcing his earlier remarks. He selected a bony segment from the accepted structure of the now reduced and purified corpus of sacred myth—a segment that places the cavern in which the narration occurred as the site of its central episode. This episode represents the sternum of the selected mythic segment, and Trumeng noted the anomalous images of this episode; for in the mythic events of the cave there are the birth of twins, androgynous figures (including Afek and Yomnok), acts of incest, and lunar elipses obscuring the cavern entrance. He emphasized an analogy between these anomalous images and the images of sheet lightning discerned in the divinations of the damaged *sacrae* from Telefolip, noting that the mysterious sheet lightning was originally produced by an incestuous mating of the androgynous twins thunder and lightning, who fuse images in the rainbows that form a bridge between the ancestral underworld and the world of the living. Their offspring, sheet lightning, however, is known as the 'destroyer of rainbows' *(wiirbaar kooru'khaanak)* and, thus, has sometimes been expelled from its celestial home to wander the landscape when storms are present.[62] It is thought to be entirely capricious, and its presence is always sudden, momentary, and unpredictable. Neither the effect nor the cause of its presence in some particular place is ever certainly known or knowable. Once again, Trumeng noted by way of commentary that the recent historical events at Telefolip were anomalous and mysterious in a manner akin to the character and wanderings of the unfathomable sheet lightning, which had been seen at Telefolip at the time of the great destruction.

From the central sternum segment, Trumeng proceeded along two narrative paths in tracing the course of this segment of sacred myth. First, he narrated the episodes associated with the sacred bones of the left ribs and then returned to the sternum. These three episodes portray various forays made by Afek when the great ancestor was secluded in the cavern during her time of menstruation and wandered abroad by moonlight to found certain traditions of the center-place. Both her newfound menstrual capacity and the weakening effect on her ritual strength to invest these traditions with aspects of her powerful *finiik* left Afek vulnerable to mysterious and debilitating forces already active in the center-place. Thus, the traditions that she instituted in the center-place—especially in their ritual aspects— were incomplete in certain ambiguous ways, and they would subsequently and forever require the periodic ritual constitution of a sacred time-place connecting the worlds of the living and the dead. The efficacy of the problematic ritual traditions of the center-place could be enhanced only by being anchored to the full efficacy of the complete ritual traditions which she eventually created in the ancestral underworld.

Trumeng recounted that once Afek traveled to a great waterfall which rushed from a hole in a cliffside and bathed there to wash the menstrual blood from her loins. In the torrent of the waterfall, she saw shadows and reflections of cassowaries and echidnas following the path of a giant rainbow. Being cold afterwards, she turned in anger toward the waterfall for weakening her state of ritual hotness and plugged the hole in the cliff with her bloody menstrual moss. Soon after she departed to begin the first hunting of frogs by torchlight in a nearby swamp, the cliffside sprang numerous tiny holes through which the once great rush of the waterfall was weakened and diminished into myriad trickles of gently flowing water. Amidst many tiny, less radiant rainbows, dim images of fragments of the bodily parts of cassowaries and echidnas appeared and gushed blood. By analogy, Trumeng noted that the waterfall, itself an image of reflections and shadows, had been forever weakened when its mighty stream was fragmented, as had the illuminating qualities of the shattered crystals from Telefolip. The sacred images of cassowaries and echidnas too had been weakened, as had their charred skulls at Telefolip.

Again, Afek ventured abroad to begin the hunting of marsupials but encountered a strange, unknown creature armed with bow and arrows who pursued her as though she were a hunted animal. In anger, she turned and transformed the creature into a boulder with her saliva and then hunted marsupials in the high forest. Yet the sounds of mysterious chants emanated from within the boulder, and the tracks of the marsupials suddenly disappeared when this chanting was heard. Soon, she became too weak to pursue the hunt and slept in a forest glade. In her fitfull dreams, she again saw shadowy images of the mysterious creature which had sought to kill her in the forest, but it was like no animal that she had known. Trumeng observed a linkage between the mysterious creature changed into a boulder and the unknown fossil that had puzzled the Telefolmin elders. Both, he claimed, were forest spirits who masquerade as ancestral spirits, surprise unwary wanderers in the forest by emerging from stones, and fling spirit arrows at their intended victims. By way of commentary, he noted that the strange fossil, although known in the center-place, was an inauspicious contamination of the ritual center at Telefolip, for the presence of forest spirits in the sacred time-place wreaks havoc with the ordained temporal rhythms of ritual performances.

Finally, Afek departed from the cavern in search of the cassowary and, seeing a giant one, followed its tracks to a stand of pandanus trees, where she saw it shed its feathered skin and underlying flesh and turn to bone. Its tracks in the surrounding forest then disappeared, and its bones were enveloped by a dense mist—a sign that its *finiik* was preparing to begin its journey to the ancestral underworld. She quickly covered its skeleton with the black blood of her menstrual flow mixed with the powerful fertile fluids from her vagina, and the cassowary returned to life and strode into the forest. Afek then continued to follow its tracks through the forest, collecting and devouring its droppings to revitalize her own ritual strength. As she ate this substance, she herself was transformed into a giant black cassowary. Trumeng then suggested that the charred cassowary skulls found in the debris of Telefolip has been stripped of their ritual adornment of black pigment—a loss of sacred protection which had produced the decay of the crumbling skulls and the loss of their capacity to hold ritual heat.

Returning to the sternum segment, however, Trumeng traced a path from sternum to spine through the heart, which is the locus of *finiik* and of all thinking/feeling. Afek once remained in the cavern for many months as she prepared the first performance of the great rites of taro, which had first grown from her menstrual residues. But, as she began the rituals, a wind entered the cavern, and she suddenly fell ill with a strong fever. In her fever, her heart began to palpitate, and the *sacrae* that she had created for the taro rite turned to dust and lost their reflective qualities. By an extended analogy, Trumeng noted that the crumbling, nonreflective quality of the ancestral skulls and boys' bones from Telefolip was due not only to the charring effects of the great fire, but also to the gradual weakening of the *finiik* that had been occurring since the end of the time of the first ancestors. To illuminate this course of events, he suggested that he had noticed a difference in the images of the ancestral skulls and of the boys' bones as reflected in the great crystal, and that the former still contained traces of a more powerful but diminished *finiik* that clung tenaciously to the ruined bone of the skulls. The boys' bones, in contrast, exhibited no trace of *finiik*, although they had been alive more recently.

Second, he portrayed the mythic episodes linked to the sacred bones of the right ribs and then again returned to the sternum. These three episodes depict the journeys of Yomnok, the younger brother and consort of Afek, in his quest for strength after being polluted by intercourse with the menstruating Afek in the cavern and being ill there for many days. In his delirium, he had frightening dreams in which he saw the reflections and shadows of wild boars in the surrounding forest. The shadows and reflections of the boars rushed at him ferociously and then disappeared into the mists of the forest. These dreams left him terrified and further weakened. On several occasions, nonetheless, Yomnok left the cavern in search of wild boar blood in the heat of midday, encountering various obstacles to his efforts and causing much destruction on the paths of his travels. What he destroyed along the path of his hunt were subsequently found to be powerful ritual *sacrae* which then had to be reconstituted by Afek.

Initially, Yomnok journeyed to a great ravine where the tracks of a wild boar disappeared beneath a tangle of giant spiderwebs. Being increasingly weak, hungry, and eager for wild boar blood, he rushed toward the spiderwebs in anger and ripped them apart with his bow. When he turned to follow the tracks of the boar, however, they had disappeared, for they had been only a luminescent reflection in the spiderweb. He placed the fragments of torn spiderweb in his netbag and departed from the ravine to begin again the search for boar tracks. As he entered the low forest, he suddenly found himself entangled in great nets of spiderwebs, but the webs fell away at the first light breeze and were carried into a nearby stream. He was puzzled at how they had lost their strength, but he knew how he had lost his own. By an anology, Trumeng observed that the spiderweb, also an image of reflections and shadows, had been forever weakened when its delicate weavings were torn, as had the reflective qualities of the fragmented crystals from Telefolip been weakened or destroyed when they were shattered by fire.

Again abroad, Yomnok set a trap on a forest path known as the haunt of large wild boars and then lay in hiding nearby. Suddenly, a giant, strange, and unknown creature burst from the underbrush and pursued him as though he himself were a hunted wild boar. In fear, he ran quickly and then circled behind and killed the creature, which was transformed into a wild boar in its death throes. But, as he approached, the boar suddenly returned to life and then transformed itself once again into another kind of terrifying but unknown creature, who attacked him and drank blood from his wounds. Trumeng noted the connection between this creature who repeatedly changed form and was always highly aggressive and the unidentified fossil that the Telefolmin elders had found among the ruins of Telefolip. Both, he claimed once again, were malevolent forest spirits, who transform themselves into various other kinds of spirits and creatures, attack unsuspecting travelers and hunters in the forest by emerging from hidden places, and often weaken their victims by drawing blood. In commentary, he noted again that the fossil represented a corruption of the ritual center at Telefolip, for the presence of forest spirits in the sacred time-place is known to destroy the integrity of ritual performances in inappropriately drawing vital substances from the bodies of ritual participants and, thus, weakening their *finiik*.

Finally, Yomnok left the cavern once again in search of a wild boar and followed its tracks to a grove of pandanus trees, where he saw it feed upon the scattered nuts and then fall ill, convulse, and die. As its death agonies progressed, however, its tracks mysteriously began to disappear, and its dying gasps became audible gurgles. Its *finiik* was beginning to leave its body in the final stages of dying. While its body was still quivering Yomnok anointed its skin with the red blood of his many scratches from the underbrush, and the boar suddenly revived and fled into the forest. Trumeng then suggested, in parallel to the rib segment portraying Afek, that the charred echidna skulls found at the site of the destruction of the ritual structure at Telefolip had been stripped of their ritual decoration of red pigment—a desecration which had resulted in the rotting of the crumbling skulls and the loss of their reflective qualities.

Returning again to the sternum segment, however, Trumeng traced another path from sternum to spine through the heart. Yomnok also once remained in the cavern for many months as he prepared the first performance of the great rites of sweet potato. But, as he began these rituals, a new wind entered the cavern, and he, like Afek, fell ill with a strong fever. In his fevered state, his heart began to race, and the *sacrae* that he had created turned to viscous mud and ceased being reflective. By the same analogy he had drawn before, Trumeng noted that the crumbling quality of the ancestral skulls and boys' bones from Telefolip was due not only to their immolation in the great fire, but also to the incessant weakening of the *finiik* that had been occurring ever since the advent of suffering and death. To demonstrate the relevance of this claim, he once again maintained that he had observed a difference in the crystal reflections of the ancestral skulls and the boys' bones, and that the former continued to exhibit traces of a more powerful but weakened *finiik* that still adhered to the bone of the skulls. The boys' bones, however, showed no sign of the presence of any *finiik*, despite the fact that they had been living in more recent times.

In emphasizing the parallels and linkages between the episodes of the sacred myth and the artifacts of the historical event, Trumeng retraced the structure of this bony segment once again, but this time in reference to various parts of the ritual house which had been destroyed in the fire at Telefolip. Two intertwined sets of analogies formed the structure of this facet of the mythic interpretation, for the episodic bones of the mythic narrative were focused on the skeletal structure—the central doorway, the three decorated houseboards on the sides, and the sacrificial hearth at the center—of the ritual house, on the one hand, and the skull, ribs, and sternum of the skeletal structure of the body, on the other. Interwoven with this analogic portrait was attention to the elaborate symbolism of ritual houses, which is bound up with understandings of human anatomical structures as the bodily encasements of the power of the *finiik*. Indeed, Trumeng soon focused the interpretation once again on the theme of the ever-weakening *finiik* 'spirit or life-force' in terms of fundamental matters of self, person, and agency as reflected in the present condition of humans and the entailments and consequences of that condition for both communal and cosmological aspects of tradition in the center-place. In this context, he once again enunciated his imaginative view of the ambiguous character of historical events, which were sometimes wrought by human action. Then, by way of conclusion, he reiterated his view that the great destruction at Telefolip and elsewhere among the ritual centers of the Mountain-Ok region was not only, or perhaps even primarily, a matter of ancestral intention or design, or a newly emergent pattern hidden among the great secrets of the first ancestors and lost to subsequent ancestors who were beset by suffering and death and a weakening of *finiik,* or a matter of enduring patterns and propensities of the sacred time-place. The remedy to shield the sacred things of the center-place from such calamitous harm, he boldly suggested, lay within the province of human ritual action. What remained of the sacred time-place among Bimin-Kuskusmin, now that the western pillar of ritual knowledge at Telefolip had been irrevocably weakened, must be secured by new forms of the imagination of the nature of sacred myths and historical events if the confluence of the lessening winds of the first ancestors and the quickening first winds from a new source were to be understood. Trumeng's long discourse on such new forms of imagination is often recounted. And he forcefully added that to secure these things would require the ritual work of mortal men and perhaps would involve new forms of ritual previously unimagined and not ordained by discernible ancestral design.

Shortly after the completion of this famed and often recounted mythic interpretation, the elders launched a massive and self-conscious effort to strengthen the remaining eastern pillar of ritual knowledge within the Mountain-Ok—their own ritual complex—by beginning deliberately to alter their traditions of myth and ritual—a process perhaps begun in the purification of the corpus of sacred myth in the aftermath of the time of the great destruction and continued into the present. In many senses, the arenas of Bimin-Kuskusmin performances that focused on the sacred time-place became more rigidly marked and bounded, with rules of access and trespass becoming richly elaborated. At that time, the exchanges of ritual *sacrae* with other ritual centers of the Mountain-Ok region ceased, and the tradition of encouraging ritual elders from other areas to attend local performances of rites and narrations of myths and to witness displays of other *sacrae* was abandoned. A previously somewhat fluid sociology of knowledge was given considerable structural rigidity, with hierarchical categories of persons entitled to various corpora of mythic-ritual knowledge becoming more precisely defined and increasingly encompassed by myriad rules of secrecy, food taboos, behavioral restrictions, and other symbolic markers of categorical difference, entitlement, and access. Vast arrays of ritual paraphernalia were refurbished, replenished, or created anew, and unprecedented *sacrae* were imaginatively created. New caverns became ritual sites; new shrines were established throughout the landscape of the center-place; and new ritual groves and gardens were begun. Hundreds of new crystals were harvested and sanctified for placement in revitalized cult houses. The already complex decade-long, ten-stage male initiation cycle was elaborated, with the ninth stage becoming partitioned into two parts, to counterbalance the diminution of the length, intricacy, and efficacy of the Telefolmin rites of initiation.

In turn, the further purification of sacred myth proceeded in diverse ways. The exegetical traditions surrounding mythic-ritual practices became vastly more complicated and self-conscious, with the increasing efflorescence of detailed elaborations of diverse concepts being expanded and reworked and made more precise, of rich displays of intricate images of many kinds, and of intricate classificatory systems that enfold both image and concept. However, and of special importance in this matter, the role of the imagination—now seen by the elders as being, in part, a *praxis* no longer exclusively bound to the patterns and charters of sacred myth but being more reflective and reflexive in a broader sense—was harnessed to intentional designs to protect an important ritual center from further erosion and to keep at a deliberative distance from that center the threat of various historical events. In areas of their mythic-ritual complex where marked conceptual development was already the case, concepts were further expanded, elaborated, and systematized. In other domains where conceptual development did not directly intrude upon the efflorescence of images, concept and image became more powerfully and intricately interconnected. Yet, certain realms of imagery were embellished without conceptual elaboration—remaining a deliberately bounded area of sacred tradition from which to launch mythic narrations and ritual performances. Thus, it is perhaps no accident that the first attempts by local Christian missions to gain a foothold in the center-place were met by a long deliberated and anticipated, well rehearsed, and elaborately philosophical denial of the request, and that recent conversion to Christianity, in turn, has been a careful, collective decision that is protective of the sanctity of the sacred time-place, now increasingly shielded also by a more mortal and worldly sense of the protective force of Afek's mantle. Of course, Trumeng, a man of remarkable traditional sensitivity, of profound understanding of the forces of change in a transforming world, and of innovative capability, has been at the forefront of the imagination of and response to both changes.

Trumeng, like Bosuurok who figures prominently in my complementary essay,[63] is a paramount ritual elder of his clan and ritual moiety and, thus, also a paramount curer-diviner and political-economic leader, for economic, political, and ritual authority and power are intricately interconnected among Bimin-Kuskusmin.[64] Indeed, Trumeng and Bosuurok, representing the highest ranked clans of the Kuskusmin and Bimin ritual moieties, are the politically and ritually most powerful elders in the center-place. Yet, the primary focus of authority and source of power is high ritual status and the experience, knowledge, understanding, entitlement, skill, talent, and genre of personhood attributed to its incumbents. Mythic-ritual knowledge is, for such ritual elders, a resource to be deployed in a variety of social transactions, but its very deployment is an emblem and index of their entitlement, authority, and power to reveal and to interpret its secrets. Such knowledge implicates at once understanding, authority, and power, centered on myth and ritual but pervading most domains of Bimin-Kuskusmin social life. It is by virtue of such knowledge that they symbolize the unity, exclusiveness, and essential values of Bimin-Kuskusmin tradition and represent those ancestral elders who have borne and protected that tradition over countless generations since primordial times. In a sacred state of ritual purity, they embody an immanent force derived from ancestral beings whose voice they articulate in archaic forms of ritual speech. In mediating between the realms of mortals and ancestors, they regenerate tradition by invoking its primordial and enduring foundations through their invocations of the authority of ancestral wisdom and power. Wrapped in the cloak of such traditional authority and power, however, they also hold special entitlements and resources to provoke change by articulating their imagination of its inevitability, necessity, or desirability, of the forms that change should take, and of ritual accommodations of such change.

As the paramount ritual elder of the Imoranmin clan and Kuskusmin ritual moiety, Trumeng has not only an ordained entitlement and responsibility to engage in mythic interpretation, but also a privileged access to semantic creativity in his authority to interpret—to nominate, mark, and signify some sense of a deciphered reality and its entailments and consequences for ritual action. Although his mythic interpretations are formally empowered by his exalted ritual status, his personal reputation is also involved in his credibility. He is renowned for his mastery not only of mythic narratives, but also of mythic narration—not only of ordained mythic metaphors, but also of the creative potentials of the figurative discourse of myth telling. Performatively, his skill in innovatively constructing metaphoric assemblages in mythic interpretations lends an aura of ambiguity, magicality, aesthetic ingenuity, and power to his discourse. It is recognized that his power of mythic interpretation rests, in part, on some privileging of concept, which can be discursively constituted, unpacked, condensed, metaphorically cast, and so on, in highly innovative fashion, over image, which tends to be more fixed and less malleable in its anchorage to tradition. Power, which is ultimately predicated on esoteric 'ritual knowledge' *(ben'khaa baasok akaaraak'sakhaan)* and on 'ritual understanding' *(ben'khaa khaim'khraakkhaan'naam),* is at issue in the acceptance (or modification or rejection) of a mythic interpretation, and power, knowledge, and understanding may converge in a tacit or masked problem of ideology cast in terms of regional ritual pre-eminence. Ritual elders have significant ideological stakes in the politics of ritual and in the political arenas beyond, but importantly linked to, the domain of ritual.

Like Bosuurok in another context, Trumeng has embedded in his interpretation of the great destruction his own ideological agenda for making sense of the dramatic new events in his world and for ensuring and even enhancing his authority and power within them. Implicit in his interpretation but well known to his audience is the ever-encroaching presence of the European who first appeared among the Telefolmin. Indeed, sheet lightning had already become a metaphor for the muzzle flash of a rifle—the most feared symbol of the power of these alien beings. Thus, he implies, the great destruction at Telefolip was, for the Telefolmin, a new wind that could not be turned aside and would never cease. The position of this long-revered ritual center in the Mountain-Ok region had been irrevocably, irremediably eroded. Yet, for Bimin-Kuskusmin, who now held hegemonic ritual dominance in the region in their own view, the implications of the great destruction could be dealt with through an innovative recasting, strengthening, and protecting of the mythic-ritual traditions of the center-place. In this elaboration of tradition and in its entailments and consequences for understanding and contending with the fall of Telefolip and the rise of European influence, Trumeng's authority would reach its greatest heights. With Bosuurok, his peer, comrade, and brother-in-law, he would most profoundly and influentially articulate the rationale and the shape of Bimin-Kuskusmin elaborations of ritual and reactions to the European presence.

A given mythic interpretation, nonetheless, is subject to internal critiques within the privileged sphere of ritual elders on any of several grounds. The interpreter may be recognized as inappropriate in recognized ritual status, purity, skill, or talent and, more subtly, in acquired reputation. The versions of sacred myths selected as the framework of the endeavor may be seen as somehow inappropriate to the interpretive task. The historical events to be interpreted may be deemed insignificant or already well understood through ordinary analogy and, thus, not an appropriate subject for such profound interpretation. Some aspect of the interpretive performance—the *praxis* of mythic interpretation—may be flawed in any of myriad ways in the context of traditional canons governing this performative genre, its ordained forms, and its innovative possibilities. The interpretation may contradict some set of prior interpretations that remain valid by strong social consensus among elders. On all grounds, Trumeng's masterful mythic interpretation of the great destruction was consensually accepted among other important ritual elders, many of whom had attained, not incidentally, their exalted statuses in important measure through his support. His project of response to the great destruction was soon carried forward by the entire Bimin-Kuskusmin community, with enormous investment of time and effort.

In the idiom of an account—or, indeed, in the interweaving of several accounts—of the great destruction at Telefolip and of its significance, this essay has explored how the Bimin-Kuskusmin conceptualize the imagination and how, in terms of that notion and related images and concepts, they may have become more skeptical and self-conscious in their understanding of a sense of tradition through an appraisal of their *praxis* of mythic interpretation of historical events in a moment of crisis. This skepticism and self-consciousness has partially illuminated for them how that *praxis* is predicated on and instantiated in the unstable, shifting contours of sacred myth and historical event and how central the fragilities and imponderables of human action are to such *praxis.* These changes, both in the idea of the imagination and in its *praxis* in institutional forms, have seemingly wrought at least the rudiments of a new sense of time and place, of self, person, community, region, and cosmos, that has become all the more elaborated, sometimes in yet different ways, as the coming of the European early in this century has slowly led to the recent opening of the mountain fastness of the Bimin-Kuskusmin to the forces of a colonial presence, of the proselytizing activities of missions and schools, and then of an independent nation-state. The account of the great destruction, nonetheless, exhibits important resonances with mythic accounts which portray the great time of darkness and the first appearance of the elder brother of the sun, as well as many other cataclysmic turnings of the tides of tradition that have punctuated and perhaps reshaped the time of sacred myth from the epoch of the great first ancestors to the era of the culture heroes that marks the far boundaries of the reach of living memory. There is, then, something of an enduring mythic model for viewing the great destruction in a more or less time-honored way as a catastrophic harbinger of profound change.

Perhaps, it might be argued, the *ethno-historical* account of the great destruction is no more than a myth of cataclysm and of change in the making, but seen from a vantage point that is privileged, albeit only in some ways, in its proximity to events which are still richly a part of the memories of the living. That very proximity may somewhat disable a grasp of the enduring patterns in the recent dislocations, for how the great destruction will appear to scholars of *myth, history,* and *reason* conducting research among Bimin-Kuskusmin in this remote region in generations to come is uncertain; and the Bimin-Kuskusmin whom they will encounter will not be the same. Indeed, Trumeng and Bosuurok—the last great ritual elders in living memory—are already gone, and Christianity has now become a new force in the community. The long-recognized processes of structural amnesia, telescoping, and other aspects of the reshaping of genealogical time are perhaps better understood, or seemingly so, than the processes which give shape and meaning to mythico-historical time because the refashioning of genealogical constructs is more readily seen in the contexts of ongoing sociopolitical disputes and in a relatively shorter temporal span within which living and variable memory is transformed into a more constant and less disputatious traditional form. Yet, a general problem of the character and boundaries of *myth* and *history* pervades this understanding as well,[65] as does the politics of the mythic interpretation of historical events which has been addressed in this essay only in brief summary. In the study of nonliterate societies, however, it has always been rather easy to overplay the force of timeless *myth* and enduring local *tradition* and to underplay the force of other senses of *history* and a philosophically developed sense of *reason*. In turn, it is also easy to ignore both the changing and the enduring aspects of the foundational *myths* that are the legacy of modern Western academic senses of *myth, history,* and *reason*,[66] and to assume that the Western cultural imagination somehow readily transcends its historical moments. In the West, *myth* has often been relegated by *reason* to a realm of the imagination distinct from *history* in a particular configuration of genres of understanding. Among Bimin-Kuskusmin, however, the imagination has yielded a different portrait of *myth, history,* and *reason,* yet the directed force of the Bimin-Kuskusmin imagination toward understanding the entailments and consequences of catastrophic events for the course of human life is somehow not beyond the Western imagination.

Notes

1. The elaborate, powerful image of Afek, who is known by various sacred names in distinctive hierarchical strata of mythological discourse and is often associated with the mysterious cassowary, represents the primordial founding ancestral figure *par excellence.* Emerging from the decay of a primordial lizard who carved the riverine system of the land with its tail, she is portrayed as an androgyne, a surviving twin of the lizard who bore her, as well as the incestuous mate of her brother Yomnok, who is associated with the anomalous echidna monotreme. Afek created the first human and "totemic" ancestors, established the foundations of Bimin-Kuskusmin tradition, revealed the secrets of myth and ritual, and subsequently departed for the ancestral underworld with her lastborn son. The myriad myths of Afek represent the core of the Bimin-Kuskusmin corpus of sacred myths and are believed to be narrated *in toto* in the performance of the final and most elaborate rite of the male initiation cycle. The narration of this ritually embedded corpus of Afek myths recorded in the field took some eighty continuous hours.

2. The 'first ancestors' *(khyrkhymin)* represent all of the "human" progeny of Afek and Yomnok, as well as the "totemic" siblings of such offspring (representing all of the mythically and ritually significant florae, faunae, geological forms, and astronomical bodies), before the advent of suffering and death. These original ancestors are portrayed as the most powerful, pure, knowledgeable, and otherwise idealized forms of humanity and are depicted as immortal, although they are also said to be incomplete. Ideally, such completion was to be effected through rituals, which subsequently were seen to have insufficient efficacy for this purpose because of increasing decline in the moral-spiritual "human condition." Note that the "totemic" siblings, which analyti-

cally may be seen to enter into classificatory systems that mark, among other phenomena, relations among patricians in a manner recognizable from Lévi-Strauss' discussion of the matter, are believed to be endowed with personhood in the same manner as other forms of *khyrkhymin*. See C. Lévi-Strauss, *La pensée sauvage* (Paris: Plou, 1962).

3. Toward what was to become the end of the era of the first ancestors, Afek summoned these ancestors in order that she might disclose her most powerful mythic and ritual revelations. For reasons that remain obscure, however, the first ancestors, unlike their "totemic" siblings, failed to assemble. In a rage, Afek brought suffering and death to the land, made the passages to the ancestral underworld impassable to the living, and journeyed to this ancestral abode alone with her lastborn son, to whom she revealed the great secrets that she had denied to the now mortal humans. She noted that her lastborn son would return someday to the land and enlighten the Bimin-Kuskusmin with these long-withheld and profound secrets, yet humans would progressively become weaker and unable to discern the sacred meaning of myth and to perform efficaciously the rituals that she had once bestowed upon them.

4. The notion of the center-place refers not only to local images of the traditional, contiguous territory of the Bimin-Kuskusmin (including ritually consecrated land recognized to have been conquered in the remembered past), but also to local claims of the centrality of this territory in a regional ritual system. In addition, the idea of the center-place refers to the ritual and mythic integrity of this territory, which is marked at periphery and center by caverns laden with crystals and stalactites and stalagmites, cult houses, ossuary caves, ritual gardens, sacred groves, shrines, spirit paths, waterfalls, and other mythically enshrined relics of a primordial past. This mythic and ritual integrity of the center-place is elaborately represented by an image of a dense network of underground capillaries through which oil is said to flow, and the oil—the 'semen of Afek' *(maiyoob'uus afek'khaan)*—emerges through a sacred hole in the very middle of the center-place. See F. J. P. Poole, "Erosion of a Sacred Landscape: European Exploration and Cultural Ecology among the Bimin-Kuskusmin of Papua New Guinea," in *Mountain People,* ed. M. Tobias (Norman: University of Oklahoma Press, 1986), 169–82.

5. This concept of understanding refers to a capacity believed to be peculiar to the primordial first ancestors and only to be approximated in the present by senior ritual elders. It involves a distinctive form of "thinking/feeling" peculiar to the capacity of 'wisdom' *(agetnaam)* and the acquisition of 'ritual knowledge' *(ben'khaa baasok akaaraaksakaan)* and known as 'being in the same time-place with' *(kuurkhaaraniin).* It is associated with the revelatory

qualities of reflections and shadows that are imagined to be bound up with the sacred characteristics of crystals, phosphorus, rainbows, spider webs, spirit paths, and waterfalls, which are believed somehow to illuminate the totality of phenomena.

6. In this context, the 'bones of the center-place' *(abiip mutuuk kuunan)* refer to marked sites of mythic or ritual significance. They are often said to be living fossils of the bones of the first ancestors, who still dwell in the ancestral underworld. More ordinary fossils, commonly found in caves, are sometimes said to be the bones of now unknown "totemic" ancestors.

7. In primordial times, Afek's mantle, woven of iridescent spider webs and cassowary plumes, formed the canopy of the sky, which encased the center-place (then including the ancestral underworld) and was held to earth at its edges by "totemic" marsupials on the encircling mountain crests. When suffering and death came upon the land, however, the upper part of the canopy soon decayed, exposing the center-place to all manner of "natural" catastrophes. Remnants of Afek's original mantle are represented in the appearance of comets or meteors, which are said to arise from and return to the ancestral underworld.

8. Crystals, phosphorus, rainbows, spider webs, spirit paths, and waterfalls enter into the most elaborately marked metaphoric constructions that are intended to illuminate the nuances of the understanding of the 'sacred meaning' *(aiyem'khaa)* of sacred myths. See F. J. P. Poole, "Wisdom and Practice: The Mythic Making of Sacred History among the Bimin-Kuskusmin of Papua New Guinea," in *Discourse and Practice,* ed. Frank Reynolds and D. Tracy (Albany: State University of New York Press, 1992), 13–39.

9. The first great time of darkness, in which there was no light, and ash and stone fell from the sky, may well have coincided with known volcanic eruptions in the Southwest Pacific over the millennia, and the image appears in various forms in the myths of diverse communities throughout the New Guinea Highlands. See R. Blong, *The Time of Darkness* (Canberra: Australian National University Press). In turn, images of the first appearance of the elder brother of the sun seem to refer to the phenomenon of a lunar elipse of the sun. Together, these two cataclysmic events are generally interpreted as omens—especially significant in their fusing, respectively, of night and day and of sun and moon—of the coming of suffering and death to the center-place. Both phenomena are said to require extraordinarily elaborate and prolonged ritual action to counteract the consequent weakening of the *finiik* 'spirit or life-force' of humans and the efficacy of the rituals in which they engage.

10. The time of the 'great destruction' *(daraata'koruun miitan)* refers to a set of seemingly unprecedented disasters that befell various sacred sites throughout the Mountain-Ok region—that ritual region of culturally similar and socially interacting ethnic groups which extends approximately from the Star Mountains (to the west), to the headwaters of the Fly River (to the south), to the Strickland Gorge (to the east), and to the Om River (to the north)—and that eventually came to be associated with the increasing intensity of the appearance of the European in the area.

11. The great destruction, the subsequent divinations, and the varied mythic-ritual attempts to understand these divinations and to shield the sacred things from harm, all of which seem to have occurred in the mid-1940s, resulted in a perception of profound change among Bimin-Kuskusmin in regard to their "philosophical" stance concerning fundamental matters of myth and ritual in interpreting and affecting the 'winds' *(iniim,* in reference here to matters of change) of the center-place.

12. The field research among Bimin-Kuskusmin upon which this essay is based (1971–1973) was generously supported by the National Institutes of Health, the Cornell University/Ford Foundation Humanities and Social Sciences Program, and the Center for South Pacific Studies of the University of California, Santa Cruz. The primary debt of gratitude, however, is owed to the Bimin-Kuskusmin people, in general, and to their ritual elders, in particular, for their attempts to impart something of the profound *mythologiques* that form a cornerstone of their sense of wisdom. For mostly wise comments on the present analysis, special thanks are due to A. Al-Azmeh, F. Bantly, R. Bernstein, S. Collins, S. Gressens, P. Griffiths, M. Meeker, R. Parmentier, L. Patton, P. Powers, F. Reynolds, R. Shweder, S. Tambiah, C. Taylor, D. Tracy, and L. Yearley.

13. In this essay a number of Bimin-Kuskusmin concepts are indexed by their linguistic expressions. Such terms or phrases are given English glosses, often of some complexity, without explicit attention to the problematic nature of such translation, which is inevitably itself a critical aspect of comparison. This approach is taken for two reasons. First, some of the subtlety of the Bimin-Kuskusmin sense of these terms or phrases—and the discourse in which they are embedded—is intended to be conveyed in the text (or in Poole, "Wisdom and Practice," 13–39), and detailed attention to the ethno-semantics of these terms or phrases would be inappropriate in this essay. Second, the deliberate juxtaposition of Bimin-Kuskusmin and English terms or phrases denoting (or connoting or indexing) complex concepts implicated in both languages is intended to be provocative in evoking attention to the nature of the similarities and the differences between them. Such translations are constructed by draw-

ing tentative analogies through both glossing and positioning in the narrative, anchoring meaning to more or less densely descriptive contexts, realigning the trajectories and refocusing the lenses of the analogies, and so on, in order to weave an ever-richer web of analogic connections between their terms or phrases (concepts) and those more familiar. The endeavor seeks to bend the creative potential of the conceptual repertoire of each language in the direction of the other by narratively constructing a mode of analytic discourse that uses the semantic resources of English to encounter, engage, envelop, and illuminate something of the resources of the Bimin-Kuskusmin imagination in its linguistic manifestations.

14. See F. J. P. Poole, "Melanesian Religions: Mythic Themes," in *The Encyclopedia of Religion,* ed. M. Eliade, et al. (New York: Macmillan, 1987), 359–65. As I note elsewhere, analyses of mythology in Melanesia have rarely explored the problem of myth vis-à-vis history, although there are now some illuminating studies of the cultural constitution and social force of local genres of myth and other narrative forms. See K. O. L. Burridge, *Tangu Traditions* (Oxford: The Clarendon Press, 1969); J. LeRoy, *Fabricated World* (Vancouver: University of British Columbia Press, 1985); R. Wagner, *Lethal Speech* (Ithaca: Cornell University Press, 1978); J. F. Weiner, *The Heart of the Pearl Shell* (Berkeley: University of California Press, 1988); M. W. Young, *Magicians of Manumanua* (Berkeley: University of California Press, 1983). In turn, recent studies of Melanesian history and ethno-history represent a new sensitivity to the complexities and subtleties of what constitutes historical knowledge in local societies of the region, but again the puzzle of myth vis-à-vis history is generally addressed only obliquely, if at all. See N. McDowell, "Past and Future: The Nature of Episodic Time in Bun," in *History and Ethnohistory in Papua New Guinea,* ed. D. Gewertz and E. L. Schieffelin (Sydney: Oceania Monographs, University of Sydney, 1985), 26–39; E. L. Schieffelin, "The Retaliation of the Animals: On the Cultural Construction of the Past in Papua New Guinea," in *History and Ethnohistory in Papua New Guinea,* ed. D. Gewertz and E. L. Schieffelin (Sydney: Oceania Monographs, University of Sydney, 1985), 40–57; E. L. Schieffelin and R. Crittenden, *Like People You See in a Dream* (Stanford: Stanford University Press, 1991), 1–43; E. L. Schieffelin and D. Gewertz, "Introduction," in *History and Ethnohistory in Papua New Guinea,* ed. D. Gewertz and E. L. Schieffelin (Sydney: Oceania Monographs, University of Sydney, 1985), 1–6; E. L. Schieffelin and H. Kurita, "The Phantom Patrol: Reconciling Native Narratives and Colonial Documents in Reconstructing the History of Exploration in Papua New Guinea," *Journal of Pacific History* 23(1) (1988):52–69.

15. For a preliminary discussion of certain aspects of the character of comparison in the anthropology of religion(s), see F. J. P. Poole, "Metaphors and

Maps: Towards Comparison in the Anthropology of Religion," *Journal of the American Academy of Religion* 54 (1986): 411–57. For a set of elegant specifications of the nature of comparison and demonstrations of the power of comparative inquiry in accord with my own perspective, see J. Z. Smith, *Map Is Not Territory* (Leiden: E. J. Brill, 1978); J. Z. Smith, *Imagining Religion* (Chicago: University of Chicago Press, 1982); J. Z. Smith, *To Take Place* (Chicago: University of Chicago Press, 1987); J. Z. Smith, *Drudgery Divine* (Chicago: University of Chicago Press, 1982). For a general portrait of the problem of comparison in the conferences on "Religion(s) in Culture and History" that are the original context of this essay, see F. C. Bantly and F. E. Reynolds, "Hedgehogs and Foxes: Rethinking the Philosophy and History of Religions," *Criterion* 27 (1988):2–6.

16. See Fortes, "On the Concept of the Person among the Tallensi," in *La notion de personne en Afrique noire,* ed. G. Dieterian (Paris: Éditions du Centre National de la Recherche Scientifique, 1973), 283–319. By personhood, following Fortes, I refer to those culturally recognized attributes, capacities, and signs that mark a moral career and its jural entitlements in a particular society. An interest in personhood invokes a concern with the cultural forms and social forces that together publicly render the individual present in a culturally constituted "human nature" that is socially encompassed, and in some array of social positions that are the contexts, entitlements, and emblems of the achievement of particular kinds and degrees of personhood. Indeed, social personhood endows the culturally recognized individual with those powers or capacities upon which human agency depends, enables and constrains his proper actions, casts him as possessed of judgement and thus responsibility, and calls him to account in a sociomoral order. Although the capacities of personhood may be anchored to the powers and limitations of the human body and thus may be seen as "natural" attributes, they are at once judgemental, social, and often mystical capacities; persons are essentially social beings who develop in different ways and to differing degrees over the course of the social life-cycle. Thus, a person is fundamentally a social being with a certain moral status and is a legitimate bearer of rights and obligations. A person has a sense of self and of individually, a notion of past and future. He can hold values, perceive goals, recognize resources, acknowledge constraints, make choices, and thus adopt plans that are attributable to him as a being with the conscious, reflective capacity to frame culturally appropriate representations of phenomena and to have purposes, desires, and aversions which require judgement and propel and guide action. To be a person, or a moral agent, is to be sensitive to certain standards of the sociomoral order of the community and to suffer a sense of shame when their breach may be

attributed to one's judgement and responsibility. Personhood, thus, is basically a conceptual adjustment of a culturally constituted sense of "human nature" to a socially constituted jural-moral order. For discussion of some aspects of mythic portraits of dimensions of personhood, see F. J. P. Poole, "Morality, Personhood, Tricksters, and Youths: Some Narrative Images of Ethics among Bimin-Kuskusmin," in *Anthropology in the High Valleys,* ed. L. L. Langness and T. E. Hays (Novato: Chandler and Sharp, 1987), 283–366.

17. A note on the character of the ethnographic data presented in this essay is in order. Both the historical events of the time of the great destruction and the mythic interpretation(s) of them occurred some twenty-five to thirty years before the time of the original field work in 1971 to 1973. Nonetheless, the detail of accounts of these events and particularly of interpretive efforts to make sense of them is extraordinary. What, then, is the nature of a collective memory that has produced in the early 1970s this kind of detail in images from the mid-1940s? Although Bosuurok, Trumeng, and Maakeng, as well as other, less prominent ritual elders, were all directly involved in the history of these interpretive endeavors from their very beginnings, images of the first concerted attempts to make sense of the great destruction have been recast again and again over the intervening years and into the ethnographic present as the foundation of successive and continuing efforts to interpret these historical events in a dramatically changing historical context. Thus, reconstructions of earlier events and interpretations are inevitably and subtly shaped by the history of their recastings and by their role in contemporary mythic understandings of that reconstituted "past." They are also shaped by the present ideological investments in them of now old ritual elders in matters that occurred when they were much younger, differently positioned politically in the Bimin-Kuskusmin ritual domain, and armed with a less rich portrait of historical changes wrought by an alien outside world on their mountain fastness. In consequence, the cultural lens on that "past" in the present has been progressively reground and refocused by a variety of Bimin-Kuskusmin experiences during the intervening decades, despite the illusion created by the use of elaborate mnemonic designs of recapturing some veridical past. However much ideological claims may insist that such images depict an untransformed "past," therefore, they portray a "past" of and in the present and significantly shaped by present interests in that "past."

18. See F. J. P. Poole, "Wisdom and Practice: The Mythic Making of Sacred History among the Bimin-Kuskusmin of Papua New Guinea," 13–39.

19. See D. Tracy, *The Analogical Imagination* (New York: Crossroads, 1981), 446–57.

314

20. See J. M. Soskice, *Metaphor and Religious Language* (Oxford: The Clarendon Press, 1985).

21. Cf. F. Barth, *Ritual and Knowledge among the Baktaman of New Guinea* (New Haven: Yale University Press, 1975); F. Barth, *Cosmologies in the Making* (Cambridge: Cambridge University Press, 1987).

22. Other profound changes in Bimin-Kuskusmin understandings of sacred myth and historical events may well have occurred in a more remote past that is now cast in the images of a sense of enduring tradition. The changes that are the focus of this essay, however, took place within the living memory of ritual elders who were already embedded in the ritual hierarchy of "offices" (in Fortes' sense) or "commisions" (in McGaffey's term) and were privy to the esoteric debates surrounding the time of the great destruction. Indeed, these elders were the primary informants for this study. See Fortes, op. cit.; W. McGaffey, "African History, Anthropology, and the Rationality of Natives," *History in Africa* 5 (1978):101–20. Of course, it must be recognized that representations of these changes, and of their significance, are ideological and are bound up with intricate relationships of knowledge and power that inform the shape of the present political landscape of the Bimin-Kuskusmin community, yet the character and importance of these changes continue to be a matter of debate among the elders, who sometimes portray somewhat different images of the changes.

23. For present purposes, I use *ethno-history* to refer to indigenous concepts and images of knowledge of the past, with attention to how and why such cultural knowledge is constituted and socially deployed in a particular way. See R. Borofsky, *Making History* (Cambridge: Cambridge University Press, 1987); H. Morphy and F. Morphy, "The 'Myths' of Ngalakan History: Ideology and Images of the Past in Northern Australia," *Man* 19 (1984):459–78; R. J. Parmentier, *The Sacred Remains* (Chicago: University of Chicago Press, 1987); J. Y. D. Peel, "Making History: The Past in the Ijesha Present," *Man* 1 (1984):111–32; P. Rigby, "Time and Historical Consciousness: The Case of Ilparakayo Maasai," *Comparative Studies in Society and History* 25 (1983):428–56; R. Rosaldo, "Doing Oral History," *Social Analysis* 4 (1980):89–99; M. D. Sahlins, "Other Times, Other Customs: The Anthropology of History," *American Anthropologist* 85 (1983):517–44. In contrast, others tend to see ethno-history as involving the critical use of the resources of oral tradition to distill from its cultural constructions some confirmation of a "true historical record" otherwise constituted in Western historical documents. See B. S. Cohn, "Anthropology and History in the 1980s: Toward a Rapprochement," in *The New History*, ed. T. K. Rabb and R. I. Rotberg (Princeton: Princeton University Press,

1981), 227–52; McGaffey, op. cit.; J. Vansina, *Oral Tradition* (Chicago: Aldine, 1965); J. Vansina, *Oral Tradition as History* (Madison: University of Wisconsin Press). For useful discussions of the traditional character of ethno-history, see R. M. Carmack, "Ethnohistory: A Review of its Development, Definitions, Methods, and Aims," *Annual Review of Anthropology* 1 (1972):227–46; I. McBryde, "Ethnohistory in an Australian Context: Independent Discipline or Convenient Data Quarry?" *Aboriginal History* 3 (1979):128–51.

24. All 'paramount ritual elders' *(kunum aiym ser)* among Bimin-Kuskusmin are also 'paramount curer-diviners' *(kunum kusem ser)* and 'paramount political-economic leaders' *(kamok ser)* within the context of their respective clans. Thus, their ideological stakes in the mythic interpretation of these historical events are provoked not only by their positions and investments in the ritual arenas of clan, community, and region, but also by other political stances, often cast in a mythic-ritual idiom, focused on broader and more secular concerns in societal and regional affairs.

25. See R. Horton, "Tradition and Modernity Revisited," in *Rationality and Relativism,* ed. M. Hollis and S. Lukes (Oxford: Basil Blackwell, 1982), 227–60.

26. See A. N. Whitehead, *Adventures of Ideas* (New York: The Free Press, 1933); A. N. Whitehead, *Science in the Modern World* (New York: New American Library, 1948).

27. See J. Engell, *The Creative Imagination* (Cambridge: Harvard University Press, 1981). See also R. L. Brett, *Fancy and Imagination* (London: Methuen, 1969); E. S. Casey, *Imagining* (Bloomington: Indiana University Press, 1976); H. Osborne, *Aesthetics and Art Theory* (New York: E. P. Dutton, 1970); M. Warnock, *Imagination* (Berkeley: University of California Press, 1978); A. R. White, *The Language of Imagination* (Oxford: B. H. Blackwell, 1990).

28. See J.-P. Sartre, *L'imaginaire* (Paris: Gallimard, 1940), 233. Thus, with respect to the complex relationship of the "imagination" and "reality," Sartre notes,

> Poser une image c'est constituer en objet en marge de la totalité du réel, c'est donc tenir le réel à distance, s'en affranchir, en un mot le nier. Ou, si l'on préfère, nier d'un objet qu'il appartienne au réel, c'est nier le réel en tant qu'on pose l'objet; les deux négations sont complémentaires et celle-ci est condition de celle-là. Nous savons, par ailleurs, que la totalité du réel, en tant qu'elle est saise par la conscience comme une *situation* synthétique pour cette conscience, c'est le monde. La condition pour qu'une conscience puisse imaginer est donc double: il faut à la fois qu'elle

puisse poser le monde dans sa totalité synthétique et, à la fois, qu'elle puisse poser l'objet imaginé comme hors d'atteinte par rapport à cet ensemble synthétique, c'est-à-dire poser le monde comme un neant par rapport à l'image.

29. Cf. S. Gearhart, *The Open Boundary of History and Fiction* (Princeton: Princeton University Press, 1984).

30. For an interesting historical discussion of the shifting nature and role of "closed" and "open" concepts in philosophy and the arts, see M. Weitz, *The Opening Mind* (Chicago: University of Chicago Press, 1977); M. Weitz, *Theories of Concepts* (London: Routledge, 1988).

31. Current debates on the epistemological status of images, especially visual images, are usefully summarized in S. M. Kosslyn, "The Debate about Imagery," in *Image and Mind* (Cambridge: Harvard University Press, 1980), 11–28. See also M. Johnson, "Toward a Theory of Imagination," in *The Body in the Mind* (Chicago: University of Chicago Press, 1987), 139–72; A. R. White, *The Language of Imagination* (Oxford: B. H. Blackwell, 1990). There is considerable controversy concerning the epistemological status of images. Thus, Ryle, who conceived the imagination as encompassing a broad spectrum of heterogeneous phenomena, wished to deny mental images as having any status beyond an unwarranted reference to internal events. See G. Ryle, *The Concept of Mind* (London: Hutchinson, 1949); cf. D. C. Dennett, *Content and Consciousness* (New York: Humanities Press, 1969).

32. See L. Wittgenstein, *The Blue and Brown Books* (Oxford: B. H. Blackwell, 1964), 40 ff.

33. See ibid., 43.

34. See Poole, "Wisdom and Practice," 13–39.

35. See R. Verbrugge and N. McCarrell, "Metaphoric Comprehension," *Cognitive Psychology* 9 (1977): 530. Cf. E. R. Mac Cormac, *A Cognitive Theory of Metaphor* (Cambridge: MIT Press, 1985).

36. See Johnson, *op. cit.,* 139.

37. See ibid., 140.

38. See M. Turner, *Death Is the Mother of Beauty* (Chicago: University of Chicago Press, 1987), 16.

39. Cf. T. Beidelman, *Moral Imagination in Kaguru Modes of Thought* (Bloomington: Indiana University Press, 1986). The common anthropological assumption that culture is somehow a tightly and uniformly integrated "seam-

less web" has often led to notions that people in so-called simple societies, in which the homogeneity and "seamlessness" of culture is said to be especially pronounced, lack the capacity to formulate abstractions, to recognize contradictions, and to exercise "imagination" beyond traditional prescriptions. The recognition of the importance of ambiguity, inconsistency, contradiction, and imaginative innovation in cultural concepts and in their varied kinds of organization, and of their entailments and consequences for understanding alien "modes of thought," has only recently been recognized in theoretical terms. See E. Gellner, "Concepts and Society," in *Cause and Meaning in the Social Sciences,* ed. E. Gallner (London: Routledge and Kegan Paul, 1973), 18–46; D. N. Levine, *The Flight from Ambiguity* (Chicago: University of Chicago Press, 1985). It is perhaps in terms of the general significance of cultural ambiguity that the occasionally recognized plasticity or flexibility of myth makes most general sense. See R. Firth, "The Plasticity of Myth: Cases from Tikopia," *Ethnologica* 2 (1960):181–88; Th. P. van Baaren, "The Flexibility of Myth," *Studies in the History of Religions* 22 (1972) 199–206.

40. See R. Wagner, *Habu* (Chicago: University of Chicago Press, 1972), 8. See also R. Wagner, *The Invention of Culture* (Englewood Cliffs: Prentice-Hall, 1975); R. Wagner, *Lethal Speech* (Ithaca: Cornell University Press, 1978); R. Wagner, *Symbols That Stand for Themselves* (Chicago: University of Chicago Press, 1986).

41. In regard to the character of myth and mytho-poetic language, the notion of cultural imagination has often been deemed central and significant. See Beidelman, op. cit.; R. Friedrich, "Poetic Language and the Imagination: A reformulation of the Sapir Hypothesis," in *Language, Context,* and the Imagination, ed. P. Friedrich (Stanford: Stanford University Press, 1979), 441–512; P. Friedrich, *The Language Parallax* (Austin: University of Texas Press, 1986). Indeed, the very notion of mytho-poetic language alludes to the richly figurative nature of many mythic narratives.

42. See R. G. Collingwood, *The Idea of History* (New York: Oxford University Press, 1961), 242. In regard to the constructed nature of history, Collingwood notes that "the *a priori* imagination" shapes history as a form of the "perceptual imagination."

43. This class of sacred illnesses is generally believed to be caused by ancestral beings to enhance the perceptive powers of male ritual elders, who alone may be afflicted by such illnesses in contexts of ritual performances or mythic narrations. This genre of sacred illnesses is contrasted with another class of sacred illnesses, brought about by ancestral wrath under circumstances of ritual pollution, which blunt perceptive capacities. Both kinds of sacred ill-

nesses affect the state of the *finiik* 'spirit or life-force' and, thus, processes of "thinking/feeling."

44. See J. Z. Smith, *Map Is Not Territory* (Leiden: E. J. Brill), 300.

45. These crystals, which are central to all major ritual performances (including important divinations), are harvested from enormous caverns throughout the center-place—caverns sometimes reaching twenty or more miles in length and believed eventually to descend to the ancestral underworld. Indeed, the crystals are said to be the omnipotent 'eyes of the first ancestors' *(kiin khyrkhymin)*. Because crystals are endowed with important aspects of personhood and are possessed of agency, the ritual elder who cuts one from its geological matrix in a cavern must undergo a special form of mortuary rite, having already undergone rites of purification before entering the cavern. On rare occasions, divinations, accompanied by unusual sacrifices of cassowary or echidna flesh (representing the great ancestors Afek and Yomnok), may be performed in the caverns themselves. Under such circumstances, the object of concern, or some sign of it, is placed on a scaffold above the sacrificial fire and is consumed or scorched by the fire, which is reflected throughout the crystalline canopy and outcroppings of the cavern. The combined smoke of the flesh of echidna or cassowary and the burned object wafts toward the crystals, which are observed for the particular patterns of light that they reflect. Ordinarily, however, harvested crystals are stored in clan cult houses and brought into other ritual settings and are believed to store the ancestral wisdom distilled from countless generations of ritual performances, which they somehow bring to bear on the efficacy and power of the divinations in which crystals are used.

46. The sacrificial hearths in these caverns are positioned near particularly dense arrays of stalactites, stalagmites, and crystals that reflect the light of their fires. The stalactites and stalagmites are etched with generations of designs (always containing a series of concentric circles surrounding an abstract sign of the focus of a divination) that are believed to represent a chronology of divinations held since primordial times. One side of the hearth is lined with human skulls, which are said to portray all human forebears subsequent to the first ancestors, and the other side is lined with the alternating skulls of cassowaries and echidnas, which represent here the first ancestors. Separating these lines of skulls are fossils (largely of trilobites), which are associated both with unknown "totemic" ancestors whose spirits no longer rise from the ancestral underworld and with the still living but never-born fetuses of the first ancestors who continue to dwell in the ancestral underworld.

47. See F. J. P. Poole, "The Voice of 'Thinking/Feeling' and the Power of Speech: Ethno-psychological Discourse among Bimin-Kuskusmin" (paper presented at the 86th Meeting of the American Anthropological Association, Chicago, 1987).

48. See F. J. P. Poole, "Ritual Rank, the Self, and Ancestral Power: Liturgy and Substance in a Papua New Guinea Society," in *Drugs in Western Pacific Societies,* ed. L. Lindstrom (Lanham: University Press of America, 1987), 149–96.

49. Thus, all phenomena that become the foci of divination or mythic interpretation are subjected to some sense of removing this nonreflective dry dust of ordinary things from some aspect of them. Note that this external sense of 'surface' *(bangep'khaan magaang),* which is believed to contain the dust and illusory qualities of the phenomenon, is contrasted with another sense of 'surface' *(bangep'khaan sauk'khaan),* which refers to the linkage between surfaces in the former sense or to the relational position of bounded event entities in some classificatory scheme that is deemed relevant by virtue of divination or mythic interpretation. See Poole, "Wisdom and Practice," 13–39. A surface in the first sense, however, may obscure a surface in the second sense.

50. See Lévi-Strauss, op. cit. Cf. T. O. Beidelman, "Lévi-Strauss and History," *Journal of Interdisciplinary History* 1 (1971): 511–26; Bloch, "The Past and the Present in the Present," *Man* 12 (1977): 278–292; Parmentier, op. cit.; Rigby, op. cit.

51. Cf. Gearhart, op. cit.

52. Cf. P. Ricoeur, *Time and Narrative,* vol. 3, trans. K. Blamey and D. Pellaver (Chicago: University of Chicago Press, 1988). Ricoeur explores other senses in which time is refigured by narrative.

53. See Poole, "The Voice of 'Thinking/Feeling.' "

54. These bubbles, often said to be similar to bubbles on the surface of a river or in a swamp but to be invisible to all not in ritual trance, are believed to capture images of various ordinary phenomena and to transport them to extraordinary contexts. Thus, such bubbles, peculiar to the sacred time-place, are thought to reveal that the apparent "natural" order of the world is always, at least in some ways, uncertain, problematic, and different from its ordinary appearances.

55. The image of the 'wind' *(iniim)*—its force and coolness or warmth, what it bears, from whence it comes, the course it follows through the center-place, and its place of departure or time of disappearance—is a primary idiom for

representing many aspects of potential and actual change of different orders of significance.

56. Within their sociocentric cultural perceptions of structure of their ritual region, Bimin-Kuskusmin view the ritual center of Telefolip to be the western pillar of a vast ritual system encompassing the Mountain-Ok region and their own ritual traditions to represent the eastern pillar of that system. This destruction of a crucial ritual site and its *sacrae,* as well as the destruction of the living representation of an age-grade coming into being, were seen to be the most dire of omens, with profound consequences for the integrity of the ritual traditions of the Bimin-Kuskusmin.

57. The divinatory scrutiny of charred remains, especially of bone, implicates a common sequel to sacrifice. Indeed, it was seen to be necessary to determine whether or not the destruction at Telefolip had been an ancestral sacrifice of some order in response to a breach of the sacred time-place that had provoked ancestral wrath. It was determined that the cause was not ancestral intervention—or, at least, not ancestral intervention in any ordinary sense.

58. Sheet lightning is believed to be embers of an ever-burning celestial fire behind the sun that are driven earthward by forces which do *not* emanate from the ancestors. It is held to be an altogether mysterious phenomenon, of no known cause and not associated with Afek as is ordinary lightning. Yet, ordinarily, sheet lightning does no harm. Thus, why sheet lightning seemed to be implicated in the destruction remained a puzzle to be explored. But see also note 62.

59. Indeed, the Telefolmin have ceased to perform this ill-fated phase of male initiation and have truncated their initiation cycle accordingly.

60. The patch of taro garden in this context is associated with making the site more ordinary in sense, with domesticating its once sacred qualities. Yet, taro is also endowed with *finiik* 'spirit or life-force' and is itself sacred and an integral part of ancestral designs of tradition.

61. See Poole, "Wisdom and Practice," 13–39.

62. That sheet lightning is identified with the destruction of rainbows, which both contain and reveal aspects of ancestral wisdom and sacred meaning, marks its appearance as a sometimes ominous sign, for it is said to possess the capacity to sunder some of the myriad connections between the center-place and the ancestral abode which constitute the possibilities of ritually creating a sacred time-place in the world of the living.

63. See ibid.

64. See note 24.

65. See Rigby, op. cit.

66. See Gearhart, op. cit.; I. Strensky, *Four Theories of Myth in Twentieth-Century History* (Iowa City: University of Iowa Press, 1987); Weitz, op. cit.

References

Bantly, Francisca C., and Frank E. Reynolds. 1988. "Hedgehogs and Foxes: Rethinking the Philosophy and History of Religions." *Criterion* 27:2–6.

Barth, Fredrik. 1975. *Ritual and Knowledge among the Baktaman of New Guinea.* New Haven: Yale University Press.

———. 1987. *Cosmologies in the Making.* Cambridge: Cambridge University Press.

Beidelman, Thomas O. 1971. "Lévi-Strauss and History." *Journal of Interdisciplinary History* 1:511–26.

———. 1986. *Moral Imagination in Kaguru Modes of Thought.* Bloomington: Indiana University Press.

Bloch, Maurice. 1977. "The Past and the Present in the Present." *Man* (n.s.) 12:278–92.

Blong, Russell. 1982. *The Time of Darkness.* Canberra: Australian National University Press.

Borofsky, Robert. 1987. *Making History.* Cambridge: Cambridge University Press.

Brett, Raymond L. 1969. *Fancy and Imagination.* London: Methuen.

Burridge, Kenelm O. L. 1969. *Tangu Traditions.* Oxford: The Clarendon Press.

Carmack, Robert M. 1972. "Ethnohistory: A Review of its Development, Definitions, Methods, and Aims." *Annual Review of Anthropology* 1:227–46.

Casey, Edward S. 1976. *Imagining*. Bloomington: Indiana University Press.

Cohn, Bernard S. 1981. "Anthropology and History in the 1980s: Toward a Rapprochement." In *The New History*, edited by Theodore K. Rabb and Robert I. Rotberg, 227–52. Princeton: Princeton University Press.

Collingwood, Robin G. 1961. *The Idea of History*. New York: Oxford University Press.

Dennett, Daniel C. 1969. *Content and Consciousness*. New York: Humanities Press.

Engell, James. 1981. *The Creative Imagination*. Cambridge: Harvard University Press.

Firth, Raymond. 1960. "The Plasticity of Myth: Cases from Tikopia." *Ethnologica* 2:181–88.

Fortes, Meyer. 1973. "On the Concept of the Person among the Tallensi." In *La notion de personne en Afrqieu noire*, edited by Germaine Dieterflen, 283–319. Paris: Éditions du Centre National de la Recherche Scientifique.

Friedrich, Paul. 1979. "Poetic Language and the Imagination: A Reformulation of the Sapir Hypothesis." In *Language, Context, and the Imagination*, edited by Paul Friedrich, 441–512. Stanford: Stanford University Press.

———. 1986. *The Language Parallax*. Austin: University of Texas Press.

Gearhart, Suzanne. 1984. *The Open Boundary of History and Fiction*. Princeton: Princeton University Press.

Gellner, Ernest. 1973. "Concepts and Society." In *Cause and Meaning in the Social Sciences*, edited by Ernest Gellner, 18–46. London: Routledge and Kegan Paul.

Horton, Robin. 1982. "Tradition and Modernity Revisited." In *Rationality and Relativism*, edited by Martin Hollis and Steven Lukes, 201–60. Oxford: Basil Blackwell.

Johnson, Mark. 1987. "Toward a Theory of Imagination." In *The Body in the Mind*, 139–72. Chicago: University of Chicago Press.

Kosslyn, Stephen M. 1980. "The Debate about Imagery." In *Image and Mind*, 11–28. Cambridge: Harvard University Press.

LeRoy, John. 1985. *Fabricated World.* Vancouver: University of British Columbia Press.

Levine, Donald N. 1985. *The Flight from Ambiguity.* Chicago: University of Chicago Press.

Lévi-Strauss, Claude. 1962. *La Pensée sauvage.* Paris: Plon.

Mac Cormac, Earl R. 1985. *A Cognitive Theory of Metaphor.* Cambridge: MIT Press.

MacGaffey, Wyatt. 1978. "African History, Anthropology, and the Rationality of Natives." *History in Africa* 5:101–20.

McBryde, Isabel. 1979. "Ethnohistory in an Australian Context: Independent Discipline or Convenient Data Quarry?" *Aboriginal History* 3:128–51.

McDowell, Nancy. 1985. "Past and Future: The Nature of Episodic Time in Bun." In *History and Ethnohistory in Papua New Guinea,* edited by Deborah Gewertz and Edward Schieffelin, 26–39. Sydney: Oceania Monographs, University of Sydney.

Morphy, Howard, and Frances Morphy. 1984. "The 'Myths' of Ngalakan History: Ideology and Images of the Past in Northern Australia." *Man* n.s. 19:459–78.

Osborne, Harold. 1970. *Aesthetics and Art Theory.* New York: E. P. Dutton.

Parmentier, Richard J. 1987. *The Sacred Remains.* Chicago: University of Chicago Press.

Peel, John Y. D. 1984. "Making History: The Past in the Ijesha Present." *Man* n.s. 1:111–32.

Poole, Fitz John P. 1986. "Erosion of a Sacred Landscape: European Exploration and Cultural Ecology among the Bimin-Kuskusmin of Papua New Guinea." In *Mountain People,* edited by Michael Tobias, 169–82. Norman: University of Oklahoma Press.

———. 1986. "Metaphors and Maps: Towards Comparison in the Anthropology of Religion." *Journal of the American Academy of Religion* 54:411–57.

———. 1987. "Melanesian Religions: Mythic Themes." In *The Encyclopedia of Religion,* edited by Mircea Eliade et al., vol. 9, 359–65. New York: Macmillan.

————. 1987. "Morality, Personhood, Tricksters, and Youths: Some Narrative Images of Ethics among Bimin-Kuskusmin." In *Anthropology in the High Valleys,* edited by Lewis L. Langness and Terence E. Hays, 283–366. Novato: Chandler and Sharp.

————. 1987. "Ritual Rank, the Self, and Ancestral Power: Liturgy and Substance in a Papua New Guinea Society." In *Drugs in Western Pacific Societies,* edited by Lamont Lindstrom, 149–96. Lanham: University Press of America.

————. 1987. "The Voice of 'Thinking/Feeling' and the Power of Speech: Ethno-psychological Discourse among Bimin-Kuskusmin." Paper presented at the Eighty-sixth Annual Meeting of the American Anthropological Association, Chicago.

————. 1992. "Wisdom and Practice: The Mythic Making of Sacred History among the Bimin-Kuskusmin of Papua New Guinea." In *Discourse and Practice,* edited by Frank Reynolds and David Tracy, 13–50. Albany: State University of New York Press.

Ricoeur, Paul. 1988. *Time and Narrative,* vol. 3. Translated by Kathleen Blarney and David Pellauer. Chicago: University of Chicago Press.

Rigby, Peter. 1983. "Time and Historical Consciousness: The Case of Ilparakayo Maasai." *Comparative Studies in Society and History* 25:428–56.

Rosaldo, Renato. 1980. "Doing Oral History." *Social Analysis* 4:89–99.

Ryle, Gilbert. 1949. *The Concept of Mind.* London: Hutchinson.

Sahlins, Marshall D. 1983. "Other Times, Other Customs: The Anthropology of History." *American Anthropologist* 85:517–44.

Sartre, Jean-Paul. 1940. *L'imaginaire.* Paris: Gallimard.

Schieffelin, Edward L. 1985. "The Retaliation of the Animals: On the Cultural Construction of the Past in Papua New Guinea." In *History and Ethnohistory in Papua New Guinea,* edited by Deborah Gewertz and Edward Schieffelin, 40–57. Sydney: Oceania Monographs, University of Sydney.

Schieffelin, Edward L., and Robert Crittenden. 1991. *Like People You See in a Dream.* Stanford: Stanford University Press.

Schieffelin, Edward L., and Deborah Gewertz. 1985. "Introduction." In *History and Ethnohistory in Papua New Guinea,* edited by

Deborah Gewertz and Edward Schieffelin, 1–6. Sydney: Oceania Monographs, University of Sydney.

Schieffelin, Edward L., and Hiroyuki Kurita. 1988. "The Phantom Patrol: Reconciling Native Narratives and Colonial Documents in Reconstructing the History of Exploration in Papua New Guinea." *Journal of Pacific History* 23(1):521–69.

Smith, Jonathan Z. 1978. *Map Is Not Territory.* Leiden: E. J. Brill.

———. 1982. *Imagining Religion.* Chicago: University of Chicago Press.

———. 1987. *To Take Place.* Chicago: University of Chicago Press.

———. 1990. *Drudgery Divine.* Chicago: University of Chicago Press.

Soskice, Janet M. 1985. *Metaphor and Religious Language.* Oxford: The Clarendon Press.

Strenski, Ivan. 1987. *Four Theories of Myth in Twentieth-Century History.* Iowa City: University of Iowa Press.

Tracy, David. 1981. *The Analogical Imagination.* New York: Crossroads.

Turner, Mark. 1987. *Death Is the Mother of Beauty.* Chicago: University of Chicago Press.

van Baaren, Theodorus P. 1972. "The Flexibility of Myth." *Studies in the History of Religions* 22:199–206.

Vansina, Jan. 1965. *Oral Tradition.* Chicago: Aldine.

———. 1985. *Oral Tradition as History.* Madison: University of Wisconsin Press.

Verbrugge, Robert, and Nancy McCarrell. 1977. "Metaphoric Comprehension." *Cognitive Psychology* 9:494–533.

Wagner, Roy. 1972. *Habu.* Chicago: University of Chicago Press.

———. 1975. *The Invention of Culture.* Englewood Cliffs: Prentice-Hall.

———. 1978. *Lethal Speech.* Ithaca: Cornell University Press.

———. 1986. *Symbols That Stand for Themselves.* Chicago: University of Chicago Press.

Warnock, Mary. 1978. *Imagination.* Berkeley: University of California Press.

Weiner, James F. 1988. *The Heart of the Pearl Shell.* Berkeley: University of California Press.

Weitz, Morris. 1977. *The Opening Mind.* Chicago: University of Chicago Press.

———. 1988. *Theories of Concepts.* London: Routledge.

White, Alan R. 1990. *The Language of Imagination.* Oxford: B. H. Blackwell.

Whitehead, Alfred N. 1933. *Adventures of Ideas.* New York: The Free Press.

———. 1948. *Science and the Modern World.* New York: New American Library.

Wittgenstein, Ludwig. 1964. *The Blue and Brown Books.* Oxford: B. H. Blackwell.

Young, Michael W. 1983. *Magicians of Manumanua.* Berkeley: University of California Press.

Part IV

Practical Reason and the Negotiation of Difference

Chapter 8

The Rhetoric of Revolution: Comparative Ethics after Kuhn and Gunnemann

Jeffrey Stout

Comparative ethics tends to focus on two kinds of comparisons. The first kind moves across cultural boundaries: *here* people think and talk in one way about ethical topics, but *there* people think and talk differently. Questions arise about how a culturally distant (and often oppressed) "other" is to be understood in comparison with familiar patterns of thought and speech. The second kind of comparison stays within a cultural tradition while traversing temporal boundaries: *before* some moment of revolutionary change people thought and talked in one way about ethical topics, but *after* that time they thought and talked differently. Questions arise about how to describe and explain such transitions and, in particular, about the part reasoning plays in them.

This essay is about the second kind of comparison, the before-and-after kind. Among the questions it considers are the following: What is it that changes when an ethical tradition undergoes a revolutionary transformation, and what stays the same? What sorts of differences are generally most important in explaining revolutionary moral change and thus deserve the closest comparative scrutiny? What role does reasoning play in bringing about such transitions, and what role is played by nonrational or irrational forces? Does it even make sense to speak of the principal participants in revolutionary episodes as reasonable or justified in committing themselves as they do?

My starting point will be the most fully developed treatment of these questions in comparative ethics, Jon P. Gunnemann's 1979 book, *The Moral Meaning of Revolution*.[1] Because Gunnemann was working primarily in an idiom drawn from Thomas Kuhn's *The Structure of Scientific Revolutions*,[2] we will need to come to grips with that idiom if we want to understand and assess his work properly. While Kuhn's work is "arguably the most frequently cited book in the humanities and social sciences in the last twenty-five years,"[3] it has long ceased to be the center of controversy in the philosophy of science, and there are signs that Kuhn's particular terminology has begun to lose its appeal outside that field. One author well known for his use of Kuhn's vocabulary has recently declared that the Kuhnian "wars now seem to be drawing to a close."[4] When undergraduates discuss before-and-after comparisons, they are now as likely to be talking about "ruptures" and "transgressive discourses" as about "revolutions" and "paradigm shifts." How much difference this change in vocabulary will make remains to be seen, but it is sometimes hard to avoid the impression that some of the old Kuhnian battles are merely being refought in uniforms imported from France. It therefore seems a good time to reexamine what was at stake in the debate over Kuhn and to reflect on the rhetoric of revolutionary discontinuity Kuhn employed.

I will begin by making some general remarks about the significance of Kuhn's work for cultural criticism. I will then look closely at Gunnemann's adaptation of Kuhn's rhetoric. Finally, I will propose a way of taking Kuhn seriously and learning from his example while moving beyond preoccupation with his terminology.

My proposal will be that it is less fruitful to borrow Kuhn's terms than to emulate the creativity of his borrowing. He borrowed the term "revolution" from political historiography, the term "conversion" from religious studies, and the term "paradigm" from rhetorical criticism. He used these terms to suggest unsettling analogies between science and other domains of culture. The map of cultural domains will never look quite the same again. We students of comparative ethics have sometimes borrowed these terms, in turn, from him, and used them to discuss practical reasoning, ignoring his warnings and regrets. The results have rarely been edifying, and they have often left Kuhn himself bemused. Why should we limit ourselves to a few terms that served his purposes, expecting them to serve ours as well, when we can go directly to his sources with our own (ethical) purposes explicitly in mind?

The Cultural Significance of Thomas Kuhn

Kuhn sees a certain irony in the influence *The Structure of Scientific Revolutions* has enjoyed outside the history and philosophy of science:

> A number of those who have taken pleasure from it have done so less because it illuminates science than because they read its main theses as applicable to many other fields as well. I see what they mean and would not like to discourage their attempts to extend the position, but their reaction has nonetheless puzzled me. To the extent that the book portrays scientific development as a succession of tradition-bound periods punctuated by noncumulative breaks, its theses are undoubtedly of wide applicability. But they should be, for they are borrowed from other fields. Historians of literature, of music, of the arts, of political development, and of many other human activities have long described their subjects in the same way.[5]

Kuhn locates his originality mainly in his attempt to apply these rather standard historiographical tools "to the sciences, fields which had been widely thought to develop in a different way." He was assuming what he took to be a fairly standard model of how change occurs in areas like politics, applying that model where most people had assumed it could not be applied—namely, to science. No one but the most hidebound natural lawyer ever doubted that political development involved relatively stable periods of normalcy, on the one hand, and episodes of revolutionary departure from what had gone before, on the other. Many, however, had tended to view scientific development as gradual and cumulative. Kuhn aimed to write scientific history as political historians have long written political history—by showing that not everything in science can be understood as gradual, cumulative progress. Science has revolutions, too, he held, and they need to be understood more or less as political revolutions are.

This may seem like a rather mild-mannered thesis, and for some time that is how Kuhn has wanted it to seem. Just as he has been puzzled over why scholars in neighboring disciplines should find his use of ideas borrowed from political historiography especially exciting for political theory or ethics, he has also expressed surprise over the stir his book caused among philosophers of science. To understand the stir, we need first to understand what Kuhn's major thesis—that science undergoes noncumulative breaks—implied for the received view of science and the tradition of cultural criticism in which that view of science played an essential role.

A dominant tradition of thought in our culture since the Enlightenment has taken science—especially natural science—as its model of rationality, while portraying other spheres of culture, such as art, religion, morality, and politics, in a series of contrasts and comparisons. Kuhn's cultural significance derived from the role he played as a symbol of a powerful challenge to the conception of science that made this tradition of cultural criticism possible. Any such challenge to the received view of science and the associated model of rationality was bound to provoke reassessment of the other domains of culture as well. Therefore, Kuhn's project had ramifications beyond his own field, for his work implied not only a new conception of science, but also a new map of the culture as a whole.

According to the received empiricist view, scientists proceed by gathering evidence through experiment and observation and erect upon a basis of such evidence the scientific theories they take to be justified by it. The observational data, if they are to support the theories, must not presuppose them. Therefore, observation must itself, be pre- or nontheoretical—equally accessible in principle to all, no matter what their theories. Only thus, according to the received view, can observational data settle the question of which theories to accept. Science makes progress, then, by accumulating more and better observational evidence and by erecting new and improved theories on that progressively improving basis of fact. Its history is therefore an essentially uniform story of gradual, cumulative progress. We can demonstrate straightforwardly and decisively why new theories are better than old ones by appealing to theoretically neutral facts. The better theory is the one that either follows from or better accommodates the gradually accumulating observational evidence.

If you make something like this view of science your model of rationality per se, you should be able to map out the rest of culture by showing the extent to which nonscientific domains approximate this model. You will be inclined to ask of ethics, for example, whether there is anything to play the role of the observational basis in moral reasoning. If you find something to play that role, ethics will count as a rational endeavor. Otherwise, you may be forced to see ethics as nonrational at bottom—as based not on evidence, properly speaking, but rather on unreasoned commitments (to be explained either as essentially arbitrary individual choices or as reflections of underlying power relations). And so on, for other spheres of culture.

Any sphere, like art or politics, the history of which cannot be narrated convincingly as a uniform progression constrained by theoretically neutral evidence, will tend to be counted as nonrational (at least to some significant degree). In politics, for example, we speak of revolutions because there seem to be turnabouts of fairly radical proportions in our reasoning and behavior, turnabouts that cannot be captured in talk of progressive improvements of theory based on more or less steady accumulation of evidence. In a political revolution, there is no neutral evidence to which we can appeal to settle a dispute. What counts as evidence is itself under question; each revolutionary or established ideology will have its own account of what ought to be considered evidence for judging political proposals. The ideology involves what might be called a way of seeing the world. It recognizes one set of descriptions as "facts" and rejects as biased the so-called facts of its opponents. People might abandon one ideology for another. They might be "converted" to the revolutionary cause. They do not, however, adopt an ideology because it follows from or comports well with ideologically neutral facts. There are no such facts to be found.

When Kuhn said that much the same holds for science—that scientists' theories help determine how they see the world, that there aren't any theoretically neutral facts to appeal to in judging scientific theories, and that scientists use some of the same rhetorical devices that political revolutionaries do in justifying their more radical departures from established theory—he seemed to be saying that not even science was rational. He seemed to be saying that science, like art and politics, is fundamentally nonrational because it presupposes an ultimately arbitrary or merely ideological choice of some theory or world view, which in turn determines how you see the evidence against which that theory or world view will be judged.

But—at least on the reading of his position that Kuhn eventually came to prefer—he was not saying this at all, for to say this would be to accept the received model's conception of rationality and then to use it to denigrate science's claim to rationality. Kuhn later insisted that he did not accept that conception of rationality.[6] He still thought of science as a rational enterprise, one in which practitioners are largely justified in believing and acting as they do, but he did not think either science or any other sphere of culture had to measure up to empiricist ideals in order to be a rational endeavor. For Kuhn's view of science to entail irrationalism, one must assume that the old image of rationality was correct. Largely because many of his readers held that image of rationality close to their hearts—and ascribed it to Kuhn as well—his book was bound to cause the stir it did.

Kuhn was not the first to challenge the received view of science. By the time Kuhn's book appeared, Karl Popper had been attacking parts of the received view for several decades. While Popper did defend a revised conception of rationality, he did more to reinforce than to challenge the established tradition of cultural criticism. His conception of rationality as open-minded "conjecture and refutation" was still designed to draw a "line of demarcation" between science and pseudo-science in a way that would not require reworking the old map of culture. It was not so much Popper as W. V. O. Quine and Ludwig Wittgenstein who prepared the philosophical groundwork for Kuhn. Stephen Toulmin and N. R. Hanson, both working under Wittgenstein's influence, were the first to make use of this groundwork in books about science. Michael Polanyi and Paul Feyerabend were among those who sought to bring out the broader implications for cultural criticism.[7]

Viewed in historical perspective and as a contribution to a specialized field of research, Kuhn's ideas begin to recede somewhat into the surrounding landscape. His book attracted by far the most attention, but it was neither a completely novel departure from contemporary philosophical writing nor a work meant to foment conceptual revolution throughout the human sciences. The stir it caused was largely the unintended consequence of its manifold lacunae and ambiguities.[8] Controversy over the book began to die down within the philosophy of science as Kuhn's critics and defenders gradually succeeded in identifying the lacunae and sorting out the ambiguities. The resulting clarifications have had regrettably little effect, however, in the neighboring disciplines that were quick to adopt Kuhn's vocabulary but loathe to enter too deeply into the technicalities of the relevant philosophical literature.

The most important lacuna in the book was that it did not address the issue of rationality in any detail. This left readers free to fill in the blank as they saw fit, ascribing a conception of rationality to Kuhn that he did not explicitly endorse. Three infamously ambiguous claims associated with the book's major thesis made it virtually inevitable that Kuhn would be read as an irrationalist. The claims are as follows: (1) that what changes in a scientific revolution is the "paradigm" to which scientific practitioners are committed, (2) that a revolutionary scientific paradigm is "incommensurable" with its predecessors, and (3) that "after a revolution scientists work in a different world."[9] The first of these claims seemed to mean that when scientists convert to the revolutionary cause, they commit themselves to something for which neither reasons nor evidence can be given. The second seemed to imply that revolutionaries and their opponents are unable even to discuss or understand one another's theoretical differences. The third seemed to cut scientific inquiry off from the real world.

In the second edition of his book and in later essays, Kuhn explicitly repudiated the charge of irrationalism and attempted to distance himself from the more radical readings of his previous claims about paradigms, incommensurability, and "different worlds." As we will see in the next section of this chapter, when Kuhn tried to repair the damage caused by his careless use of the term *paradigm,* he sharply diminished the extent of discontinuity initially associated with the idea of paradigm shifts. When it simultaneously became clear that the difficulty of translating a revolutionary scientific theory into the terms of its predecessors "does not entail unlearnability, and that learnability is all that is required to make discussability possible,"[10] Kuhn's claim about incommensurability began to seem less worrisome. As for the claim about different worlds, most of Kuhn's defenders argued that it could readily be dispensed with as a misleadingly metaphysical figure of speech.[11] This move tended to isolate realism-versus-idealism as a side issue. Meanwhile, as a more permissive, pragmatic conception of rationality made gains among Kuhn's philosophical colleagues, it became increasingly plausible to see his thesis of noncumulative breaks as compatible with the view that science is a rational endeavor.[12]

By this point, as Rorty puts it:

> Most of Kuhn's critics have conceded that there is no ahistorical metavocabulary in terms of which to formulate algorithms for theory-choice (algorithms which might actu-

ally be useful to practicing scientists, rather than being *post factum* constructs). Most of his defenders have conceded that the old and the new theories are all "about the same world." So there is little left for them to quarrel about.[13]

With this thought in mind, I turn now to Gunnemann.

Gunnemann on Revolution

Revolutionaries and their opponents, according to Gunnemann, do not stand within a shared framework of principles and values. Revolutionaries have undergone something like a religious conversion; this conversion gives them a perspective sufficiently different from their opponents' to prevent adjudication of their competing claims. It is because revolutionaries and their opponents do not share a common framework or perspective, as Gunnemann saw it, that

> the language of justification seems as unsuited to revolution as it does to conversion: it offends our sense of what is appropriate to ask whether a conversion is justified or unjustified. Conversions can, of course, be evaluated in other ways. We may speak of authentic and inauthentic conversions and even of the adequacy of the content or direction of someone's conversion. We may also reasonably make moral judgments about the consequences of conversion and the actions of those who stand in some relation to the converted person. But in none of these cases are we weighing the justice of the conversion itself, and the person who is converted would find it strange indeed if the question were raised.[14]

Gunnemann implied in this passage that there is something not only odd but inappropriate about judging a revolutionary's position justified or unjustified. This is a weighty conclusion to draw from epistemological premises. If the language of justification is "unsuited" to the topic of revolution, are we barred from asking whether we would be justified in promoting or frustrating the most dramatic changes in our patterns of thought and ways of life? Apparently so.

Gunnemann took for granted in this passage that the language of justification assumes the existence of some higher standard or neutral ground to which we could appeal to settle what is "justified." The phenomena of revolutionary change make evident, according to Gunnemann, that quite different perspectives or frameworks of evaluation come into conflict with one another. In response to these phenomena, Gunnemann made the Kuhnian point that there is no higher standard or neutral ground to appeal to in adjudicating the conflict, and he alluded to Kuhn's use of the term "conversion." Because there is no higher standard or neutral ground and neither side can justify its position to the other in its own terms, Gunnemann assumed that the language of justification has no place. One either converts to the revolutionary cause, or one does not. Because conversion is a nonrational phenomenon, on Gunnemann's view, it does not make sense to speak of justification in connection with conversion.

Given the absence of a neutral framework of adjudication, there are surely many circumstances in which a revolutionary group will be unable to justify its complaints, perceptions, and proposals *to* opponents whose social and epistemic context differs substantially from their own. But "justifying one's position to someone" is only one of the notions at work in the language of justification. Another is "being justified in accepting a position." Neglect of this distinction is one of the things that made the first edition of Kuhn's *Structure* seem irrationalist in its implications for science. For glossing over the distinction makes it seem that an inability to justify one's position to one's opponent in rationally compelling terms entails being rationally unjustified in accepting that position. In contrast, underlining the distinction (and coupling it with a permissive, pragmatic conception of rationality) allows us to endorse Kuhn's skepticism about neutral adjudication without barring the language of justification from revolutionary discourse altogether.

Suppose I am an Algerian in the 1950s and have come to believe that nothing short of revolutionary transformation of Algerian society and the termination of French rule can satisfy the requirements of justice. Yet I find myself faced with reasonable opponents who do not believe this. They, too, abhor the oppression of Algeria by the French, but they propose reform rather than revolution as a remedy. They attach higher hopes to the success of reform than I do and see revolution as certain to make matters much worse for all concerned. Now, even if I have an opportunity to reason with these antirevolutionary reformers, the best arguments I construct may fail to persuade them. I might find that I cannot justify my position to them, given the extent to which their social and epistemic context differs from mine. They do not start from the same premises as I do, or reason along the same lines, or employ precisely the same concepts. So my arguments fall flat, as Gunnemann would predict. Does it follow that I am not rationally justified in holding my belief about the necessity of revolutionary struggle? Only on the assumption that being justified in holding a position entails being able to justify it (in rationally compelling terms) to one's opponents. But this assumption is, to say the least, highly questionable.

Being justified in holding a position involves a relation between a person, the propositions defining the position, and the context within which the position is adopted. A revolutionary situation, in Gunnemann's terms, is one in which two parties have conflicting positions while differing to such an extent in their respective epistemic contexts that neither party can justify its stance to the other. A permissive conception of rationality leaves room for reasonable people to disagree over matters where reason does not compel them to take the same position. Where their contexts differ in certain relevant respects, it will be all the more likely that they can diverge without ceasing to be rationally justified in going their separate ways. Why not simply say, about such cases, that someone standing in a context unlike mine is likely to be justified in disbelieving some of the things I believe? Especially when we start in different contexts, my opponent and I may find ourselves reasoning faultlessly to opposed conclusions.

Under such circumstances, it makes sense to say that we are both justified in believing what we believe.[15] This means, however, that I can condemn my opponent's conclusions as incorrect, and reject some of the premises he employs as false, without implying that he has made improper or negligent use of the evidence, concepts, and inferential patterns available to him in his context. I can grant that my opponent is justified (given his context) in rejecting my conclusions and admit my inability to justify those conclusions to him, while claiming nonetheless that I am justified in taking the position I do and behaving accordingly.

Some philosophers might deny this. They might claim that in matters of moral importance we are all (so to speak) in the *same* context, a universal one, defined by immutable laws we all can know. Or they might claim that being justified in believing something depends, in the final analysis, on being able to justify it to a potentially universal audience of rational agents. The first claim is implausible, in part for the historical reasons Gunnemann offers against it. The second is equally so, for reasons I have developed at length elsewhere.[16] Given the suspicions he expresses about an ethics of natural law, one would expect Gunnemann to reject the second claim as well as the first. But, ironically, it is hard to make sense of what he says about just-war criteria without ascribing it to him. He says that "any attempt to apply categories from the just-war tradition" is bound to distort the phenomena of revolution. If being justified in accepting the criteria required being able to justify them to one's opponents, then this conclusion, like Gunnemann's sweeping doubts about the language of justification, would be in place. If not, however, then his own evidence supports only a much weaker (and more plausible) conclusion—namely, that the just-war criteria lack the universal adjudicatory powers some ethical theorists have attributed to them.

We need now to return to the issue of whether it is ever possible, in revolutionary situations, to justify one's stance *to* an opponent. Gunnemann seemed to imply that complete perspectival discontinuity separates the revolutionary from anyone who would presume to stand in judgment of revolutionary conduct. If so, then moral discourse with the opposition—let alone the hope for neutral adjudication—would seem to have little point.

As we shall see, however, Gunnemann's explicit remarks on Kuhn suggest a very different picture indeed, one in which even revolutionary discontinuity is not total, a picture that makes more room for rational persuasion across the revolutionary barricades than he explicitly allows.

The several pages Gunnemann devoted to summarizing Kuhn comport well with the account I gave in the previous section of this chapter. In particular, Gunnemann carefully avoided ascribing irrationalism to Kuhn; he also took note of Kuhn's insistence that not everything changes in a scientific revolution. The crucial thing that changes in a scientific revolution, according to Kuhn's later writings, is the accepted paradigm of successful scientific practice, where a paradigm is an exemplar or model of solving puzzles in the area in question. Kuhn now confesses that he was insufficiently clear in distinguishing this notion of a paradigm from certain other things that might be meant by the term, but it is this notion (in its strict sense) that he takes as his own contribution to the tools historians have for studying revolutions.

Scientists never change their minds about everything, but they do occasionally abandon one exemplar for another. When they do, Kuhn speaks of this as a revolution. The change characteristically entails some revision of theoretical vocabulary—and thus the vocabulary used for describing and recognizing "facts." It also entails some change in the theoretical principles scientists are willing to accept. Above all, however, the change is a matter of commitment to imitating a new model, some apparently successful puzzle solution that seems to lend itself to fruitful extension, by analogy, to other puzzles. "What changes dramatically in a scientific revolution," wrote Gunnemann in his account of Kuhn, "is not the entire belief structure of scientists—for clearly many scientific commitments and values persist through revolutionary turmoil—but rather a specific puzzle-solving paradigm that had given coherence to a scientific community and its research."[17] As Gunnemann added in a footnote to this passage, Kuhn's clarification of this point "in the second edition of his book has helped to answer the charge by some of his critics that he does not give enough attention to the continuities of science throughout revolutionary change."

The clarification proves most important, for it is in part by bringing out the continuities that persist even in the midst of revolutionary change that Kuhn intends to avoid the charge of irrationalist relativism. When Kuhn originally spoke of scientists being "converted" to a new paradigm, he was commonly taken to mean that they had switched—lock, stock, and barrel—from one basic framework of reasons to another, and that in the middle of the switch they were simply without reasons because they were "between" frameworks. If a revolutionary conversion consists in changing one's basic principles—beyond which there is no further appeal—then it seems one could never *have reason* for this sort of change in view. The process would have to be essentially nonrational, a matter of arbitrary choice.

Kuhn, however, thinks there aren't any foundational principles in the relevant sense of principles on which everything else depends for its justification but which themselves do not depend upon anything else. He thinks there are just families of more and less general beliefs about various sorts of things and that we revise these beliefs as we go along—more or less reasonably—the better to resolve the problems, puzzles, and anomalies we confront. Even a revolution changes only a few beliefs, though the difference that makes may give a new cast to the whole. Revolutionary moments notwithstanding, then, we always have many beliefs in place to help us decide nonarbitrarily whether we would be justified in making a given change. The beliefs we have in place necessarily possess whatever advantages they needed to survive the process of criticism and revision up to this point.

We may not be able to appeal to essentially fixed rules or perfectly neutral observations to adjudicate the conflict between a revolutionary scientific proposal and the established theory. So long as the conflict continues, we will have trouble justifying our own commitments *to* the other side, whatever that happens to be. We nonetheless have plenty to go on in making up our own minds, in arriving at beliefs we might be justified in holding. In fact, we have almost everything to go on—just not as much as usual—and there is no telling, in advance, whether some of the arguments and considerations we find persuasive might succeed in winning over the opposition. We should not consider ourselves beyond the pale of reasoning simply because the issue cannot be settled by appeal to theory-independent observations or by applying rules built into reason as such.

In any event, says Kuhn, the kind of reasoning involved relies less upon "rules," which supposedly "determine choice," than upon "maxims, norms, or values," which "influence it." It relies, in other words, upon a sort of practical wisdom educated by previous experience and shaped by the history of the community. Moreover, we know the revolutionary moment has passed not when choice-determining rules have displaced the necessity of practical wisdom but rather when the community once again settles into imitation of a common model of excellence, a new paradigm.[18]

Gunnemann rightly emphasized Kuhn's recognition of continuity—some of the time. He got into trouble when he tried to adapt Kuhn's discussion of scientific paradigms to the moral sphere. He was true to his own account of Kuhn when he stressed that there is no neutral ground on which revolutionary conflict could be adjudicated, no set of choice-determining rules above the ideological fray to which we can appeal in settling disagreements. But he sometimes fell back into the practice of making the discontinuity seem total—a practice which, on his own account, must be called un-Kuhnian—and he never paid adequate heed to the distinction between being justified in believing something and being able to justify it to someone else.

When Gunnemann introduced his negative assessment of just-war criteria by saying that "there are no rules of the game [the revolutionary] can share with the enemy,"[19] he did not say what he meant by rules, nor did he show sensitivity to Kuhn's distinction between rules, on the one hand, and norms, maxims, and values, on the other. From a Kuhnian point of view, we should not expect just-war criteria to serve as neutral rules capable of determining choices among competing proposals in revolutionary disputes. This leaves open, however, a possibility Gunnemann did not explore—namely, that just-war criteria function not as rules in Kuhn's narrow sense but rather as norms.[20] Norms, in Kuhn's usage, influence choice without determining it. They may have universal scope (in the sense that we can apply them to everyone's conduct) without being unrevisable or foundational. They may also, to some significant extent, prove useful in discourse between revolutionaries and their opponents.

In Kuhn's view, the parties to a revolutionary dispute will inevitably have overlapping norms, maxims, and values. It is prudential application of norms, maxims, and values not yet in question, along with practical reflection on what we are striving for, that can guide debate in the revolutionary situation. Because norms influence choice without determining it, and because the overlap between one party's norms and another's may not be perfect, there will often be room for reasonable people to choose differently. A permissive conception of rationality holds that reason does not always dictate which positions one ought to accept. In some situations, more than one position is rationally permissible. Indeed, where contexts differ in the relevant respects, each of two parties can be expected to find her own position rationally compelling. This is not to say, of course, that everyone does behave reasonably or choose wisely in revolutionary situations. Often, parties to a revolutionary conflict are rationally unjustified in holding the positions they do. But this too is something we can determine only by employing the language of justification. The point is that we need to move case by case while remaining sensitive to details of context all along. It is a mistake to abandon the language of justification from the start simply because the hope for neutral adjudication has come to seem delusory.

When Gunnemann expressed his own suspicions about various revolutionaries and their proposals, he himself invoked the concept of justice and criticized those who declare a complete break with the past in the name of absolute freedom, liberation, or hope. His critique of Frantz Fanon in the chapter called "Revolutionary Dualism" remains, I think, an especially incisive example of argumentation across the barricades. Yet I wonder whether Gunnemann could have pressed his conception of justice very far without arriving at something like the traditional criteria of just cause, just conduct, and just ends, the unworkability of which he had alleged many pages earlier. For the central claim against Fanon's dualism seems to be indistinguishable from the familiar just-war claim that the justice of one's cause should not be allowed to engender a "crusade mentality" of unconstrained and unlimited struggle against evil. Moreover, I doubt that Gunnemann's critical arguments can be squared with the passages in which he made his strongest claims about the language of justification. Was he not assuming throughout that he was *justified* in making his claims against Fanon?

We have seen that Kuhn describes himself as taking an approach to science that had already been taken to the study of political history, at least in its essentials. His claim to originality as a historian of revolution is his notion of paradigms or exemplars. The main thing that changes in a scientific revolution is the model of scientific achievement scientists hold up for imitation. Kuhn uses his notion of paradigms to describe and explain what makes science unique as well as what makes it similar to other cultural domains. He explicitly cautions against careless overemphasis on similarities and, in particular, the common tendency to analyze all sorts of revolutions as paradigm shifts. Gunnemann, however, in hope of making maximal use of Kuhn's book as his exemplar, feels he needs to find something analogous to scientific paradigms in the moral-political sphere.

With this purpose in view, he turns to Max Weber and Peter Berger on theodicy. *Theodicy* is a term theologians have used to describe that part of theology in which one tries to show how it could be that a benevolent, all-knowing, and all-powerful God could allow evil and suffering in his creation. Sociologists like Weber and Berger have taken over the term as a name for any society's attempt to deal with, justify, or explain the existence of evil, suffering, and death—especially as hardships to be endured by people who seem not to deserve them. A society's theodicy, then, is its response to "the problem of evil" and, for Gunnemann, the sociopolitical equivalent of the scientist's paradigmatic puzzle solution. Political revolutions, according to Gunnemann, are to be explained as theodicy shifts, the transition from one paradigmatic solution of the problem of evil to another.

This is an interesting idea, but Gunnemann did something very un-Kuhnian with it when he endorsed Berger's idea that we have a "primordial" or "pretheoretical" experience of evil. This would be analogous, from Kuhn's point of view, to the old doctrine of pretheoretical facts or theoretically neutral observations in response to which all theorizing begins. For Kuhn, there is no such thing as pretheoretical experience. When Gunnemann said that our raw experience of evil is antecedent to all social legitimations and that the choice of a theodicy in effect brings society into being, he was opening up the very possibility of absolute discontinuity he elsewhere consciously resisted.

For on this model, borrowed from Berger, our submission to the patterns of subordination and domination implicit in a given theodicy is necessarily nonrational. It must be, because it is antecedent to the creation of the framework of reasons or legitimations we require to justify choices. Once a theodicy is in place, we can appeal to the reasons it supplies, but moving from one theodicy to another in a revolution involves moving into the "abyss" between frameworks. The discontinuity between social frameworks is total. Thus Gunnemann wrote as follows:

> If revolution is an innovative response to the problem of evil, and if the problem of evil is, as Berger suggests, antecedent to social legitimations, then the process of revolution resembles the actual or imagined emergence of human association itself—it is not simply the transition from one form of social order to another. Revolution is, of course, a transition from one form of social order to another, but it has features that distinguish it from other forms of social transition, features that we at least imagine to have been present at the beginning of human association.[21]

A few sentences later, Gunnemann warned against the dangers of apocalyptic language—that is, language implying that "we do not merely evolve from one order to another" but rather should expect a completely "new heaven and a new earth." It should now be clear, however, that Gunnemann built precisely such an emphasis on discontinuity into his account of revolution by borrowing as heavily as he did from Berger. Either the Berger or the Kuhn must go. They stand at odds.

If Gunnemann's more Bergerian passages were correct, then we ought to conclude that revolutions are completely beyond the limits of meaningful moral debate. There would then be no point in using either just-war criteria or anything else to help persuade opponents in revolutionary situations. Edmund Burke and Thomas Paine, it would seem, must have been wasting their time in trying to win over one another's followers by arguing whether the means employed in the French Revolution were just and whether the benefits of "cashiering" the Old Regime were enough to justify the costs of the fighting.[22] But these men were not wasting their time, for they did succeed, now and again, in converting those one would expect to be most firmly tied to the opposition's ideology or theodicy. Burke was, after all, nearly driven to distraction by hearing Paine's arguments and conclusions from the lips of the English noblemen for whose privileges Burkean Whiggism was meant to provide the ideal justification. And the reasoning Paine offered seems, as a matter of historical fact, to have played some role in the process of conversion. Has not the same been true for other great writers debating the merits of other revolutions?

Revolutions are often conceptually intimate affairs, fought on the ideological plane between parties who are bending much the same ideas in different directions.[23] In the heat of the moment, their defenders and critics often depict them as complete breaks with the past. But a retrospective view teaches that this is not so, at least if the cases of Burke and Paine are any indication. Both of these men saw the French Revolution as utterly discontinuous with what had gone before. In fact, we may owe the theme of revolutionary discontinuity to them. Looking back, however, it is easy to locate them both within the same broad tradition of European political thought—Burke struggling to hold several different strands of that tradition together, and Paine convinced that the republican strand he favored was ultimately incompatible with the others. The two men shared more assumptions and concepts than anyone could innumerate. Recall in this connection the surprise and shock Paine felt when Burke, the man who had written the "Speech on Conciliation" with the American colonies, published *Reflections on the Revolution in France.*

Similarly, only several decades after Fanon's *Wretched of the Earth* appeared in the early 1960s, no one who has read Rousseau, Marx, Lenin, and Sartre can get very far into the book without sensing that stock ideas from European radicalism are being recycled. When one encounters his demand for the complete rejection of everything European and the complete recreation of man, the unintended irony of continuity could hardly be stronger. So we ought to be suspicious of the claim of complete conceptual discontinuity, even in making sense of its most famous defenders. This is one moral of the Kuhnian wars worth keeping in mind now that other, more exotic and openly irrationalist, vocabularies of discontinuity are making the rounds.

Paradigms, Persuasion, and Practical Wisdom

Where should comparative ethics go from here? If we want to make the most of Kuhn as an exemplary figure, I propose that we view him as an Aristotelian ethnographer (of sorts) doing fieldwork among the scientists, not an epistemologist theorizing about the gaps between conceptual schemes. If this idea seems bizarre at first, it may be because nobody's conception of science seems less like Kuhn's than Aristotle's. The idea seems less bizarre, I think, when Kuhn is viewed as part of a modern effort to break down classical distinctions between theoretical and practical reason and between logical demonstration and rhetorical art. One consequence of this effort—to which philosophers as different as John Dewey, Hans-Georg Gadamer, Jürgen Habermas, Charles Taylor, and Stephen Toulmin have also contributed—is the application of categories from Aristotelian ethics and rhetoric to phenomena classical Aristotelians had consigned to the spheres of theory and logic. So, in effect, attacks on Aristotle's way of dividing theory from practice and logic from rhetoric have ironically made the *Politics,* the *Nicomachean Ethics,* and the *Rhetoric* seem relevant to virtually all of human life. Kuhn may be less conscious of his Aristotelian roots than someone like Gadamer is, but he is nonetheless skilled in finding new uses for classical ethical and rhetorical themes.

Stanley Fish has rightly pointed out that Kuhn's terminology is "rhetorical through and through."[24] *Structure* was about cases of disagreement in which "each party must try, by persuasion, to convert the other" and in which "there is no standard higher than the assent of the relevant community."[25] The book specified the means of persuasion typically used in such cases, and its author later took pains to argue that those means could be a matter of *rational* persuasion even when they fell short of being logically compelling demonstrations. Like a rhetorician, he sought to understand the factors influencing choice. He was interested in rational persuasion and sound reasoning, as engaged in by actual human beings, not in the requirements of reason, construed as a universally shared human faculty.

When he explained the major difference separating scientific revolutionaries and their opponents, Kuhn spoke of their commitment to conflicting paradigms. The term *paradigm* (like the term *maxim*) can itself be traced back to Aristotle's *Rhetoric,* where *paradeigma* is used to name the figure Latin authors called *exemplum.*[26] When Kuhn later apologized for the ambiguous use of this term in his book's first edition and vowed to make amends, it was the rhetorician's sense of the term that he decided, wittingly or not, to favor. He thus made a rhetorical figure the central component in his account of scientific revolution.

If a scientific paradigm, in Kuhn's preferred sense, is an exemplary puzzle solution, what might be the closest moral analog? One thinks immediately of casuistical traditions in which some authority's exemplary puzzle solution comes to function as a paradigm for applied ethical theory. Consider, for example, the rule of double effect as introduced by Aquinas in his treatment of homicide (*Summa Theologiae,* 2a2ae.64.7) and its subsequent extension, by analogy, to a wide variety of other issues by later Roman Catholic moralists. Among the Thomists, this bit of casuistry was treated as a model puzzle solution for imitation and application. Within this tradition of moral theology, ethics has at times approximated the condition Kuhn would ascribe to normal science. Perhaps it would make sense to speak of the recent uprising of liberal proportionalists as the beginning of a revolution in Catholic moral theology. We might then investigate the extent to which they are united by commitment to some other exemplary puzzle solution.

These are suggestive thoughts, but even if they enabled us to write detailed and illuminating histories of certain casuistical traditions (rabbinical and Confucian, for example, as well as Roman Catholic), it seems clear that we could not make sense of all epochal transitions in the history of ethics in the same way. Some such transitions, if they have to do with paradigm shifts at all, involve paradigms of a different kind (dear to the heart of contemporary Aristotelians like Alasdair MacIntyre)—namely, exemplary persons and communities, examples of the good life. Paradigms of this kind are not puzzle solutions but stories and images: narratives about Jesus or Gautama, lives of the saints, legends about mythic heroes, biblical visions of God's kingdom, nostalgic portrayals of the early church or the Greek polis as a model community, and so on. Arguably, some major transitions in the history of ethics can be explained as shifts in the use or function of such stories and images.

Gunnemann's moral paradigms are model solutions to the problem of evil, not figures of moral excellence. Because he interprets them in Bergerian fashion, theodicies occupy a structural position in Gunnemann's account of revolution more like that of "disciplinary matrices" than that of "paradigms as exemplars" in Kuhn. But my purpose is not to convict Gunnemann of un-Kuhnian tendencies, nor to demonstrate that revolutions of the sort he describes should always be explained in Aristotelian, as opposed to Weberian, terms. It would surprise me if *anything* ended up playing the same role in comparative ethics that exemplary puzzle solutions play in Kuhnian philosophy of science. I see no reason to suppose, at this early stage of comparative ethical inquiry, that all major transitions in the history of ethics involve the same kind of shift. It seems certain that paradigms of various kinds play significant roles in some historic episodes of moral transformation. By the same token, however, many things besides paradigms probably play significant roles too.

The best way to improve upon Gunnemann's account of revolution, I conclude, is to remind ourselves not only that there are many kinds of moral paradigms (only some of which pertain to theodicy) but also that paradigms are only one among a variety of rhetorical vehicles at the disposal of ethical thought and speech. If I am right about this, the most productive way to advance beyond Gunnemann and Kuhn is to be more rigorously rhetorical than either of them. This would entail being prepared to study the full array of means by which people persuade one another (and themselves) to adopt ethical convictions: the tropes of example, metaphor, irony, and hyperbole, among various others; the levels of diction, ranging from the technical to the conversational, from the dignified to the vulgar, from the foreign to the familiar; the modes of arranging linguistic material in narrative, argumentative, and fragmentary forms; and such rhetorical tactics as the appeal to authority, the invocation of maxims, and the citation of statistics. What better way could there be to explore these matters than by delving deeply into the tradition of rhetorical criticism? And if we want help in doing so, do we not have more to learn from a lifelong student of rhetorical tradition like Kenneth Burke than from a philosopher of science who borrowed from the tradition only for relatively limited purposes?[27]

To Kuhn's credit, the thing that draws him to the tradition of rhetorical criticism, while nonetheless steering him clear of irrationalism, is the Aristotelian notion that practical wisdom has the capacity to make reasonable choices in matters that cannot be determined simply by consulting agreed-upon rules. If practical wisdom were merely the ability to apply agreed-upon rules or if the scientific community were unable to sustain a subculture in which the right kind of practical wisdom continued to flourish, scientific progress, in Kuhn's view, would be impossible. When scientists respond to revolutionary proposals in their disciplines, the legitimacy of their choices cannot be proved or disproved by appeal to agreed-upon rules. As we have already noted, Kuhn thinks rational deliberation and persuasion remain possible under such circumstances in part because so much of any intellectual heritage is left in place even during a revolution. In many cases, especially in the early stages of a revolution, there will be enough latitude in the available evidence for reasonable people to move in different directions, each with his or her own sufficiently good (sometimes highly personal) reasons. In other cases—Kuhn cites Joseph Priestly as an example[28]—we will recognize clear instances of decision unjustified by good reasons. But to understand the deliberation and persuasion that do take place under such circumstances, Kuhn adds, we need to look at the "characteristics [most] scientists share by virtue of the training which licenses their membership in one or another community of specialists."[29] We must look at the skills and habits good scientists acquire and the "special kind of community" in which the inculcation of such skills and habits takes place.[30] Without the right kind of community, those skills and habits would not flourish.

I would like to make several analogous points with respect to morality and politics. First of all, we should expect there to be circumstances—especially but not only in the midst of revolutions—in which contestable background assumptions, disputable calculations of proportionality, or uncertainty over how to apply criteria to new cases will leave enough room for reasonable people to disagree. Under such circumstances, contending parties will be unable to justify their positions to the opposition simply by invoking agreed-upon rules. But this does not mean that lawlike norms become irrelevant under such circumstances, that we will lack justification in accepting them or applying them, that there will be no point in offering reasons to the opposition, or that clear instances of unjustifiable decisions will cease to be discernible.

Still, we have no guarantees. Why? Because rational deliberation and persuasion depend upon the exercise of practical wisdom—the virtue of *phronesis* or *prudentia*. And this virtue, like all acquired skills and habits, is likely to flourish only in a "special kind of community." It will not be a community of specialists, for moral reasoning is not an art reserved for a few. It will, however, be a community of a specific kind, one in which models of excellence are made available for reflection and in which all the moral virtues are, to some significant degree, nourished by practice and rewarded by honor. A severely unjust society, in which the acid of vicious practices eats away at the moral fibre of oppressor and oppressed alike, is not such a community. In a severely unjust society the habits of just conduct, made costly by oppression, will atrophy in all but the most courageous. In giving its members just cause for revolution and closing down the avenues of peaceful reform, it is no more hospitable to practical wisdom or rational persuasion than it is to justice, for wherever injustice is practiced, rationalization, wishful thinking, and suppression of evidence are in store. Severe injustice, manifested in gross inequality among classes, tends to corrupt the citizenry as a whole, threatening the possibility of reasoned debate and eventually the virtue of practical wisdom itself.

Such corruption is often the seed of dualistic rhetoric and apocalyptic imagery among the oppressed. Tutored daily in the distinction between one class and another, the oppressed will be strongly tempted to imagine themselves caught up in an ultimate struggle with evil itself. Much apparently confirming evidence will come their way. To fall under the influence of such tropes under such circumstances is not to plunge into the primordial depths of society, beneath the ground of all grounds, and to emerge again with a new theodicy, arbitrarily and mysteriously chosen. It is to accept the most salient social distinction of one's life, that between oppressor and victim, as the single fact around which to organize all moral experience. With attention focused by force on their own suffering, the oppressed will be virtuous indeed if they do not lose sight of other evils, including those of their own doing. Put in their place, and held there by the chains of injustice, they may easily forget what else besides chains they have to lose. Driven down by despair, the urge will be strong to transport themselves, through wishful thinking, to a future in which they inherit the earth and vengeance is wrought upon their enemies. Deprived of all other means of realizing their dreams, it will be easy to rationalize striking out at the innocent, creating more victims like themselves.

If the oppressed do succumb to these temptations or become corrupted in similar ways, we know what is likely to happen to the rhetoric of their opponents. It too will harden into progressively more vicious forms of dualistic thinking, and the spiral of violence and injustice will worsen. The most worrisome difficulties for moral reasoning in revolutionary situations actually start here, in the corrupting effects of injustice on the communities in which we do our thinking and talking, not in the conceptual distance between rival premises from which argument can begin. For it is typically when they are singled out as a group for unjust treatment by their oppressors that the oppressed not only first configure themselves rhetorically as a collective body but also first acquire the resentment, despair, and dualistic imagery that make tragedy the most likely outcome of whatever collective action they initiate.

Fanon was right when he said that compromise and adjudication are going to be unacceptable to such people, but he did great harm by glorifying even the most murderous forms of violence undertaken by them as something that "invests their characters with positive and creative qualities" and by rationalizing it as a "cleansing force."[31] The moral meaning of revolution, painfully often, is that the vices of the oppressors meet their match in the vices of the oppressed. It is better to call the relevant traits *vices,* even when speaking of the oppressed, than to speak unjustly or to drain our language of its capacity for invective altogether. To speak of vices in this context is to acknowledge that some traits of character, however they may have been acquired, tear apart the fabric of social life, undermining the common good. Those traits, evaluated in relation to the common good, are an essential part of the explanation of what transpires as the spiral goes deeper.[32] Tyranny breeds terror, one form of injustice begets another.

The *moral* meaning of revolution, then, is to be sought principally in moral, not epistemological, causes. We need ethical and rhetorical categories to understand it, not epistemological theories. When the conceptual gap opens between oppressors and oppressed—when, as Fanon puts it, "the Manicheism of the settler produces a Manicheism of the native"[33]—the ethical rhetoric of each side shows the marks of moral harm previously inflicted. Then the rhetorics do moral harm of their own, locking the participants into habits of thinking and acting from which only tragedy can result. That is why comparative ethics has something of moral import to say about the rhetoric of revolution, something we ought to think about and our fellow citizens might want to hear. It is no merely academic matter. It is a matter of how we can break out of the Manichean rhetorical cycle without becoming quietistic.

As Philip Quinn has remarked,[34] once the spiral of injustice gets beyond a certain point, it creates "tragic dilemmas both for individuals and for communities that are beyond the power of reason to resolve or even ameliorate." It was surely such a dilemma that Albert Camus and others like him faced in Algeria in the late 1950s, and which colonial oppression and the "cleansing" violence of native terrorists conspired to create. When Camus fell silent, he may have been moved in part by self-serving motives, but he was not mistaken in thinking that the scope for just action and reasoned debate had become extremely narrow. The proposals he had worked out a few years earlier, which were designed to allow all groups involved to survive and to pursue the genuine goods of their respective ways of life, had been made unrealistic by the course of events. It had come to pass that the only likely outcomes would be severely unjust to someone.What more was there to say? What more was there to do but care for and weep with the victims?

Even revolutionary circumstances are often better than that, and perhaps there was more for a just person to say and do in Camus' Algeria than he came to think. Yet his silence can still remind us that the "special kind of community" required to sustain the virtues is a fragile thing, always in danger of falling apart, and that nothing contributes to its disintegration more effectively than injustice itself. It would be foolish to take too much comfort in the dissimilarities between our situation and his, for there is always enough actual injustice in the communities we live in or have dealings with to place practical wisdom, and thus rational deliberation and persuasion, at risk. All the more reason to commit ourselves to justice, in all its dimensions, not least of all the rhetorical, before the hour is too late, and to hope that it is not too late for our community already.

Concluding Exhortation

Comparative ethics is less a discipline than a sort of floating seminar in which scholars from various fields trade information and discuss methodology. Because most people around the seminar table know only one or two traditions intimately and are rightly anxious to resist hasty generalization, most of the information being exchanged is introductory and fragmentary in nature. Anyone who is brave or rash enough to make a substantive comparative claim is likely to be greeted by a long series of counterexamples and cautionary remarks. Discussion therefore typically moves from historical substance to method before long, for it is at the methodological level that the seminar most readily finds common ground.

Most of us feel a mixture of relief and dissatisfaction when this shift occurs; we're happy to be back on familiar footing but disappointed to have learned so little. Some of us compensate by looking forward to a day when comparative ethics can take its place in the academy as a unified discipline. If we could somehow produce a generation of scholars who knew much more than any of us knows about the history and variety of ethical traditions, then the conversation would surely be worthwhile. But it seems doubtful that the hope for a generation of renaissance comparativists will ever be realized. Life is short, and human minds are finite. So there is some danger that the next generation's comparativists will know less than we do about anything in particular and that they will have even more trouble than we have had explaining why anyone outside the guild ought to take their pronouncements seriously. The temptation to take comfort in "methodological sophistication," and to insulate themselves from the risks and responsibilities of addressing a public audience, may be stronger than ever.

Comparativists may someday have a more secure niche within the academic bureaucracy than we have had; they may congratulate themselves for being more "sensitive to difference" and less "philosophically naive" than their teachers. But what of moral and historical substance will they have to offer their students and readers? When the professors alternate between collating facts and manipulating jargon, who outside the profession has reason to listen in? One way to earn a broader audience is by clarifying the moral import of what we are saying. And that means having something that is morally important to say, as well as an apt way of saying it. We still haven't given our fellow citizens a reason for being interested. Our style repels them.

A comparative ethics worth having will be *about* ethical rhetoric in its many varieties, good and bad, as they manifest themselves in various contexts, happy and grim. But it will also *be an ethical rhetoric,* in the sense of being a complex rhetorical performance that expresses and advances genuinely ethical concerns. The point of inquiring into the patterns of ethical language is not to catalog those patterns neutrally, recording their causes and effects, but rather to instruct ourselves in the ethics of speaking, writing, and thinking about ethical topics. The public study of ethical rhetoric is itself a rhetorical act. May it also be an ethical one, practicing what it praises.

Notes

1. Jon P. Gunnemann, *The Moral Meaning of Revolution* (New Haven: Yale University Press, 1979). For a perceptive treatment of Gunnemann's book that touches on some of the matters developed at length here, see Cornel West's review in *Journal of Religion* 61 (1981): 218–19.

2. I will refer to the second edition (Chicago: University of Chicago Press, 1970). For a collection of Kuhn's later writings, see *The Essential Tension* (Chicago: University of Chicago Press, 1977). For a more recent discussion of related issues, see his essay, "The Natural and the Human Sciences," in *The Interpretive Turn: Philosophy, Science, Culture,* ed. David R. Hiley, et al. (Ithaca and London: Cornell University Press, 1991), 17–24.

3. Stanley Fish, "Rhetoric," in *Critical Terms for Literary Theory,* ed. Frank Lentricchia and Thomas McLaughlin (Chicago: University of Chicago Press, 1990), 210.

4. Richard Rorty, *Objectivity, Relativism, and Truth* (Cambridge: Cambridge University Press, 1991), 48. Rorty's earlier book, *Philosophy and the Mirror of Nature* (Princeton: Princeton University Press, 1979), made extensive use of Kuhnian vocabulary to discuss philosophy. The publication date is the same as Gunnemann's.

5. *The Structure of Scientific Revolutions,* 208. For a useful account of this irony, see Richard J. Bernstein, *The Restructuring of Social and Political Theory* (New York and London: Harcourt Brace Jovanovich, 1976), 84–106.

6. See the essays collected in *The Essential Tension.*

7. For a relevant bibliography and a useful account of Kuhn and Popper in relation to the received view of science, see Harold I. Brown, *Perception, Theory and Commitment: The New Philosophy of Science* (Chicago: Precendent Publishing, 1977).

8. For a historical parallel, consider the reception of D. F. Strauss's *The Life of Jesus, Critically Examined,* another highly controversial text that acquired a cultural significance far more radical and determinate than anything intended by its author.

9. *The Structure of Scientific Revolutions,* 148, 135.

10. Rorty, *Objectivity, Relativism, and Truth,* 48.

11. See, for example, my treatment of this issue in *The Flight from Authority* (Notre Dame, Ind.: University of Notre Dame Press, 1981), ch. 8.

12. Bas van Fraassen has contrasted two conceptions of rationality: "The difference is analogous to that between (or so Justice Oliver Wendell Holmes wrote) the Prussian and the English concept of law. In the former, everything is forbidden which is not explicitly permitted, and in the latter, everything permitted that is not explicitly forbidden." According to the more rigid, "Prussian" conception of rationality, "what is rational to believe is exactly what one is rationally compelled to believe." According to the more permissive, "English" view, "what is rational to believe includes anything that one is not rationally compelled to disbelieve. And similarly for ways of change: the rational ways to change your opinion include any that remain within the bounds of rationality—which may be very wide." The permissive view, says van Fraassen, was advocated by the American pragmatists (Bas C. van Fraassen, *Laws and Symmetry* [Oxford: Clarendon Press, 1989], 171 f.).

13. Rorty, *Objectivity, Relativism, and Truth,* 48.

14. *The Moral Meaning of Revolution,* 2.

15. For further discussion of this sort of possibility and a general treatment of the distinction between justification and truth, see my book, *Ethics after Babel* (Boston: Beacon Press, 1988), pt. 1.

16. See my paper, "On Having a Morality in Common," in Gene Outka and John P. Reeder, Jr., eds., *Prospects for a Common Morality* (Princeton: Princeton University Press, 1993), ch. 9.

17. *The Moral Meaning of Revolution,* 19.

18. *The Essential Tension,* 293–339.

19. *The Moral Meaning of Revolution,* 44.

20. Experiment: Read Wittgenstein on following a rule, and then try to imagine something that qualifies as a rule in Kuhn's narrow sense.

21. *The Moral Meaning of Revolution,* 38.

22. Interestingly, both Burke and Paine rely heavily on just-war criteria, despite their other differences. See, for example, *Reflections on the Revolution in France,* ed. J. G. A. Pocock (Indianapolis: Hackett, 1987), 26–27, 34–35, 41–42, 72–73. In these passages Burke claims that the "Revolution of 1688 was obtained by just war," quotes Livy's version of the criterion of necessity or "last resource," applies that criterion to the French Revolution, inquires into the intentions and putative authority of the Jacobins, declares that the "punishment of real tyrants is a noble and awful act of justice," and reflects at length on the disproportionality of revolution in the French case. Throughout *Rights*

of Man, Paine tries to refute Burke on many of these points, but he assumes that just-war criteria are pertinent. He invokes them more explicitly in *Common Sense,* ed., Karl Heinz Schönfelder (Halle: Niemeyer, 1956), 67, 73–80, 92. Paine's arguments in these passages pertain to the questions of last resort ("The peaceful methods which we have ineffectually used for redress"), the justice of his own intentions as a revolutionary ("I am not induced by motives of pride, party, or resentment to espouse the doctrine of independence"), proportionality ("The object contended for, ought always to bear some just proportion to the expense"), just cause ("Thousands are already ruined by British barbarity"), and the need to establish just authority by declaring independence and adopting plans for just self-government ("While we profess ourselves the subjects of Britain, we must, in the eyes of foreign nations, be considered as Rebels").

23. As Michael Walzer stresses, following Antonio Gramsci, social critics speaking out on behalf of the oppressed are typically making use of the very ideas that ruling-class ideologues have used in attempts to justify the established order. Defenders of the establishment, because they feel a need to justify extant practices and institutions *to* the disadvantaged, provide them with concepts and ideals that can also be used for purposes of social criticism. For this reason, the conceptual gap between establishment and revolutionary ideologies is often narrow, especially when compared to that between the outlooks of two warring nations that have had relatively little cultural influence on one another. See Walzer, *Interpretation and Social Criticism* (Cambridge: Harvard University Press, 1987), esp. 40–44. See also Gunnemann, *The Moral Meaning of Revolution,* ch. 3, esp. 63–65.

24. Fish, "Rhetoric," 210. Unfortunately, Fish fails to handle the term "paradigm" with any subtlety and neglects even to single out the sense of the term that derives from Aristotle's *Rhetoric.*

25. *The Structure of Scientific Revolutions,* 198, 94.

26. For a historical discussion of this figure, see John D. Lyons, *Exemplum: The Rhetoric of Example in Early Modern France and Italy* (Princeton: Princeton University Press, 1989).

27. See, for example, Kenneth Burke, *The Philosophy of Literary Form,* 3d ed. (Berkeley, Los Angeles, and London: University of California Press, 1973), and *A Rhetoric of Motives* (Berkeley, Los Angeles, and London: University of California Press, 1969).

28. *The Structure of Scientific Revolutions,* 159.

29. *The Essential Tension,* 320.

30. *The Structure of Scientific Revolutions,* 167.

31. Frantz Fanon, *The Wretched of the Earth,* trans. Constance Farrington (New York: Grove Press, 1968), 93–94.

32. "These vices are the *causes* of these storms" (Edmund Burke, *Reflections on the Revolution in France,* 124).

33. *The Wretched of the Earth,* 93.

34. In his valuable comments on the draft of this chapter that I read at the University of Chicago in the spring of 1988.

References

Bernstein, Richard J. 1976. *The Restructuring of Social and Political Theory.* New York and London: Harcourt Brace Jovanovich.

Brown, Harold I. 1977. *Perception, Theory and Commitment: The New Philosophy of Science.* Chicago: Precendent Publishing.

Burke, Edmund. 1968. "Speech on Conciliation." In *Edmund Burke: Selected Writings and Speeches,* edited by Peter J. Stanlis, 147–185. Gloucester, Massachusetts: Peter Smith.

————. 1987. *Reflections on the Revolution in France.* Edited by J. G. A. Pocock. Indianapolis: Hackett.

Burke, Kenneth. 1969. *A Rhetoric of Motives.* Berkeley, Los Angeles, and London: University of California Press.

————. 1973. *The Philosophy of Literary Form.* 3d ed. Berkeley, Los Angeles, and London: University of California Press.

Fanon, Frantz. 1968. *The Wretched of the Earth.* Translated by Constance Farrington. New York: Grove Press.

Fish, Stanley. 1990. "Rhetoric." In *Critical Terms for Literary Theory,* edited by Frank Lentricchia and Thomas McLaughlin, 203–22. Chicago: University of Chicago Press.

Gunnemann, Jon P. 1979. *The Moral Meaning of Revolution.* New Haven: Yale University Press.

Kuhn, Thomas P. 1970. *The Structure of Scientific Revolutions.* 2d ed. Chicago: University of Chicago Press.

———. 1977. *The Essential Tension.* Chicago: University of Chicago Press.

———. 1991. "The Natural and the Human Sciences." In *The Interpretive Turn: Philosophy, Science, Culture,* edited by David R. Hiley, et al., 17–24. Ithaca and London: Cornell University Press.

Lyons, John D. 1989. *Exemplum: The Rhetoric of Example in Early Modern France and Italy.* Princeton: Princeton University Press.

Paine, Thomas. 1956. *Common Sense.* Edited by Karl Heinz Schönfelder. Halle: Niemeyer.

———. 1984. *Rights of Man.* New York: Penguin.

Rorty, Richard. 1979. *Philosophy and the Mirror of Nature.* Princeton: Princeton University Press.

———. 1991. *Objectivity, Relativism, and Truth.* Cambridge: Cambridge University Press.

Stout, Jeffrey. 1981. *The Flight from Authority.* Notre Dame, Ind.: University of Notre Dame Press.

———. 1988. *Ethics after Babel.* Boston: Beacon Press.

Strauss, D. F. 1972. *The Life of Jesus Critically Examined.* Translated by George Eliot and edited by Peter C. Hodgson. Fortress Press: Philadelphia.

van Fraassen, Bas C. 1989. *Laws and Symmetry.* Oxford: Clarendon Press.

Walzer, Michael. 1987. *Interpretation and Social Criticism.* Cambridge: Harvard University Press.

West, Cornel. 1981. Review of Gunnemann's *The Moral Meaning of Revolution,* in *Journal of Religion* 61:218–19.

Chapter 9

The Fear of *Qing*: Confucian and Buddhist Discourses on Desire

Francisca Cho Bantly

In considering the modern academic scene, Richard Bernstein has recently stated, "There is scarcely a cultural discipline today, including the comparative study of religions, that does not gravitate to the complex of issues concerning alterity and 'the Other.' "[1] The question of "the Other," as Bernstein elaborates, has obsessed Anglo-American thought traditions, particularly the philosophical disciplines, since the late nineteenth century. At the center of this concern, the so-called incommensurability thesis has held the spectre of cultural relativism over both the philosopher who seeks the pathway to atemporal truth and the historian in search of a foundation for cross-cultural understanding. Philosophers have fought hard against the implications of the incommensurability thesis, charging that its premises are caught up in a "myth of the framework"[2] or a "myth of systems,"[3] which fallaciously suggests that we are all imprisoned within our individual cultural boundaries.

The evolution of the debate on cultural relativism and its infiltration into the modern academy's scholarly practices is of

significant historical interest in and of itself, and some would
have us believe, singularly unprecedented. To be sure, the powers of modern technology have caused its benighted beneficia-
ries to bump up against each other harder and more frequently
than ever before. One might also plausibly assert that modern
thought traditions, carried out by those empowered to codify
and articulate our existence, have seldom been matched in the
self-consciousness and vigor with which they have carried out
their hermeneutical tasks. It is also true, however, that the model
conscientiousness which marks current discussions of cultural
pluralism (at least in the professional salons) is a matured species which has seen more ignoble days. Perhaps in this respect,
the modern encounter with Otherness can be traced to scenarios
that are all too common. Let us consider an analogous example
from a very different time and place. In the late fifth century,
the Chinese scholar-official Gu Huan considered the relative
merits and demerits of Buddhism—a foreign religion from India—and determined that

> Buddhism originated in the land of the barbarians; is that
> not because the customs of the barbarians were originally
> evil? The Tao originated in China; is that not because the
> habits of the Chinese were originally good? . . . Buddhism
> is not the way for China, Taoism is not the teaching of the
> western barbarians. Fishes and birds are of different ori-
> gins, and never have anything in common. How can we
> have Buddhism and Taoism intermingle to spread to the
> extremities of the empire?[4]

Despite Gu Huan's preference for Taoism, his argumentative
strategy was echoed in Confucian tracts which formed the historical mainstay in the Chinese opposition to Buddhism. Hence
almost four centuries later, Han Yu (768–824), whose *Memorial
on the Buddha Relic* forms the locus classicus of such texts,
evoked the argument that "the Buddha was by origin a barbarian" (who didn't even speak Chinese!),[5] further equating un-
Chineseness with immorality.

It is possible to see a glimmer of early China's own incommensurability thesis in Gu Huan's metaphor of birds and fish,

albeit one openly beholden to issues of political power and preference. Any proper Chinese would have sided with Gu Huan's
implicit assumption that the pursuit of knowledge was not an
end in itself but was for the purpose of establishing and perpetuating orthodoxy. The tangible benefits of such endeavor
would be the cultivation of citizens capable of upholding a moral
society built on the foundations of orthopraxis, or proper moral
and ritual behavior. Consequently, it is not surprising that most
attacks against Buddhism refused to engage that tradition on an
intellectual level, preferring instead to attack its social and political practices as being opposed and detrimental to China's
own.[6] The hermeneutically sophisticated question, or doubt,
about the integrity of one's understanding of the Other, then,
appears irrelevant in this context. If Confucian eagerness in upholding established ethical norms exacted the price of philosophical finesse, we must nevertheless ask if brandishing bra-
zen political agendas throughout encounters with Otherness is
any more invidious than past Western claims of religious and
racial superiority disguised as scientific discourse.

   Leaving these ultimately normative judgments aside, it is
the task of this essay to discover what the process of analogical
mapping—that is, comparison—could possibly say about our
present concern with cross-cultural discourse. Whatever the assumptions that determined the contours of the initial Buddhist
encounter by the Chinese, the reality of this encounter persisted
for centuries and displays a range of permutations. I will focus
on a relatively late point in this evolution, the late Ming dynasty, which is a period when Buddhist-Confucian dialogue not
only reached substantive intellectual heights, but self-consciously
harmonized through the doctrine that Buddhism and Confucianism (and Taoism) were essentially the same teachings *(san
jiao qui yi)*. By examining this period's strategies for cultural
and intellectual synthesis, it may be possible to garner some
insights into the modern cross-cultural situation.

   The basic point of this exercise is perhaps to show that
cross-cultural encounters hardly constitute a new chapter in the
human story. The purpose of telling the story of the late-

sixteenth-century Buddhist-Confucian encounter in China is to suggest that what happened there might have something to say about how late-twentieth-century comparative scholars in the West should proceed in their own work. The possibility that this comparative study can formulate action guides for modern scholars, and even illuminate something of the processes by which action guides are derived, conforms to this volume's concern with the notion of practical reason.

My use of the term "practical reason" is inspired by Lee Yearley's discussions in *Mencius and Aquinas: Theories of Virtue and Conceptions of Courage*. Deriving the term from Aquinas, Yearley's use of the notion of practical reason renders it into a cognitive skill which makes judgments about the world, formulates ends regarding that world, and evaluates the means by which such ends can be achieved.[7] It is important to note that Yearley carries out his discussions of practical reason within the realm of ethical theory. As such, his application of the term does not perfectly coincide with my own. I am interested in the notion of practical reason as an intellectual practice of the academy—particularly of comparative scholars who confront the task of understanding other cultures. Thus the distinctive function that I attribute to practical reason as an intellectual skill is the ability to integrate world views in meaningful ways rather than the ability to make ethical choices.

I choose to use Yearley's definition of practical reason as the foundation for my own discussions because of Yearley's idea that practical reason is a cognitive skill. The term "skill" suggests a methodological ability that can be applied to innumerable cases. Practical reason is a tool or instrument that can be wielded within the context of a comparative encounter in order to accomplish certain ends. In what is to follow, I will demonstrate the workings of practical reason in Ming dynasty China when certain intellectual and literary groups offered a synthesis of Buddhist and Confucian notions of desire. Drawing this picture of practical reason in action makes it possible to suggest salient characteristics of this intellectual skill.

These characteristics can be best described by building on Yearley's original definition of practical reason as the ability to make judgments about the world, to formulate ends regarding that world, and to evaluate the means by which those ends can best be achieved. The use of practical reason in the comparative context calls for making judgments, formulating ends, and evaluating means. The formulation of *ends* is pregiven in this situation. The ends always involve the attempt to integrate seemingly disparate theoretical structures which suggest difference and possibly conflict. The impetus for such integration necessarily differs with each historical context, as the comparison between China and the modern academy will make clear. The ultimate goal of integration, however, can be argued to be essentially the same. In the service of this goal, making *judgments* about the comparative situation requires flexing certain intellectual muscles in order to adequately understand the meaning of each theoretical structure. This effort naturally converges with the *means* of practical reason which enables the process of integration to be actually completed. The nature of this means is perhaps the most interesting fact that this essay has to reveal and is the most salient characteristic of practical reason.

The means by which the late Ming discourse on desire synthesized Buddhist and Confucian conceptions plays on the notion of "practical" in the sense of an expedient pragmatism that bends ideas to the demands of current agendas. Thus practical reasoning involves a process of reinterpretation or representation that subverts the sacred cow of pure description, of presenting "just the facts." The worst instance of practical reasoning would involve a misrepresentation of a cultural or thought system. This result is not innate to practical reason itself but stems from an inadequate exercise of that part of practical reasoning that makes *judgments* about the comparative context, as explained above. The best instance of practical reasoning offers a creative picture of that other reality which is honed to say something significant about the current reality, the one in which the user of practical reason is working.

Two statements can be made about the nature of practical reasoning as a means. First, one should call attention to its pragmatic creativity in the representation of others. The case study contained within this essay will demonstrate this creativity.

Second, the idea that practical reason should be utilized in order to make other contexts speak to one's own expands the aims of practical reason beyond my initial stipulation of them as the integration of disparate world views. The reason why such an integration should be attempted at all is intimately bound up with the possibility for meaningful self-understanding and action in the present.

Here, my use of the term *practical reason* further draws upon Yearley's discussions and links up with his notion of practical *theory*—a term which also operates within ethical speculations and whose "aim is to explain human activities to guide people's practices, and therefore lead them to a more complete flourishing."[8] The active principle of explaining and guiding people's practices can be applied directly to my own use of practical reason. My ultimate aim in stipulating practical reason as an intellectual practice of comparative scholars is to suggest that this practice not only describes the comparativist's activities, it also provides a rationale and justification for those activities.

Just as in Yearley's formulations, the use of practical reason can explain the scholars' activities, guide their practices, and thus lead them to a more complete flourishing. Explicit in this notion of flourishing is a justification of what comparative scholars do—that is, make assertions about other cultures with reasonable protection against charges of Orientalism. The laxative effects of much soul-searching in the academy over Otherness encounters have tended to vitiate, rather than charter, the practices of comparative scholars. The greatest recommendation of practical reason in this situation is its potential for offering a metapractical understanding that explains the comparativist's enterprise in a way that both enfranchises and guides it.

The Comparative Context

Pronouncements of Buddhist-Confucian syncretism in the late Ming are quite commonplace. They were espoused not only by various schools of neo-Confucianism that flourished in the era and by their Buddhist counterparts, but by scholars who have made this period their object of study. To offset such repetition, it is worthwhile to bear in mind that the impetus for this mutual embrace originated in certain neo-Confucian quarters—particularly Wang Yangming's (1472–1529) school of mind *(xin xue)* and its various offshoots—whose position of relative power was capable of elevating Buddhism's own status. In other words, the revival of Buddhism—which had suffered institutional decline since the late Song—in the late Ming owed much to Wang Yangming's patronage. Of course, it has been rightfully claimed that the entire neo-Confucian tradition, including the bulwark of orthodoxy embodied by Zhu Xi and the Cheng brothers' school of principle *(li xue)* constituted a response to Buddhism—particularly its complex ontological and epistemological challenges. The acknowledgement of Buddhism's implicit presence, however, does little to mitigate its obvious political weakness—a weakness which also extends to its late Ming revival.

In order to offset this imbalance of power, an imbalance which often resulted in the expedient use of Buddhist language to prove the existence of a Confucian world, I will further narrow my inquiry into Buddhist-Confucian syncretism to the most Buddhistic of neo-Confucian movements, the so-called Taizhou school founded by Wang Gen (1483–1540). A direct student of Wang Yangming, Wang Gen established a movement (named for his place of origin in the lower Yangtze Valley) unprecedented for its class, political, and religious ecumenism. Wang Gen and his followers invigorated the Confucian tradition of sixteenth-century China by spreading it to the popular level—a concern little exhibited by its prior, elitist adherents. Wang Gen himself was a salt maker by trade with little formal education who never achieved officialdom even after his pursuit of the sagely path. With its primary concern for education and mass proselytization, the Taizhou school, in Wm. Theodore DeBary's estimation, allowed Confucianism to become "heavily involved in the sphere traditionally occupied by the popular religions."[9]

The Taizhou school, however, amounted to more than a popular movement. Its egalitarian thrust was propelled by definable doctrines which were articulated by its educated literati members. The school's philosophical foundations derived from extending Wang Yangming's emphasis on one's "innate knowledge" (liang zhi), which departed from Zhu Xi orthodoxy by insisting that moral knowledge was innate to one's heart and mind rather than external to the self. A logical consequence of this view articulated by Wang Gen was the necessity of conferring sagehood (or at least its possibility) upon the common man. In his sociopolitical awareness, Wang Gen divorced sagehood from the appurtenances of the ruling class, which had been erroneously identified with Confucian virtue.[10] This form of sagehood also tended to emphasize its development within the context of everyday, ordinary reality rather than the elusive niches of rulership. It is in this context that the influence and language of Chan Buddhism is most evident. Wang Gen focused on the concept of "spontaneity" (ziran) in all of one's actions as proof of and response to one's innate moral nature. Like the use of the gongan in Chan, the emphasis on "right" and "wrong" knowledge gave way to natural expressions of self: "Instead of the truth being defined in a set of doctrines it was seen as a living Way and a highly personal experience, culminating in a personal encounter between master and disciple which recognized the personality, capabilities, and insights of the individual."[11] Hence the philosophical and sociopolitical directions of the Taizhou school suggest a certain degree of distance from the automatic positions of privilege assumed by adherents of Confucianism.

An extensive social and intellectual history of the Taizhou movement would undoubtedly provide fascinating reading. Regrettably, modern Western scholarship on this topic is limited, and I can claim little in the way of intent or expertise to fill this lack. My concern with this late Ming neo-Confucian school will be primarily limited to its discussion of qing, or desire. Qing is a term which took on a peculiar significance in the Ming period and which considerably transcends the boundaries of Taizhou discourse. We might do best to assert, in fact, that although the Taizhou school provides a sociopolitical locale for the Ming discourse on desire, this discourse actually represents the convergence of several intellectual traditions.

In order to provide a road map of this intellectual territory, it should be stated at the outset that this chapter will consider four streams of tradition. In addition to and conjunction with the Taizhou school, a look at contemporary poetic and literary trends is indispensable to any consideration of *qing*. The "Gongan School" of literary criticism exhibited a particular affinity with the Taizhou movement; the two streams in fact shared a significant voice in the person of philosopher Li Zhi.

These intertwined strands of thought which emerged in the sixteenth century, however, must be set over and against an earlier and ongoing set of discourses. These are the pre-Han (206 B.C.E. to 220 C.E.) Confucian discussions of human nature, particularly as embedded in the philosophers Mencius and Xunzi, and the rival Buddhist doctrines of desire and suffering which formed the basic components of Buddhism's religious framework. I believe that these two antagonistic perspectives comprise the intellectual heritage that was creatively fused in the Ming discourse on desire. Our standard notions of cultural syncretism are inadequate to suggest how this fusion worked. Neither does the politically controlled realm of neo-Confucian–Buddhist dialogue begin to approximate the cultural strategies that were operative here.

A preliminary indication of the forces at work in the Ming context can be given through a consideration of my own methodology in this paper. It will perhaps strike some scholars as rather unseemly of me to breeze in and out of a plethora of immense traditions—pre-Han philosophy, Buddhist doctrine, neo-Confucianism, Chinese literary criticism—when many scholars have dedicated their whole careers to studying minute slices of these cultural edifices. We benignly tolerate sweeping surveys as a necessity in certain intellectual contexts but disparage the results as unavoidably simplistic and reductionistic. As inured as we are to this judgment, it would perhaps do us well to remember that the desire to amass and consolidate a bewildering array of cultural phenomena was not first spawned in the modern academy, with its sometimes pragmatic and limited formats. It is very possible to attribute the same kind of pragmatism to Ming philosophers. Hence if the exigencies of my intellectual enterprise force me to be freewheeling and ostensibly arbitrary in what I examine, perhaps such expedience actually reflects, rather than reduces, my object of inquiry. With this sympathetic attitude, we can perhaps begin to understand one viable way in which Chinese culture got over the incommensurability thesis of Gu Huan. My own methodology, in other words, simply replicates the late Ming discourse's implementation of practical reason. In particular, it highlights that aspect of practical reason that I have identified as its means—its means of using a pragmatic creativity in order to bring about a synthesis of diverging world views for broader ends. I will explicitly examine this kind of cultural strategy at the end of this study.

The Realm of Desire in the Ming

Although I render the term *qing* loosely as "desire," its prevalence and importance in Ming philosophy demands greater nuancing through a string of translations ranging from "emotion," "feeling," "passion," and "affinity," to "love." As A. C. Graham informs us, this understanding of the term *qing* begins in the Song dynasty and therefore cannot be applied to the pre-Han philosophers.[12] The exaltedness of *qing* and its various states contrasts decidedly with another conception of desire, rendered in the Chinese as *yu*, which is consistently identified with coarse physical appetites such as the desire for food, wealth, and sex. The concept of *yu* has undoubtedly had the longer and more consistent meaning in Chinese thought. In the third century B.C.E., the philosopher Xunzi declared that "man is born with the desires of the eyes and ears, with a fondness for beautiful sights and sounds. If he indulges these, they will lead him into license and wantonness, and all ritual principles and correct forms will be lost."[13]

The link between man's material appetites and social degeneration is a consistent theme in Confucian thinking. Many centuries later, the neo-Confucian philosopher Zhu Xi asserted a distinction between principle *(li)*, which is the supreme realization of the sage, and material force *(gi)*, which contains the desires and serves as an obstruction to the attainment of *li*.[14]

Interestingly, many scholars have pointed out that Zhu Xi's dualism of principle and material force reveals the most incisive Buddhist influence, reflecting as it does the Buddhist distinction between "the world of stability *(nirvana)* and the world of fluidity *(anitya),*"[15] or what some might render simply as the dualism of nirvana and samsara.[16] To be sure, the role of desire in both dualistic systems exhibits a substantial affinity. If desire leads the self away from the cultivation and practice of moral knowledge for Zhu Xi, the culpability of desire has been long asserted by basic Buddhist doctrine which roots the sufferings of the world in ignorance *(avidya)* and desire *(trsna)*—terms that function synonymously. It is important to note that in the Buddhist universe, desire encompasses both the Chinese sense of *yu* and *qing.* Sometimes translated as "craving," *trsna* does not ultimately discriminate between material and mental-emotional longings.

In Chinese traditions, the separation between *yu* and *qing*—particularly in the pre-Han era—manifests an intricacy in the view of desires and emotions that we will explore. This intricacy reveals certain ambiguities in the Confucian view of desire (along with Buddhist ambiguities) which germinate into the later celebration of *qing,* understood as passion and emotion. Xunzi points concisely to the Confucian ambiguity when he suggests that both desires *(yu)* and *qing* are derived from heaven as essential parts of man:

> The basic nature of man is that which he receives from Heaven. The emotions *(qing)* are the substance of the nature and the desires *(yu)* are the responses of the emotions. It is impossible for the emotions not to believe that their desires can be satisfied and to refrain from seeking to satisfy them. But when they have decided that their desires can be satisfied, it must then be the function of the intellect *(dao zhi zhi)* to guide the search for satisfaction.[17]

Despite the implied "naturalness" of desires and emotions here, Confucians—along with Buddhists—exhibit an impulse to control and eventually quell the demands of desire on the basis of moral practices.[18] Despite its relevance, it is not this general point of similarity between Confucian and Buddhist thinking that I wish to explore. The notion of *qing* which developed in the Ming, and which was expressed equally in literary as well as philosophical writings, offers an assessment of desire which is not immediately recognizable either in the Confucian or the Buddhist context. In an anthology of love stories collected in the early seventeenth century called the *History of Qing (Qing shi)*, a preface written by Feng Menglong offers a *gatha* which reads in part:

> Had heaven and earth had no *qing* they would not have produced the myriad of things. Had the myriad of things had no *qing* they would not have eternally given each other life. Life gives birth to life, and never is extinguished because *qing* itself never becomes extinguished.
>
> The four great elements all are but illusion; only *qing* is neither empty nor false. When there is *qing* the separated are close; when there is no *qing* the intimate become estranged. The distance between that with *qing* and that without *qing* is immeasurable.
>
> I intend to establish a school of *qing* to teach all who are living, so that a son will face his father with *qing* and a vassal will face his lord with *qing*. One can, then, deduce the relations of all the various phenomena from this single point of view.[19]

What is singularly striking about this pronouncement is its unbridled enthusiasm for *qing,* coupled with an expression of its ontological and ethical role which skews rather than reflects Buddhist and Confucian tenets. It is perhaps best at this point to diverge from strictly Buddhist and Confucian sectarian lines of analysis and look instead at the literary movement which gave rise to Feng Menglong's words.

The Ming discourse on *qing* is embedded within a literary debate (ongoing in Chinese history) about the function and purpose of poetry. Although the question about the relationship between literature and religious goals (whether defined as sagehood or enlightenment) is too complex to be adequately addressed here, suffice it to say that the current debate added a practical element to neo-Confucian intellectualism by offering poetry as a vehicle by which the attainment of sagehood or principle could be expressed. Thus, understandably, the detail as to what the poetic process actually embodied became of significant interest insofar as the conclusion affected the notion of sagehood itself. Therefore it is not surprisingly that certain members of the Taizhou school, most notably Li Zhi (1527–1602), threw themselves wholeheartedly into the debate.

Before examining the details of Li Zhi's position, we should take time to note the import of the neo-Confucian embrace of aesthetic vehicles (which included painting and calligraphy as well as poetry) as a way of expressing its ideals. The turn to aesthetic practices reveals the neo-Confucian tradition's fundamental concern with going beyond mere intellectual speculation to a level of praxis capable of leading to true self-cultivation. This goal of concrete realization was not limited to artistic practices. It also focused on the interactions of the master and student relationship and prescribed activities such as quiet sitting *(jing zuo)*.[20] Li Zhi himself emphasized the importance of praxis at the expense of intellectual activities through denunciations of book learning, which directly echoed Chan Buddhist textual iconoclasm. It is in the context of aesthetic practices, however, that neo-Confucianism displays its greatest spiritual capacity. The language of "enlightenment" *(wu)* and "awakening" *(jue)* was often employed to describe the poetic process not only as an expression of self-realization, but as the embodiment of it.[21] Neo-Confucianism's aesthetic dimension helped to assure the tradition's efficacy beyond the confines of a narrow moral intellectualism.

The overriding drift of the literary theory which emerged in the Ming must be characterized in relation to its antecedent: the "orthodox" criticism founded on the philosophy of Yen Yu (1180–1235) of the Song and carried out by the so-called Former Seven Masters *(qian qizi)* and Latter Seven Masters *(hou qizi)* who spanned the Ming. In brief, this school articulated the belief that enlightenment *(wu)* could be attained through poetry, but that this state could be arrived at only through sustained and diligent study of the classics of the Han, Wei, and the High Tang. This approach essentially espoused a classicism which believed that the pinnacle of poetic endeavor had already been achieved in the past and that this standard must be maintained as a constant model for the present.

In the late sixteenth century, the rise of an alternative school of interpretation known as the *Gongan pai,* or the Gongan school (named for the region in Hubei), vehemently challenged the predominance of antiquarianism in literature, a predominance which often produced works of lifeless imitation in the name of poetic enlightenment. In its stead, the Gongan school sought to promote a more sincere form of literature which some scholars have labeled neo-Romantic in its glorification of local flavor and personal emotion.[22] Each age, it was asserted, evinces its own particular style and point of view. Literature should be appreciated as a genuine expression of its age rather than forced into unnatural molds. The historically significant impact of this school's views was manifested in the positive appreciation of vernacular fiction and the relaxation of scholarly writings, both in form and content.

As a close associate of leaders in the Gongan fiction, Li Zhi was perhaps one of the most vocal in his call to shake off the tutelage of the ancients and to give free reign to individual expression. It was this general focus on self-expression that led to the glorification of *qing,* defined as human emotion and "the spontaneous expression of inner feelings." For Li Zhi, this spontaneity of emotion was directly opposed to the kind of moral instruction imposed by neo-Confucianism. Indeed, any moral teaching was an imposition on the individual and the free flow of his spontaneous nature. The basis of one's spontaneous nature, Li asserted, is one's original purity—a Buddhistic concept clothed in his own phrase of the "childlike mind" *(tongxin).* Most important to the preservation of *tongxin* was to shield it from "moral principles" *(daoli)* and "impressions" (*wenjian,* literally, "to hear and see"). Li Zhi suggested that literary creations flow from the preservation of the childlike mind, that each period and person had its own literary capacity, and that each should be recognized as worthy.[23]

Amongst his contemporaries, Li Zhi's extreme views led to his frequent repudiation. Not only did he go too far in his disdain for Confucian intellectual traditions, but his embrace of *qing* also earned him a reputation as a licentious, immoral man. Although such censure was often abbreviated to the accusation that he was "Chan crazy" *(chan kuang)*, it is interesting that he received similar criticisms from Buddhist quarters. The example of the monk Zhuhong (1535–1615), one of the foremost reformers of Ming Buddhism, is notable and representative.[24] Li Zhi defended his views on *qing* through the *Heart Sutra,* one of the most significant Buddhist texts in the Chinese tradition. Faithfully echoing the work, Li Zhi claimed, "In truth, that which I call passion *(se)* is none other than emptiness; outside of passion there is no emptiness."[25] Such views led Zhuhong to accuse Li Zhi of using Buddhist exegesis for the sake of self-indulgence.[26] The clash of the two figures is understandable given Zhuhong's primary concern to reform the morals of the monastic community, which deservedly suffered from ill repute. Li Zhi's decision to enter the Buddhist monastery towards the end of his life still did little to render him representative of the Buddhism of his age.

Li Zhi's marginality in both Confucian and Buddhist quarters should not obscure the profound impact of the ideas—especially concerning *qing*—that he espoused. As seen in the *Qing shi* which was prefaced, and most likely compiled, by Feng Menglong, the centrality of *qing* is underscored by having it take on cosmic proportions. To be exact, Feng Menglong's preface suggests a cosmogonic narrative in which the force of *qing* gives birth to the world. Given the union of the themes of desire and procreation in this context, it seems only logical that the somewhat abstracted concept of *qing* became concretely rendered as the love between man and woman. For Li Zhi, it is in fact the union of man and woman that forms the ultimate cosmogonic force. The other social relationships—that of father and son, older and younger brother, lord and subject—follow from it. More grandiosely, the myriad things of the world are also engendered by it, because the dual principle of man and woman is homologous to that of heaven and earth.[27] The cosmic proportions of *qing* imbue it with a certain transcendence, yet it responds to and determines the lives of those who will open themselves up to it. In chapter 10 of the *Qing shi,* whose thematic concern is the efficacy of *qing ("qing ling"),* the compiler comments,

> After a man is born, *qing* can make him die; after a man is dead, *qing* can resurrect him. . . . *Qing* can bring the desires of this life to their fulfillment after one's death, and bring the uncompleted affinity of one's previous life to its completion in the next life. Then, is not the efficacy of *qing* quite evident? If that *qing* which arises from the merest of desires on the part of a man and a woman can be everlasting like this, then is it not the more so regarding that *qing* which binds the essences together, unites the spirits, and designs and creates the splendid, grandiose universe itself?[28]

The power of love and its transcendence over life is a theme which saturates not only short stories but, most exemplarily, the work of the great playwright Tang Xianzu (1550–1616). His most famous piece, the *Peony Pavilion (Mudan Ting),* evinces the power of *qing* through the love of a woman for a man, her passion enabling her to resurrect him from the dead.

The following is an excerpt from the "Transformation of *qing*" *(qing hua):*

> *Qing* sometimes transforms itself into stone, a hard substance. At other times it may transform itself into birds or plants, i.e., things without intelligence. . . . The camphor tree can intertwine its branches; and two flowers can bloom on a single stem. Although plants are devoid of intelligence, when they imitate human emotion it seems that they too have intelligence. Should a man have no emotion, he would be even lower than the plants.[29]

Aside from the further testimonial this commentary offers to the control that *qing* holds over life, those familiar with Chinese fiction will immediately recognize in this the frame premise of the classic *Story of the Stone.* The novel tells the story of how the love between a stone and a plant in the celestial sphere caused their reincarnation into the human realm in order to play out their love destiny. This tale not only sustains the poetic theme of inanimate objects sparked to life by love, it maintains the discourse on *qing* as a cosmic force animating the existence of life as a whole.

The Confucian Discourse on Qing

If the cosmic persona of *qing* within the Ming literary context elevates the term to a hitherto unknown and exalted status, the cultural building blocks of this pygmalion transformation still remain to be seen. So far, we have focused only on the departures of Ming thought from both Confucian and Buddhist mainstays. DeBary's disapproving assessment of Li Zhi concludes that "the original moral basis of Confucian sagehood has disappeared, while the Buddhist awareness of egoism and selfish craving, which is the starting point of all its philosophy and discipline, has been largely ignored."[30] The links of continuity to prior religious traditions are indeed rather opaque but, nevertheless, I believe, fundamentally represented.

In the Confucian mindset, a nuanced attitude towards human desires can be seen in the fact that it seeks to satisfy desires through the very act of controlling and transforming them. In this respect, Confucian impulses directly oppose the Buddhist's. If we look back to Xunzi's words quoted above, we see that *qing* (and by consequence, even *yu*) is rooted in human nature *(xing)*, a nature which is given by heaven and hence by definition is good. Xunzi, of course, is famous for having argued against Mencius that human nature is originally evil. One must bear in mind, however, that Xunzi deployed this rhetoric in an effort to focus on the centrality of social and ritual conditioning for the proper education of the gentleman. Xunzi was primarily concerned with the conditioning process ("Environment is the important thing!"), but this focus is based on the assumption of human perfectibility. The educational process legitimately included the careful channeling of human feeling through rituals for the purpose of cultivating social sentiments that would bind individuals together. It is understandable that within this context, the Buddhist ideal of complete detachment—put into practice by monks who would leave family and society behind—was looked upon as a monstrous moral aberration. Han Yu denounced the Buddha, claiming, "He did not understand the proper loyalty between prince and subject nor the proper affection between father and son."[31] Han Yu's words not only complain about the disruptive nature of monasticism as a social institution, they also point to his inherited belief in the basic goodness of the world—a goodness brought out by the work of the conscious mind exerting itself on the raw materials of human feeling.

It is Mencius, of course, who spoke most confidently for the innate goodness of human beings by locating human nature beyond the physical appetites and in the primary instincts of compassion, shame, propriety, and righteousness. His most famous illustration of this is the story of the baby about to fall into a well (*Mencius* 2A.6). Mencius claims that a man's instincts propel him to save the child because of his compassionate nature rather than a calculation of reward or praise. Although Mencius would have no grounds to dispute Xunzi's stress on social inculcation, his concerns go beyond moral process to moral ontology, seeking the ground which makes the good world possible.

It is for this reason that Mencius offers a more fruitful context for exploring Confucian ambiguity in its attitude toward human desires. To be sure, both Mencius and Xunzi are united and representative in their belief that one should always seek to control and reduce one's desires. For Xunzi, this process ensures that basic human needs will be satisfied. Hence one might aver that a society based on adherence to the rites is actually the best means for responding to the demands of the desires. For Mencius, limiting the desires allows instinctive human feelings, such as compassion, to be nurtured. This process is guided by a rational calculation which decrees that since not all desires can always be satisfied, one must choose between them by their greater and lesser values. On the point of self-preservation, Mencius states, "The parts of the person differ in value and importance. Never harm the parts of greater importance for the sake of those of smaller importance, or the more valuable for the sake of the less valuable."[32] Distinguishing between greater and lesser values sets the stage to allow Mencius to argue that in some cases, moral goods take precedence over all sensual desires, including the desire for life itself. In making this point about the priority of moral goods, however, Mencius does not compel us to reject the coarser desires altogether.

Unlike Xunzi, Mencius recognizes both the sensual appetites and the moral impulses as constituent parts of the human person. This duality allows for greater complexity in the treatment of human passions. Passion may be rooted in material instincts and desires, but as an emotion, it also possesses an implicit (or at least potential) moral power. The challenge is to maintain the balance of regulating human feeling while it is being cultivated. The fear here, of course, is that emotions may overstep proper boundaries and erupt into unbridled, antisocial passion. The fear is well summarized by Confucius' lament: "I have yet to meet the man who is as fond of virtue as he is of sex *(se)*" (*Analects* 9.18 and 15.13). The twice-articulated complaint, with the added murmur in 15.13 of "I suppose I should give up hope!" seems to assume the mutual incompatibility between the pursuit of virtue and the pursuit of women. Later perspectives, however, attempted to navigate between these two courses by exploring the multifaceted nature of human feelings. Mencius himself suggests a strategy in the following passage:

> When a person is young he yearns for his parents; when he begins to take an interest in women, he yearns for the young and beautiful; when he has a wife, he yearns for his wife; when he enters public life he yearns for his prince and becomes restless if he is without one. A son of supreme dutifulness yearns for his parents all his life. In Shun I have seen an example of a son who, even at the age of fifty, yearned for his parents.[33]

The verb to consider is *mu,* which D. C. Lau renders as "yearn" and others have given as "desire."[34] The term's general definition as "yearn," "long for," "desire," and "admire" seems to be broadly applicable, but Mencius' range is particularly interesting. The passage seeks to make a point about filial piety; specifically, that the truly filial son will not stop loving and honoring his parents beyond the period of his dependency on them and after other claimants have made their appearance. These others take the form of women, who claim sexual devotion, and rulers, who demand political loyalty. By rendering these emotions, along with filial piety, by the singular term *mu,* a homology across all three kinds of relationships is suggested. The feelings which bind a man to his parents are not significantly different from those which draw him to a lover or ruler. It is important to note that these three configurations comprise three of the five basic relationships that form the basis of Confucian society. Although this particular passage seems to suggest the primacy of the parent-child relationship—whereas Li Zhi much later upheld the priority of the male-female one—the greater point we must consider is the underlying sameness of all the relationships—their rootedness in human feeling.

What the *Mencius* passage presages is the Confucian strategy, borne out in history, of taming the hotter, more impetuous side of human emotions—most often manifest as the passion between man and woman—through ritually governed and regulated interactions. Homologizing more passionate relationships to duty-bound relationships was a notable detail of this method. Perhaps to our post-psychoanalytic consciousness there is something peculiar about positing that one can desire one's parents like one desires a lover. This should not set Freudian adherents salivating as much as it should suggest the extent to which cultural homologies can act as agents of behavioral control. Lee Yearley has underscored Mencius' belief in the possibility of using moral education to create rational values which in turn can alter emotions into appropriate forms.[35] In this respect, Mencius speaks for Xunzi and the entire Confucian tradition in stressing the importance of cultivating the moral will. The role of rationality within this will goes beyond mere calculation of how one's desires can be most prudently satisfied. The moral will can actually reinvent the nature and direction of one's desires so that "they have no reality apart from the cognition or interpretation that produces them."[36] The taming of sexual passion by conflating it with the nobler virtues of filial piety and political constancy formed a dominant pattern through which this moral rationality operated.

The homology between the male-female and the ruler-subject relationships has had a particularly long and visible career. It has been a common practice for political officials to assume poetically the role of a rejected wife on the occasion of falling out of disfavor with their monarch. The long history of this poetic association suggests a convention for self-perception actualized over and over again by historical beings. Again, it perhaps strikes us as incongruous for a minister to address his lord as "My Fair One," or "My Fragrant One,"[37] even in poetry. The regulatory role of such associations, however, is particularly manifest in the Ming and Qing when the male-female and ruler-minister homology refracted back on the real conjugal situation. The particular target of this effort was young widows. In the explosion of biographies of "virtuous wives" that were composed in this period, women were exhorted to bind themselves to their husbands in the same manner that their husbands bound themselves to their sovereigns. The relevant expression of virtuosity was wifely chastity, or the refusal to rewed (or even look upon another man) after widowhood. This chastity was analogized to male political loyalty. The shared trait was the subject's refusal to switch political/sexual allegiance—no matter how expedient—even at the cost of one's life.

To be sure, the celebration of female chastity in the late Imperial era involves much more than the desire to regulate the behavior of women. The Manchu rulers of the Qing, for example, saw in this practice a convenient way of reinforcing political behaviors which would stabilize their own dynasty.[38] Here moral homologies quite clearly converged with power concerns, underscoring Chinese culture's general tendency to blur moral and political boundaries. This kind of patterned cultural behavior represents one dominant strategy for controlling instinctive emotional expressions. It is a strategy which desiccated the marriage institution, changing it from one based on romantic feeling and love to one based on duty and obligations. The burst of celebration over these arid romantic sentiments in certain schools of the Ming may challenge the mainstay of Confucian efforts, but it is itself a reaction anchored deeply in prior appreciations of the power of emotion.

The Buddhist Discourse on **Qing**

If the Confucian mind recognized the power of human feeling and its ambiguous force as both a creator and a destroyer of social order, then the Buddhist attitude is much less ambivalent. The power of desire, in fact, plays a key role in fundamental

Buddhist doctrine—to wit, the second and third noble truths which attribute all the sufferings of the world to human cravings *(trsna)*. The truth of the origin of suffering states that "It is craving that leads to rebirth, is pleasurable, connected with passion and takes delight here and there, namely: craving for lust, craving for becoming, craving for destruction."[39] The third noble truth serves as an antidote to this condition; a prescription for quelling the ravages of suffering in this world by extinguishing these very flames of desire. At this level of doctrine, Buddhism clearly demarcates itself from Confucian policy by exhorting complete detachment from and transcendence of the realm of desire. This forms an intrinsic devaluation of the world as a whole, rendering it a realm of suffering *(samsara)* which can only be conquered by quitting it altogether. This was at least the initial Chinese understanding of Buddhism, before the exegetical powers of Chinese Buddhists set about to soften this affront to world-affirming Confucians.

This initial understanding of Buddhist doctrine requires agreement with DeBary's accusation that Li Zhi largely overlooked "Buddhist awareness of egoism and selfish craving." This assessment, however, gives rather short shrift to Buddhist powers of perception. While indeed Buddhist attitudes seem to convey a wariness and even a fear of *qing,* even at its earliest stages of formulation the Buddhist world view evinced its own form of ambivalence towards desire. The ambivalence differs from the Confucian version, but it is distinctly recognizable in the Ming's celebration of *qing:* specifically, the Buddhist assessment of *qing* also comprises a homage to its cosmogonic powers.

The second noble truth is perhaps the single most identifiable source of this position when it states that craving is what leads to rebirth. *Samsara,* in turn, forms the arena of rebirth and the entire phenomenal world as we know it. Desire, then, is the fuel that drives *samsara,* the creative force which ensures that the cycle will continue to revolve. To be sure, this scenario hardly comprises a cosmogonic myth in the sense that it accounts for the creation of the world from nothing or from primordial ingredients into a something. One might even posit that Buddhism offers no genuine creation myth because it lacks a sense of beginnings. The suffering which is made synonymous with the world is only said to have existed from the "beginningless beginning," thus hardly fulfilling the function of myth to explain why the world is the way it is.

Frank Reynolds has already argued the possibility of a broader conception of cosmogony which can classify the Buddhist scenario examined here as what he calls a "samsaric cosmogony."[40] The point of this cosmogony is to account for the maintenance of the world—its cosmological ground, so to speak—rather than its origins. Understood in this sense, any perusal of Buddhist literature immediately identifies desire or ignorance *(avidya)* as the creative matrix of the world. Although the "Four Noble Truths" focus on desire and grasping, the Pali canon's twelve-fold chain of dependent origination, which offers a step-by-step sequence of the evolution of psychophysical existence, roots this process in ignorance. It is generally thought that the focus on *trsna* preceded the identification of *avidya* as the cause of suffering, but most texts are content to feature them together.[41] The parity of these two causes can also be seen in the classical formulation that greed, hatred, and delusion keep *samsara* in motion. Greed (sometimes rendered as lust) and hatred are the reverse but complimentary sides of *trsna,* and delusion is equivalent to ignorance.

The cosmogonic creativity of desire defines it as an autonomous force irrespective of, and in spite of, the negative emotional value that Buddhist doctrine might give it. As an agent of cosmic law, the power of desire can be examined as its own entity, rather than as an epiphenomenal construct to give justification to the Buddhist path. It is this sense of observation that is clearly apparent in the *Qing shi* and in Li Zhi. Their elevation of *qing* into a singular cosmic force goes far beyond any Confucian concession, which still insists on the primacy of Heaven *(tian)* as the ultimate source of life. It is quite telling in this context that Buddhists in fact claimed superiority over Confucians in their ability to account for the world and its workings. The Buddhist's relative ease with cosmological discourse may help to identify the glorification of *qing* as the result of Buddhist pathways.

A significant tactic of Buddhist intellectual warfare in China has been the contention that the Confucian understanding of the human being, which is limited to ethical and social contours, is no match for Buddhist metaphysical conceptions. In the ninth century, Zongmi wrote a short treatise known as "On the Original Nature of Man" (*Yuan Ren* T.45, 707–10) supposedly in reply to the anti-Buddhist polemic of Han Yu. In it, Zongmi exposes Confucianism's restricted explanatory powers by posing the classical problem of theodicy:

> To be rich or poor, noble or base, wise or foolish, good or bad, lucky or unlucky, fortunate or unfortunate—all this depends on the Will of Heaven. Why does Heaven decree that there should be so many poor and so few rich, so many base and so few high-born, so many unfortunate beings and so few fortunate ones, and so on? If the allotment lies in the Will of Heaven, why is it not equitable?[42]

As Zongmi points out, the Confucian concept of the will of heaven is incapable of responding to this question, whereas the lowest of Buddhist teachings can explain it in full. The doctrine of karma accounts for the seeming vagaries and unjustness of individual lives by explaining that they are rewards and punishments for prior actions meted out across lifetimes.

The fact that the doctrine of karma seeped into the Chinese consciousness almost as an explanatory reflex seems to suggest that this Buddhist tenet filled a real gap in the indigenous world view. If Zongmi was capable of reducing the notion of heaven to a relatively humble place in the contest for cosmological interpretability, this should not obscure the Buddhist tradition's own continuing struggles. The doctrine of karma, in fact, was liable to rather facile explanations of events and did not adequately address the question of the origins of suffering.

In our examination of *qing* as a cosmogonic force in Buddhist theory, we noted two features: the role of *qing* lacks a genesis scenario, and its valorization in the Ming is at odds with Buddhism's initial efforts to transcend *qing*. I believe these two points can be simultaneously resolved by reviewing the subsequent efforts of Chinese Buddhists to absolutize their metaphysical understanding. This effort included in large part an attempt to explain the existence of suffering in the world on an ontological basis as well as through the causal explanation of *qing*. Was suffering real or merely an illusion of the unenlightened? The issue is perhaps akin to that raised by Manichaean dualism which suggested that evil was as real and powerful as the forces of good. In the Buddhist case, to rest content with the assertion that suffering had existed from "the beginningless beginning" also risked the implication that despite the ability of some individuals to overcome it, the state of suffering was a permanent and self-existing feature of the world.

The outcome of this debate was more than predetermined, for the Buddhist tradition in China had resolutely come to affirm that the world and all individual beings were actually pure and enlightened despite their perception of suffering. This conclusion quite plainly altered the Buddhist outlook on the phenomenal world into a positive and affirming stance. In Zongmi's words: "From the beginningless beginning this mind has been constant, pure, luminous, and unobscured; it has always been characterized by bright cognition; it is also called the Buddha Nature or the Womb of Tathagata."[43] In concession to the experience of suffering in the world, Zongmi continues:

> From the beginningless beginning, man's delusions have obscured it so that he has not been aware of it. Because he recognizes in himself only the ordinary man's characteristics, he indulges in a life of attachment, increases the bond of karmic power and receives the suffering of repeated births and deaths.[44]

Zongmi is representative in his final accounting of suffering as a delusion which arises from the phenomenal aspect of the originally pure and one true mind. In other words, suffering does not arise from a separate and opposing force. The basis of purity and enlightenment also gives rise to the function of delusion, but this delusion is not the mind's fundamental essence. *Samsara* itself reveals itself as intrinsically pure once seen through the enlightened eye.

The phenomenology of how the experience of suffering arises within the ground of purity was the subject of much greater exegesis than we can give it here.[45] Our interest lies in the effect of this theodical resolution on the concept of desire. If desire is the cause of suffering in the world, it seems cogent enough to curtail and restrain one's desires. But if this world is claimed to be actually pure, and suffering a deluded state of mind, then what role do the desires play? For the unenlightened, craving and grasping can still form the vehicles for a misguided life. But perhaps for the true seer, it is possible to embrace human feeling, love, and even sex as a part of spiritual liberation.

Can Li Zhi's valorization of *qing* then be said to stem from the Buddhist affirmation of the world as pure and enlightened? The urge to answer positively is mitigated by the fact that although Buddhist theology denies the ontological reality of suffering, its path is still anchored in suffering's experiential verity. The final Buddhist pronouncement of *qing* must then be somewhat tempered. Although suffering is not ultimately real, desire, as suffering's causal agent, still has the capacity to bring about the experience of suffering. It takes an epistemological breakthrough—that is, the power of knowledge—to see the illusoriness of suffering. But in the quest for this knowledge, it is possible to assert that desire can act as an agent of this spiritual transformation. Here, too, as in the Confucian case, a double assessment of *qing* is suggested. As Li Zhi's astute usage of the *Heart Sutra* shows, the notion that one could reach emptiness through the vehicle of the passions was indeed an orthodox—albeit dangerous—path.

Although the idea of harnessing passion in a religious capacity may be more familiar to us as an element of Tantric scripture and ritual, the pervasiveness of this theme becomes apparent at the level of popular practices. In popular Song images of the Bodhisattva Guanyin, accompanying tales told of how the Bodhisattva would appear to men in the form of a young nubile woman who used the promise of sex as a lure to Buddhahood. The promise is not merely used as a carrot on a stick, for it is often fulfilled. Sometimes she is depicted as an outright whore.[46] The impetus for this image is plainly explained by a Chan poem, many of which were written as eulogies to paintings of the Bodhisattva: "She looks at everyone equally with compassion. She entices people and draws them to her with desire. One knocks out a wedge with another wedge and fights one type of poison with another type of poison."[47] The notion of fighting fire with fire, or desire with desire, is plainly espoused as part of a potent arsenal of Buddhist soteriology.

Another story about Guanyin in the Korean compilation of legends and anecdotes known as the *Samguk Yusa* (compiled by the Buddhist monk Ilyon [1206–1289]) tells of how she enters the woods to tempt two hermit monks. The first turns her away, while the second allows her into his hut. After bathing together, the fragrant and golden liquid in the tub transforms the monk into a Bodhisattva. The depiction of Guanyin as a temptress suggests a convergence between the desires of the flesh and the desire for liberation. This paradoxical note is sounded in Ilyon's concluding comments to the story: "In her song of temptation she might have said, 'The winds of heaven mingle forever in sweet emotion; why can I not mingle with thee into a single being?' But because she was a goddess she could not allow herself to sound like a vulgar woman in a ballad."[48]

There are notable differences, of course, between these tale traditions and that of the *Qing shi*. Here, desire is depicted more as a Buddhist skillful means than a cosmic power. A greater association between the two genres is offered by their uniform recognition of desire's positive and constructive force. One might say that Feng Menglong's conception of *qing*, however, is more comprehensive in linking itself back to prior Buddhist illustrations of desire as a cosmogonic principle.

Intercultural Dialogue: The Tool of Practical Reason

If the Ming discourse on desire represents an instance of Buddhist-Confucian syncretism, it is apparently not based on the convergence of ready similarities between the two traditions. Each tradition acknowledges the power of desire from within its self-contained perspective. For the Confucians, the restraint of *qing* through the exercise of the moral will amounted to an homage to the force of this impulse, an impulse which was rooted in human nature. For the Buddhist, desire was the root of all dissatisfaction human beings experienced in the world but nevertheless comprised its own autonomous cosmogonic and ultimately, soteriological, force. Perhaps both Confucianism and Buddhism can be said to display a form of ambiguity in their assessments of desire, but these are ambiguities which have cogency only within their respective systems of meaning.

To support this thesis, one may note that each tradition's contribution to the conversation derives from aspects of its intellectual history, aspects that often existed in mutual antagonism throughout Chinese history. Thus the Confucian belief in human feeling as the basis of the moral perfectibility of the world was challenged by the Buddhist doctrine of *samsara* and the monastic path. On the other hand, the Chan celebration of this-worldly action and the ideal of giving free reign to one's spontaneous nature elicited a most puritanical response from Zhu Xi and his school of mind. Charging that the Buddhist celebration of the mundane amounted to a perverse sanctioning of immorality, Song neo-Confucianism championed the need for strict moral discipline.

This situation has prompted the need to dig within the framework of each tradition's own constructs in order to pinpoint the elements of Buddhist and Confucian theories contributing to the celebration of desire. What this suggests about the Gongan and Taizhou schools as examples of syncretism is important. Despite the reality of factionalism, readily attested to by epithets such as "wild Channist" *(kuang chan)* and "fake moralist" *(jia daoxue)*, the concept of *qing* displays a free eclecticism rather than a steady sectarian rigor. This eclecticism itself, I suggest, is more adventitious than studied. Only the fastidious mindset of the academician seeks its variegated roots. Accomplishing the task, however, promises more than its own reward. For it is this adventitious Buddhist-Confucian dialogue that may serve as an analogical model for our concern with cultural encounter.

Lee Yearley has pointed out that the realm of pure theoretical discourse is a difficult one for making cultural comparisons.[49] A significant part of the problem is that theoretical systems tend to articulate highly evolved and intellectually loaded terms which defy easy translation into other systems. Any sustained attempt to substantiate the claim that the Confucian concept of principle *(li)* is equivalent to the Buddhist term *nirvana* will quickly make this evident. The academy's preference for theoretical discourses probably accounts for the sustenance of the incommensurability thesis with its myth of the framework or of systems. In any case, it is apparent that at the level of cultural encounter as well—as in the Buddhist-Confucian case—fundamental frameworks are apt to clash even after repeated attempts to negotiate differences.

In light of this fact, many have turned to a more concrete level of thought known as "primary theory" or as plain "everyday discourse" in their search for common ground.[50] As Yearley states, primary theories, which all cultures possess, are turned towards immediate concerns and give off the air of common sense:

> The explanations they provide allow people to predict, plan, and thereby often control important aspects of life. Moreover, they usually appear to be obviously truthful to people within the culture and even to many outside it. These theories can then be said to have a universal character; that is, they often speak in one voice, they are similar in nature and content.[51]

Whatever the difference in Buddhist-Confucian moral frameworks, surely the primary tier of concern that supports the Ming discourse on *qing* is the problem of desires at a fundamental material and emotional level. One might in fact assert that the problem of desire represented a primary-level moral concern in the Chinese context. Buddhists and Confucians, in any case, agreed on the universality of this problem by positioning desire at the foundation of their theoretical systems. The scholarly efforts of early thinkers such as Mencius and Xunzi always remained trained on the question of how a moral society could be maintained given one's natural impulse to satisfy one's sensual appetites. The first two noble truths of the Buddha are together one of the most satisfying psycho-poetic analyses of the fundamental human condition. The experience of life as suffering and desires as the cause of suffering articulates the unquenchable feelings of want and deprivation experienced by all individuals regardless of their actual material and social condition.

This chapter's investigation of each tradition's independent theories of desire, however, suggests something important about the Chinese attempt to merge the two. The Buddhist and Confucian analyses of desire may seem to refer to a universally shared and immediately recognizable human condition, but their frameworks of analysis are locked into divergent assumptions, values, and strategies. Whereas Buddhists attempted to control and ultimately overcome desire in all its manifestations, Confucians sought to channel desire in order to establish an ideal social order.

If the synthesis of theories of desire in the late Ming represents an instance of practical reason in action, this example would seem to suggest that the pragmatic, adventitious nature of practical reason exacts the cost of fundamental misrepresentation—to the point where the Ming synthesis misrecognized diverging theoretical discussions as a primary-level synthesis. From the comparative scholar's point of view, this result represents her worst nightmare—the spectre of two irreconcilable terms being forced together. Given this situation, it would seem odd to suggest that practical reason is an intellectual skill of comparative scholarship. The Ming case would seem to indicate that practical reason is a tool of groups or societies that encounter others, but that this model of encounter is quite distinct from and even contrary to the ideal of scholarly comparisons.

If I am to substantiate my claim that the modern comparativist has something to learn from this case study, then the operative definition of practical reason needs further elaboration. My earlier stipulation that practical reason has formulating action guides—what Yearley technically defines as practical *theory*—as its ultimate goal supplies the extra ingredient. In Yearley's ethical speculations, the use of practical reason is aimed at obtaining the kind of knowledge that results in desirable ethical actions. In this model, there is a fluid progression from knowledge to action, or at least to action guides in the form of practical theory, whose applicability to the comparative discipline may ultimately be questionable. The present goal, however, is to establish the initial link between practical reasoning and the justification of actions. The use of practical reason for the purpose of addressing larger issues of community and action is historically attested to in the Ming context.

The Taizhou and Gongan schools were not scholarly currents relegated to the intellectual salons. They represent a historical expression of both a community and an ideal of community, which, significantly, championed the need to integrate the life of the mind into everyday reality. The literary aspect of this movement, which sanctioned vernacular styles and subjects as reflective of the real lives of the populace, put this ideal into practice. The schools I have examined, however, were not unique in their goals. They represent a growing impatience around the end of the sixteenth century towards the aloof intellectualism of Song-Ming neo-Confucianism which exploded in the rise of the "practical learning" or "realistic pragmatism" *(shixue)* movement.[52] As such, the Taizhou school represents only one competing vision which was in vehement contention with others. The school's most ardent critics were from communities that proclaimed the same ideals. Thus it is important to note that the Taizhou synthesis of the concept of desire occurred within a greater historical debate about how the scholar-official should fulfill his ideal as a moral leader of the people.

Like the Taizhou school itself, the critical voices of this era launched a two-pronged attack. The first was directed against the lack of effective government which, second, was blamed on a legacy of theoretical scholarship whose highly abstract moral discourse failed in its task of producing the ideal scholar-official.[53] In this respect, the intellectual and social upheaval of the late Ming was inspired by Wang Yangming's vision of the unity of moral knowledge and action. This vision was translated into a demand that theoretical discourse be capable of impinging upon the behavior of individuals, particularly the scholar-official who acted as a guide and a model to the people. Similar to Yearley's notion of practical theory, the "practical learning" movement conceptualized knowledge as an ultimately pragmatic entity in which attainment would lead to right actions. Both practical theory and practical learning reinforce the basic Confucian assumption that cultivation and development of the self will lead to the creation of a moral society.

In this era's contest for visions, the Taizhou school implemented practical reason most virtuously by drawing freely and expediently upon the materials of an ongoing past. Its strategy of utilization does not bother much about academic consistency. Qing, as a theoretical construct, is the convenient creation of praxis, but nevertheless a construct for the regulation and explanation of behavior.

In drawing out the symmetry between the Chinese context and the present day academy, some may feel that I have committed an act of misrecognition in identifying the problem of the "Other" as a common primary issue. There are many arguments about the differences between the two societies' historical contexts, values, and pragmatic motivations that might be adduced to support this accusation. And yet, our present intellectual environment intuitively allows for recognizing the problem of cultural plurality as a fundamental one—fundamental in the sense that the situation poses a threat to meaningful and justified action within our own community. Thus, my extension of the Otherness problem to the Chinese Buddhist-Confucian context is not an attempt to say something about Chinese culture *in vacuo,* nor an attempt to reconcile (what some consider) irreconcilable differences. Rather, it is for the purpose of exploring a rationale for our own actions. In this case, however, such a rationale must go beyond a historical analysis of our communal and institutional situation. It must extend into examining practical reason as a metapractice—in addition to an intellectual practice—which supplies an understanding and justification of our actions.

For the comparative scholar, the existence of primary levels of human experience which offer greater cross-cultural commensurability may or may not be an explicit consideration in his or her own work. Although some have engaged in speculations about primary theories, such discussions tend not to comprise a significant part of the comparativist's work as much as the thick descriptions of the locale in which she claims expertise. The recourse of submerging oneself in the rich details of the native setting and experience cannot be total, however, for it is institutionally tempered by one's need to translate this knowledge to the larger scholarly community. Thus the comparativist must utilize conceptual categories that are shared by other scholars and which are necessarily imposed on the comparative context. This is because she must operate at a certain level of theoretical reflection, particularly if the comparison is going to say anything of interest to those outside of the traditions in question.

The comparativist's activity is distinct from that of perpetuating indigenous theoretical discourses. As a translator, the comparativist must break down native theoretical terms in order to make them relatively commensurate to the comparativist's own, taken from her home culture. This process involves better or worse syntheses of two disparate secondary terms, much like the Taizhou school's integration of Buddhist-Confucian ideas about desire. The impetus to bring together such terms may, for some, be driven by a misrecognition of secondary concepts for primary ones. Indemic to practical reason as I define it, however, is the drive within intellectual communities to identify and refine such terms, not for the purpose of faithfully perpetuating past usages of them, but for the purpose of creating and perpetuating academic discourse.

The exercise of practical reason as an intellectual skill in this context is comparable to the Ming instance. For again the use of practical reason makes adventitious, although not arbitrary, choices in what is highlighted and what is ignored in the representation of a system in order to conform with and advance discussions that are historically external to the comparative object. The comparative scholar's indentureship to the broader theoretical constructs of her discipline guides the contours of her selective perceptions of her topic. Practical reason can be demonstrated to be a supreme intellectual virtue when it is wielded in such a manner that its necessary expediency is converted into a creative and synthetic contribution to ongoing discussions in the field.

The metapractical dimension of my use of the notion of practical reason entails a self-reflexive awareness of the process described above. That is, the comparative scholar must remain explicitly conscious of the fact that her understanding and translation of the Other is the product of practical reasoning. This consciousness extends practical reason beyond an intellectual skill into an actively affirmed interpretive principle. By an interpretive principle, I mean a view of practical reason as a tool of interpretation that has a particular notion of the nature of understanding itself. What practical reason as an intellectual instrument implies about the nature of knowledge is that pragmatic and adventitious renditions of truth are not necessarily reduced to being pale imitations of the real thing. The point here is not merely to cast another stone at the objectivity of truth. The ideal of truth is still a relevant and animating principle as scholars contend with one another about better and worse examples of practical reasoning in a given context. Such debates are necessary components of practical reason as a metapractice.

In the final analysis, one might be tempted to ask what, if any, difference exists between the actual practice of practical reason in the Chinese discourse on *qing* and the kind of comparative critique I have offered of it. The Chinese interpretation of desire in the late sixteenth century was mandated by broader issues of action and community. My analysis of this interpretation, which has pointed out some misappropriations of the Confucian and Buddhist traditions in the service of these larger goals, is also determined by my goal of articulating practical reason as a metapractical principle for my own scholarship. The result is that the respective portrayals of Buddhism and Confucianism differ, but our practices are nevertheless the same: the exercise of practical reason as an intellectual skill is guided by the demands of a broader context of justified actions.

There is a significant difference, however, between the two contexts just described—a difference that inheres in the nature of the "justified actions" that each setting strives for. The late Ming Chinese setting offers a direct example of Lee Yearley's understanding of practical reason as a method for obtaining and articulating a practical theory. That is, the intellectual process of practical reasoning is utilized for framing a context in which one can ethically act in the world. What is peculiarly "ethical" about this process is that actions constitute the goal, the end to which the tool of practical reason is applied. The justification of these actions is presumed in the prior phase of obtaining knowledge of the world—the kind of knowledge whose own structures make proper actions within this context self-evident.

Within an ethical system, then, justified action is a final product which comprises the goal of that system. As such, justified action in this context does not imply the level of meta-practical examination that is crucial to the academic setting. Although ethical-practical theory seeks to ground the notion of justified actions in a broader world view, this world view pre-determines what comprises ethical action. In the case of the academy, the recognition of practical reason as an interpretive principle similarly justifies our actions in light of our growing commitment to the hermeneutical belief that conceptions of truth are constructed in response to the demands of the times. What is different here, however, is the rejection of the simple linearity from knowledge to action that can be so easily assumed in the other model. What is added is an explicit recognition that the context of one's actions is likely to determine what counts as interesting or valid knowledge. Practical reason as an intellectual tool that leads to knowledge bears this recognition within itself.

Finally, my use of the term *practical reason* as a comparative method encompasses ethical issues relevant to our current situation. The category of practical reason may improve on the notion of "syncretism" which has often proved problematic in the study of cultural diversity. Past paradigms of the interaction between Buddhism and native traditions in China have be-fuddled the normative connotations of the term *syncretism*. Its various formulations as the Buddhist "conquest of China" and the Chinese "transformation of Buddhism" has rendered the concept of syncretism a power issue, played out as ongoing reversals in the struggle for cultural dominance. The virtue of practical reasoning as a model of cultural encounter is that it nuances the power issue into pragmatically mediated instances of contingency and creativity. I hope future applications of practical reason to contexts in which ideological systems clash will reveal that the process of understanding is not wrought by zero-sum strategies of intellectual warfare. Rather, understanding is gained through the creation of options whose best recommendation is a rationale for action.

Notes

1. Richard Bernstein, "Reconciliation and Rupture: The Challenge and Threat of Otherness," *Discourse and Practice,* ed. Frank Reynolds and David Tracy (Albany: State University of New York Press, 1992), 296.

2. Karl Popper, "Normal Science and Its Dangers," *Criticism and the Growth of Knowledge,* ed. I. Lakatos and A. Misgrave (Cambridge: Cambridge University Press), 56.

3. Stephen Toulmin, "Beyond Anti-Anti-Relativism" (unpublished paper, 1986).

4. Quoted by Kenneth Ch'en in "Anti-Buddhist Propoganda during the Nan-Ch'ao," *Harvard Journal of Asiatic Studies* 15 (1952):172.

5. Homer H. Dubs, "Han Yu and the Buddha's Relic," *The Review of Religion,* vol. 11, no. 1, 12.

6. The major exception to this generalization is the debate over the doctrine of *karma* and the question of whether or not the soul is commensurate with or separate from the body. See Ch'en's discussion of Fan Zhen in "Anti-Buddhist Propoganda," 180–83.

7. Lee Yearley, *Mencius and Aquinas: Theories of Virtue and Conceptions of Courage* (Albany: State University of New York Press, 1990), 98. See 95–102 for Yearley's overall discussion of practical reason.

8. Ibid., 177.

9. Wm. DeBary, ed., "Individualism and Humanitarianism in Late Ming Thought" in *Self and Society in Ming Thought* (New York: Columbia University Press, 1970), 174. For a general discussion of Wang Gen and the Taizhou school, see pp. 157–78 of this article.

10. Ibid., 160.

11. Ibid., 175.

12. See A. C. Graham, "The Background of the Mencian Theory of Human Nature," *Studies in Chinese Philosophy and Philosophical Literature* (Albany: State University of New York Press, 1990), and the appendix on the meaning of *qing,* where he defines the term in the pre-Han era as meaning "the genuine," and "the essential quality of something."

13. Burton Watson, trans., *Hsun-tzu: Basic Writings* (New York: Columbia University Press, 1963), 156.

14. For an informative discussion of Zhu Xi and his notion of principle, matter, and desire, see Chung-ying Cheng, "Reason, Substance, and Human Desires in Seventeenth-Century Neo-Confucianism," in *Unfolding of Neo-Confucianism,* ed. Wm. Theodore DeBary (New York: Columbia University Press, 1975).

15. Ibid., 470.

16. See Gregory's discussion in *Tsung-mi and the Sinification of Buddhism* (Princeton: Princeton University Press, 1991), 310.

17. Watson, *Hsun-tzu,* 151–52.

18. Actually, A. C. Graham asserts that the pre-Han definition of *qing* is not "emotion" or "passion" but something on the order of the essential quality of a thing that makes it that thing (see n. 12). Graham's definition strongly reinforces the idea that *qing* was not a pejorative category but rather something implicit to human beings, on the order of human nature itself.

19. Translated in full by Hua-yuan Li Mowry, *Lover Stories from Ch'ing-shih* (Hamden: Archon Books, 1983), 13.

20. Judith Berling examines exactly this question of neo-Confucianism as a praxis-oriented, as opposed to solely intellectual, tradition in her article "Embodying Philosophy."

21. See Richard John Lynn, "Orthodoxy and Enlightenment: Wang Shih-chen's Theory of Poetry and Its Antecedents," in *Unfolding of Neo-Confucianism,* ed. Wm. Theodore DeBary (New York: Columbia University Press, 1990) especially pp. 218–19.

22. Jonathan Chaves actually argues that the label of "Romantic," or "neo-Romantic" in the Gongan context is superficially applicable at best. For his specific arguments see "The Expression of Self in the Kung-an School: Non-Romantic Individualism," in *Expression of Self in Chinese Literature,* ed. Robert E. Hegel and Richard C. Hessney (New York: Columbia University Press, 1985).

23. *Fen Shu,* 3/98 Tongxin Shuo.

24. See DeBary, "Individualism and Humanitarianism," 218–19.

25. *Fen Shu,* 3/99 Xinjing Tigang.

26. DeBary, "Individualism and Humanitarianism," 218.

27. Li Zhi, *Chutanji* (Beijing: Zhang hua Shuju, 1974), 1 Fufu Yi.

28. Mowry, *Ch'ing-shih,* 84.

29. Ibid., 87.

30. De Bary, "Individualism and Humanitarianism," 219.

31. Dubs, "Han Yu," 12.

32. D. C. Lau, trans., *Mencius* (London: Penguin, 1970), 168/4A.14.

33. Ibid., 139/5A.1.

34. James Legge, *The Sacred Books of China: Mencius* (Oxford: Oxford University Press, 1926), 345.

35. *Mencius and Aquinas,* 95–111.

36. Ibid., 97.

37. See Qu Yuan's "Li Sao" ("On Encountering Sorrow"). Qu Yuan is the forth-century B.C.E. poet who perhaps originated the poetic convention of addressing one's master as a rejected lover. In David Hawkes' *Songs of the South* (Harmondsworth: Penguin, 1985).

38. T'ien Ju-k'ang offers an in-depth social analysis of the rise of female chastity practices in *Male Anxiety and Female Chastity: A Comparative Study of Chinese Ethical Values in Ming-Ch'ing Times* (Leiden: E. J. Brill, 1988). T'ien looks primarily to political and economic factors which created an upsurge in the number of frustrated scholars in the Ming and Qing. T'ien claims that these would-be bureaucrats encouraged the cult of female chastity for both financial and psychological reasons. Interestingly enough, T'ien's psychological analysis points to the homologization process in which disappointed scholar-officials compared themselves to suffering women. See in particular ch. 5, "Scholars' frustration and roundabout way of emotional expression."

39. Quoted by Hans Wolfgang Schumann in *Buddhism: An Outline of Its Teachings and Schools* (Wheaton: First Quest, 1974), 55.

40. Frank E. Reynolds, "Multiple Cosmogonies and Ethics: The Case of Theravada Buddhism," in *Cosmogony and Ethical Order,* ed. Robin Lovin and Frank Reynolds (Chicago: University of Chicago Press, 1985), 205–9.

41. Schumann, 57.

42. Translated by Yoshito Hakeda in *The Buddhist Tradition in India, China and Japan,* trans. Wm. DeBary (New York: Vintage, 1969), 184.

43. Ibid., 191.

44. Ibid.

45. Peter Gregory devotes a whole chapter to Zongmi's formula in *Tsung-mi.* See "A Cosmogonic Map for Buddhist Practice," 173–205. Matthew Kapstein offers a Tibetan version of the same question in his examination of the myth of Samantabhadra. Kapstein offers this as a cosmogonic myth which attempts to speculatively work out the paradox of "the passage from the indeterminacy and atemporality of the ground to the temporal projection of numberless sentient beings, without implying that the primordial Buddha must himself fall from his primordial enlightenment" ("Samantabhadra and Rudra," 65).

46. Chun-fang Yu, "Images of Kuan-yin in Folk Literature" *Proceedings of the International Conference on Chinese Folk Literature* (Taibei, Taiwan, 1989), 23.

47. Translated by Chun-fang Yu in ibid., 56 n.7.

48. Tae-Hung Ha, trans., *Sanguk Yusa: Legends and History of the Three Kingdoms of Ancient Korea* (Seoul: Yonsei University Press, 1972), 242.

49. See his overall discussion in *Mencius and Aquinas,* 175–82.

50. The terminology of "primary theory" is derived from Robin Horton, who has been the most explicit about this kind of speculation. See the citation of his 1986 article, "Tradition and Modernity Revisited."

51. Ibid., 176.

52. Ian McMorran gives an account of the "practical learning" movement in his article on Wang Fu-chih, an intellectual whose concerns anticipated the movement. See "Wang Fu-chih and the Neo-Confucian Tradition," in *Unfolding of Neo-Confucianism,* ed. Wm. DeBary.

53. For a helpful account of the general intellectual upheaval of the late Ming era, see the volumes by Cynthia Brokaw (1991) and Joanna Handlin (1983) cited in the bibliography.

References

Bernstein, Richard. 1992. "Reconciliation and Rupture: The Challenge and Threat of Otherness." In *Discourse and Practice.* Edited by Frank Reynolds and David Tracy. Albany: State University of New York Press.

Berling, Judith. 1992. "Embodying Philosophy: Some Preliminary Reflections from a Chinese Perspective." In *Discourse and Practice.* Edited by Frank Reynolds and David Tracy. Albany: State University of New York Press.

Brokaw, Cynthia J. 1991. *The Ledgers of Merit and Demerit: Social Change and Moral Order in Late Imperial China.* Princeton: Princeton University Press.

Chaves, Jonathan. 1985. "The Expression of Self in the Kung-an School: Non-Romantic Individualism." In *Expression of Self in Chinese Literature.* Edited by Robert E. Hegel and Richard C. Hessney. New York: Columbia University Press.

Ch'en, Kenneth. 1952. "Anti-Buddhist Propaganda during the Nan-Ch'ao." *Harvard Journal of Asiatic Studies* 15:166–92.

Cheng, Chung-ying. 1975. "Reason, Substance, and Human Desires in Seventeenth-Century Neo-Confucianism." In *Unfolding of Neo-Confucianism.* Edited by Wm. Theodore DeBary. New York: Columbia University Press.

DeBary, Wm. Theodore. 1970. "Individualism and Humanitarianism in Late Ming Thought." In *Self and Society in Ming Thought.* Edited by Wm. Theodore DeBary. New York: Columbia University Press.

Dubs, Homer H. 1946. "Han Yu and the Buddha Relic: An Episode in Medieval Chinese Religion." *The Review of Religion.* Vol. 11, no. 1: 5–17.

Elvin, Mark. 1984. "Female Virtue and the State in China." *Past and Present.* No. 104:111–52.

Graham, A. C. 1990. "The Background of the Mencian Theory of Human Nature." *Studies in Chinese Philosophy and Philosophical Literature.* Albany: State University of New York Press.

Gregory, Peter N. 1991. *Tsung-mi and the Sinification of Buddhism.* Princeton: Princeton University Press.

Ha, Tae-Hung, trans. 1972. *Samguk Yusa: Legends and History of the Three Kingdoms of Ancient Korea.* Soeul: Yonsei University Press.

Hakeda, Yoshito, trans. 1969. "On the Original Nature of Man," by Zongmi. In *The Buddhist Tradition in India, China and Japan.* Edited by Wm. Theodore DeBary. New York: Vintage.

Handlin, Joanna Flug. 1983. *Action in Late Ming Thought: The Reorientation of Lu Kun and Other Scholar-officials.* Berkeley: University of California Press.

Hawkes, David. 1985. *Songs of the South.* Harmondsworth: Penguin.

Horton, Robin. 1986. "Tradition and Modernity Revisited." In *Rationality and Relativism.* Edited by Martin Hollis and Steven Lukes. Cambridge: MIT Press.

Hsia, C. T. 1970. "Time and the Human Condition in the Plays of T'ang Hsien-tsu." In *Self and Society in Ming Thought.* Edited by Wm. Theodore DeBary. New York: Columbia University Press.

Kapstein, Matthew. 1992. "Samantabhadra and Rudra: Innate Enlightenment and Radical Evil in Tibetan Rnying-ma-pa Buddhism." In *Discourse and Practice.* Edited by Frank Reynolds and David Tracy. Albany: State University of New York Press.

Lau, D. C., trans. 1970. *Mencius.* London: Penguin.

Legge, James, trans. 1926. *The Sacred Books of China: Mencius.* Oxford: Oxford University Press.

Li Zhi. 1961. *Fen Shu.* Beijing: Zhonghua Shuju.

———. 1974. *Chutanji.* Beijing: Zhonghua Shuju.

Lynn, Richard John. 1975. "Orthodoxy and Enlightenment: Wang Shih-chen's Theory of Poetry and Its Antecedents." In *Unfolding of Neo-Confucianism.* Edited by Wm. Theodore DeBary. New York: Columbia University Press.

McMorran, Ian. 1975. "Wang Fu-chih and the Neo-Confucian Tradition." In *Unfolding of Neo-Confucianism.* Edited by Wm. Theodore DeBary. New York: Columbia University Press.

Mowry, Hua-yuan Li. 1983. *Love Stories from Ch'ing-shih.* Hamden: Archon Books.

Popper, Karl. 1970. "Normal Science and Its Dangers." In *Criticism and the Growth of Knowledge.* Edited by I. Lakatos and A. Misgrave. Cambridge: Cambridge University Press.

Reynolds, Frank E. 1985. "Multiple Cosmogonies and Ethics: The Case of Theravada Buddhism." In *Cosmogony and Ethical Order.* Edited by Robin Lovin and Frank Reynolds. Chicago: University of Chicago Press.

Schumann, Hans Wolfgang. 1974. *Buddhism: An Outline of Its Teachings and Schools.* Wheaton: First Quest.

T'ien Ju-k'ang. 1988. *Male Anxiety and Female Chastity: A Comparative Study of Chinese Ethical Values in Ming-Ch'ing Times.* Leiden: E. J. Brill.

Toulmin, Stephen. 1986. "Beyond Anti-Anti-Relativism." Unpublished paper.

Watson, Burton, trans. 1963. *Hsun-tzu: Basic Writings.* New York: Columbia University Press.

Yearley, Lee. 1990. *Mencius and Aquinas: Theories of Virtue and Conceptions of Courage.* Albany: State University of New York Press.

Yu, Chun-fang. 1989. "Images of Kuan-yin in Folk Literature." *Proceedings of the International Conference on Chinese Folk Literature.* Taibei, Taiwan.

Concluding Reflections

Comparison, Pragmatics, and Interpretation in the Comparative Philosophy of Religions

Richard J. Parmentier

There exists a very strong, but one-sided and thus untrustworthy, idea that in order better to understand a foreign culture, one must enter into it, forgetting one's own, and view the world through the eyes of this foreign culture. This idea, as I said, is one-sided. Of course, a certain entry as a living being into a foreign culture, the possibility of seeing the world through its eyes, is a necessary part of the process of understanding it; but if this were the only aspect of this understanding, it would merely be duplication and would not entail anything new or enriching. *Creative understanding* does not renounce itself, its own place in time, its own culture; and it forgets nothing. In order to understand, it is immensely important for the person who understands to be *located outside* the object of his or her creative understanding—in time, in space, in culture.

—Mikhail Bakhtin, *Speech Genres and Other Essays,* p. 7

Models and Strategies of Comparison

A notable feature of contemporary intellectual discourse in the "human sciences" is the flowering of the comparative perspective in both disciplinary and interdisciplinary domains.[1] The emergence of publications, journals, and conferences in fields such as comparative politics, comparative literature, comparative philosophy, comparative history, and comparative sociology, building on earlier endeavors such as comparative mythology and comparative philology, necessarily raises reflexive theoretical and methodological issues about the nature of the comparative enterprise. The multidisciplinary conferences "Religions in Culture and History" held at the University of Chicago Divinity School, and the corresponding essays and books published in the *Toward a Comparative Philosophy of Religions Series,* raise a critical question for all these comparative activities: Is the current trend toward comparative studies the fulfillment of the ultimate Western hegemony in which scholarly discourse becomes a powerful regimenting metalanguage, or is it a sign of global, multicultural, dialogic conversation and empathetic understanding that mirror the cultural heteroglossia of the modern world?[2] While these extreme poles of regimentation and dialogue are rarely manifested so boldly, they remain asymptotic options, each with serious implications for empirical work in the comparative vein.

Despite the apparent newness of much comparative discourse, it would be an error to assume that comparison itself has no historical lineage. In fact, some form of comparative thinking can be located in almost any intellectual milieu, especially if the assertion of noncomparability is taken as a negative modality of comparison. Today, forms of comparison are typically distinguished by the absence or presence of historical connectedness: similar phenomena that are remote in space and time can be compared by a logic of analogy or parallelism, whereas phenomena that are known to share a developmental source or to have been in contextual interrelationship can be analyzed genealogically or historically.[3] This clear-cut distinction between analogy and genealogy does not, however, fully characterize previous models of comparative discourse.

It is easy to forget that for millenia the dominant mode of cross-cultural understanding, whether dealing with religion or with any other cultural phenomena, was ethnocentrism, that is, the view that other societies can be placed on a continuum of familiar to strange, calculating out from one's immediate neighbors to the most remote peoples. Herodotus, commenting on the customs of Persia, notes that ethnocentrism frequently correlates with an assumption of moral superiority:

> Most of all they [the Persians] hold in honor themselves, then those who dwell next to themselves, and then those next to *them,* and so on, so that there is a progression in honor in relation to the distance. They hold least in honor those whose habitation is furthest from their own. This is because they think themselves to be the best of mankind in everything and that others have a hold on virtue in proportion to their nearness; those that live furthest away are the most base.[4]

Herodotus himself, on the other hand, was quick to locate the source of much of Greek culture, especially its religion, in "barbarian" traditions of Persia and Egypt, proposing thereby a model of borrowing and diffusion that angered Greek chauvinists like Plutarch, who complained, "not only is he [Herodotus] anxious to establish an Egyptian and a Phoenician Herakles; he says that our own Herakles was born after the other two, and he wants to remove him from Greece and make a foreigner out of him."[5]

In medieval Arabic culture strictly linear ethnocentrism was modified by a systematic ecological determinism according to which societies were located in zones starting just above the equator.[6] Those peoples enjoying the temperate climes of the middle zones (China, Arabia, India, etc.) are most favored, while those existing at the southern and northern extremes are victims of distemper—lethargy for black-skinned Africans and indolence for pale-skinned Slavs. According to Al-Azmeh, the rigor of application of this deterministic model of cross-cultural typology was itself conditioned by the Arab evaluation of the societies to be understood: "It was a social judgement which ultimately determined the degree to which credence would be given to geographical determinism, and this determinism was applied mercilessly only in the construction of sheer barbarism, which was not merely a distemper with varying degree of severity, but fully a disnature."[7]

The inherent difficulties of comparative understanding were well articulated by Jean-Jacques Rousseau, who, despite being described by Lévi-Strauss as the "founder of the science of man,"[8] warned that the period of European exploration would not likely yield reliable knowledge of other cultures because of the ethnocentric blinders of the observers:

> I am persuaded that we have come to know no other men except Europeans; moreover it appears from the ridiculous prejudices, which have not died out even among men of letters, that every author produces under the pompous name of the study of man nothing much more than a study of the men of their own country. . . . One does not open a book of voyages without finding descriptions of characters and customs, but one is altogether amazed to find that these authors who describe so many things tell us only what all of them knew already, and have only learned how to see at the other end of the world what they would to have been able to see without leaving their own street, and that the real features which distinguish nations, and which strike eyes made to see them, have almost always escaped notice.[9]

Rousseau did not, however, give up on comparison, for he thought that it would be possible to replace the biased vision of these "sailors, merchants, soldiers, and missionaries"[10] with a true scientific study of other cultures that would yield increased self-knowledge. His own reflections on the origins of inequality, for instance, performed a shocking inversion of the more usual ethnocentrism by arguing that the degree of human inequality radically increases with civilization and that individuals eager for the institutional benefits of progress in fact "all ran toward their chains believing that they were securing their liberty."[11]

With the expansion of European colonialism and its supporting ideological matrix of evolutionism in the nineteenth century, comparison of cultures frequently involved the paradoxical principles of differential development and genetic explanation. According to the first, societies pass through a sequence of stages of evolutionary progress ("savagery," "barbarism," and "civilization," in the terms of several key writers) culminating in the scientific rationalism of modern European culture; according to the second, inexplicable phenomena later in time are accounted for by uncovering their rational origins at an earlier point in time. The paradox arises because instances of failed progress, whether in spatially distant "primitive" societies or in local irrational superstitions or residual social inequalities, are problematic "survivals" or "remnants" of modernity's historical trajectory. Our knowledge of the past, thus, depends on the contemporary persistence of societies and customs that once had coherent meaning.[12] Whereas in the late eighteenth century Johann Gottfried Herder[13] could argue that "remnants of the old, true folk poetry" of Europe ought to be collected before they vanish with the "daily advance of our so-called culture," nineteenth-century evolutionists were more likely to urge that such survivals should, in the spirit of enlightened rationalism, be either reformed or eradicated. Applied as a general principle of comparison, then, the doctrine of survivals stipulates the following:

> The fragmentary and disjointed nature of certain customs—their poor integration into a people's way of life, and the nonsensical nature of people's rationales for them—is itself one of the telltale signs that they are a survival from earlier times when they formed a more nearly seamless part of the web of life. In the West, it is this same fragmentary nature of certain customs that is taken as justifying the comparativist in arranging them serially across cultures: the less a custom appears to be integrated into life, that is, the less intelligible it is per se (or to those who now practice it), the more legitimate becomes the writer's assimilation of it into a list of similar customs practiced around the world.[14]

I have mentioned linear ethnocentrism, self-critical reflex-
ivity, and evolutionary survivals as three models for comparison that permeate cross-cultural understanding with moral evalu-
ations. In much contemporary discourse, in contrast, such blatant
evaluative stances are out of favor, as comparativists attempt to
ground their work in more principled research strategies, perhaps reflecting the fact that scholarship takes place in a
(post)modern world characterized more by the collage of what
Geertz calls "clashing sensibilities in inevitable contact"[15] than
by autonomous cultural isolates. Without attempting to give a
comprehensive listing here, several prominent strategies—
typology, reconstruction, hermeneutics, and reductionism—need
to be briefly characterized.[16]

Comparison by typology involves generating a set of analytical parameters, the values of which enable the analyst to
locate different cultural systems on one or more continua of
difference. As comparative work proceeds, both the values and
the parameters are modified, refined, and expanded as additional data are gathered. Anthropologists are particularly prone
to dichotomize the societies they study into poles such as hot
and cold, classificatory and instrumental, egalitarian and hierarchical, Aristotelian and Heraclitean, and group and grid; similarly, comparative philosophers still struggle with the simplistic
Hegelian opposition between Western subjectivism and Oriental universalism.[17] Clyde Kluckhohn provides a more sophisticated account of the typological strategy:

> Such enquiry, exposing the principles of cultural struc-
> ture, would take us some distance toward ranging cul-
> tures in an orderly way as to their respective similarities
> and differences. It would also help us to isolate wherein
> rests the distinctiveness of each particular culture at a given
> time level—the "without-which-not" of that culture. . . . For
> typological models of structure and process we need to
> abstract from immediately visible "reality," disengaging
> the accidental by including in the models only those as-
> pects of the observable that are relevant to the model be-
> ing constructed.[18]

Typologies can also be constructed by specifying the implicational relations among a set of variables, such that one variable presupposes a second variable but not vice versa: for example, *do ut des* ("give in order to receive") ritualism and macrocosm-microcosm cosmology,[19] or "denaturalized" philosophical discourse and the assertion of universal truth claims.[20] All empirical cases are consistent with the direction of the implication, but the posited universal regularity does not predict the presence of the variables in specific cases. A third kind of typology, in addition to those based on dichotomization and implicational relations, is semiotic typology, which organizes cultural data in terms of some "master trope," such as metonymy or metaphor, textuality or rules, prescriptive or performative, and signifier or signified.[21] The logical danger here is that the analyst must locate the comparative enterprise itself in one of the hypothesized typological spaces, which implies that comparison is just another trope.[22]

The most famous exponent of the comparative method of reconstruction in religious studies is Georges Dumézil. Without understanding the situational creativity and intercultural borrowings from outside the Indo-European heritage, Dumézil postulates the persistence of "common underlying structures"[23] throughout the Indo-European world, from Vedic India to Celtic Ireland, particularly the representation in cosmology and history of deities, powers, and social formations belonging to three distinct functions, "magical sovereignty," "warrior power," and "peaceful fecundity."[24] Dumézil asserts,

> The comparative study of the most ancient documents from India, Iran, Rome, Scandinavia, and Ireland has allowed us to give [Indo-European civilization] a content and to recognize a great number of facts about civilization, and especially religion, which were common to these diverse societies or at least to several of them. . . . It seems hardly imaginable that chance should have twice created this vast structure, especially in view of the fact that other Indo-European peoples have homologous accounts. The simplest and humblest explanation is to admit that the Romans, as

well as the Scandinavians, received this scenario from a common earlier tradition and that they simply modernized its details, adapting them to their own "geography," "history," and customs and introducing the names of countries, peoples, and heroes suggested by actuality.[25]

According to this method, comparison is made possible by the recognition of similarities among traditions known to have been genetically related. The specifics of local variation from the reconstructed prototype cannot, however, be explained without invoking additional arguments of a sociological or historical nature.[26] In clever hands, of course, similarities to an imputed prototype can be used to hypothesize historical connection, as in Carlo Ginzburg's[27] attempt to trace, following the principle that "isomorphism establishes identity," early-modern ecstatic beliefs and practices to an origin in the nomadic shamanism of Scandinavian and Siberian paleolithic peoples.

Reflective hermeneutics, especially as defined and practiced by the philosopher Paul Ricoeur, is an important recent development in comparative scholarship in the humanities and social sciences. By modifying the classic "hermeneutical circle" from being a part-to-whole relationship *within* the domain of understanding to being the reciprocal dialectic *between* textual explanation (i.e., linguistics) and textual understanding, Ricoeur's method of interpretation appropriates the texts of temporally distant cultures in the service of self-understanding.[28] Through interpretation, people living in a scientific world view are able to recapture a lost dimension of human understanding, the mythico-symbolic world of archaic cultures.[29]

> No interpreter in fact will ever come close to what his text says if he does not live in the aura of the meaning that is sought. And yet it is only by understanding that we can believe. The second immediacy, the second naivete that we are after, is accessible only in hermeneutics; we can believe only by interpreting. This is the "modern" modality of belief in symbols; expression of modernity's distress and cure for this distress. . . . But thanks to this hermeneutic circle, I can today still communicate with the Sacred by explicating the preunderstanding which animates the interpretation.

Hermeneutics, child of "modernity," is one of the ways in which this "modernity" overcomes its own forgetfulness of the Sacred.[30]

Of course, the modern effort to think through primordial symbols, metaphors, and allegories entails a demythologization in which critical objectivity resists an equal dialogue with the "alien" text, since this earlier text contains only a pretheoretical level of interpretation. This kind of comparative enterprise can easily become self-serving, especially if the myths of other cultures are studied not with the intent of grasping their meaning and function in their original context, but rather for personal needs of acquiring pearls of ancient wisdom.[31]

Various works of comparison, finally, are based on kinds of reductionism, that is, on the finding of extra-systematic factors that account for the underlying patterns of similarity of cultural phenomena. These factors can be located in, for example, ecological variables, biological constraints, sociobiological adaptations, imputed facts of human nature, or the structure of the human mind, but all of these arguments share the limitation of treating variation as both random and epiphenomenal.

Comparative Philosophy of Religions as a Discipline

This account of three early patterns and four more recent strategies of comparison provides a methodological backdrop for examining the potentials and problems of the newly constituted discipline of the comparative philosophy of religions. The papers presented in the conference series offer three differentially weighted ways that this new discipline can be operationalized. For some, the discipline is the comparative *philosophy* of religions, that is, the strictly philosophical study, grounded in a comparative perspective, of the phenomena of religion. While this perspective takes a relatively narrow view of the analytical discourse required, it allows a broad acceptance of the range of phenomena to be considered "religion." And, according to this perspective, the motive for comparison lies primarily with the philosophically oriented analyst, rather than within the realm of religion. For others, the discipline is the *comparative* [study of] philosophies of religions; this implies a well-delimited object of the investigation, namely, texts (or discourse, in the case of nonliterate cultures) created by philosophers of religion (including esoteric specialists and ritual elders), yet it allows for considerable flexibility in the analytical methods used, including history, ethnography, and philology. Finally, for several participants the discipline can be characterized as the comparative philosophies *of religions,* that is, the study of the explicit doctrines or implicit stances of various philosophers, theologians, and religious traditions toward other cultural traditions.[32] In contrast to the other two approaches, this view implies that the comparative impulse comes from the religious thinkers or communities under study. Much of the debate that made the Chicago conferences so lively was caused by fundamental disagreements as to how to accent the very name of the discipline being constructed. But, more important, the rich cross-disciplinary fertilization that is revealed in the final papers results from a tacit agreement that these three perspectives should be held in "essential tension,"[33] a collective decision that allows for a "preventive pluralistic methodology"[34] in which historians, philosophers, ethnographers, and theologians are all welcome.

A critical consequence of this debate over the definition of the discipline is the vital importance of the unifying recognition that the motive for comparison and construction of comparative discourse belong *both* to the work of analytical scholarship and to the world of philosophical and religious traditions being studied. At the obvious level, if we set out to compare the philosophy of religion articulated by, say, Hume and Hegel, it will be important to grasp the conclusions about comparative understanding found *in* their philosophical texts. At the less obvious level, if we are to compare the implicit philosophies of, say, medieval Islam and medieval Christianity, part of the task will be to discover the stances toward other religions embodied *in* these religious traditions.

This is not to say, of course, that our scholarly comparison will be identical, in intellectual motive or written discourse, to the comparative positions or stances under study. While philosophical texts and religious traditions may provide modern schol-ars with useful tools for comparative analysis—the notions of analogy,[35] metaphor,[36] and "superimposition"[37] have proven par-ticularly helpful—I do not think that we can simply borrow *their* models of understanding as *our* models of understanding. To the degree that research increasingly reveals the richness of the interpretive, comparative, metapractical, or metapragmatic[38] resources of philosophical and religious discourses, this stric-ture becomes increasingly difficult to obey. Three options seem to be open to those who confront this dilemma: (1) to appropri-ate local interpretive, comparative, and metapragmatic models as our analytical tools (e.g., using Thomistic analogy to under-stand Mencius); (2) to take the discourses under study as equal dialogic partners with reference to our analytical discourses (e.g., comparing their metaphors with our metaphors)—leading ide-ally, as Hallisey argues, to the "preservation" of the other's dis-course and the sharpening of our conceptual tools; and (3) to find in these local discourses necessary yet revealing limitations and biases which in principle exclude them from sharing in the task of analysis yet which expand the range of things the ana-lyst is forced to comprehend.[39]

Why is it so dangerous to dignify local "theories" of com-parison with the status of explanatory models? First, these kinds of local theories are often rationalizations, justifications, or sec-ondary elaborations that must themselves be penetrated in the act of analysis. Second, they often lack time perspective and thus cannot begin to account for changes in either historical situation or ideological assumptions. Third, they tend to be decontextualized abstractions that "iron out" the contextual or indexical dimensions of experience, ignoring precisely those pragmatic aspects of philosophical reasoning and religious ac-tion that are subject to only limited self-awareness.[40] Fourth, they often focus on semantic, propositional, or referential di-mensions of discourse and miss the significance of rhetorical, organizational, and structural dimensions of texts and actions. Finally, they are inherently positional within society, whether the product of elites, radicals, or world renouncers, and need to be linked to alternative, competing, or contradictory theories from elsewhere in the heteroglossic social order. Taken together, all these considerations point to the same general principle: to the degree that a philosophical or religious discourse approaches in either formal shape or declared purpose the status of an abstract, complete, or true account of comparison, this discourse fails to achieve critical self-awareness of its own pragmatic features.

So both comparative analytics and comparisons within traditions have *pragmatic* dimensions that need to be critically identified. As a first approximation, several things might be included in an account of the pragmatics of any discourse: the personal motives or institutional interests behind the production of texts; the contextually grounded presuppositions and implications of texts; the strategic design or rhetorical organization of texts that contributes to their function or efficacy; the social dispersion of texts within a culture, such as the evaluative opposition between high and low culture, official and carnivalesque,[41] or scholarly and popular;[42] explicit text-internal metapragmatic devices, such as performatives and *verba dicendi,* and implicit metapragmatic forms grounded in a discourse's textual properties, both of which provide a commentary on the function of the discourse in context;[43] the real-time dynamics of interpretive acts as socially realized practices; and the intertextual relationship among texts in a culture, including the chain of commentaries on texts.[44] In sum, the pragmatics of discourse comprehends almost every kind of meaningfulness *other than* the decontextualized, distantiated, semantic meaning that Ricoeur[45] labels the "said" of the text.

Despite the fact that many philosophical texts attempt to claim that they are decontextualized discourses asserting universal truths, just as many religious traditions claim unique access to the "really real," one of the jobs for analysts is to discover the pragmatics of these discourses or claims. But the analyst's discourse is itself not free from pragmatics. One of the great dangers of modern scholarship—and the discipline of the comparative philosophy of religions is no exception—is to assume that our own intellectual models, research techniques, and academic writings are not themselves subject to pragmatic considerations.[46] The ultimate irony of the position advocated here is that, although our scholarly acts of comparison can be fundamentally homologous to the comparative doctrines, stances, and encounters revealed in cross-cultural study, there is no reason in principle to model our comparative analytics on the *specific* comparative maneuvers we observe in religious or philosophical traditions. While the ubiquity of comparative discourse and cross-tradition interface can lead us to the universal set of pragmatic conditions and implications of comparison, our comprehension, though itself an act of comparison, is not compelled by any particular discoverable model.

Comparison and Interpretation as Practical Reason

At first glance, this volume's application of the notion of "practical reason" to the field of religion seems to be an uneasy juxtaposition of opposites, since the division between religious practice and philosophical or theological discourse can correlate with the distinction between effective action and discursive reasoning. In other words, the field of religion seems to have pragmatics in the field of ritual while reason seems to have pragmatics in the realm of doctrine or philosophical argumentation, thus leaving little room for a unified notion of practical reason. Furthermore, what is practical, namely, ritual action, is not particularly subject to efficient articulation or philosophical scrutiny. Also, *both* ritual, with its tendency toward decontextualized semiotic form, *and* religious discourse, with its attention to transcendent realities, often place religion at the opposite pole from the utilitarian or functional concerns of everyday life, which can be taken to be the locus of practical rationality.[47]

On closer inspection, however, practical reason does play a critical role in religious traditions. In general cross-cultural terms, religious phenomena that could be listed under the rubric of practical reason include the embodiments of divinity in material tokens such as sacraments, amulets, icons, and masks; religious practices of socialization, indoctrination, initiation, and discipline; ritual acts with effective or even performative force, such as blessing, anathematization, and healing; rhetorical devices in religious communication, preaching, and conversion;

the normative, ethical dimension of religious life and religious thinking; and the explicit philosophical expression of the religious validity of practical reason as an alternative to theoretical reason in notions such as mystical participation, *coincidentia oppositorum,* and the absurdity of belief.[48]

To this rather obvious list of dimensions of practical reason in religion needs to be added *comparison,* seen both as the historical interface of religious traditions and as a topic for philosophical and theological discourse about religion. In fact, if there is a tendency for the discipline of the comparative philosophy of religion to fission between the study of the cultural-historical dimension of religious traditions and the study of philosophical discourses about religion, careful attention to the importance of comparison can be a useful experiment in self-critical dialogue, since there appears to be a complex dialectic or reciprocal feedback between historical circumstances and philosophical reflections: on the one hand, the historical encounter between religious traditions can compel philosophical and theological theorizing about comparison; on the other hand, philosophical positions and theological doctrines can play powerful roles in pre-structuring the experience of religious interface.

In commenting on her ethnographic fieldwork in New Guinea, where small-scaled societies live in close proximity with interlocking exchange relationships, Margaret Mead generalized: "It can, I believe, be demonstrated that contiguity and close interrelationship between groups with differing communicational styles increase awareness that various aspects of the communicational system are learned, can be taught, and are transmissible to others who are not born with them."[49] This heightened sensibility to the conventionality of cultural systems as a result of historical encounter presents certain difficulties for religious and philosophical traditions, both of which, in many cases at least, try to make a claim of uniqueness and absoluteness. Thus, when religious traditions come into historical contact, the encounter often becomes part of broader political and economic power relations put into play, though it is a mistake to analyze these situations solely from the point of view of the agency of the dominant force in the interface. The range of historical stances

runs from fanatical exclusivism dictating the rejection and con-
demnation of the Other so that no communication is deemed
possible;[50] to the zealous proselytizing of missions to convert
the Other; to respectful juxtaposition facilitated by a thorough-
going allegorizing of the Other's texts and doctrines in an effort
to make the foreign seem "the same";[51] to creative forms of
syncretism, blending, and hierarchical layering; to efforts at
multicultural dialogue predicated either on the relativist assumption of the formal equivalence of deities, cosmologies, or ritual
practices or on the inclusivist assumption of the constructive
benefit of modifying the "reading" of the local tradition through
the perspective of an alien tradition.[52]

Walker's analysis of al-Farabi, a tenth-century Islamic philosopher, illustrates a particularly clear case of comparison by
hierarchical synthesis.[53] In the confrontation—real or hypothetical—between Greek philosophy, personified by Aristotle, and
Islamic religion, epitomized by its founder, Muhammad, al-
Farabi maintains the formal identity of the great philosopher
and the great religious founder, but only on the condition that
each of the two roles operates according to the guidelines of
"theoretical" reason, the principles of which were discovered by
Aristotle. Theoretical reason leads to universal, logically demonstrated knowledge, while practical reason depends on the
linguistic expressions, representational forms, and rhetorical techniques of particular cultures. Al-Farabi writes,

> There are two ways of making a thing comprehensible: first,
> by causing its essence to be perceived by the intellect, and
> second, by causing it to be imagined through the similitude
> that imitates it. . . . Now when one acquires knowledge of
> the beings or receives instruction in them, if he perceives
> their ideas themselves with his intellect, and his assent to
> them is by means of certain demonstration, then the science
> that comprises these cognitions is *philosophy*. But if they
> are known by imagining them through similitudes that imi-
> tate them, and assent to what is imagined of them is caused
> by persuasive methods, then the ancients call what com-
> prises these cognitions *religion*. . . . In everything demon-
> strated by philosophy, religion employs persuasion.[54]

Thus, the philosopher and the religious leader are brought into a hierarchical relationship, since Aristotle and Muhammad can only enter into a nonlinguistic dialogue, that is, a kind of transparent communication anchored in universal knowledge. Several centuries later the vector of this hierarchy was severely challenged by Ibn Khaldun, who argued that philosophers such as al-Farabi and Avicenna, in putting primacy on intellectual knowledge of corporeal existants, completely overlook "spiritual essences."[55] Rather, argues Ibn Khaldun,

> When Muhammad guides us toward some perception, we must prefer that to our own perceptions. We must have more confidence in it than in them. We must not seek to prove its correctness rationally, even if (rational intelligence) contradicts it. We must believe and know what we have been commanded (to believe and to know). We must be silent with regard to things of this sort that we do not understand. We must leave them to Muhammad and keep the intellect out of it.[56]

In contrast to this theoretical encompassment of Greek and Islamic traditions, Bantly's account of the loose synthesis of Buddhism and Confucianism in sixteenth-century China suggests that practical reason can also be a model for "conversation" across religious or philosophical systems. At the level of official doctrine, Buddhism's stress on monastic world rejection and its location of the origin of suffering in human desire clearly contrast with Confucianism's focus on the world-affirming ritual conditioning for public life and its valorization of desire as a positive part of human nature. The synthesis of these two traditions attained in certain neo-Confucian schools of the Ming period, however, largely avoided theoretical dispute by formulating a response in terms of everyday social life, popular folklore, and literary forms. This uneasy synthesis combined a creative notion of desire as a means for spiritual liberation with a claim that sagehood cannot be restricted to the ruling class. In this case, then, it is the concrete historical experience of Chinese Buddhism that provides a useful model for the "adventitious" quality of cross-cultural dialogue.

Several essays in this volume explore a second dimension of the operation of practical reason in the philosophy of religion, namely, the dynamic process of *interpretation*. In some cases, this dynamism involves the historical trajectory of the "work" of hermeneutical practices; in other cases, the dynamism lies in the cultural attitudes toward history, time, and change entailed by philosophical positions or religious doctrines. What is remarkable, though, is that interpretive *praxis* is frequently a creative and structuring response to the comparative encounter, either with other religious traditions or with an earlier moment of the same tradition.[57]

Poole's account of the history of the Bimin-Kuskusmin's confrontation with the West details the powerfully conservative interpretive practices of ritual elders prior to the events of the "great destruction" of the 1940s.[58] The elders were able to provide satisfying explanations of various experienced anomalies by relying on the rich metaphorical resources of their "mythic imagination": a strange phenomenon or threatening event that cannot be modeled by one of several existing plant metaphors (e.g., root as source, intertwining as intertextuality, and husk-core as shallow-deep meaning) is defined away as not culturally significant, that is, not leaving a "scar" on the culture's ritual "center-place." This situation of interpretive adequacy changed dramatically after a group of ritual initiates burned to death in a fire at Telefolip and after the region experienced unusual sheet lightning. No longer able to maintain the position that anomalies do not scar the center, Trumeng, a prominent ritual elder, created a new mode of religious interpretation as a middle way between hermetic denial and cultural self-destruction. In contrast to the previous hermeneutic of holism, Trumeng advocated a new interpretive method grounded in the assertion of the *analogy* of anomaly; that is, Trumeng found in the corpus of myths a dimension of historical praxis (including transformations, corruptions, and the progressive weakening of spirit) that was not previously focused on. The crisis situation of cultural encounter could now be modeled, since an anchored homology (or "indexical icon")[59] can be established between the interpretation of praxis (the dynamism in the myths) and the praxis of interpretation (the hermeneutical actions of the ritual elders). In effect, Trumeng reasserted at a higher logical level the encompassment of history by the center-place in his recognition that change is an essential feature of *both* traditional myth and current experience, yet still without admitting the possibility of the Other's power to forever scar the sacred center.[60]

Interestingly, this strongly pragmatic encompassment of history launched the Bimin-Kuskusmin elders on an interpretive path leading in the opposite direction—both geographically and semiotically. Now that the sacred site at Telefolip to the west had been tarnished, they worked to protect their own sacred site by severing ties with the wider interpretive community (by stopping the exchange of *sacra* and ritual personnel) and by elaborating an inward-looking, intentionally reflexive interpretive program. This, too, can be seen as an icon on the comparative situation, for the Bimin-Kuskusmin responded to the next historical incursion of missionaries with "philosophical" rather than ritual discourse.

In contrast to this analogical application of mythic metaphors, Patton's discussion of the history of commentaries on *Ṛg Veda* 9.112 as a "practice of reading" within the Indian tradition illustrates a process involving both the making explicit of what was initially presupposed in the Vedic text and the recontextualization of the locus of textual performativity. The chant sets out multiple occupational roles (carpenter, physician, smith, miller, priestly poet) that strive with diverse means for the same ultimate goal, namely, gold or material wealth. Despite the overt parallelism and consequent equality of these paths toward wealth, the chant implies a fundamental hierarchy, since the utterance of *this mantra* in a sacrificial context (e.g., the pounding of Soma) is the performative means by which the priestly group gains its wealth and asserts its social pre-eminence.[61] Many centuries later one commentator counters the possible implication that members of the priestly or brahminical caste might undertake different occupational activities by framing the *mantra* with the question about a hypothetical circumstance: What can priests legitimately do during a famine? An even later commentary continues this theme by adding the idea that the *man-*

tra was actually uttered "during" a drought, thus removing the text from its previous ritual context. In the first of these commentaries the performative force of the *mantra* is undermined by the process of literalizing the contextual presuppositions of the text; in the second, performativity is reintroduced when the commentator notes that the *mantra* is performed by priests who, having been forced into un-brahminical labors, utter it to purify themselves. Finally, the diverse social roles mentioned in the Vedic *mantra* receive official codification in the *Laws of Manu*. Operating at a tangent to these legitimizing commentaries, however, are other occurrences of the theme of the "myth of exigency" in folklore and epic, which, as Patton argues, reverse the officializing tendency by narrating instances where other castes, even untouchables, can act toward the goal of ending the drought. As this case makes clear, the Indian tradition must be seen as a fundamentally diachronic (Vedic and post-Vedic) and essentially intertextual (*mantra,* commentary, statute, folktale, epic) field of interpretation.

Finally, Al-Azmeh's analysis of the hermeneutical parallels in medieval Arabic thought between the fields of religion and jurisprudence provides an excellent example of the linkage between practical reason, comparison, and interpretation. Theological interpretation is grounded in a genealogical typology whereby historical events are rendered significant by being considered replicas or simulacra of archetypal foundational acts; thus, chronological time is subsumed by salvation history in such a way as to deny the contingency, randomness, chaos, and uniqueness of instances, which are all brought into identity through their being performative results of the original types.[62] In jurisprudence, the relationship between religious textual precedent and consequent legal judgment is, likewise, viewed as one of causal iconicity; in situations where the particular case is not transparently assimilable under an explicit Koranic passage, a mechanism of analogy intervenes as an interpretive tool to "extend the purview of nomothetic discourse to previously uncharted domains."[63]

The indexical ground of the analogical correlation of textual authority and particular judgment is not, however, located in either natural law or social convention, since only God's wisdom knows the causal relation between the two and since only God's command has true juridical force.

> Having no compelling necessity, the concordance of the one with the other, and the compulsion of the index linking the two in an analogical relation, is a matter which lies beyond rational certainty, but is guaranteed by the authority of the text and its hermeneutician. The final arbiter who decrees the ineffable to be operative is therefore equally the final cause of this decree; and the concordance which assures the assonance of humanity and divinity and thus evades the horrors of infernal eternity is one whose custodian is the authority that decrees it.[64]

A consequence of these principles is that identical legal postulates found in non-Islamic cultures, or in Arabic societies prior to Islam, are by definition invalidated. In other words, a hermeneutic of total encompassment correlates with a comparative stance of radical exclusivism.

Directions for Future Research

By way of conclusion I point to two issues, one substantive and the other methodological, which might serve as a challenge for future research in the comparative philosophy of religions. After a careful review of the articles in the three edited volumes in this series, I think that more systematic attention needs to be directed to the bi-causal relationship between philosophical discourse and the cultural traditions in which that discourse emerges. On the one hand, the surrounding tradition can provide an overarching, general ideology that influences the character of philosophical reasoning, as in the effect of evolutionary (if not imperialistic) ideologies on Hegel's typology of religions. Or, the existing social order might provide a foundation for intellectuals in certain social roles to think in similar ways, as in Humphreys'[65] linkage of philosophies of transcendence and interstitial and solitary intellectuals, and as in Smith's[66] correlation of local notions of ritual as exact repetition with the social context of archaic urban elites. Or, there may be a patterned relationship between the predominance of implicit metapragmatic discourse and the nonscriptural basis of the religious tradition, and, inversely, the development of explicit metapragmatics might correlate with scriptural literacy.[67] One might, in this way, draw on the papers of Poole and Hallisey and juxtapose the metapragmatic devices of Bimin-Kuskusmin ritual practices with the textually highlighted metapragmatic distinction between commonplace yet indirect instrumental language and abstract yet direct language in the medieval Buddhist thinker Gurulugomi.

On the other hand, it may well turn out, as Griffiths[68] argues, that it is in the nature of philosophical reasoning to exist in a relatively decontextualized state, that is, not dependent upon cultural traditions, so that religious discourse responds to metaphysical commitments but not vice versa. This reversed causality would suggest research into the impact of philosophical discourse on religious traditions, along dimensions such as systematization (e.g., promoting local typologies of traditions in India), rationalization (e.g., the increasing attention to exegetical rules and interpretive principles in religious contexts), and regimentation (i.e., the development of official, standardized, or codified norms of religious practice, feeling, and expression). Of particular interest here would be to study changes in religious traditions across shifts in philosophical world views.

Second, in my opinion the comparative philosophy of religions needs to become clearer about its methodology of comparison, along at least three axes: modality, scope, and ground. By modality I refer to the status of the terms of comparison, whether imputed by the analyst, as in Schrempp's[69] comparison of Maori cosmology and Kantian philosophy, Yearley's[70] comparison of Mencius and Aquinas, and Patton's comparison of Benjamin's reading of Parisian arcades and Indian interpretations of Vedic mantras, or motivated by historical linkages, as is the case in the papers by Poole, Bantly, Al-Azmeh, and Stout. The analyst must take extra care in making explicit the motivation for creating artificial juxtapositions. Imputed comparisons across cultural levels (India/Paris, Maori/Kant) and comparison between well articulated systems (Plato/Kūkai, Mencius/Aquinas) are particularly difficult. By scope I mean the range of the units of comparison: are the units entire philosophical systems, key interpretive mechanisms (analogy, typology, metaphor), or specific religious doctrines or philosophical principles (good action, miracles)? Given that philosophical discourse tends toward systematic formulation, comparison operating at a lesser scope requires vigilance against atomization or fragmentation. Finally, by ground I mean the metric, criteria, or reason upon which the comparison is based. Whereas some authors take the ground from one of the units to be compared (usually from the Western one), others attempt comparative analysis without realizing, as the present commentary has insisted, that their scholarly activities have deep historical roots *and* find echoes in the traditions under study.

Notes

1. As the final presentation in the multi-year conference series, my task as discussant was to provide a general summary perspective on the issues of comparison and interpretation that would link the papers presented at this and at earlier conferences. I am grateful to Frank Reynolds for inviting me to participate in these conferences and to the conference participants for the opportunity to share in their multidisciplinary conversation. The written version has benefitted from the comments of Robert Hunt, Frank Reynolds, and Paul Powers.

2. Hans-Georg Gadamer, "Practical Philosophy as a Model of the Human Sciences," *Research in Phenomenology* 9 (1979):74–84; Erik Schwimmer, "The Taste of Your Own Flesh," *Semiotica* 46 (1983):126. Charles Taylor ("Comparison, History, Truth," in *Myth and Philosophy,* ed. Frank Reynolds and David Tracy [Albany: State University of New York Press, 1990], 47), notes that the presence in the West of rational discourse about the equal value of other traditions seems, ironically, to be an argument for the West's claim to cultural superiority, since this spirit of equality is missing in many other cultures.

3. Maurice Bloch, "Symbols, Song, Dance and Features of Articulation: Is Religion an Extreme Form of Traditional Authority?" *Archives européenes de sociologie* 15 (1967):47; Stephen Jay Gould, *Wonderful Life: The Burgess Shale and the Nature of History* (New York: W. W. Norton, 1989), 213.

4. Herodotus, *The History,* trans. David Grene (Chicago: University of Chicago Press, 1987), 96.

5. Plutarch, *De Herodoti Malignitate,* quoted in Martin Bernal, *Black Athena: The Afroasiatic Roots of Classical Civilization* (New Brunswick, N.J.: Rutgers University Press, 1987), 113.

6. Aziz Al-Azmeh, "Barbarians in Arab Eyes," *Past and Present* 134 (1992).

7. Ibid., 8.

8. Claude Lévi-Strauss, *Structural Anthropology,* vol. 2, trans. Monique Layton (New York: Basic Books, 1976), 33.

9. Jean-Jacques Rousseau, *A Discourse on Inequality,* trans. Maurice Cranston (London: Penguin, 1984), 159.

10. Ibid.

11. Ibid., 122; see Juliet Flower MacCannell, "The Semiotic of Modern Culture," *Semiotica* 35(3/4) (1981).

12. George W. Stocking, Jr., *Victorian Anthropology* (New York: Free Press, 1987), 230.

13. Johann Gottfried Herder, "Correspondence on Ossian and the Songs of Ancient Peoples," in *The Origins of Modern Critical Thought,* ed. David Simpson (Cambridge: Cambridge University Press, 1988), 75.

14. Robert F. Campany, " 'Survival' as an Interpretive Strategy: A Sino-Western Comparative Case Study," *Method and Theory in the Study of Religion* 2(1) (1990):16.

15. Clifford Geertz, "The Uses of Diversity," *Michigan Quarterly Review* (1986):114.

16. For a record of penetrating discussions of the typology of comparison, see Francisca Cho Bantly, ed., *Deconstructing/Reconstructing the Philosophy of Religions* (Chicago: University of Chicago Divinity School, 1990), 3–21 (summary by Robert Campany) and 123–44 (summary by Laurie L. Patton).

17. Georg Hegel, *Lectures on the Philosophy of Religion,* vol. 2, *Determinate Religion,* ed. Peter C. Hodgson (Berkeley: University of California Press, 1987), 572.

18. Clyde Kluckhohn, "The Use of Typology in Anthropological Theory," in *Men and Cultures: Selected Papers of the Fifth International Congress of Anthropological and Ethnological Sciences,* ed. Anthony Wallace (Philadelphia: University of Philadelphia Press, 1960), 137–39.

19. Betty Heimann, "The Supra-Personal Process of Sacrifice," *Revista degli Studi Orientali* 32 (1957).

20. Paul J. Griffiths, "Denaturalizing Discourse: Abhidharmikas, Propositionalists, and the Comparative Philosophy of Religion," in *Myth and Philosophy,* ed. Frank E. Reynolds and David Tracy (Albany: State University of New York Press, 1990), 80.

21. Frederic Jameson, "Marxism and Historicism," *New Literary History* 11(1) (1979):68.

22. Jonathan Z. Smith (*Imagining Religion: From Babylon to Jonestown* [Chicago: University of Chicago Press, 1982], 22) even postulates a typology of comparative thinking, in which various writers on religion are positioned relative to four types: ethnographic, encyclopedic, morphological, and evolutionary.

23. C. Scott Littleton, "Georges Dumezil and the Rebirth of the Genetic Model," in *Myth in Indo-European Antiquity,* ed. Gerald James Larson (Berkeley: University of California Press, 1974), 173.

24. Georges Dumézil, *Mitra-Varuna: An Essay on Two Indo-European Representations of Sovereignty,* trans. Derek Coltman (New York: Zone Books, 1988), 121.

25. Georges Dumézil, *Archaic Roman Religion,* trans. Philip Krapp (Chicago: University of Chicago Press, 1970), 1:73.

26. Bruce Lincoln, *Death, War, and Sacrifice: Studies in Ideology and Practice* (Chicago: University of Chicago Press, 1991), 123.

27. Carlo Ginzburg, *Ecstasies: Deciphering the Witches Sabbath,* trans. Raymond Rosenthal (New York: Pantheon Books, 1991), 18.

28. Paul Ricoeur, *Interpretation Theory: Discourse and the Surplus of Meaning* (Fort Worth: Texas Christian University Press, 1976); Paul Ricoeur, "What Is a Text?" in *From Text to Action: Essays in Hermeneutics, II,* trans. Kathleen Blamey and John B. Thompson (Evanston: Northwestern University Press, 1991), 118. Cf. Gadamer's notion of "alienation," in Schweiker 1990, 42.

29. Paul Ricoeur, *The Symbolism of Evil,* trans. Emerson Buchanan (Boston: Beacon Press, 1967), 350–52.

30. Paul Ricoeur, *The Conflict of Interpretations: Essays in Hermeneutics* (Evanston: Northwestern University Press, 1974), 298.

31. Wendy Doniger O'Flaherty, "The Uses and Misuses of Other People's Myths," *Journal of the American Academy of Religion* 54 (1986):226.

32. David Tracy, "On the Origins of Philosophy of Religion: The Need for a New Narrative of Its Founding," in *Myth and Philosophy*, ed. Frank Reynolds and David Tracy (Albany: State University of New York Press, 1990), 15.

33. Thomas S. Kuhn, *The Essential Tension: Selected Studies in Scientific Tradition and Change* (Chicago: University of Chicago Press, 1977).

34. David Zilberman, "Understanding Cultural Traditions through Types of Thinking," in *The Birth of Meaning in Hindu Thought*, ed. Robert S. Cohen (Dordrecht: D. Reidel, 1991), 300.

35. Lee Yearley, *Mencius and Aquinas: Theories of Virtue and Conceptions of Courage* (Albany: State University of New York Press, 1990).

36. Fitz John Porter Poole, "Metaphors and Maps: Towards Comparison in the Anthropology of Religion," *Journal of the American Academy of Religion* 54(3) (1986); William Schweiker, "The Drama of Interpretation and the Philosophy of Religions," in *Discourse and Practice*, ed. Frank Reynolds and David Tracy (Albany: State University of New York Press, 1992), 271.

37. Francis X. Clooney, *Theology after Vedanta* (Albany: State University of New York Press, n.d.), ch. 5.

38. Thomas P. Kasulis ("Philosophy as Metapractice," in *Discourse and Practice*, ed. Frank Reynolds and David Tracy [Albany: State University of New York Press, 1992]), introduced the term *metapractical* to refer to philosophical reflection on religious practices that arises from the character of those religious practices; Michael Silverstein ("Shifters, Linguistic Categories, and Cultural Description," in *Meaning in Anthropology*, ed. Keith H. Basso and Henry A. Selby [Albuquerque: University of New Mexico Press, 1976], 48–51; "Metapragmatic Discourse and Metapragmatic Function," in *Reflexive Language: Reported Speech and Metapragmatics*, ed. John Lucy [Cambridge: Cambridge University Press, 1993], 330) uses the term *metapragmatic* to refer to any form of discourse that takes as its object and thereby frames or regiments the pragmatic or indexical functioning of signs in context.

39. Charles Taylor, "Understanding and Ethnocentrism," in *Philosophical Papers* (Cambridge: Cambridge University Press, 1985).

40. Michael Silverstein, "The Limits of Awareness," *Working Papers in Sociolinguistics* no. 84 (Austin: Southwest Educational Development Laboratory, 1981).

41. Mikhail Bakhtin, *Rabelais and His World*, trans. Helene Iswolsky (Cambridge: MIT Press, 1968), 9–10.

42. Aaron J. Gurevich, "Popular and Scholarly Medieval Cultural Traditions: Notes in the Margins of Jacques Le Goff's Book," *Journal of Medieval History* 9 (1983).

43. This distinction comes from Silverstein's many lectures and papers on pragmatics and metapragmatics; see especially Silverstein, "Metapragmatic Discourse."

44. Wendy Doniger, "Rationalizing the Irrational Other: 'Orientalism' and the *Laws of Manu*," *New Literary History* 23 (1992):39–41.

45. Ricoeur, *Conflict*.

46. Two excellent demonstrations of the pragmatic background to comparative analytic work are Jonathan Z. Smith, (*Drudgery Divine: On the Comparison of Early Christianities and the Religions of Late Antiquity* [Chicago: University of Chicago Press, 1990]) and Howard Eilberg-Schwartz (*The Savage in Judaism: An Anthropology of Israelite Religion and Ancient Judaism* [Bloomington: Indiana University Press, 1990]).

47. Bloch, "Symbols," 78.

48. Several scholars have noted that comparison at the level of practical reason might help avoid the generalization that the more developed a philosophical theory is, the more remote the chance of finding suitable comparative parallels in other theories; see, e.g., Thomas P. Kasulis, "Reference and Symbol in Plato's *Cratylus* and Kūkai's *Shōjijissōgi*," *Philosophy East and West* 32 (1982), 403; Yearley, *Mencius*, 179.

49. Margaret Mead, "Vicissitudes of the Study of the Total Communication Process," in *Approaches to Semiotics*, ed. Thomas A. Sebeok (The Hague: Mouton, 1962), 281.

50. Paul Tillich, *Christianity and the Encounter of World Religions* (New York: Columbia University Press, 1963), 31.

51. Smith, "Map," 101.

52. Francis X. Clooney, "Evil, Divine Omnipotence, and Human Freedom," *Journal of Religion* 69 (1989):547; Francis X. Clooney, "Reading the World in Christ," in *Christian Uniqueness Reconsidered*, ed. Gavin D'Costa (Maryknoll, N.Y.: Orbis Books, 1990).

53. In the discussion of the volume's papers in this and the following paragraphs, I am primarily interested in drawing out material relevant to the joint theme of comparison and interpretation, which in several cases misses the

author's central concerns. Also, space restrictions preclude dealing fully with all of the conference papers here.

54. Al-Farabi, "The Attainment of Happiness," in *Alfarabi's Philosophy of Plato and Aristotle,* trans. Muhsin Mahdi (New York: The Free Press of Glencoe, 1962), 44–45.

55. Ibn Khaldun, *The Muqaddimah: An Introduction to History,* trans. Franz Rosenthal (Princeton: Princeton University Press, 1967), 402.

56. Ibid., 390.

57. The argument proposed by MacIntyre (357) that traditions are rational to the degree that they engage in historically layered self-criticism overlooks the important role of *cross*-cultural engagement.

58. Fitz John Porter Poole, "The Erosion of a Sacred Landscape: European Exploration and Cultural Ecology among the Bimin-Kuskusmin of Papua New Guinea," in *Mountain People,* ed. M. Tobias (Norman: University of Oklahoma Press, 1986); Poole, "Wisdom," 1992.

59. Michael Silverstein, "Metaforces of Power in Traditional Oratory," (lecture, Dept. of Anthropology, Yale University, 1981); Richard J. Parmentier, "The Political Function of Reported Speech: A Belauan Example," in *Reflexive Language,* ed. John Lucy (Cambridge: Cambridge University Press, 1993).

60. The Bimin-Kuskusmin case is fruitfully compared to the myth of Hainuwele from Ceram analyzed by Jonathan Z. Smith (1978, 304; 1982, 96–101), where the incongruity of the encounter with Europeans and foreign goods is coded by indigenous motifs in mythological narratives.

61. On this performative function, see Francis X. Clooney, "Why the Veda Has No Author: Language as Ritual in Early Mimamsa and Post-Modern Theology," *Journal of the American Academy of Religion* 55 (1987):672.

62. Sheryl L. Burkhalter, "Completion in Continuity: Cosmogony and Ethics in Islam," in *Cosmogony and Ethical Order: New Studies in Comparative Ethics,* ed. Robin W. Lovin and Frank E. Reynolds (Chicago: University of Chicago Press, 1985), 245.

63. Aziz Al-Azmeh, *Arabic Thought and Islamic Societies* (London: Croom Helm, 1986), 87.

64. Ibid., 91–92.

65. S. C. Humphreys, "Transcendence and the Intellectual Roles: The Ancient Greek Case," *Daedalus* 104 (1975), 112.

66. Smith, "Map," 293.

67. Ernest Gellner, *Plough, Sword, and Book: The Structure of Human History* (Chicago: University of Chicago Press, 1987), 75.

68. Paul J. Griffiths, "Buddha and God," *Journal of Religion* 69 (1989):527–29.

69. Gregory Schrempp, "Autinomy and Cosmology: Kant among the Maori," in *Myth and Philosophy,* ed. Frank Reynolds and David Tracy (Albany: State University of New York Press, 1990).

70. Yearley, *Mencius.*

References

Al-Azmeh, Aziz. 1986. *Arabic Thought and Islamic Societies.* London: Croom Helm.

———. 1992. "Barbarians in Arab Eyes." *Past and Present* 134:3–18.

al-Farabi. 1962. "The Attainment of Happiness." In *Alfarabi's Philosophy of Plato and Aristotle,* 11–50. Translated by Muhsin Mahdi. New York: The Free Press of Glencoe.

Bakhtin, Mikhail. 1968. *Rabelais and His World.* Translated by Hélène Iswolsky. Cambridge: MIT Press.

———. 1986. "Response to a Question from the *Novy Mir* Editorial Staff." In *Speech Genres and Other Essays,* 1–9. Translated by Vern W. McGee. Austin: University of Texas Press.

Bantly, Francisca Cho, ed. 1990. *Deconstructing/Reconstructing the Philosophy of Religions.* Chicago: The University of Chicago Divinity School.

Bernal, Martin. 1987. *Black Athena: The Afroasiatic Roots of Classical Civilization.* Vol. 1, *The Fabrication of Ancient Greece 1795–1985.* New Brunswick, N.J.: Rutgers University Press.

Bloch, Marc. 1967 [1928]. "A Contribution Towards a Comparative History of European Societies." In *Land and Work in Medieval Europe,* 44–81. Translated by J. E. Anderson. New York: Harper Torchbooks.

Bloch, Maurice. 1974. "Symbols, Song, Dance and Features of Articulation: Is Religion an Extreme Form of Traditional Authority?" *Archives européenes de sociologie* 15:55–81.

Burkhalter, Sheryl L. 1985. "Completion in Continuity: Cosmogony and Ethics in Islam." In *Cosmogony and Ethical Order: New Studies in Comparative Ethics,* edited by Robin W. Lovin and Frank E. Reynolds, 225–50. Chicago: University of Chicago Press.

Campany, Robert F. 1990. " 'Survival' as an Interpretive Strategy: A Sino-Western Comparative Case Study." *Method and Theory in the Study of Religion* 2(1):2–26.

Clooney, Francis X. 1987. "Why the Veda Has No Author: Language as Ritual in Early Mīmāṃsā and Post-Modern Theology." *Journal of the American Academy of Religion* 55:659–84.

———. 1989. "Evil, Divine Omnipotence, and Human Freedom: Vedānta's Theology of Karma." *Journal of Religion* 69:530–48.

———. 1990. "Reading the World in Christ: From Comparison to Inclusivism." In *Christian Uniqueness Reconsidered: The Myth of a Pluralistic Theology of Religions,* edited by Gavin D'Costa, 63–80. Maryknoll, N.Y.: Orbis Books.

———. n.d. *Theology after Vedānta.* Albany: State University of New York Press.

Doniger, Wendy. 1992. "Rationalizing the Irrational Other: 'Orientalism' and the *Laws of Manu.*" *New Literary History* 23:25–43.

Dumézil, Georges. 1970 [1966]. *Archaic Roman Religion,* 2 vols. Translated by Philip Krapp. Chicago: University of Chicago Press.

———. 1988 [1948]. *Mitra-Varuna: An Essay on Two Indo-European Representations of Sovereignty.* Translated by Derek Coltman. New York: Zone Books.

Eilberg-Schwartz, Howard. 1990. *The Savage in Judaism: An Anthropology of Israelite Religion and Ancient Judaism.* Bloomington: Indiana University Press.

Gadamer, Hans-Georg. 1979. "Practical Philosophy as a Model of the Human Sciences." *Research in Phenomenology* 9:74–84.

Geertz, Clifford. 1986. "The Uses of Diversity." *Michigan Quarterly Review* (Winter):105–23.

Gellner, Ernest. 1988. *Plough, Sword, and Book: The Structure of Human History.* Chicago: University of Chicago Press.

Ginzburg, Carlo. 1991 [1989]. *Ecstasies: Deciphering the Witches' Sabbath.* Translated by Raymond Rosenthal. New York: Pantheon Books.

Gould, Stephen Jay. 1989. *Wonderful Life: The Burgess Shale and the Nature of History.* New York: W. W. Norton.

Griffiths, Paul J. 1989. "Buddha and God." *Journal of Religion* 69:502–29.

———. 1990. "Denaturalizing Discourse: Abhidhārmikas, Propositionalists, and the Comparative Philosophy of Religion." In *Myth and Philosophy,* edited by Frank E. Reynolds and David Tracy, 57–94. Albany: State University of New York Press.

Gurevich, Aaron J. 1983. "Popular and Scholarly Medieval Cultural Traditions: Notes in the Margin of Jacques Le Goff's Book." *Journal of Medieval History* 9:71–90.

Hegel, Georg Wilhelm Friedrich. 1987. *Lectures on the Philosophy of Religion.* Vol. 2; *Determinate Religion,* edited by Peter C. Hodgson. Berkeley: University of California Press.

Heimann, Betty. 1957. "The Supra-Personal Process of Sacrifice." *Revista degli Studi Orientali* 32:731–39.

Herder, Johann Gottfried. 1988 [1773]. "Correspondence on Ossian and the Songs of Ancient Peoples." In *The Origins of Modern Critical Thought: German Aesthetic and Literary Criticism from Lessing to Hegel,* edited by David Simpson, 71–76. Cambridge: Cambridge University Press.

Herodotus. 1987. *The History.* Translated by David Grene. Chicago: University of Chicago Press.

Humphreys, S. C. 1975. "Transcendence and the Intellectual Roles: The Ancient Greek Case." *Daedalus* 104:91–118.

Jameson, Frederic. 1979. "Marxism and Historicism." *New Literary History* 11(1):41–73.

Kasulis, Thomas P. 1982. "Reference and Symbol in Plato's *Cratylus* and Kūkai's *Shōjijissōgi.*" *Philosophy East and West* 32:393–405.

————. 1985. "The Incomparable Philosopher: Dogen on How to Read the *Shobogenzo.*" In *Dogen Studies,* edited by William R. LaFleur, 83–98. Honolulu: University of Hawaii Press.

————. 1992. "Philosophy as Metapraxis." In *Discourse and Practice,* edited by Frank Reynolds and David Tracy, 169–95. Albany: State University of New York Press.

Khaldun, Ibn. 1967. *The Muqaddimah: An Introduction to History.* Translated by Franz Rosenthal. Princeton: Princeton University Press.

Kluckhohn, Clyde. 1960. "The Use of Typology in Anthropological Theory." In *Men and Cultures: Selected Papers of the Fifth International Congress of Anthropological and Ethnological Sciences,* edited by Anthony F. C. Wallace, 134–40. Philadelphia: University of Pennsylvania Press.

Kuhn, Thomas S. 1977. *The Essential Tension: Selected Studies in Scientific Tradition and Change.* Chicago: University of Chicago Press.

Lévi-Strauss, Claude. 1976. *Structural Anthropology,* Vol. 2. Translated by Monique Layton. New York: Basic Books.

Lincoln, Bruce. 1991. *Death, War, and Sacrifice: Studies in Ideology and Practice.* Chicago: University of Chicago Press.

Littleton, C. Scott. 1974. "Georges Dumézil and the Rebirth of the Genetic Model: An Anthropological Appreciation." In *Myth in Indo-European Antiquity,* edited by Gerald James Larson, 169–79. Berkeley: University of California Press.

MacCannell, Juliet Flower. 1981. "The Semiotic of Modern Culture." *Semiotica* 35(3/4):287–301.

MacIntyre, Alasdair. 1988. *Whose Justice? Which Rationality?* Notre Dame: University of Notre Dame Press.

Mead, Margaret. 1962. "Vicissitudes of the Study of the Total Communication Process." In *Approaches to Semiotics,* edited by Thomas A. Sebeok, 277–87. The Hague: Mouton.

O'Flaherty, Wendy Doniger. 1986. "The Uses and Misuses of Other Peoples' Myths." *Journal of the American Academy of Religion* 54:219–39.

Parmentier, Richard J. 1993. "The Political Function of Reported Speech: A Belauan Example." In *Reflexive Language: Reported Speech and Metapragmatics*, edited by John Lucy, 261–86. Cambridge: Cambridge University Press.

Poole, Fitz John Porter. 1986. "The Erosion of a Sacred Landscape: European Exploration and Cultural Ecology among the Bimin-Kuskusmin of Papua New Guinea." In *Mountain People*, edited by M. Tobias, 169–82. Norman: University of Oklahoma Press.

———. 1986. "Metaphors and Maps: Towards Comparison in the Anthropology of Religion." *Journal of the American Academy of Religion* 54(3):411–57.

———. 1990. "Wisdom and Practice: The Mythic Making of Sacred History among the Bimin-Kuskusmin of Papua New Guinea." In *Discourse and Practice*, edited by Frank Reynolds and David Tracy, 13–50. Albany: State University of New York Press.

Reynolds, Frank E., and David Tracy, eds. 1990. *Myth and Philosophy*. Albany: State University of New York Press.

Reynolds, Frank E., and David Tracy, eds. 1992. *Discourse and Practice*. Albany: State University of New York Press.

Ricoeur, Paul. 1967. *The Symbolism of Evil*. Translated by Emerson Buchanan. Boston: Beacon Press.

———. 1974. *The Conflict of Interpretations: Essays in Hermeneutics*. Evanston, Ill.: Northwestern University Press.

———. 1976. *Interpretation Theory: Discourse and the Surplus of Meaning*. Fort Worth: Texas Christian University Press.

———. 1991 [1971]. "What Is a Text?" In *From Text to Action: Essays in Hermeneutics, II*, 105–24. Translated by Kathleen Blamey and John B. Thompson. Evanston, Ill.: Northwestern University Press.

Rousseau, Jean-Jacques. 1984 [1753]. *A Discourse on Inequality*. Translated by Maurice Cranston. London: Penguin Books.

Schrempp, Gregory. 1990. "Antinomy and Cosmology: Kant among the Maori." In *Myth and Philosophy*, edited by Frank Reynolds and David Tracy, 151–80. Albany: State University of New York Press.

Schweiker, William. 1990. *Mimetic Reflections.* New York: Fordham University Press.

———. 1992. "The Drama of Interpretation and the Philosophy of Religions: An Essay on Understanding in Comparative Religious Ethics." In *Discourse and Practice,* edited by Frank Reynolds and David Tracy, 263–94. Albany: State University of New York Press.

Schwimmer, Erik. 1983. "The Taste of Your Own Flesh." *Semiotica* 46(2/4):107–29.

Silverstein, Michael. 1976. "Shifters, Linguistic Categories, and Cultural Description." In *Meaning in Anthropology,* edited by Keith H. Basso and Henry A. Selby, 11–55. Albuquerque: University of New Mexico Press.

———. 1981. "The Limits of Awareness." *Working Papers in Sociolinguistics* no. 84. Austin: Southwest Educational Development Laboratory.

———. 1981. "Metaforces of Power in Traditional Oratory." Lecture, Department of Anthropology, Yale University.

———. 1993. "Metapragmatic Discourse and Metapragmatic Function." In *Reflexive Language: Reported Speech and Metapragmatics,* edited by John Lucy, 33–58. Cambridge: Cambridge University Press.

Smith, Jonathan Z. 1978. "Map Is Not Territory." In *Map Is Not Territory: Studies in the History of Religions,* 289–309. Leiden: E. J. Brill.

———. 1982. *Imagining Religion: From Babylon to Jonestown.* Chicago: University of Chicago Press.

———. 1990. *Drudgery Divine: On the Comparison of Early Christianities and the Religions of Late Antiquity.* Chicago: University of Chicago Press.

Stocking, George W., Jr. 1987. *Victorian Anthropology.* New York: Free Press.

Taylor, Charles. 1985. "Understanding and Ethnocentrism." In *Philosophical Papers.* Vol. 2, *Philosophy and the Human Sciences,* 116–33. Cambridge: Cambridge University Press.

—————. 1990. "Comparison, History, Truth." In *Myth and Philosophy,* edited by Frank Reynolds and David Tracy, 37–55. Albany: State University of New York Press.

Tillich, Paul. 1963. *Christianity and the Encounter of World Religions.* New York: Columbia University Press.

Tracy, David. 1990. "On the Origins of Philosophy of Religion: The Need for a New Narrative of Its Founding." In *Myth and Philosophy,* edited by Frank Reynolds and David Tracy, 11–35. Albany: State University of New York Press.

Yearley, Lee H. 1990. *Mencius and Aquinas: Theories of Virtue and Conceptions of Courage.* Albany: State University of New York Press.

Zilberman, David. 1991. "Understanding Cultural Traditions through Types of Thinking." In *The Birth of Meaning in Hindu Thought,* edited by Robert S. Cohen, 299–329. Dordrecht: D. Reidel.

Index